ASHES TO ASHES

ASHES TO ASHES

THE PHOENIX PROGRAM AND THE VIETNAM WAR

BY

DALE ANDRADÉ

Lexington Books

D.C. Heath and Company • *Lexington, Massachusetts* • *Toronto*

This book is published as part of Lexington Books
Issues in Low-Intensity Conflict series, Neil C. Livingstone, consulting editor.

Library of Congress Cataloging-in-Publication Data
Andradé, Dale.
Ashes to ashes : the Phoenix program and the Vietnam War / by Dale
Andradé.
  p.   cm.
ISBN 0-669-20014-X (alk. paper)
1. Vietnamese Conflict, 1961–1975—Underground movements.
  2. Counterinsurgency—Vietnam.   I. Title.
     DS558.92.A67   1990
       959.704'34—dc20   90-30979
                                                   CIP

Copyright © 1990 by Lexington Books

All rights reserved. No part of this publication
may be reproduced or transmitted in any form or
by any means, electronic or mechanical, including
photocopy, recording, or any information storage
or retrieval system, without permission in writing
from the publisher.

Published simultaneously in Canada
Printed in the United States of America
Casebound International Standard Book Number: 0-669-20014-X
Library of Congress Catalog Card Number: 90-30979

The paper used in this publication meets
the minimum requirements of American National Standard
for Information Sciences—Permanence of Paper
for Printed Library Materials, ANSI Z39.48-1984.

Year and number of this printing:

90 91 92 8 7 6 5 4 3 2 1

To Kim:
Her patience and support are my inspiration

Contents

Preface IX
Acknowledgments XIII
Introduction XV

1. Threat: Viet Cong Infrastructure 1
2. Phoenix Rising: Anti-infrastructure Antecedents 15
3. Bureaucrats and Soldiers: Creating a System 47
4. From the Ashes of Tet: 1968 71
5. Three Operations: A Study in Contrasts 99
6. Coming of Age: 1969–1970 123
7. Police Work: The National Police Field Force and the Police Special Branch 147
8. Dirty Work: PRUs and SEALs 171
9. Long Arm of the Law: Courts and Detention Systems 201
10. Return to Ashes: 1971–1972 229
11. Enemy Strikes Back: Communist Reaction to Phoenix 255

Epilogue	281
Appendix	287
Notes	293
Glossary	311
Selected Bibliography	315
Index	321
About the Author	333

Preface

> They have also another sacred bird called the Phoenix, which I myself have never seen, except in pictures. Indeed it is a great rarity even in Egypt, only coming there once in five hundred years.
>
> —Herodotus, *The Histories*

THE PHOENIX Herodotus wrote of represented man's preoccupation with immortality—in this case, the ability to rejuvenate. During the Vietnam War the Phoenix program sought to rejuvenate life from a dying effort. American troops and firepower had been unable to stop communists in North Vietnam from taking the war south in an attempt to unify the country. Perhaps most importantly, the United States had failed to prevent the tide of domestic public opinion from turning against the war effort. And like the ancient myth of the phoenix, Vietnam's Phoenix exited its last life amid controversy over interpretation and translation.

The phoenix of old renewed itself in many ways, depending on which account is read. Herodotus believed the phoenix came from Arabia, carrying the body of its dead father wrapped in a ball of myrrh. The younger phoenix built a funeral pyre and then died, whereupon a new phoenix arose from the flames that consumed the parent.

The Assyrians saw the recreation of the phoenix differently. After five hundred years the phoenix built itself a nest of fragrant branches. Upon completion of the nest the phoenix died and a young bird issued forth.

Vietnam's Phoenix program, too, seemed to lead different existences, depending upon who told the story. To many in the military, the Phoenix program was just another Rube Goldberg plan designed to strip the Army of its ability to conduct the war on its own terms. To counterinsurgency advocates who saw Vietnam as a proving ground for the future of what would become known as low-intensity conflict, Phoenix was an important program that came on the scene much too late. To antiwar protesters Phoenix was a logical—and criminal—extension of an immoral foreign policy; a program of secret murder peopled with clandestine agents, corrupt Vietnamese officials, and sadistic thugs who rarely discriminated between Viet Cong agent and innocent villager during their deadly forays. To other observers of the war Phoenix was a bad joke, a comedy of errors that accomplished little except to create paperwork behind which to hide its failure in a bewildering tangle of numbers and statistics.

Which interpretation is correct? None of them and all of them. Not surprisingly, a bit of truth is in every interpretation of the Phoenix program. But, unfortunately for history, much is false. Polemics seem to have clouded the reality of Phoenix to a greater degree than any other aspect of the Vietnam War. But considering the controversial nature of the program, that is not surprising.

Phoenix represented shades of warfare that Americans would prefer not to think about. Most of the Viet Cong Infrastructure (VCI) targeted by Phoenix were, strictly speaking, civilians. That is to say, they were not part of a military organization. Yet without them the communist effort in South Vietnam never would have gotten off the ground. Americans don't like to see noncombatants killed. But it must be remembered that the VCI were not noncombatants. In a revolutionary war virtually everyone is involved in some way and the VCI was no exception. In fact, the VCI provided the central figures in the communists' strategy in South Vietnam. They carried out Mao Tse-tung's dictum that revolutionaries should be like fish swimming in the sea of the people. The VCI—not the North Vietnamese Army or the Viet Cong military units—were the fish. They were the men and women who used every possible means to assure that communist ideology took hold in the countryside and that the Saigon government was discredited in the eyes of the people. Without them the main-force military units of the Viet Cong would have had no more luck in penetrating the hearts and minds of the peasants than did the Americans and the South Vietnamese government.

America had no reason to foresee that Vietnam would be the place of its first defeat. No army had yet stood up to America's military might and the motley assortment of black-clad Viet Cong guerrillas in South Vietnam did not seem to be an exception. But the war planners did not understand the political nature of this conflict and they were loath to modify their strategy to deal with it. Only gradually did Washington realize the need for some sort of plan that would address the political problems in South Vietnam's countryside. That meant two things: the injection of a benevolent government presence into the villages, and a means of providing the people with security from communist retribution. Neither could be accomplished as long as the VCI ran free.

Far from being a sideshow or "the other war," the Phoenix program's attempt to strike at the VCI represented final recognition that "conventional" military might alone could not win the war. In many ways that recognition was too little too late, but there are lessons from the experience that should be examined. Unfortunately, it will not be simple merely to step back and look because the Phoenix program remains mired in myth and misunderstanding. A decade and a half of allegations, half-truths, and outright lies have framed the picture the public sees when it hears the name "Phoenix."

Acknowledgments

Hᴜ̲ɪsᴛᴏʀʏ doesn't come easy. We are sometimes led to believe historians are the keepers of facts; they simply lay them out end to end for all to see. Of course, it is never that easy. As time marches on works of history become more and more intricate, particularly when they attempt to describe and analyze a complex and controversial subject.

The Vietnam War is probably the best-documented conflict of all time, if best-documented can be defined by sheer volume. There is so much paper lying out there in various archives, libraries, and private collections that anyone willing to take up the trail is bound to come away with some new aspect of the war. But all this documentation has become a researcher's bane. For example, the National Archives in Washington, D.C. has so many Vietnam-era documents that workers there do not realistically hope to have it all cataloged for decades. In some cases they do not even know exactly what they have.

My research trail led straight into untracked territory. I have chosen a topic that has been hotly debated, but remains largely misunderstood—in many cases largely unknown. No one had attempted to sort through the material and examine the facts and myths of the Phoenix program. When I first embarked on this study I was skeptical that it could be done at all. I believed the old story that Phoenix was a closely held national secret and I expected a dearth of documents providing at best an incomplete picture. Nothing could have been further from the truth.

So many documents had already been declassified that finding a starting point was a difficult decision. Where there were gaps, the Freedom of Information Act helped fill them, though slowly.

To the people who helped me search and sift through this mass of paper, my thanks. They all thought they were just doing their jobs, but to a researcher innocent in the ways of official archives, their patience and understanding was appreciated. I only wish I could list them all here.

A few must be mentioned by name. Dr. Richard Hunt, a historian at the U.S. Army Center of Military History, was never too busy to leave his desk and dig through files for documents, or answer endless questions. William Getshell, Richard Boylan, and Cary Conn helped me wade through the holdings at the National Archives' largely untapped wealth of Phoenix program documents. Thanks also to the people who answered my Freedom of Information Act requests, declassifying most of what I asked for.

Naturally, this book could not have been completed without the cooperation of dozens of participants in the Phoenix program, from top officials to field advisers. Robert Komer and William Colby provided invaluable insight on the evolution of the Phoenix program. Colonel Stuart Herrington sacrificed some of his precious weekend mornings educating me on the finer points of being a Phoenix adviser in Vietnam. Frank Brown pointed me toward many new avenues of research and provided a valuable glimpse of the day-in–day-out life of the Phoenix program in his province. Other advisers, most of whom wish to remain in the background, gave willingly of their valuable time and endured countless phone calls, letters, and questions.

A special thanks goes to Neil Livingstone for helping get a new writer started and to Robert Bovenschulte, publisher of Lexington Books, for not pushing too hard on deadlines. They both provided a steady stream of constructive criticism and were always there for me to lean on.

This book couldn't have been written without the help of others, but the responsibility for its content belongs with the author. Any errors in fact or interpretation are my own.

Dale Andradé
Alexandria, Virginia

Introduction

AN AIR of great solemnity vibrated tangibly through the halls of the Rayburn House Office Building. It was 10:00 A.M., 2 August 1971, the scheduled beginning of the final day of hearings on U.S. Assistance Programs in Vietnam. An innocuous-sounding subject, just one of many turgid sessions churned out by a Congress more and more involved in putting an end to U.S. involvement in Vietnam. But one of the main topics was the controversial Phoenix program, considered to be a prime reason to suspend U.S. participation in the war. Better still, one of the final witnesses called before the subcommittee was said to be a hands-on participant in the Phoenix program, a man who had seen Phoenix at work and its effects on the enemy. To many, this was more enlightening than testimony by high-ranking officials who—it was argued—were out of touch with the Phoenix program's realities.

The hearings had begun on 15 July and were conducted by the Foreign Operations and Government Information Subcommittee, part of the House Committee on Government Operations. William S. Moorehead (D–Mass.) chaired the subcommittee.

Congressman Moorehead took his seat and stared for some moments at the stack of papers before him. Silence reigned as questioners, witnesses, and staff members awaited the first barrage of questions. At Moorehead's side were two of his fellow committeemen: Congressman Ogden R. Reid (R–N.Y.) and Paul N. McCloskey, Jr. (R–Calif.). The other six members were not present.

Facing them was one of the subjects of today's anticipation. His name was K. Barton Osborn, a former serviceman and Vietnam veteran allegedly involved in the Phoenix program. His position on the Phoenix program pointedly contradicted earlier testimony by high-ranking pacification officials.

Moorehead looked up from his papers and studied the man sitting before him. Osborn seemed to have consciously shed any connection to his military past. He lacked the ramrod bearing of a man proud of his martial service and he had grown a mop of curly reddish hair and long bushy sideburns. But Moorehead wasted no time on such trivial observations. He curtly asked Osborn to explain his connection with the Phoenix program.

Osborn said that while in Vietnam he was involved in both military intelligence and with the CIA. Before that he attended intelligence school at Ft. Holabird, Maryland, where he was trained in a classified program of "illegal agent handling" which included "terminating" people.

Reid jumped into the act. He did not seem to care about Osborn's training, or about his connection with the Phoenix program. He was more concerned about a single word.

"Could you explain what you mean by 'terminate'?"

Osborn must have been expecting the question because he quickly answered. It meant "releasing agents when they were no longer of use." A simple enough explanation, but Reid knew a good opening when he saw one and he was not about to let go.

"Do you imply by that 'with extreme prejudice'?" The term had become popular in these days of CIA-bashing and Reid could scarcely contain his satisfaction with this line of questioning.

Osborn replied in a measured tone. "With prejudice is sub-categorized into two areas. With prejudice may mean simply that the agent did a bad job; in some way was judged not loyal or whatever, and was not to be hired again and was to be put on a list of undesirable personalities which they call a 'black list.'"

"With extreme prejudice is to murder the individual right out because he or she constitutes a knowledgeable person who may be compromising to present or future operations. That is a termination process," he said.

Later in the questioning Osborn was asked to explain what was meant by "neutralize." His answer was unequivocal. "Killed on the spot," he said flatly. He claimed this in spite of days of testimony and documentation defining neutralization as "capture, kill, or rally."

Osborn also characterized the Phoenix program as "a sterile, depersonalized murder program." This opinion was based on his limited experience in a single city within a single province of South Vietnam. How could he possibly make that claim based on the evidence at his disposal? The answer was simply that the facts did not matter; the allegations alone were enough to convict Phoenix.

With his hands carefully folded on the table in front of him, Osborn went on, calmly answering questions and explaining his role in Vietnam. In the end he cleared up nothing. He only helped perpetuate many of the myths that grew to surround the Phoenix program. Osborn came to personify a popular (though untrue) image of the Phoenix program in those waning days of the Vietnam War and the next generation would remember only the allegations, not the facts.

For all the seriousness implied by Osborn's presence before Congress, his testimony was a sham. Osborn never was really associated with Phoenix, but like many others who believed that Phoenix was a sort of Murder, Incorporated, he had heard stories, most of them during training. After enlisting in the Army in 1966 Osborn had been trained at Ft. Holabird, Maryland as an intelligence specialist and in September 1967 he was sent to Danang to report to the 525th Military Intelligence Group. Almost immediately Osborn claimed he began to witness atrocities. He left Danang in December 1968, only six months after the Phoenix program really got off the ground.

What did Osborn see that convinced him Phoenix was an assassination program? He related a story about Viet Cong prisoners thrown out of a helicopter by U.S. Marine Corps personnel; he said he saw a woman starved to death in a cage in the First Marine Division Counterintelligence Team complex near Danang; and he said he saw the body of a prisoner being carried out of an interrogation room where he had died when a six-inch dowel was pushed through his ear and into his brain.

All are gruesome stories and all are inexcusable in any war. But Osborn never brought forth a shred of evidence to support his allegations. He refused to name names and he could provide no documentation. Most importantly, even if these atrocities did occur, they could not be laid at the feet of the Phoenix program. First, the Marines never were more than tangentially involved with the Phoenix program. Second, I Corps, where Osborn allegedly witnessed these acts, was always a war of big units with relatively little emphasis placed on programs like Phoenix. Third, and perhaps most important, Phoenix was not a well-organized program in late 1967 and early 1968. Osborn had fallen into the same trap as many before and after him: he blamed the name Phoenix for all the unsavory deeds that came to represent the war. The reputation was simplistic and unrealistic.

Two years later Osborn returned to testify again, this time before the Senate Committee on Armed Services. The occasion was the July 1973 hearings on William E. Colby's nomination as director of Central Intelligence. Once again, Phoenix was on trial and Osborn sat in as a witness for the prosecution. The impact of the Phoenix program's image on the American people played a large part in the proceedings, often overshadowing Colby's long and diverse career in the CIA, most of which had nothing to do with Phoenix. In the end he was confirmed, but not without a fight. Even today, Colby is mostly remembered as the man who presided over the Phoenix program.

Although K. Barton Osborn quickly and quietly faded from sight following his brief moment in the spotlight, he had become the personification of all the allegations and half-truths that emerged about the Phoenix program. Worst of all, men like Osborn provided the final comment on Phoenix. And in the rush to forget Vietnam and all that it meant, only that last word burned a permanent image into the public imagination. Because the nation's mood was antiwar, rational voices that tried to explain that Phoenix was an integral part of counterinsurgency were shouted down. As the war gradually faded into America's collective consciousness, the glimmer of memory that recalled Phoenix would attach to it the false label of "assassination program."

The myth was largely undeserved.

1

Threat: Viet Cong Infrastructure

The war in Vietnam began as a people's war, a struggle among the population for control of political allegiance rather than territory. Americans liked to call it the battle for hearts and minds, although the military was neither prepared nor willing to fight that kind of war. Only gradually did it become clear that more than firepower would be needed to win. Saigon would have to inject a benevolent presence into the villages and provide a means by which the people could be protected from communist retribution.

The enemy, seeking to make it impossible for the government of South Vietnam (GVN) to protect the people, maintained a clandestine presence among the population. This shadowy presence came to be called the Viet Cong Infrastructure (VCI) and was basically a miniature government reproduced down to the village level throughout South Vietnam. This infrastructure allowed the Viet Cong to maintain a presence in all of South Vietnam's approximately 250 districts, even if the main-force guerrilla units were destroyed by American firepower. And as long as the VCI remained in the villages, few people would be foolhardy enough to cooperate with the government.

Life of a VCI

Tran Van Tem did not fit the popular image of a formidable guerrilla. He was about forty years old, was married, had seven children, and worked off and on as a canal construction laborer and rice harvester. But then Tem was not a fighter. He was a member of the Viet Cong Infrastructure.[1]

Like many of his Viet Cong compatriots, Tem became involved with the revolution because there was no alternative. In early 1962 he lived in a small village in Duc Hue District, Hau Nghia Province, and, like many of the other peasants, Tem hired himself out as a field hand to rich farmers to make a meager living. Cash was scarce, and the field hands were paid in rice, though never enough to adequately feed their families.

One day, feeling the pinch of hunger, Tem asked the farmer if he could be paid a little more. The farmer was not in a charitable mood and he accused Tem of being a communist. The Viet Cong had been through the village on a number of occasions and one of their promises to the people had been that they would force the rich farmers to give a bigger share of the crops to the workers. To this farmer, Tem's request for more rice seemed like an admission of adherence to VC ideology and he reported Tem to the hamlet chief.

In his anger, the farmer embellished Tem's request, adding that he had threatened to bring VC revenge on the farmers if more rice was not forthcoming. To the hamlet chief this was proof enough of Tem's association with the Viet Cong. Some of the villagers learned of the farmer's report and warned Tem that he was to be arrested. Knowing the fate that surely awaited him, Tem fled into the jungle.

The Viet Cong soon learned of the incident and the next day discovered where Tem was hiding. That night the leader of the local VC cell, a man named Sau Tau, came to visit Tem in his hideaway. Given Tem's predicament, Sau Tau had little trouble convincing him the GVN was a puppet government that did not have the people's interests at heart. Tem agreed to work for the Viet Cong as a hamlet guerrilla.

During the next year the guerrillas avoided contact with the few government forces in the area. They were armed only with a few old U.S. carbines and insufficient ammunition, so they devoted their time to performing propaganda sessions in the local villages. In early 1963, after a year of work with the Viet Cong, Tem was appointed finance and economy chief for An Thuan

Hamlet and was given membership in the People's Revolutionary Party.

Because the guerrillas were still weak in 1963 they were unable to collect much money in taxes. In An Thuan Hamlet the Viet Cong taxed individual families by their ability to pay, but because they lacked the power to enforce their will, very little money came into the VC coffers during 1963. Tax money was turned over to the Party and cadre were paid a small cash stipend and some rice. In 1964 the Viet Cong had grown stronger and few people escaped the tax net. The guerrillas now had the guns to back up their demands.

During the early 1960s the GVN, under the rule of Ngo Dinh Diem, paid only passing attention to the Viet Cong in the villages, preferring instead to consolidate power in Saigon and guard against coup attempts. After Diem's death in November 1963 there was an effort to develop the capability to fight the Viet Cong in the villages, on their own terms. Part of this tactic were the Provisional Reconnaissance Units (PRUs), paramilitary groups developed in 1964 to strike at the guerrillas in the villages. They lived in the countryside and were tasked with seeking out and destroying the VCI. Tem suddenly became a target.

In June 1965 Tem and a number of other cadre fled to Cambodia to escape the PRUs, which, along with a few American advisers, had set up base in an old sugar mill. The PRUs regularly swept the area searching for VC and by this time it was common knowledge that Tem was working for the Viet Cong. Cambodia was a haven because the Americans had ruled that it was off limits to military operations.

In late December 1967 Tem was told he would have to return to his village in Duc Hue and prepare for a massive offensive. In January Tem was back in Vietnam. Like many of the other cadre, Tem believed this offensive would finally end the war and they could all return to normal, peaceful lives. They were wrong. Many cadre were lost in the Tet Offensive of January and February 1968 and the Party was forced to promote many cadre of lesser quality to high political posts.

Throughout the rest of 1968 and into 1969 the situation remained tense for Tem and the other cadre in Duc Hue. Tax revenues fell because the people were disenchanted with the Viet

Cong, which had promised the war would soon be over with the "final offensive." In October 1969 the military pressure on the VCI in Duc Hue was, in Tem's words, becoming unbearable. He contracted malaria and returned to Cambodia for rest and recuperation. The increase in military operations, a new emphasis on pacification, and the fledgling Phoenix program combined to force other VCI out of their haunts and into Cambodia, many of them simply abandoning their posts without permission from the Party. In Hiep Hoa Village in Duc Hue only three cadre remained: the farmers association chief, the deputy unit leader, and the deputy secretary.

In April 1970 U.S. and ARVN troops pushed over the Cambodian border in an attempt to crush the Viet Cong sanctuaries. The communists had received warning and were able to move their highest-ranking cadre out of danger. But the invasion disrupted their secure lines of supply and devastated the cadre rest areas. Tem and some of the other cadre who escaped were forced to steal from Cambodian peasants just to survive.

This was the last straw for Tem—he decided to rally to the GVN at the first opportunity. At the end of July 1970 he infiltrated Vietnam along with some NVA returning to their units. Because the Viet Cong were in bad shape in Duc Hue, Tem was immediately put back on tax collection duty. On 19 August, while moving through a swamp on their way to a hamlet tax collection point, Tem and his party were ambushed by an ARVN patrol. They managed to escape, but tax collecting was becoming hazardous duty that yielded fewer and fewer revenues.

On 1 September 1970 Tem rallied. The GVN had a program called Chieu Hoi (Open Arms), which promised freedom and repatriation for any Viet Cong or NVA soldier who turned himself in and gave up the fight. The Chieu Hoi program brought in almost one hundred sixty thousand deserters between 1963 and 1973, about thirty thousand of them VCI.[2]

Tran Van Tem's war was over. He discovered the GVN was willing to treat him well, contrary to stories he had heard from his comrades. Tem was not a high-level VCI, nor was he dogmatic in his adherence to the Party line. Tem simply wanted a better life than the one he had under the GVN. The Viet Cong had promised that, but things had only gotten worse. Like many other VCI, Tem had joined because he didn't want to become a guerrilla and fight. The life of a political cadre seemed much safer. But after the Tet Offensive, Tem was certain if he continued along his present course he would be captured or killed. That was not part of the plan.

Throughout his career with the Viet Cong, Tem did not realize the importance of his part in the communist war effort. Although he answered only to the district cadre, they, too, were part of an organization that formed a great web all over South Vietnam. After his desertion Tem came to realize that even though the situation he and his comrades faced was desperate, such was not necessarily the case throughout the country. He began to see that he had been a building block in a flexible structure designed to exert communist control all over South Vietnam. Like most deserters, Tem was not part of the elite cadre that remained in secure areas tightly controlled by the Viet Cong. Tem's job actually was much more dangerous than that of his bosses: he and his comrades were to remain in the contested villages under the guns of the military in an effort to keep close to the people. Without tight and constant contact with the population the revolution would have withered on the vine.

Formation of an Infrastructure

Although American policy makers and military planners argued over whether the center of the war lay in Hanoi or in the guerrilla movement in South Vietnam, the communists never had any doubt. The core of the revolution was the ability to extend a presence throughout the countryside. This was to be accomplished with the careful construction of a political infrastructure, not with a guerrilla army. The guerrillas were to keep the GVN off balance and, most importantly, protect the infrastructure.

The infrastructure, which became known as the VCI, formed the roots of Ho Chi Minh's revolution. After the Geneva Convention in July 1954 created a divided Vietnam, Hanoi recalled its soldiers in partial compliance with the Geneva Accords, but left in place an infrastructure of three thousand political and five thousand armed military cadre. This hardcore element would keep close to the people and assure that a shadow communist government remained in place. The Geneva Accords specified that elections were to be held in North and South Vietnam no later than July 1956. Because Ho Chi Minh was by far the most well-known figure in Vietnam, and because he was identified closely with the anti-French movement dating before WWII, there was little doubt he would win the elections. "Stay-behind" cadre were instructed to organize people in the South, capitalizing on the legitimate grievances brought on by a decade of war and an inequitable social system perpetuated by the new Diem regime. The communists exploited and exacerbated the problems, avoiding any mention of Marxist doctrine. The cadre formed cells, village committees, and small, loosely knit military units. A program of limited terror began, aimed at GVN officials, but also at those individuals necessary for a functioning society: teachers, doctors, and agricultural workers.[3]

By 1959 it was clear to Hanoi that there could be no peaceful takeover of South Vietnam and the insurgency began in earnest. After two years of increased terrorism and general violence the communists formally created a front organization in the South with an announcement on Hanoi Radio in January 1961. It heralded the formation of a National Front for the Liberation of South Vietnam (NLF).

The NLF actually had been formed on 20 December 1960, although it was a paper organization. Instead of drawing organizations together under a front in standard Leninist fashion, the NLF first created the front and then began drawing up organizations. In early 1961 the NLF was but a shadow waiting for a solid shape to bring it to life.[4]

The strength of the NLF burst forth from its gun barrels. By the mid-1960s as much as 40 percent of the rural population had been forced to pay taxes, supply warm bodies to fill Viet Cong ranks, and shelter and feed guerrillas and cadre. Reports became widespread that the NLF had authorized cadre to shoot recalcitrant villagers. Thought reform sessions and propaganda shows were a constant part of village life. The villagers began to resent the Viet Cong, but they were powerless to resist.[5] Despite growing hostility the NLF was able to grow and expand at an alarming rate, filling a vacuum the GVN had been unable and unwilling to fill, preferring instead to guard against coups in Saigon. Despite weapons and support from the United States, the GVN had been unable to accomplish anything approaching such a level of control in the countryside because their focus was misguided. While Saigon trained to meet an invasion from North Vietnam, the real enemy was creeping in the back door. The Viet Cong were devoting all effort to develop a superb organization down to the lowest levels.

The emergence of the NLF marked the beginning of open political revolution in South Vietnam, but it was not the true center of political power that many believed. Hanoi had intended to create an illusion, leading casual observers to conclude that the NLF was a spontaneous uprising of Southern discontent, while still controlling the reins. Those reins formed the crucial link between North and South Vietnam.

Link between North and South: The People's Revolutionary Party

The construction of a political link between North and South Vietnam became crucial because, from Hanoi's point of view, the NLF began to show signs of severe internal problems. First, the NLF had been created with a broad outline designed to appeal to Southern nationalists who might not favor reunification with the North. Second, the NLF expanded rapidly, outstripping the resources of available cadre. Third, Hanoi needed a way to firmly but quietly control and direct the Southern insurgency.

By 1961 guerrilla operations had expanded to a point where the military and political aspects of the NLF were on an equal footing. Consequently, policy considerations became the responsibility of a "new" organization, the People's Revolutionary Party (PRP). Official acknowledgment by Hanoi of the existence of the PRP came in January 1962. The PRP was formerly the southern branch of North Vietnam's Worker's Party (Dang Lao Dong, or Lao Dong Party) and represented the desire of leaders in Hanoi to place the NLF "under the guidance of veteran revolutionaries."[6]

The PRP was organized to be independent of, but enmeshed with, the NLF, which was the subordinate entity. The PRP had three functions: to provide the NLF with political guidance; to carry out general administration; and to act as logistics manager for the increasing infiltration of arms and men down the Ho Chi Minh Trail.

The PRP's most important command apparatus was at the province. From there the Party supervised policy at the district, village, and hamlet level. But the district-level committees were probably the most important because they oversaw day-to-day contact with the people and operations against the GVN. Before 1964 the district committees were the lowest operating level of the PRP and had considerable decision-making latitude, especially in the formation of new cells down to the hamlet level. After 1964 a massive effort was made to extend cells to the village and hamlet level.[7] By the time the Phoenix program appeared on the scene in late 1967 the PRP had extended its influence to the lowest levels of South Vietnamese society.

Even an organization as pervasive as the PRP did not have the manpower or resources to place committees in every village. It was logistically impossible. Rather, one village committee controlled from five to a dozen branches that made their way to various villages at various times. The village-level executive committee was made up of five to seven members commanded by a single PRP leader.

The PRP and the NLF worked side by side down to the lowest levels of South Vietnamese society. However, the NLF was not a mere puppet or a hollow shell designed to give an appearance of indigenous roots. The PRP did dominate the NLF, but their goals were parallel. The objective of the PRP was to make sure the NLF continued to have goals compatible with those of Hanoi, and if the day were to come when those goals diverged, to make sure that it had weeded out any potential troublemakers. So, while the NLF was Southern-based, it was Northern-controlled.[8]

American and ARVN forces were convinced that the PRP had a central headquarters somewhere in South Vietnam. In 1962 there were reports that the PRP Central Committee was operating from the area north of Saigon in Binh Duong Province. Other reports placed the headquarters just inside the Cambodian border west of Hau Nghia Province. Then in January 1966 a joint U.S.–ARVN operation overran the headquarters, capturing some six thousand pounds of documents. The raid proved conclusively that the PRP itself was linked to Hanoi by another outside organization.

Hanoi's Unseen Hand

The insurgency in the South received marching orders from Hanoi through the Central Office for South Vietnam (COSVN). This highest echelon of the revolution was made up of the most senior regional and provincial PRP and NLF members. They elected from their own members some thirty to forty men to become members of a Central Executive Committee. This committee in turn appointed ten members for the Current Affairs Committee. It was this small group that had day-to-day control over the Party's activities in South Vietnam. Naturally, its decisions were tailored to Hanoi's wishes.[9]

The Current Affairs Committee met continuously and controlled the activities of the next lower rung, made up of the Political Section and the Military Section, both of equal stature. Below them were various lesser sections, most of which fell under the Political Section. COSVN also maintained Regional and, most importantly, Provincial Party Committees that controlled local front organizations, associations, and military units.[10]

COSVN first appeared in 1959, following closely on the heels of the Lao Dong Party as successor to the old Indochinese Communist Party. Immediately following its creation the Lao Dong Central Executive Committee acknowledged the existence of COSVN by declaring that, "As of the publication of this notice, the Central Office of South Vietnam will be in Cambodia." To insure its continued survival, though, COSVN moved constantly. By the end of 1959 it was reported that COSVN had moved from Cambodia to the southern tip of South Vietnam, the Ca Mau Peninsula.[11]

Before March 1962, communist efforts in South Vietnam were divided into two zones, called Intersector V and the Southern Region, or Nam Bo. Each was responsible to the Central Committee of the Lao Dong Party in Hanoi. Then in March 1962 both zones were combined into a single operations center—COSVN.

Stories about the elusive nature of COSVN circulated throughout South Vietnam. Generally, it was believed that COSVN headquarters remained in the area west of Tay Ninh Province inside Cambodia. A former cadre told GVN officials in late 1959 that COSVN was actually in Tay Ninh. He said both the headquarters and the trails leading to it were camouflaged and that top COSVN leaders had separate houses with underground shelters and escape tunnels. After its reorganization in the early 1960s COSVN was reported to be northeast of Saigon, but within a year it alternated between Tay Ninh or just over the border in Cambodia. In December 1968 other defectors reported that COSVN "occupied a site in Cambodia six square kilometers in area." It was built in thick jungle, was bordered on the east and west by streams, and on the south it reached almost to the Vietnamese border.[12]

COSVN headquarters was always a target for the American and South Vietnamese military although they never succeeded in destroying it. At least once they did damage COSVN. In 1967 General Nguyen Chi Thanh died in a B-52 bombing raid, although Hanoi announced that he had died of a heart attack. Thanh was the overall commander of the Viet Cong and North Vietnamese forces in South Vietnam, the communist equivalent of General William Westmoreland. Thanh was replaced by Pham Hung, one of the most powerful men in North Vietnam.[13] Hung was also the secretary for the PRP and chief political officer of the Liberation Army, an indication of the interwoven relationships between the various organizations, all ultimately controlled by Hanoi.

Operations and Activities

Cadre in the villages and hamlets could expect to regularly receive instructions from the province level via commo-liaison agents who traveled regularly between the province committee and the various villages and hamlets. The routes taken by these cadre as they tirelessly trekked between various cadre cells became well-established and were a prime target of GVN anti-infrastructure operations.

The ruling committees of district and province chapters generally met once a month. The Current Affairs Committees at each level met frequently and often carried on daily operations. The regularity of these meetings depended upon the degree of Viet Cong control: in contested areas meetings were sporadic; in VC-controlled areas meetings might occur on a regular schedule. Commo-liaison cadre were told of the meetings a few days in advance so they could plan out their transportation route.[14]

To protect themselves, VC cadre had to build their activities around security in the villages. In communist-controlled areas cadre lived in their own houses by day, moving to alternate quarters each night. No matter how secure a village seemed, there was always the possibility that the enemy might learn where cadre members lived and send special teams to capture or kill them.

District cadre operated out of the most secure village in the area. Even so, top district cadre changed sleeping places as often as three times a night. The houses they chose had tunnels or holes in the floor or out in the garden and were selected with an eye toward convenient escape routes. Top Party officials at the district and province level lived in remote base areas even if the population was considered strongly Viet Cong.

Cadre awoke early in the morning, cooking meals long before daylight so the smoke would not be noticed. After breakfast cadre returned to their hideouts and remained there until midmorning. GVN sweep operations almost always occurred at dawn, so by noon it was fairly safe to come out of hiding knowing that no more enemy operations were likely until the next morning.

Whenever high-level cadre met in person they chose the most remote hamlet in a Viet Cong village, preferably one close to a secure base area to which they could flee if danger approached. Such areas were riddled with tunnels and escape routes and guarded by a platoon of guerrillas who ringed the hamlet and engaged any attacking force long enough for the cadre to escape. Guerrillas often led the enemy on a chase designed to draw them away from the meeting area.[15]

High-level province and regional cadres rarely left their bases. If travel was necessary it was only under heavy guard to VC villages on Party business. District cadre were sometimes required to make the journey to province and region base areas to report on district activities. When important cadre traveled they were accompanied by two or three armed bodyguards and carried a concealed pistol. The pistol was often a badge of rank and GVN forces that found pistols on captured or killed Viet Cong knew they had eliminated someone important. The general rule of thumb was that the higher the rank of the cadre, the larger the bodyguard retinue and the more sophisticated the weaponry that backed them up.

Paramount Target

As the U.S. military troop buildup progressed in the early 1960s, more and more resources went toward battling Viet Cong, and later North Vietnamese Army (NVA), regular forces. The CIA remained in charge of the PRU, a small program conducted behind a dark curtain of secrecy. Pacification—to which the PRUs and any other anti-infrastructure operations should have been inextricably tied—was virtually a separate program that was often little more than a conduit for funneling rice, medicine, and building supplies into South Vietnam's rural countryside. Unfortunately, many of those supplies ended up on the black market, or worse, in the hands of the Viet Cong.

There was little cooperation between pacification in general and the CIA's PRU program. Everyone seemed to be operating in their own little world. But anti-infrastructure operations were the teeth that gave bite to the jaws of pacification and any effort that did not combine the two was doomed to failure.

Nor did MACV do much to remedy the problem. General Westmoreland, who served as COMUSMACV (commander, U.S. Military Assistance Command, Vietnam) from June 1964 to June 1968, did not regard the VCI as the center of conflict in South Vietnam. Westmoreland acknowledged that the political infrastructure was an important part of the communists' war plan, but he considered it secondary to main-force units. Westmoreland illustrated his priorities with an analogy. The VCI, he said, were "termites" that slowly gnawed away at the foundation of the GVN. Waiting in the wings with crowbars poised to demolish the weakened structure were the "bully boys," the Viet Cong and NVA military units. Westmoreland believed that "only by eliminating the bully boys—or at least harrying them so as to keep them away from the building—was there a possibility of eliminating the termites. . . ."[16]

Westmoreland's reasoning showed precisely the military's quandary in Vietnam. Although Army planners recognized the existence of both the political infrastructure and the main-force units, they were unable to distinguish which was paramount. Why couldn't Westmoreland just as easily use his "termite" and "bully boy" analogy to illustrate that the main strategy should have been to destroy the "termites" first? Then the "bully boys" would have had a more difficult time knocking over the GVN with their crowbars. The answer was that Westmoreland, like the rest of the Army, had been trained to believe that war would always be conventional. When the situation in Vietnam did not conform to the concept, they tried to make it fit.

The military could not bring itself to view the VCI as the most important foe. They had trained the ARVN to counter an invasion by North Vietnam and from the beginning refused to recognize the role played by the VCI in paving the way for main-force units. The CIA and a few civilian agencies were left to monitor and combat the VCI, while Army intelligence concentrated on enemy order of battle data. The military's neglect of the VCI was particularly foolhardy given the experiences of those who had battled insurgencies before them—particularly the French, who had fought the same enemy and had failed to recognize the heart of the conflict.

2

Phoenix Rising: Anti-infrastructure Antecedents

THE AMERICAN experience with political infrastructure in Vietnam was not a new phenomenon. Since World War II the importance of dealing with pacification became clear in a number of conflicts, but the lessons were not easily learned. The Americans in particular had a wealth of lessons they could look back on to define the shape of the new conflict they were getting into on the Asian mainland. The French had lost to a guerrilla army that had built its strength by first controlling the countryside. In the Philippines, American advisers had seen a conventionally trained Filipino army change its ways and adapt to guerrilla warfare. The result was victory over the guerrillas. In Malaya the British handled their "Emergency" with pacification techniques, including strategic hamlets and police primacy.

Yet in Vietnam the American military insisted the war was basically conventional and could be won by conventional means. It chose to disregard many of the lessons learned by those who preceded them in Asia.

French Lesson in Indochina

The Viet Minh victory at Dien Bien Phu on 7 May 1954 marked the end of French involvement in Indochina. France had played out her hand as a colonial power in Asia, but the defeat also heralded a rebirth of sorts for the French military. As their American successors in South Vietnam would later come to realize, this war could not be won by military might alone. Even during the First Indochina War the French had made some attempts at pacification—with some success in the south, but almost nothing of note in the north. As was to be the case with American involvement in Vietnam, there was considerable debate between military men over the correct method to be used in fighting the communist insurgency. Some believed in conventional combat as a means of bludgeoning the Viet Minh into surrender, while others felt some form of pacification would provide the best results.[1]

When French forces began their postwar redeployment into Vietnam in October 1945 they were emboldened by the fact that Viet Minh forces simply retreated into the countryside, abandoning one town after another with hardly a fight. But as Bernard Fall noted, the French really only controlled Vietnam "to the extent of 100 yards on either side of all major roads."[2]

During the early days of the war the French were convinced the war would be over in a matter of weeks, so "pacification" really only meant hammering the Vietnamese populous into cooperation. But even with such an attitude prevailing within the French military, there was a realization that pacification needed to be refined. It would take more than the thirty-five thousand French troops already in Vietnam during late 1945, however. Some French planners felt one hundred thousand was a more realistic figure.[3]

Fortunately for the French, or perhaps not, as events would come to show, the war in Cochin-China (southern Vietnam) provided an ideal stage for trying out a new pacification program. Cochin-China was basically devoid of main-force Viet Minh units, so French forces could concentrate on winning hearts and minds. General Pierre Boyer de la Tour, the commander of French forces in Cochin-China, was well aware of the need for pacification, writing that, "The military man in Cochin-China must be, above all, a pacifier. He must restore confidence, little by little, among the people."[4] And true to the general's word, French troops engaged in a rudimentary pacification program beginning in 1946. The guiding principle was the *tauche d'huile* ("oil spot"), which, in theory, yielded twin benefits.

First, the army went into an area that was relatively secure and began using it as a base from which to attack the Viet Minh in other areas. From a conventional standpoint this made sense—logistics were simpler to maintain and the enemy was faced with less predictable movement from French forces operating out of nearby urban areas.

Secondly, the oil spot method allowed French forces to stay in a village and provide a sense of security, which was the first step toward coaxing the people away from Viet Minh propaganda. Civic action was the basic component of the pacification phase of the oil spot. As the army established control, it set up an administration that managed the maintenance of roads and the building of schools and hospitals. Taxes and the local legal system also were administered under this system.[5]

The oil spot was not something concocted by the French just for Vietnam. In the late nineteenth century, future Marshals Gallieni and Lyautey developed the method in Madagascar and North Africa. The plan called for a string of forts to serve as a sign to the people of the region that the French were close by to provide protection. The forts also served French troops as a stepping-off point for actions against the enemy.[6]

Between 1946 and 1950 the French devoted a substantial effort toward pacification in the south. Indeed, the war there converted some French officers into believers in pacification. One French general wrote, "For a province to be considered pacified, it is necessary [for] . . . the legal government to manifest itself by the restoration of normal political institutions, for the clearing of the area to have been completed by the people themselves, and, finally, for the centers of population to have organized self-defense units." There was by this time a realization on the part of the French that the people themselves had to be the real work force behind any pacification effort.[7]

The Viet Minh infrastructure became an important objective for the French as early as 1945, but they seemed to be unclear as to how to go about the task of eliminating it. French pacification operations were largely a process of *cloisonnement* ("partitioning off"), combined with a grid-square of garrisons and forts called *quadrillage*. This process was the essence of the oil spot and in its midst was the attempt to seek out and neutralize the Viet Minh infrastructure. In July 1947 General de la Tour became commander of the *Forces Terrestres Sud-Vietnam* ("Ground Forces in South Vietnam," or FTSV) and with his appointment orders for the elimination of the enemy infrastructure "became more explicit."[8]

Orders called for the "closest civil–military coordination from the highest level in Saigon all the way down to the humblest villages in the paddy country." The civil authority—not the military—was charged with purging elements of the infrastructure, the equivalent of what would become known as Phoenix when the Americans came to Vietnam. The civil authorities also ran the rallying program (from the French word *rallier*, "to win over"). Again, the Americans would adopt this twenty years later and call it Chieu Hoi.[9]

The second aspect of General de la Tour's pacification directives set forth the creation of a "Vietnamese *Garde Republicaine de Cochinchine*, which was gradually to make possible the withdrawal of French units from pacification duty."[10] The parallel to the American decision to use South Vietnamese army units for pacification duty while the Americans took on the burden of fighting the "big unit" war seems obvious.

By 1948 the French believed their pacification efforts in the south were producing results. Members of the Cao Dai and Hoa Hao religious sects were being integrated into both the French forces and the *Garde Republicaine* to *jaunir* ("yellow"), the French colonial armed forces, in an attempt to make them seem more indigenous.[11]

In late 1949 and early 1950 the French command outlined some lessons from the French experience in Cochin-China, which were then issued as directives. All of them stated in general that the "armed force must never become an end in itself; it is only a means for achieving pacification."[12]

The French followed two of their newly coined cardinal rules in at least one pacification operation carried out in what became the province of Kien Hoa. A Vietnamese half-caste named Jean Leroy organized local French and Vietnamese elements into a mobile pacification force known as Mobile Units for the Defense of Christendom (UMDC is the French acronym). This force was mainly made up of Catholic Vietnamese organized into sixty-man brigades that were assigned to clear out Viet Minh main-force units from the area, then set up garrisons in the pacified villages to provide the peasants security from communist reprisals, and finally construct and train a local self-defense force that could, in time, fend for itself. The operation followed the oil spot pattern, but also took the extra step of putting trust in the villagers for their own defense. After all, who better knew which people living in the region were the enemy infrastructure? The locals, with their security provided for by a combination of UMDC and self-defense forces, were not as likely to fear retribution for cooperating with the government and so set out to clear their own areas of the Viet Minh infrastructure. When this was accomplished the UMDC moved on. In Leroy's own words, "Once the self-defense militias were on hand and the authority of the notables well established, I would send my UMDCs a little farther on."[13]

Leroy's experience was not the norm, however. In general his success was not to be repeated anywhere else in Cochin-China. And even Leroy's success was short-lived. In 1952 he departed Vietnam, and many of the areas pacified by his troops experienced an upsurge of Viet Minh terrorism that his fledgling local self-defense forces could not contain. In the end regular French forces were sent back in to try and contain the Viet Minh resurgence and the situation was back to square one.[14]

Perhaps the most distressing aspect of the French pacification process—as far as the Vietnamese rural population was concerned—was that the French tended to bring back the same administrative system, the same law enforcement procedures, and the same landlords. While the peasants were pleased with the initial security the French presence brought to the countryside, they were not at all enthusiastic about the return of the old unequitable ways of running village affairs. The French never equated pacification with the long-term reforms that later experience in Vietnam—and elsewhere in the Third World—would show were necessary for any sort of lasting suppression of communist insurgency.

However, in 1950, the question of the success or failure of

pacification in Cochin-China became largely academic discourse when the Viet Minh intensified attacks on Tonkin (northern Vietnam) and forced the French to divert many of the troops involved in southern pacification efforts to conventional combat duty in the north. Almost immediately the situation in the villages vacated by French pacification forces deteriorated.[15]

French pacification efforts in Tonkin largely were unsuccessful. This was because of the concentration of Viet Minh regular forces in the north but there were other reasons as well. Most notable was that Tonkin contained almost no anti–Viet Minh minority groups such as the Hoa Hao and Cao Dai to help the French establish a foothold in the countryside. Simple timing was also a factor. The Viet Minh had been in place in Tonkin for a full six months before the first French troops arrived in March 1946, and it was another three months before the fighting began. That gave the Viet Minh nine months to establish an infrastructure in rural Tonkin before the French even began to respond. By 1953 the Viet Minh were estimated to have had at least partial control of "5,000 out of the 7,000 villages in the deltaic plain."[16] The Americans had the same problem twenty years later. By the time U.S. troops arrived in South Vietnam the Viet Cong had had years to infiltrate and control the villages.

Pacification took a giant step backward in Tonkin, although in fairness to the French, they were unprepared for the size and scope of the Viet Minh conventional military challenge. When General Henri Navarre became commander-in-chief of the French forces in Indochina in early 1953, he espoused the idea that all first-rate troops were needed for fighting Viet Minh regulars. Navarre felt that pacification was a secondary task in that it could really only be accomplished if the main-force threat were eliminated, or at least reduced, beforehand. Navarre did believe, however, that pacification had to be maintained, even if that meant using troops "of lower quality" for pacification duty. But on the other hand, Navarre really only viewed pacification as a means of keeping the Viet Minh out of the villages once they had been driven out. In other words, pacification meant "expelling, destroying, and cleaning out."[17]

In Tonkin's far north, along the Chinese border, the French attempted a long-range pacification program that, though unsuccessful, heralded the new thinking in French colonial counterinsurgency. In this region during the years following WWII and until 1949, French junior officers often acted as district chiefs, administering the affairs of each village in whatever way he saw fit. Beginning in 1949 these officers began acting as advisers to Vietnamese district chiefs, relying on their judgment to manage affairs, such as the identification of enemy infrastructure. The administration and pacification effort was protected by a network of forts garrisoned by about seven hundred men, 80 percent of whom were Vietnamese. Although only a rudimentary pacification program, it was a start, albeit too little too late. In 1950, Giap's Viet Minh troops wiped out the string of French forts used to protect the region and French pacification efforts collapsed.[18]

The French also formed roving administrative teams called Mobile Administrative Groups for Operations (GAMO) that were sent into regions after the French military had occupied them. Begun in 1951, the GAMOs became most active in early 1952 in the Red River Delta, where they sought to destroy Viet Minh regulars and infrastructure that had infiltrated behind the de Lattre line. They would go into a village that had been surrounded by French troops, begin a security check to locate Viet Minh political personnel, appoint new administrators from among the population, and provide supplies to reopen markets and shops. GAMOs provided a better method of keeping the Viet Minh out of the villages in the Delta, but only temporarily, because they, too, were pulled out to help stem the Viet Minh offensive first begun in 1950.[19]

As control of Vietnam began to slip through their fingers, the French relied less on pacification and more on air power. French troops began to lose their stomach for trudging through unfriendly villages on futile pacification missions when it was clear that nobody wanted them around. One French soldier put it best: "We get shot at every time we pass by on the highway and I don't feel like losing a good platoon for the sake of mopping up a bunch of mud huts. Let's get the Air Force into this and just wipe 'em off the map.... Scratch three villages with their sassy civilian population."[20]

Harkening back to the 1949 article by General Pierre Boyer

de la Tour, it is difficult to see that the French had paid his prophetic words much heed. But his six-point outline still stands up to scrutiny, especially after twenty-five years of mistakes made by French and American planners and politicians in Vietnam. Some of his most relevant points directly addressed the question of eliminating the enemy infrastructure:

> The Vietnamese government will be greatly interested in reconstituting the councils of notables, in carrying out a careful census, and in the necessary purging of the local Viet-Minh who have remained in place.[21]

In 1955 the commander-in-chief of the French forces published a treatise of lessons from the First Indochina War. Although little of it dealt with pacification, there was recognition that destroying the enemy infrastructure was crucially important. Among the lessons was a single clear sentence: "The revolutionary apparatus must be destroyed, or at least shattered, before the enemy's techniques can be countered by our own propaganda."[22]

Even General Henri Navarre, the man unfortunate enough to command the French forces in their final hour of defeat at Dien Bien Phu, wrote that "against an enemy who can succeed only with the support of the population the basic problem is to keep the latter on our side by watching over it, by reassuring it, and by protecting it." Part of watching over the population meant first eliminating the Viet Minh political infrastructure.[23]

Following the Geneva Accords of 1954, which ended French involvement in Indochina, a spate of articles and books dealing with the subject of guerrilla warfare and how to counter it were published. One particular article in the *Revue Militaire d'Information,* published in January 1957, outlined the necessary ingredients for a successful pacification program. The most important rule noted by the author was to never forget that "the key to revolutionary war, the secret of [the enemy's] effectiveness, depends upon the existence of his infrastructure," which must be "destroyed root and branch." The article went on to note that the task of pacification itself can be "achieved only when the rebel infrastructure has been dismantled."[24]

Another article, again in the *Revue Militaire d'Information*, seemed to put the entire French mauling in Vietnam into perspective. The article, written in 1957, noted that "the real strength of the enemy does not reside in his terrorist groups or in his military units, but in his political infrastructure." Perhaps more than any other French military article of the immediate post–Indochina War period, this one put forth the opinion that elimination of the enemy infrastructure was so important to the war effort that it should be considered a separate lesson that "ought to be printed in capital letters" so that future generations of French military officers would not miss the point.[25]

The realization that the enemy infrastructure was central to the success or failure of any insurgency was clearly a lesson that, on the academic battleground, at least, had been learned by the French. Not only did they have their own experiences in Indochina to provide a guiding light for future policy, they also had the British "Emergency" in Malaya and the American counterinsurgency effort in the Philipines to look to, both of which had been going on simultaneously with the French imbroglio in Vietnam.

Malayan Emergency

If for no other reason, the Malayan Emergency (1948–1960) will always be remembered in history as the counterinsurgency effort that worked. The Malayan communists were crushed and the British had won with a system that was, for the most part, untried in previous military history. The British had fired the opening shot in a kind of warfare that was born in the chaos of the Second World War and would shape the method of military thinking well into the future. Perhaps it is ironic that the British opener in the fight against communist Third World insurgencies would be one of the few successes in this new genre of combat. Succeeding counterinsurgency efforts should pick up pointers from previous ones, but that has not been the case. But perhaps more than anything else, this declining record points out differences in the circumstances surrounding each insurgency situation rather than a succession of lessons that ought to have been learned.

The differences between the insurgencies in Malaya and Vietnam were legion. First, in Malaya, there was no single well-known nationalist figure who could rally the people to the cause of throwing out the colonizers. Second, except for a tiny spit of Thai territory butting up against the northern tip of the Malay peninsula, Malaya was surrounded by ocean. As a result, the communist insurgency lacked the porous border that allowed the easy transport of weapons into the country. Third, even if they could, the Soviets were unwilling to support the fledgling Malay insurgency as they would in Vietnam. Fourth, the guerrilla movement was made up largely of ethnic Chinese in a country that was mostly Malay.[26]

The Malay insurgency relied heavily on an infrastructure, both as a means of controlling the rural population and as a tool to prevent the British security forces from separating the villagers from the guerrillas by relocating them in fortified villages—the basis for the American-sponsored Strategic Hamlet program in Vietnam beginning in 1962.

The political organization of the Malay communists was set up along Soviet lines. It was controlled by a Central Executive Committee numbering between ten and thirteen with a politburo of three. This committee commanded the Malayan Races Liberation Army (MRLA) and the regional bureaus, state, district, and branch committees. Throughout this structure was a support arm, the Min Yuen, which provided the movement with intelligence, supplies, tax collection, recruitment, and any other task set forth by the Central Executive Committee. The Min Yuen were the Malay communist infrastructure.[27]

As is the case with any underground movement, the strength of the Min Yuen was difficult to estimate. Some figures place their strength at ten thousand, others as high as five hundred thousand.[28] And as would be the case with the American experience with the VCI, the Min Yuen were easier to locate than were the fighting units of the MRLA. While the MRLA ran about the jungle striking at the British whenever they felt they had the advantage, the Min Yuen, by the nature of their responsibilities, had to remain among the villages in the countryside. But like the VCI, the Min Yuen were difficult to root out. The peasants knew who they were, but they were unwilling to turn them in until the government demonstrated its ability to protect the people from communist reprisals.

The British quickly realized the importance of destroying the enemy infrastructure—the Min Yuen—as the key to defeating the insurgency. In April 1950, Lieutenant General Sir Harold Briggs was appointed director of operations in Malaya, and Sir Henry Gurney became executive of the high commissioner. General Briggs was well-versed in unconventional warfare, having fought in the Western Desert and Burma during WWII. After spending a few weeks traveling throughout Malaya, the general thought he had the answer to the question of how to defeat the guerrillas—the Briggs Plan.

General Briggs set forth four objectives: Secure all populated areas, break up the communist infrastructure in the populated areas, deny the communists food and support from the populated areas, and seek to destroy the enemy by forcing him to fight on terms of the government's choosing. Briggs established the model for overseeing the hoped-for dismantling of the insurgency, which the Americans would later follow in Vietnam. He set up in each state and district separate War Executive Committees (SWEC in the states and DWEC in the districts), which were assigned to oversee all aspects of the counterinsurgency operations. Police, intelligence, civil, and military authorities were all represented at meetings where they discussed possible methods of defeating the insurgency.[29]

It was clear to the British that the first step in winning the war was to provide the population with the security necessary to diminish their fear of reprisals from the communists. This meant separating the guerrillas from their potential base of support—the villages. Called New Villages, the plan entailed moving entire villages into fortified areas where they could be watched over by the security forces. The key to the plan's success lay in the fact that the villagers were given land—an eight-hundred-square-yard plot per family inside the fenced perimeter and an additional two acres of farm land outside the walls. Since most of the peasants had had no land before moving into the New Villages, the plan kept most of them happy. Perhaps the best evidence of this came after the Emergency was over and most of the villagers elected to stay in their new homes.[30] The equivalent of the New Villages in Vietnam—the Strategic Hamlets—would not prove so successful for a variety of reasons.

The law was also rewritten to make life difficult for the insurgents. The death penalty was automatically given to anyone convicted of being a terrorist, which was defined as anyone "carrying arms, ammunition, or explosives without a license or consorting with such persons."[31] In addition, anyone suspected of being a terrorist could be held under arrest for twenty-eight days and then detained for up to two years without trial. Everyone over the age of twelve was required to carry an identification card. Finally, large regions of the countryside were restricted, a sort of free fire zone from which the peasants had been cleared.

Because the Min Yuen were an underground infrastructure, the primary task of the security forces was to bring them to the surface. By controlling the dispensation of food with the identity cards, the British were able to crack the Min Yuen. To survive, the Min Yuen had to break the rules, which meant surfacing and allowing security forces to identify them.

Perhaps the most important aspect of the British counterinsurgency effort in Malaya was the decision to make the elimination of the communist infrastructure a police job rather than a military one. The military concentrated its efforts on tracking down the guerrilla fighting units.

When the Emergency began Malaya had nine thousand policemen. Within six months the number was at forty-five thousand, and at the peak of the fighting police ranks had swelled to sixty thousand. In Malaya police primacy in the fight against the insurgents was given paramount attention at the beginning of the fighting, rather than waiting for years, as was the case in Vietnam. After a six-month training period police officers were sent to the New Villages, where it was their job to protect the population. In a village of one hundred to two hundred people, there could be as many as thirty policemen. With such a favorable ratio, the villagers didn't have to worry about the consequences of facing the guerrillas when the security forces left the village, as later happened in Vietnam. In the New Villages the police stayed with the people always.[32]

The core of winning the fight against the Malayan communists, as pointed out earlier, was the destruction of the Min Yuen. The actual job of hunting them down went to the Police Special Branch. To the British, the Special Branch is the investigative arm of the police force, sort of the equivalent of the American FBI. They worked in plain clothes and in the New Villages they lived among the people. Most of the Special Branch detectives in Malaya were Malayan Chinese who held the rank of corporal or sergeant. These men were not undercover—both the villagers and the Min Yuen knew who they were. They lived in posts guarded by security forces or the regular police and their job was to recruit intelligence agents who would in turn gather information on the Min Yuen. Generally, three or four Special Branch operatives would be attached to a New Village and they would be supervised by a police inspector. On the village level the inspectors were Malay; only at the district level and above were the supervisors British.[33]

With the police dominating the populated areas, the security forces were able to pursue the guerrillas in the countryside. And in some circumstances the two worked together. When the Min Yuen were thought to be strong in an area, the security forces would move in, cordon off the village, and call in the Special Branch. The police would take all the villagers into a tent and ask them to identify the members of the Min Yuen in the village. Some would cooperate and talk, but the guerrillas would never know who had done so because all the adults in the village went into the tent for interrogation, even if they didn't talk. These so-called "black tent operations" provided the security forces with much of the intelligence needed to track down the enemy infrastructure.

The years between 1955 and 1960 were the mopping-up period for the British in Malaya. Things were going so poorly for the insurgents that many of the guerrillas chose to surrender rather than spend the next few years being hunted down in the jungle. The police Special Branch was able to smash the infrastructure, although it never did eliminate it completely. About five hundred Min Yuen and MRLA fighters retreated to the tangled jungle on the Thai border.[34]

In the end the British had succeeded in eliminating the communist insurgency that threatened Malaya. As pointed out earlier, one must use caution when attempting to apply the British model in Malaya to the American experience in Vietnam; circumstances were very different. But one part of the British strategy clearly could have applied to Vietnam and the American failure to implement it is partly responsible for the communist victory. The British immediately realized the importance of destroying the enemy infrastructure. Sir Robert Thompson, the famous counterinsurgency expert who served in Malaya with the British civil service, noted that "the priority intelligence target [in Malaya] was the underground organization rather than the guerrilla units." His idea (which was the one adopted by the British security forces) was that if the "communist subversive organization" was eliminated then the main-force units would quickly fall. And the key to destroying both was to cut the infrastructure cells off from the political leadership and the military units. It worked for the British.[35]

The Americans in Vietnam did not emphasize eliminating the enemy infrastructure and so allowed the Viet Cong to infiltrate areas where they had previously not enjoyed support. Combined with the American propensity for using firepower, the ability of the VCI to operate with virtual impunity allowed the Viet Cong to gather supporters at little cost to either their political infrastructure or to the guerrilla main-force units.

The conduct of intelligence gathering also gave the British an advantage that the Americans in Vietnam were slow to realize. By giving the police Special Branch primacy in intelligence gathering and by using the SWEC and DWEC as an overseeing board, the British were able to transcend the curse that plagued the Americans in Vietnam: the inability of any single intelligence organization to get the whole picture because some sources were withheld by the jealousies or incompetence of other agencies.[36]

But here again some caution is in order. The British controlled the government in Malaya, so they could more or less dictate the terms by which the conflict would be waged. The

Americans, on the other hand, were forced to deal with an unstable sovereign government in Saigon that jealously guarded its power by limiting the capabilities of any potential rival, especially the intelligence agencies.

The period of American involvement in Vietnam between 1968 and 1971 perhaps best parallels the British experience in Malaya. In early 1968 the Saigon government, at the behest of the Americans, placed a new emphasis on pacification, and with it, on the neutralization of the VCI. It is ironic that it took the Americans some eight years to realize the potential behind emphasizing pacification, considering that they had experienced its benefits only a decade earlier in the Philippines.

Huk Rebellion

General Edward Lansdale, chief American adviser to the Philippine government during the Huk (short for Hukbalahap) Rebellion, raised an important question for those interested in pacification as the chief means of fighting a counterinsurgency: "Why was there a special effort at 'pacification' by the government in Vietnam, while the word pacification was unknown in the war in the Philippines?" The simple answer is that in the Philippines there was no "other war." All government troops in the Huk Rebellion faced only one task: win the support of the population.[37]

As in the case of the British in Malaya, it would be unwise to draw too many parallels between the insurgencies in the Philippines and Vietnam. The Huk insurgency suffered from many shortcomings the Viet Cong never had to deal with. As was the case in Malaya, the Philippines had no porous border over which to smuggle weapons, nor could the Huks retreat to a neighboring country for sanctuary. Politically, the Filipino communists were less sophisticated and less respected in the communist world. Before WWII only five Filipinos received training at Moscow's Lenin Institute, while it appears that at least thirty Vietnamese attended during the same period. In China, hundreds of Vietnamese were educated in the ways of revolution, while only one or two Filipinos could claim the same.[38]

But most importantly, the Huks lacked a climate of political inequities (although, of course, social inequities abounded) that could be exploited. In Vietnam, the colonial situation was intolerable to a great number of Vietnamese, but in the Philippines, the Americans were well on the way toward building the foundations of democracy. There existed a public school system available to all, and the Tydings-McDuffie Act of 1934 allowed the Commonwealth of the Philippines to be self-governing, with independence granted in 1945. There was no political cause for the Huks to rally the people around and no foreign oppressor to drive out of the country. The Huks could point to the corruption in the government, the gross inequities in wealth, and the heavy-handed way in which the military controlled the countryside, but, again, the government was able to address most of these grievances without having to answer the charge of imperialism.

The Huks demanded recognition of their gubernatorial and congressional seats in central Luzon after the war, but the Philippine government refused. So the Huks returned to people's war with little success until the 1949 presidential election gave the insurgency a boost. Blatant fraud caused popular resentment all over the country and swelled guerrilla ranks. By 1950 the Huks had some fifteen thousand guerrillas and a support base of about 1 million people.[39]

The Philippine army, on the other hand, was unprepared for people's war. But it was fortunate in having a man able to take necessary measures to combat the insurgency: Ramon Magsaysay. On 1 September 1950, Magsaysay became secretary of national defense. He brought to the position a keen awareness of the workings of guerrilla war and the Huks in particular. Magsaysay was a man of the people, having been trained as a mechanic, and he had fought against the Japanese in WWII, serving as a guerrilla commander. By the force of his personality and popularity, Magsaysay was able to gain control of the military against the wishes of the entrenched interests that wished to see all forms of government control fragmented.[40]

In the words of General Lansdale, Magsaysay was able to change the traditional military reputation of being "trigger-happy, overbearing soldiers . . . into brotherly protectors of the people."[41] He weeded out corruption and used military facilities to serve the people. Civilian casualties were treated in military hospitals and people were allowed to voice their concerns and offer suggestions to the military command by means of a special one-page telegram that went directly to the office of the secretary of national defense.[42]

When the fighting broke out, Magsaysay had an army that sat in static positions in populated areas. One of its main tasks seemed to be that of guarding the holdings of wealthy landowners and politicians. Magsaysay realized the futility of fighting the Huks from such a static position, so upon becoming secretary of national defense he pulled forces out of garrison duty and began offensive operations against the Huks. Because of his magnetic personality and powers of persuasion, Magsaysay changed a demoralized military into an outfit capable of carrying the fight to the enemy. Combat patrols of company size and smaller kept the guerrillas on the run and by September 1953 the Huks had lost any semblance of military initiative.[43]

Military intelligence played an important part in the destruction of the Huks. The army received information from a captured communist officer that much of the Huk politburo—the infrastructure—was hiding in Manila. An investigation followed and on 18 October 1950, twenty-one Military Intelligence Service (MIS) men surrounded a house in downtown Manila and arrested 105 people, including most of the members of the Huk politburo. Documents, radios, and weapons were found and it was clear that the communists had been crippled. However, the infrastructure left in the countryside could carry on with the fight as long as they remained in place.[44]

Magsaysay also realized the value of using the military for civic action projects. In the November 1951 elections soldiers aided the Commission on Elections by watching for fraud. Within weeks the Huks found their cause falling down around their ears. People saw the elections as fair and what little support there had been for the communists eroded. In addition, the Huks were offered the chance to surrender and make a fresh start under EDCOR (Economic Development Corps), which set up farm communities.[45]

Many Huks took advantage of the offer and surrendered. By

1953 only a small band of guerrillas was left in the hills out of some twenty-five thousand earlier in the rebellion.[46] The statistics on the Huks put out of action during the rebellion are revealing. Some 6,074 were killed in action, 4,702 were captured, and 9,458 surrendered. The Philippine government was so effective in cutting off support for the guerrillas that many of them just quit the fight. By 1953 the rebellion was over.[47]

American advisers helped the Philippines through trying times and, although the Filipinos did most of the work, American methods of government and law provided the groundwork for the emerging system of counterinsurgency as guided by Ramon Magsaysay. Yet only one year later, in 1954, the country of South Vietnam emerged and the United States found itself facing another people's war. As we have seen, the coming conflict would be different in many ways from previous guerrilla wars, but the basic methods of how to wage the battle had been shown to be successful. But in the case of South Vietnam, the United States chose to largely ignore the guerrilla war and attempt to counter what Washington saw as the real threat—a possible conventional invasion from North Vietnam. The emphasis would be on training the Army of the Republic of Vietnam (ARVN) to fight an enemy on the field of battle rather than in the village square.

Diem and Pacification

Ngo Dinh Diem had little to recommend himself as the new head of state for Vietnam. After the 1954 Geneva Conference, which established the temporary state of South Vietnam, the Americans decided that the main credentials needed by the new president must be strident nationalism, a firm record of anti-French activity, and devout anti-communism. Diem possessed all three. Unfortunately, he did not possess any sort of power base or popularity necessary to hold and consolidate power.

Diem had many problems waiting for him as he assumed power. The last emperor of Vietnam, Bao Dai, had allowed the army to fall under the control of General Hinh, who ruled it as his own private fiefdom, picking and choosing the policies he would support. Bao Dai also sold the police and other internal security forces to the gangster organization, the Binh Xuyen. Before 1954 the French had allowed the Binh Xuyen considerable latitude within Saigon, and its former leader, Bay Vien, used his contacts to wipe out much of the Viet Minh infrastructure within the city. In return for his effectiveness the French made Bay Vien a general.[48]

In addition to these private armies, Diem was also forced to contend with the nine hundred thousand or so refugees who had fled south after the Geneva Accords were signed. All this forced Diem to concentrate on consolidating power rather than tending to the welfare of the people in South Vietnam, a situation the communists were able and willing to exploit. As Diem played politics in Saigon the communists consolidated their hold on the countryside.

By late 1954 Diem had rid himself of General Hinh and was in firm control of the army. Sects such as the Cao Dai and Hoa Hao, which wielded considerable power in certain parts of South Vietnam, were brought under control, and the Binh Xuyen were largely uprooted following some bloodshed in April 1954. With these threats to his supremacy out of the way, Diem officially abolished the monarchy, proclaimed South Vietnam a republic, and appointed himself its first president.

With the task of consolidating power out of the way, Diem turned his attention toward the communists. Diem's plan was twofold. First, he sought to alleviate the refugee problem by setting up a resettlement program and tentative land reform measures. Second, the government established a campaign to counter communist activities in the countryside. Diem basically saw an opportunity to substitute one enemy—the Binh Xuyen and other groups that had stood in the way of Diem's hold on power—for another: the communists. Whereas in late 1954 every enemy had been a "feudal rebel," by 1956 they were all called communists.

Diem began his new crusade with the "Anti-Communist Denunciation Campaign" begun in mid-1955. Using typical communist-style tactics, Diem's officials would gather people in a village or town into a large audience and then have the participants recount tales of communist atrocities, trample the Viet Minh flag, and affirm their loyalty to the new Saigon government. Former Viet Minh who had repented their past sins gave public testimony to the evils of the Viet Minh and publicly denounced communism.[49]

In January 1956 Diem went further by signing a formal proclamation allowing the imprisonment of "any person considered to be a danger to the defense of the state." Under this legislation, thousands were jailed. Implementation of this law was enforced by Mutual Aid Family Groups, which operated as cells designed to watch over other members of the community. Each cell consisted of a group of five families that watched over the activities of each other and reported any irregularities.[50]

Diem can be credited with having created the administrative system responsible for the breakdown of authority in the countryside. In 1956 Diem established new provinces, bringing the total to forty-one. New province chiefs were appointed, but rather than using experience as prerequisite for leadership, Diem used loyalty. This move made the provinces, and even the districts and hamlets, directly answerable to Diem in Saigon and there was no incentive for individual initiative. Previously elected village councils were abolished and the rural population began to feel the heavy hand of Saigon in their lives, an event that had not often occurred, even under the French.

Diem realized the importance of eliminating the shadow government that was building up in the countryside, but the measures were heavy-handed and failed to distinguish between communists and those who simply felt there were alternatives to Diem's programs. All Diem accomplished by moving into the villages and brutalizing the people was to allow his regime to be held up for comparison with the communists. Although Diem used many of the same methods as did the communists, Saigon lost out in the comparison because the communists were offering an alternative, while Diem could only show that he meant to perpetuate the inequities he had largely created.

The disorder in the countryside born of over a decade of war called for both civic action and security against any threat to Diem's power. Civic Action Teams of some ten cadre each roamed the rural areas helping the peasants dig wells, build schools, plant crops, and render medical aid. These cadre dressed in traditional peasant garb and some fourteen hundred to eighteen hundred of them stayed in the countryside with the peasants.[51] In this respect the Civic Action Teams were helpful, but they often neutralized their benevolent image by taking part in the Anti-Communist Denunciation Campaign. Whether the Civic Action Teams were effective became irrelevant in late 1956 because the program was discontinued because of rivalries between the Civic Action Directorate and the ministries of health, information, and agriculture.[52]

Diem did form a Civil Guard (CG), which fell under the direction of the minister of interior. The CG consisted of forty thousand lightly armed soldiers organized into mobile companies that were meant to move about the province and react to outbreaks of communist violence. A hamlet militia called the Self Defense Corps was also formed and dispersed among the villages in ten-man squads assigned to provide the first line of defense against communist attacks. The obvious problem with both these organizations was that they were reaction forces whose entire strategy allowed the guerrillas to strike at will and then fade away as the understrengthened militias chased after them.

Diem went through a series of land reform and pacification attempts, all aimed at isolating the rural population from the communists. Perhaps the most well-known was the Agroville Program. It was a massive failure. On 7 July 1959 Diem formally launched the program with the fervent hope that it would provide "the happy compromise between hustling, teeming city life and the placid rural existence. . . ."[53] Diem hoped the agrovilles would consolidate the rural population in areas where they would be both out of the city and away from the communists. The plan ostensibly was meant to address socioeconomic problems in South Vietnam, but like much of the action taken by Diem, the major consideration was an improvement in rural security.

The agroville concept planned to regroup the rural population into communes that would have fish ponds, farm plots, and fields for raising crops. In reality the agrovilles were barely different from the previous villages the peasants lived in except that they had been moved away from their ancestral lands and into groups more manageable to the government. Implicit in the move to agrovilles was the concept of security. But it seemed the Diem government considered the agrovilles as somehow being inherently safer than the old villages because there was no provision made for defense.

The agroville program came to fruition on 12 March 1960, when the first settlement was completed at Vy Thuan in Chuong Thien Province. On 9 July the communists burned an agroville at Tan Luoc and sent letters threatening others with a similar fate. By the end of 1960 the government had ceased support for the agrovilles and they gradually disappeared from the countryside.[54] The reason was a lack of security and a misunderstanding of both the needs of the rural population and an underestimation of the guerrilla's ability to disrupt any action taken by Saigon in the countryside. Diem had been so obsessed with the process of resettlement that he had neglected taking the necessary security measures. The real problem lay not in moving the people away from the enemy, but rather in addressing the grievances of the peasants and protecting them, in place, from the communists.

Diem's brother, Ngo Dinh Nhu, had a more thorough understanding of the need for "special soldiers" who could respond to the unconventional aspects of people's war. Nhu was Diem's main political adviser and chief of the secret police. He believed the army was not the appropriate instrument for carrying the fight to the villages. Instead Nhu stressed "peasant self-sufficiency" in the form of people's militias, a Combat Youth, and special units. In many ways, however, this notion of "self-sufficiency" was disingenuous. Nhu wanted the regular army to be near the urban areas so it would be in position to protect the Diem family from any attempted coups; his concern for events in the countryside were tangential. Dissatisfaction with the army's ability to fight an unconventional war did, however, influence Nhu's feelings about popular militias. He felt that the military was only capable of large-maneuver operations and that these would be little more than a slight nuisance to the guerrillas. Only the villagers knew the location of the guerrillas, and sweep operations by the army were bound to be futile.

In addition to his dislike of the military's methods, Nhu was unwilling to put forth the funds necessary to make the concept of self-defense viable. The government would loan the volunteer militias weapons for six months, after which it was assumed that the militias would have obtained enough captured weapons from the enemy that the government weapons could be returned. It is difficult to see how Nhu could have thought this sort of tactic could work on a uniformly adequate basis throughout South Vietnam without major government input.

Perhaps the first direct Vietnamese ancestor of the Phoenix program arose out of the Diem years, going back as early as 1955. In central Vietnam another Diem brother, Ngo Dinh Can, tried his luck at controlling the countryside. But unlike the other attempts, Can aimed his efforts directly at the communist infrastructure in the villages. Can lived in the northern part of South Vietnam, in Hue. Although he held no official position within the Diem regime, Can succeeded in establishing control of the ruling apparatus in central South Vietnam. Unlike his brothers, Can truly understood the nature of the insurgent threat and he possessed the cunning and brutality necessary to run an effective program. By taking control of the intelligence apparatus as well as the political reins in the region, Can was able to move on the communists. The program was called the *Force Populaire* and it was probably the most successful operation against the enemy political infrastructure to date. The *Force Populaire* was not a formal arm of the government, so there was no need for Can to conform to any bureaucratic procedures. He took advantage of his independence and went after those accused of being communists. Of course, he made mistakes and his operations netted many innocent people as well.

In the late 1950s a team of experts on police matters from Michigan State University recommended to Diem that he begin building a strong rural police force that could deal with the problem of the insurgency in the countryside. Because raising the necessary manpower would be difficult on short notice, the Michigan State team suggested that the existing Civil Guard be turned into a rural police force. Diem rejected the proposal out of hand because he saw the Civil Guard as a force that could be used to counter the ARVN in any attempt to throw the Diem regime out of power.[55]

Instead, Diem chose to design a "counterterror" program

that could be aimed at the enemy infrastructure. In April 1959 the GVN Intelligence Service was assigned to develop a system of mobile teams that would seek out and destroy those communist officials (and supporters) who, for lack of evidence, would slip through normal judicial cracks. These teams were under the control of individual province chiefs who in turn cooperated with area military commanders. The methods of eliminating the infrastructure ran the entire gamut of brutality: kidnappings, assassination, extortion, anything Diem felt was necessary to eliminate the communists in the villages.[56]

The men who carried out the program had all the skills needed to brutalize the population—they had learned them from the French. They rounded up men and women suspected of having communist sympathies, tortured every suspect (women were routinely raped before being otherwise tortured), and finally executed them. Torture led to more names; those named were picked up and tortured, and the gruesome cycle was repeated on a larger scale as the list of suspects grew geometrically.

The Americans were fully aware of the counterterror program, as evidenced by a U.S. Embassy summary paper issued on 30 July 1959 that stated, ". . . the Surete Internal Security Action groups were notified that restrictions had been eased regarding the powers of arrest, that clearance from higher authorities need not be obtained before making arrests, and suspects could be arrested for interrogation, investigation, and exploitation . . . this directive resulted in increased arrests in mid-May. . . ."[57]

Diem failed to realize that the use of such indiscriminate methods could only result in an increase in sympathy for the communist insurgency. Diem made no distinction between Viet Minh nationalists who were not communists (most of the Viet Minh in South Vietnam became followers of Ho Chi Minh because he represented the only organized opposition to French colonialism) and the eight thousand to ten thousand communist cadres who had stayed in South Vietnam after the 1954 partition. The Diem regime viewed the politics of South Vietnam through blinders and 'Viet Minh' was just an evil word to be purged from Vietnamese vocabulary.

Unfortunately for Diem, he chose to modify the previously failed counterterror program. In the early 1960s the program went after more and more people, some with tenuous ties to the communists. However, if the end justifies the means, then the counterterror program was successful. In some provinces, such as Long An, the communist infrastructure ceased to function. In 1962, in recognition of this success, the counterterror program was officially named the Special Police and was incorporated into the newly formed National Police Force.[58]

The system was now in place—for better or worse—for the Americans to step in and try to give some direction to the pacification program in general and the attempt to neutralize the enemy infrastructure specifically. Diem would die in 1963, partly at the hands of the Americans, who felt that his lack of cooperation had hindered the fight against communism. But it was too late. Events had been set in motion and the Americans found themselves cast as the bad guys in the same way as did the French before them. Yet they acted surprised, as if only a bunch of lunatics could lump Americans together with colonialist Europeans. So, secure in their misunderstanding of the Vietnamese people and their beliefs, the American military marched off to war, first as advisers, then as foot soldiers, in an attempt to crush the enemy in the best way they knew—with the application of technology and firepower. Forgotten were the lessons of Malaya, the Philippines, and even the failed Diem regime: the people must feel they are secure and fairly treated under the government.

Pacification and the attempt to eliminate the enemy infrastructure during the Diem years were marked by overcentralization, corruption, brutality, and general ineffectiveness. Diem never realized the necessity of addressing the problems in the countryside and instead turned his efforts toward making certain that his power base, particularly in Saigon, was secure. This is not to say that during the Diem regime nothing was done to go after the enemy in the villages. In fact, in many ways Diem was very effective, although there was little direct intent to his methods. Communist officials interviewed after the fall of South Vietnam noted that Diem came close on several occasions to seriously damaging the infrastructure, and hence communist aims, in the south.[59]

Unfortunately, Diem's existence became merely a struggle to retain power. After a November 1961 trip to South Vietnam, John Kenneth Galbraith reported to President John F. Kennedy that "Diem will not reform either administratively or politically in any effective way. That is because he cannot. It is politically naive to expect it. He senses that he cannot let power go because he will be thrown out."[60] Galbraith realized early on what would gradually become more clear: Diem could never give the necessary power to the army to control the communists. To do so would risk a coup. But even if the army had been turned loose, it is unlikely it could have done an effective job of cleaning up the insurgency, largely because American training had molded it into a force that could only handle a conventional invasion from North Vietnam.

Of course, in the end, Diem's fears proved correct. He was deposed and murdered in November 1963. His rule had become little more than a mechanism to keep himself in power, ignoring the mounting insurgency around him. Diem's misuse of the military in an effort to soothe his fear of a coup became a self-fulfilling prophecy when the military stepped in to save its own interests.

American Pacification in Vietnam

The United States cannot claim that Vietnam was dumped into its lap by the French as they fled the scene following the defeat at Dien Bien Phu. The French war effort had been largely financed by Washington right up until 1954, and after the Geneva Conference, which created South Vietnam, America willingly took over the reins of the fight to stop communism from encroaching south of the seventeenth parallel.

The fighting in the south after the creation of South Vietnam was sporadic. Guerrilla war did not really begin until 1959, when it was clear the elections scheduled for 1956 would not be held, and the Viet Cong stepped up the fighting and terror.[61] But the United States was unable to direct its attention to what was happening in the countryside because of the political instability that plagued South Vietnam. The quest for a stable, legitimate regime in Saigon made progress in pacification a virtual impossibility. Because the Viet Cong were left largely to their own devices in the countryside, they were able to build up their strength to the point where they exercised open control of entire districts. By the close of 1963 it was as if the process of infrastructure elimination that had been pursued sporadically and ineffectively for years had never occurred.

The Americans got more directly into the act of pursuing the Viet Cong infrastructure after Diem's assassination. The core of the counterterror program broke down immediately after the assassination, as many of the agents in the Special Police went into hiding to escape the wrath of any incoming government members who might have in some way suffered from the indiscriminate use of terror practiced by these teams. The cadre necessary to run an effective program against the enemy infrastructure simply dried up and the program ground to a halt.

The CIA realized at this early date the value of seeking out and destroying the enemy infrastructure, even if the Army did not. In tandem with the United States Overseas Mission (USOM, the initial U.S.AID mission in Vietnam) the CIA began recruiting province special units (the beginnings of what became known as the Provincial Reconnaissance Units, or PRU), who were trained in the fledgling techniques of rooting out and eliminating the enemy infrastructure. The methods used by Diem's counterterror program made them little more than gangs of thugs following up on whatever rumors they might run across concerning the loyalties of individual members of the population. Some of the rumors were true and genuine members of the enemy infrastructure were eliminated, but as often as not, innocent people were brutalized as Diem cast his net in a wide arc as he fished for the enemy.[62]

The CIA appeared to have the right idea about going after the enemy infrastructure, but it went about it in the wrong way. After the CIA took over the counterterror program in 1964, it failed to take the first step toward changing the image as well as the methods of Diem's program—it called the new program Counter Terror Teams (CTT), a ridiculous name considering the image that already dogged the program. CTTs were organized at the province level and were controlled directly by the province chief.

Unlike the earlier counterterror program, the CTTs recruited men with combat experience and trained them specifically for the rigors of small-unit combat deep inside enemy territory. Their mission was to eliminate the communist infrastructure—not communist supporters—by capture or killing. As would later be the case with the Phoenix program, the emphasis was on capture. CTTs were trained for leadership and initiative, and for the most part, discipline and morale was high. But, as could be expected, results differed from area to area. The quality of the CTTs depended on their leadership and the support of the province chief. Sometimes the CTTs became little more than hired thugs that safeguarded the province chief and his political power, never venturing into enemy-controlled areas to do their intended jobs. Other times the mission went as planned. CTTs of half a dozen or a dozen men would slip into enemy territory and capture or kill the target. Other times they would make their presence known by suddenly appearing in a communist-controlled village where government troops had previously feared to venture, talking to the people and leaving propaganda before fading back into the bush.[63]

Along with the operational capacity to eliminate the enemy infrastructure there must be an intelligence capacity to accurately identify and target them. Along with the development of the CTTs, the CIA instituted Province and District Intelligence Coordination Centers (PICC and DICC) to more efficiently gather and collate information on the infrastructure, and provide the central planning for operations. This program was a direct descendant of the Malayan model.[64] The Phoenix program itself was born out of this system; in fact the ICCs were the forerunners of the Phoenix centers, which began in earnest in 1968.

The CTT program simply grew too fast. In less than a year, every province in South Vietnam had a PICC and a matching team of CTTs. The rapid growth also brought on the press. Stories of CTT exploits appeared in American newspapers, generally concentrating on dramatic assassinations and dead-of-night kidnappings. The day-in–day-out work of intelligence gathering was largely ignored, as was the attempt to get the GVN enthusiastically involved in the program.

The GVN itself was continuing along the traditional mindset, which called for the building and training of conventional forces that could, in the staid minds of the South Vietnamese bureaucracy, overpower the communist insurgency. The one token gesture to specifically attacking the enemy infrastructure was set forth in the Chien Tang-Hop Tac pacification plan in 1964. But it ignored the entrenched nature of the communist infrastructure in the countryside. Responsibility for pacification and infrastructure elimination was given to the territorial forces and ARVN, not the National Police, which was the operation arm of choice as far as the Americans were concerned. Because of the conventional nature of ARVN and the territorial forces, it came as no surprise that neither organization produced much intelligence on the enemy infrastructure.[65]

By 1964 there were about four hundred CIA personnel in South Vietnam, most stationed in Saigon under cover as AID employees. Their job was twofold: to upgrade the National Police and other operational arms of the effort to target the VCI, and indoctrinate the GVN in the proper attitudes and methods needed for fighting this hidden enemy. The GVN developed its own equivalent of the CIA—called CIO (Central Intelligence Organization)—which aided the agency in modernizing and streamlining the interrogation centers where VCI and other important prisoners were brought. Before the CIA enlightened them, the South Vietnamese interrogators felt the best way to pry information out of a prisoner was to beat the soles of his feet until he told them what they wanted to hear. Of course, such methods only served to elicit false information created by the victim to stop the torture. The CIA hoped to show the South Vietnamese that there were more productive methods of interrogation.[66]

In 1965, William Colby, at that time the CIA's Far Eastern Division chief, oversaw the CTTs. It was Colby who became apprehensive over the word "counterterror" and changed the name—as well as part of the structure—to Provisional Reconnaissance Units. No matter what name these teams went under, their mission was still the same and they suffered from three drawbacks. First, the CIA funded, recruited, trained, and supplied the effort to eliminate the enemy infrastructure. Although the Agency was careful to blur the paper trail leading to its involvement, the Saigon rumor mill made it common knowledge that the CIA ran the show. Because this was the case, the program was immediately tainted by the influence of foreigners and was viewed with trepidation by the general population.[67]

Second, and an outgrowth of the first, was that the South Vietnamese government was reluctant to embrace the idea of attacking the infrastructure. Saigon officials just couldn't be made to see the advantage in cutting off the head of the organization that plagued them. They preferred to hack away at the limbs with artillery and bombs, never realizing that this enemy possessed the ability to rejuvenate its body parts as long as the infrastructure remained in place.

Third, the CIA's actions were regarded as merely an extension of the Diem regime's policies, as well as the French in the years before. The CIA was aware it was being tarred with the imperialist brush and it sought to escape the name pacification because the French had used it in the First Indochina War. But it could come up with no better term and the word stuck.[68]

By 1966 the CIA, in the form of the PRU, was active in all of South Vietnam's provinces. In addition, the CIA added a new touch—the Census/Grievance and Aspiration Program, usually called Census/Grievance for short. Of course, being CIA-sponsored, the name shed absolutely no light on what the program was supposed to do. It simply allowed the province chief to make an accurate count of people in the villages so as to find out who didn't belong, and it was supposed to check on corruption and keep track of the villagers' "aspirations," presumably meaning what they wanted from the government. Census/Grievance also provided a way in which each villager could be interviewed in such a way as not to alert the Viet Cong as to who was fingering them. Everyone in the village was called individually before the Census/Grievance committee, so there was no way to tell who talked and who didn't. This system produced intelligence that was analyzed and filed by the CIA, and it certainly produced some VCI who were in turn neutralized. But by itself Census/Grievance could do nothing to eliminate the VCI.

When viewed in isolation, the CIA effort up until 1967 seemed to be the answer: a secret war waged against a secret enemy. The agency could use its resources and methods and leave the Army with the conventional war. The opposite was true, however. The Viet Cong were easily able to sidestep most operations precisely because the program was covert and small. The PRU never numbered more than five thousand men. Although there are few records concerning the subject, it is unlikely that the VCI found the program to be a serious threat. But among the various branches and agencies serving in Vietnam, the CIA alone seemed to grasp the nature of the communist infrastructure.

The CIA's major contribution was to the massive increase in intelligence available on the VCI and the Viet Cong in general. CIA intelligence added to MACV's storehouse of knowledge on Viet Cong order of battle figures and gave a more complete picture of the total communist movement. In particular, the succession of CTTs, Province Special Units, and finally PRUs, produced mountains of captured documents pertaining to the organization, operation, and status of the VCI in various provinces.[69]

The question became what to do with the information. The CIA knew about the enemy infrastructure, knew that it had to be eliminated, and even had some ideas on how to go about doing it, but MACV wasn't listening. The Army cared mostly about order of battle intelligence. Yet by 1967 the war was going no better than it had two years earlier and President Johnson began to realize that pacification, along with the social and political reforms that went with it, was the answer to South Vietnam's problems. With the president of the United States behind the "other war," events could move in a new direction, one that still battled both conventional units and guerrillas in the villages, but began to do so under a single banner. The new structure would bring all the civilian and military pacification programs together so as to make better use of MACV's resources. The program was called CORDS, for Civil Operations and Revolutionary Development Support, and it marked the beginning of a new phase in the war in Vietnam.

3

Bureaucrats and Soldiers: Creating a System

By 1966 both the political leadership in Washington and the military in Vietnam could see that pacification had to be elevated in stature. Most importantly there was a realization both in Washington and Saigon that the VCI had to be dealt with if there was to be any chance of effectively turning back the insurgency. Search-and-destroy was only partially successful and none of that strategy's gains could be exploited unless pacification was also emphasized. Unfortunately, the machinery for extending pacification consisted of various small and diverse programs run by every conceivable civilian agency in South Vietnam; the effort was getting nowhere. Those involved in pacification had neither the resources nor the leverage to prompt Vietnamese officials in Saigon to act.

President Johnson recognized the problem and after a series of conferences and policy changes began implementing a program to bring civilian pacification efforts under the control of MACV, with all the power and resources such a move would bring with it. The result was Civil Operations and Revolutionary Development Support (CORDS), a new chain of command that gave pacification direct access to the U.S. military commander, General William Westmoreland. The establishment of CORDS implied recognition that the situation in South Vietnam required more than a conventional military solution.

The Problem

In early 1967 American military and civilian advisers all over South Vietnam reported that the situation in the countryside was already bad and deteriorating rapidly. Although the United States had stemmed what appeared to be the inevitable fall of the GVN with a massive injection of troops and firepower in 1965, the countryside was still largely "unpacified." Province advisers were quick to point out in monthly reports that American support had only brought temporary security and that unless the VCI somehow was put out of business the population would remain firmly under communist control. Although variations on this theme were repeated in virtually every province in South Vietnam, the situation in one particularly strategic province brought home the point to MACV.

Gia Dinh Province was part of southern III Corps. It might have been no different from the ten other provinces that made up III Corps except for two key characteristics. First, Saigon was situated within the province boundaries (although Saigon was a separate political and bureaucratic entity), and second, the key waterways that led from the South China Sea inland to the capital ran through Gia Dinh. If Gia Dinh Province—in the heart of South Vietnam—was in danger of falling to the communists, what were the GVN's chances throughout the rest of the country?

In an effort to develop a true picture of the situation, the American Embassy prepared a study based on the observations of all key American personnel within the province. Their conclusions were unanimous: by the spring of 1967 the situation had become critical. John Paul Vann, the outspoken director of pacification for III Corps, noted that one key district, Binh Chanh, was kept from falling completely under the control of the Viet Cong only because of the American troop presence:

> The VC have effectively controlled the village and hamlet administration within Binh Chanh for over a year. The series of small canals and waterways which exist enable the VC to

move freely between Binh Chanh and Nha Be, and thus escape forces deployed against them. . . .

The VC infrastructure in Binh Chanh has been in position long enough, and is well organized enough to withstand any number of military sweeps throughout the area.[1]

Province officials were aware that the insurgency's survival and well-being depended upon the VCI, but no one seemed to know how to effectively combat it. The PRU, the Regional and Popular Forces (RF/PF), and even the Revolutionary Development Cadre (RDC) were not used effectively against the VCI, although the CIA case officer in the province capital devoted most of his time to trying to get some support for anti-infrastructure operations.[2]

The problem was not MACV's unwillingness to commit troops and resources to root out the VCI. Soldiers from the 199th Brigade were willing and able to go after either Viet Cong military or political cadre if intelligence pointed them in the right direction. Unfortunately, American troops were not trained for such operations and they resorted to cordon-and-search operations, troop-intensive affairs during which U.S. and Vietnamese forces would surround an unsuspecting village, search every dwelling, and question every inhabitant in hopes of flushing out any guerrillas or political cadre caught up in the net. The operations generally were ineffective and they angered the largely innocent villagers who were rousted out of bed in the early morning hours.

The task of anti-infrastructure operations ideally would have been handled by the RF/PF and the National Police, but neither was up to the job. One-third of the police had been ordered to guard the district's intelligence coordination center, a static task that kept them from acting as anti-infrastructure forces. The PRUs, numbering only twenty-one, were used as the district chief's personal henchmen and were regarded by the American advisers as useless.

Vietnamese intelligence nets were good in principle; however, their performance was spotty. Although some of the information on local VCI was old, the intelligence services were maintaining blacklists on local VCI in Binh Chanh. The problem was that each Vietnamese agency jealously guarded all information as if its brother agencies were enemy agents. This was a traditional Vietnamese approach to intelligence, one that would prove a great stumbling block for the Phoenix program. The American side, too, kept intelligence from other agencies that could have put it to good use. Overcompartmentalization, keeping information from those without "a need to know," made targeting the VCI very difficult.

In theory the Americans understood the need to overcome this problem and took steps to form a combined U.S.–GVN intelligence collation center to cover Viet Cong Military Region Four. It was to be commanded by Major Nguyen Van Mau, the personal assistant of National Police Chief General Nguyen Ngoc Loan, and assisted by a joint MACV/Embassy advisory effort. Although the new intelligence coordination organization was sound in principle, it was too far removed from the Saigon chain of command to be effective. Vietnamese intelligence chiefs in the capital simply bypassed the unorthodox experiment, leaving it without resources or timely intelligence directives.

The situation led Major Mau to remark that agent nets in Binh Chanh had become worthless. "Our agents in Binh Chanh are dishonest. The people are VC because of their mind, not because of the strength of VC weapons, and our intelligence is poor." Yet according to the American advisers, who agreed with Major Mau's assessment of Binh Chanh's intelligence capabilities, the situation in nearby Nha Be District was better than average.[3]

How could the situation differ so vastly between neighboring districts within the same province? The answer lay in the leadership. Nguyen Nghiem Ton, the district chief in Binh Chanh, was considered incompetent and basically corrupt by all American advisers who had dealings with him. He was more concerned with using troops to guard his interests than he was in rooting out the VCI. But Ton was merely representative of a system that had existed in Vietnam for centuries—the cult of personality.

In all of Vietnam's provinces and districts a single man often held the key to failure or success in the fight against the communists. An incompetent or corrupt official anywhere along the long line from Saigon to the countryside could ruin the process of reform and pacification. In the case of the infrastructure neutralization effort, the problem was magnified because before 1967 no single top official in Saigon handled the job, and because no one in the field seemed to know how to go about the task. Even if they did, there were many officials in the villages and districts who resented the imposition of a new program upon them. Worse still, some were profiting from the Viet Cong by selling supplies and medicine, so the last thing they wanted was a system that might end their lucrative livelihood.

Perhaps unwittingly, the Americans bought into the personality game. It was clear that new blood was needed in Saigon; without it there could be little improvement in pacification. The infrastructure neutralization effort relied on an even greater extent on the abilities of a handful of men in key places. At the district level the district chief had to be enthusiastic about the effort and at the province level the province chief had the ability to emphasize or squash any program.

At the top the problem was the same. Neither the GVN nor the MACV had the bureaucratic or operational apparatus to form a viable program. Saigon was ambivalent because GVN officials had been taught since before the Geneva Convention that the solution to the insurgency problem was a conventional one. Saigon's advisory counterpart—MACV—had done the teaching, so new guidance was unlikely to come from that quarter.

Ironically, the solution lay in Washington. The military had been blaming policy makers and bureaucrats for the gradual escalation, which, instead of smashing the communists against the ropes, only seemed to give Hanoi enough time to recover and fight another day. To a large extent the criticism was correct, but the military was misguided in much of its thinking as to where the center of the problem lay. The result was a misplaced strategy.

Many believed that the center of communist expansion lay in Hanoi and all problems stemmed from the presence of NVA troops in the South. As was so often true in Vietnam, that theory was partly true, partly false. To destroy the NVA and force Hanoi to completely withdraw from South Vietnam (an unlikely scenario) would not have solved the insurgency. The Viet Cong would have been greatly weakened, but without both a solution to the unequal social and political problems and the destruction of the communist political infrastructure, all the military force in the world would not have made South Vietnam "free." Even if U.S. troops and the ARVN had succeeded in their search-and-destroy strategy, a coherent pacification effort was still necessary to defeat the insurgency. It is true that the military could not properly execute its role under the constraints of the rules of engagement, particularly while allowing the existence of sanctuaries in Laos and Cambodia. But that is another subject.

Since MACV was established in South Vietnam in 1962 few resources went toward neutralizing the enemy infrastructure. Everyone seemed to know the infrastructure existed, that it was vital to the communist war effort, and that without its destruction the Viet Cong would never truly be defeated. But no one knew how many cadre were out there, or worse, how to get rid of them. Studies were conducted and men from Washington went to Vietnam to come up with answers.

Search for a Solution

When the troop buildup in 1965 failed to do little more than barely keep the South Vietnamese above water, officials in Washington began to seriously rethink the conduct of the war. In January 1966, at a conference in Warrenton, Virginia, the concept that would shape the U.S. war effort from 1967 onward began to emerge. Emphasis was placed on a balance between military and pacification programs, rather than primarily military. This framework would characterize the more formal efforts later in Honolulu and Manila.

It was President Johnson, the man who was afraid to escalate the war to the point where the military could win, who began to push for a renewed emphasis on pacification. This occurred for two reasons. First, Johnson was afraid of possible Chinese intervention should the United States employ a strategy of massive bombing and a widening of the war to Cambodia, Laos, and possibly North Vietnam. He believed pacification offered a way to apply more pressure on the communists without risking escalation from China or the U.S.S.R. Second, he was a genuinely compassionate man who felt that social reforms in South Vietnam were necessary if the Viet Cong were to be defeated.

A series of conferences held in Honolulu boosted pacification to a position of semi-equality with the conventional war. The most important of these meetings was held from 6 to 8 February 1966. Attending from the American side were President Johnson; Secretary of State Dean Rusk; Robert McNamara and John McNaughton from the Department of Defense; Foreign Policy Advisor McGeorge Bundy; General William Westmoreland; Special Military Consultant to the President General Maxwell Taylor; Commander-in-Chief Pacific Command Admiral U.S.G. Sharp; Ambassador Lodge; and Averell Harriman. South Vietnamese notables included President Nguyen Van Thieu, Vice President Nguyen Cao Ky, and Minister of Defense Nguyen Huu Co.

In addition to introducing a high-powered cast of players to the international press, the Honolulu Conference of February 1966 committed the GVN to a serious pacification effort. Thieu and Ky agreed to place an emphasis on four high-priority areas, one in each of the four military regions, that would include rural development, new construction projects, and a renewed emphasis on the Rural Development cadres begun over a decade earlier under Diem. The RD cadres followed the Viet Cong lead of eating, sleeping, and working with the peasants, the basics of winning hearts and minds.

The United States wanted still more from the Vietnamese at the Honolulu Conference. In particular they asked for greater authority for province chiefs in using the ARVN for pacification, a request that was refused because Thieu was reluctant to take that power away from the division commanders. Such a move might lead to another coup. General Westmoreland agreed, wanting the ARVN troops to remain a part of the big-unit war. At the close of the Honolulu Conference, the Vietnamese, backed by Westmoreland, refused to commit the ARVN to pacification. Without the security provided by a permanent troop presence in the countryside, the RD cadres were vulnerable to attack by the Viet Cong.[4]

The Honolulu Conference sent out conflicting signals about

the roles American and ARVN troops were playing in Vietnam. The basic American strategy early in the war had been to advise the ARVN. In 1965 Westmoreland's men took over the bulk of the fighting and by 1966 MACV still had not addressed the question of what Saigon's troops were to do, except to say they should not play a major role in pacification. If the conference accomplished anything it was to serve notice to the military, the GVN, and the civilian pacification programs that President Johnson no longer was satisfied with the progress of the war.

The first to see reorganization was the American Embassy in Saigon. Although Vietnam was at war the embassy maintained procedures used during peacetime. There was a "country team" headed by the ambassador, his deputy, the heads of the political and economic sections, chiefs of CIA, AID, USIS, and MACV. When General Maxwell Taylor served as ambassador beginning in July 1964, he had organized a Mission Council that met weekly in an attempt to coordinate civilian agencies involved in pacification. The program was powerless; when Henry Cabot Lodge returned to Vietnam as ambassador in July 1965 he abolished the Mission Council concept.[5]

Lyndon Johnson wanted a centralized committee that could oversee the various civilian agencies involved in pacification. Immediately after the Honolulu Conference the president created the Office of Civil Operations (OCO) as an interim solution to the problem. The OCO was to have command responsibility over all the civilian agencies and was placed under the control of William J. Porter, the incoming deputy ambassador to Vietnam. It was Porter's task to integrate all existing pacification activities that were not under the direction of MACV and he was given 90 to 120 days to produce results. As an incentive, Johnson threatened to give the entire program over to the military if it failed to meet his expectations. Porter was in an awkward position and he never possessed the power to pull the civilian agencies together. The OCO was a failure.[6]

President Johnson was especially concerned with the lack of coordination between the military, which was responsible for security, and the civilian side, the essence of nation building. He decided to take actions that would join the two factions of the American war effort into a focused effort.

Komer at the Helm

American anti-infrastructure measures in Vietnam began as many other projects spawned by the U.S. government begin—as a compromise forged of necessity and available resources, with perhaps a little political infighting thrown in. In this case the essential ingredient was Robert Komer.

Komer was destined to go to Vietnam, although his training and experience would not seem to lead him there. He was born in Chicago on 23 February 1922, and graduated from Harvard in 1942. During World War II he saw service in the Army, after which he returned to Harvard and in 1947 earned a master's degree. He then joined the CIA as a Middle East analyst, where he served for thirteen years before moving over to the National Security Council, again as a Middle East analyst. In March 1966 Komer was named special assistant to President Lyndon Johnson, where he was diverted from his specialty in Middle Eastern affairs to Vietnam. Johnson charged Komer with revitalizing the counterinsurgency effort in Vietnam, a task to which Komer devoted himself wholeheartedly. Although Komer made his name in Vietnam, his service there was but a short blip in his career: after two-and-a-half short years, one-and-a-half of them actually spent in Vietnam, Komer continued on his original course within the world of Middle Eastern affairs; he was nominated as ambassador to Turkey in November 1968.

Komer fit well within the cult of personality. His irreverent style and brash manner, combined with a no-nonsense work ethic, were exactly what were needed to operate effectively with the duplicitous South Vietnamese government, the overbearing military, and the ineffective but territorial American civilian bureaucracies. As was often the case in Vietnam, only a strong-willed, totally dedicated leader could get the job done. Ambassador Henry Cabot Lodge had named Komer "blowtorch," partly because of the smoking pipe clenched firmly between his tightened jaws, but mostly because he was abrasive and had no tolerance for those who stood in his way. Komer was always optimistic, loved statistics and a good fight, and wrote stacks of nasty memos designed to keep his staff in line. Komer was not content with simply doing his job and keeping a low profile; he wanted everyone to know he was in Vietnam to shake loose the system. Perhaps most annoying to the protocol-conscious bureaucrats and soldiers in Saigon was Komer's propensity for taking advantage of his special relationship with President Johnson and sending cables directly to the White House, often over General Westmoreland's head.

Westmoreland often had his differences with Komer, but he was forthright in his recollection of Komer's contribution to the war effort: "Bob Komer was the man for the job. He pushed himself and his people hard. He had imaginative ideas, usually sound. Striped pants might work later, but at the start, abrasion was in order and Bob Komer worked overtime at that."[7]

A Tense Situation

If Komer was the right man for the job, the civilian apparatus that waited for him in Vietnam was not the right tool. The military had felt all along that pacification was a civilian function and MACV was unconcerned by the tangle of bureaucratic tape within which the civilian agencies operated. When Komer arrived in Vietnam to take control of pacification in May 1967 he found a system in place incapable of putting into practice the ideas he had formulated after several trips to Vietnam over the years. The State Department was perhaps the biggest offender. State's pacification arm, the Agency for International Development (AID), was the largest civilian program involved in pacification, but it had none of the tools with which to accomplish its tasks. AID placed no priority on developing a Vietnamese civil administration, a counterpart to MACV's adviser program. AID also found itself bound by procedures and funding inappropriate for wartime. In 1966 supplies took an average of eighteen months to reach Saigon.[8]

Like the military, AID personnel were not equipped to perform their tasks in a far-off and culturally strange land. But unlike the situation in the military, this lack of insight and training within groups involved in pacification was potentially more damaging. The military was fighting to convince the enemy to give in, the ultimate in violent coercion. AID was part of the plan to win hearts and minds, so its lack of understanding went to the very center of whether pacification failed or succeeded. AID personnel on their way to Vietnam took courses at the Foreign Service Institute, none of which was relevant to the rapidly changing nature of the insurgency in Vietnam. In addition, AID worked within the framework of a cumbersome model based upon the American democratic experience, also irrelevant to Vietnamese society.[9] The State Department fit into its role well, though. MACV would brook no competition with its place as chief warmaker and AID was content to play a background role.

Robert Komer was not pleased by what he encountered in Vietnam. Komer felt the "other war" was really the dominant war, the one that would determine the outcome of the entire conflict. As he searched for the appropriate tools with which to wage pacification, he saw that the CIA was the only civilian organization equipped to fill the role. After all, the agency had been doing this sort of thing since the 1950s and it was clear to Komer that only the CIA had a strategy aimed at the VCI. The CIA also had the advantages of secrecy, a flexible budget, and good intelligence.

Komer took an available system—pacification, an available operation force (the PRU and the National Police), and an existing intelligence bureaucracy—and attempted to devise a method of oversight aimed at making the whole thing workable. The hybrid came to be called CORDS and enjoyed the support of Westmoreland, Washington, a relieved mass of civilian pacification agencies, and to a certain extent, the GVN. CORDS became official in May 1967, a time when the situation in the South Vietnamese countryside was rapidly deteriorating.

As deputy in charge of CORDS (DEPCORDS), Komer would head an entirely new chain of command that included both civilian and military personnel. He was answerable to Westmoreland and was basically equal in status with General Creighton Abrams, Westmoreland's deputy. Komer demanded and received a system by which American military advisers were removed from the strictly military chain of command and placed in a new situation where they answered to others in the CORDS hierarchy. Ultimately Westmoreland was the boss, but within the new system, military and civilian advisers operated side by side. Province and district advisers did not answer to the ARVN or American military commander, but rather to a pacification chain of command.[10]

Anti-infrastructure Emphasis

Robert Komer relied on the CIA for four obvious reasons. First, the Agency had been in-country for over a decade and had developed a strong network of intelligence on the enemy. Second, CIA resources in South Vietnam were the most flexible and the least constrained by bureaucracy. Third, the CIA mission was targeted toward the infrastructure rather than main-force units. Last, but not least, Komer had spent thirteen years in the CIA and felt he knew it best. On the negative side was the image projected by using a small, covert organization to run the program. Komer was well aware of this problem and he knew that an exclusively CIA anti-infrastructure program eventually would lead to a lack of flexibility.[11]

Agency involvement had produced the basic guidelines, however. In November 1966 a CIA analyst, Nelson H. Brickham, wrote a detailed memorandum that described the VCI and suggested which parts of it should be targeted. The memo recognized that rank-and-file members were not legitimate targets because they were most often unwilling participants in the revolution. Brickham also proposed that an intelligence net be woven from informants, interrogations, and agent penetrations into the VCI. Finally, Brickham called for using all available intelligence services as a focused effort to neutralize the VCI.[12]

Komer was so impressed with the report that he assigned Brickham to the Revolutionary Development office so that all future reports would be channeled directly to Komer. Komer particularly liked Brickham's suggestion that there was really no need to begin a new anti-VCI program, only that the existing ones be brought together and managed by a single bureau. Finally, there needed to be a formative period to allow the U.S. intelligence and pacification agencies to get their own houses in order before they could beg, coerce, and cajole the GVN into following suit. In many ways, Brickham deserved the credit for the Phoenix program because it was his suggestions that were implemented almost completely into the anti-infrastructure program.

A program called Intelligence Coordination and Exploitation (ICEX) became the interim period suggested by Brickham. It was a trial-and-error affair designed to give the U.S. pacification effort time to work out the bugs of the system and then later presented to the GVN as a model to follow. Komer had sent Brickham's memo to the embassy in Saigon along with a formal proposal that it be implemented. In June 1967 Komer received a response. Called "A Proposal for the Coordination and Management of Intelligence Programs and Attacks on the Viet Cong Infrastructure and Local Irregular Forces," it was the document that coined the acronym ICEX. Its central theme pointed out that ICEX was to be merely a coordinating function, not a new agency. Most importantly, it put words into action by providing more decentralization for operations at the province and district levels.[13]

Since Robert Komer had more to do than just administer ICEX he put a new man in as ICEX director. He chose Evan J. Parker, an Army reserve lieutenant colonel who had seen extensive service in the Pacific Theater during World War II, operating behind Japanese lines in Burma. After the war he joined the CIA. Parker had come to Vietnam to serve with the Agency, but he was snatched up by Komer and thrown into the breach of the fledgling anti-infrastructure effort.

"I went out to Saigon for another job," Parker recalled. "Then I was told, 'Forget about that, there's a new program and we think you're going to head it.'" Parker was to be one of the CIA's top men in Saigon and he knew something about ICEX just from being involved in the intelligence business. Komer's shifting of Parker's responsibilities from CIA to ICEX caught Parker unaware and he went into the new job cold. But the decision illustrated the acceptance of anti-infrastructure operations as a primary task.[14]

Parker recalled that Komer really had total control of the program:

I was told to discuss the new program with the MACV J-2 and some of his staff. I discovered later that it wasn't really a discussion—they weren't given an opportunity to discuss or analyze it—but in effect this was being stuffed down their throats. This was something that Komer liked and Westmoreland liked. The Ambassador bought it and ICEX was given to the military—not to consider, but to consider and *do*.[15]

Parker had his way paved by Komer, who had made sure that there would be little or no opposition from within the military to his new program. Komer instructed Parker to come up with a mission directive for ICEX to be presented at a meeting on 20 June 1967. Komer chaired the meeting and was joined by Parker; the chief of the RD Cadre, General Forsythe; Komer's deputy, William Colby; MACV J-2 and J-3; and some embassy representatives. Parker, in his capacity as CIA chief, offered the Agency's regional and provincial intelligence centers as the core of ICEX presence in the countryside. This would include CIA personnel used as agents as well as Agency programs such as the PRU, Census/Grievance, and the Revolutionary Development Cadre.[16]

ICEX in Charge

ICEX was created with MACV Directive 381-41 on 9 July 1967, although the basic structure for the program had been in place for at least a year. (MACV Directive 381-41 was approved on 16 July 1967, as good a formal date for the birth of ICEX as can be found.) American pacification teams had been building intelligence centers at the province and district level for some time, but it wasn't until ICEX was formalized that an organized plan was developed to guide the building of District Operations and Intelligence Coordinating Centers (DOICC—by late 1967 these centers became known as District Intelligence and Operations Coordinating Centers, or DIOCC, probably because it sounded better as an acronym than DOICC).

MACV Directive 381-41 set forth the guidelines for the formal implementation of ICEX on a nationwide basis, the first serious attempt by the United States to institutionalize a program to neutralize the VCI. This represented a written acknowledgment of the new-found importance VCI elimination was to be accorded in the overall scheme of pacification. The purpose was clearly stated: "To coordinate and give new impetus to U.S. and GVN operations, both intelligence collection and processing and action operations, directed toward elimination of the VC infrastructure."[17]

ICEX was placed under the direct supervision of CORDS. All of this simply meant that ICEX was given a position of prominence within the pacification hierarchy. In theory, as illustrated by the chain of command, pacification and ICEX were given the importance they deserved within the context of the Vietnam War.

Because ICEX climbed to a prominent position in the MACV hierarchy it suffered from that series of maladies that seemed to afflict all programs in Vietnam—bureaucratization, followed by deadlines and, finally, quotas. From its birth ICEX was given a deadline and part of its perceived success depended on its ability to meet it. Komer realized the constraints deadlines would impose, but he saw no other way to get fast action.[18]

A coordinating center was set up in Saigon, responsible for overseeing progress at the province level, which was the keystone to the entire operation. The Province Intelligence Coordinating Committee (PICC) was assigned to obtain effective Vietnamese agency participation and focus attention on the Viet Cong infrastructure. Obviously, MACV understood the need to get full GVN participation and yet was concerned about whether this would occur.[19]

MACV Directive 381-41 concluded with the inevitable deadlines, which were at once restrictive and necessary. Without deadlines the program might flounder on GVN and American apathy, but with them ICEX took on all the baggage of any bureaucracy and lost much of the flexibility needed to fight an unconventional enemy. ICEX was told to ". . . draft initial, basic mission and functions statements further defining responsibilities and relationships for Corps, Province, and District organizations" by 15 July 1967. Most importantly, ICEX was to "prepare initial guidelines for DOICC operations, based on experiences of existing DOICCs" by 31 July 1967.[20]

A problem that was to plague all American attempts to target the VCI was South Vietnamese unwillingness to take any such program seriously. The conflict over priorities arose because of a fear within various GVN agencies that their traditional power bases would be eroded if ICEX succeeded in bringing the intelligence-gathering apparatus together under one umbrella group. From the beginning CORDS was aware of the potential for disaster within GVN intelligence ranks. A July 1967 memo said, "The ICEX program cannot succeed without acceptance and energetic support by the Director General of the National Police and other senior GVN military, intelligence and security officials and the necessary policy direction from them to their subordinate echelons."[21]

From the political perspective of South Vietnamese officials, it was not difficult to see why there was a distrust of the ICEX concept. Since the Diem years political power stemmed from the ability of each official—whether civilian or military—to maintain a direct channel of communication with Saigon, and to control a source of intelligence that would provide a flow of information on potential rivals. The concept of pooling intelligence resources and aiming them at the enemy infrastructure was diametrically opposed to all that the South Vietnamese had become accustomed.

The Americans, understanding the difficulties that lay ahead in convincing the GVN of the importance of ICEX, wanted to first lay the groundwork for the U.S. advisory effort and then work on the GVN effort:

> The U.S. side will be developed first, to set an example and to serve as a catalyst for similar Vietnamese development, building primarily upon existing programs and resources.
>   The latter will be marshaled and concentrated to permit a 'rifle shot' rather than a shotgun approach to the real target—key, important political leaders and activists in the VC infrastructure. The ultimate attack on this elusive target is fundamentally a Vietnamese responsibility, employing essentially

police-type and other special resources and techniques. Hence for example, it is intended that the Provisional Reconnaissance Units (PRU) be especially focused and the Police Field Forces (PFF) redirected against infrastructure, with other forces and resources playing complementary roles.[22]

A later MACV directive went further by underscoring the distrust that arose between the Americans and their Vietnamese counterparts over the GVN's reluctance to wholeheartedly embrace ICEX.

"The [U.S.] counterpart officer must . . . review and verify the submissions from the Vietnamese agencies in the interest of proper reporting and accuracy."[23] This not-so-subtle jab at the Vietnamese illustrated the friction within what would later become Phoenix over the importance and goals of the program.

ICEX Organization

Apart from the problems of convincing the South Vietnamese to accept ICEX, there were also basic bureaucratic and structural hurdles to overcome. Komer attempted to accomplish this by using the assets he already had in place. Since it was established that the CIA had the necessary flexibility and programs in place to run ICEX, Komer decided to use existing CIA intelligence centers throughout South Vietnam as the skeleton that would be fleshed out until MACV was able to fill in. The CIA agreed, although this would add to the responsibilities of the agency regional officer in charge (ROIC) at the Corps level, and to the POIC at the province level. Parker represented the CIA connection with ICEX, but his deputy, Colonel Junichi Butto, was a MACV officer. Colonel Butto was a nisei (an American-educated son of Japanese immigrants) who had served with Parker during WWII, and Parker had the highest regard for him. When told by Komer to choose a deputy, Parker asked whom he could have. "Anybody you want," was the reply. Parker knew.

> I found out that a fellow I had known during WWII, Col. Butto, was still in-country, although his tour of duty was very

nearly up. I asked if I could have him as my military counterpart, assistant, deputy; I didn't care what his title was as long as I had his help because I knew he was very good. He was appalled because he already had a full-time job, but he saw the writing on the wall and in effect he kept on doing his own job plus helping me get this thing started.[24]

With the upper echelon of the ICEX organization in order, Komer and Parker could begin developing downward. On the national level ICEX was run from Saigon. A coordinating committee was made up of DEPCORDS; the special assistant to the ambassador (a CIA position); the assistant chief of staff, J-2; assistant chief of staff, J-3; and the chief of the RD Cadre. It was their job to keep track of progress at the province level.

At the lower levels—region and province—ICEX made the most headway. The CIA ROIC was designated senior adviser at the Corps level. He had a MACV military officer as his deputy for anti-infrastructure intelligence coordination. As ICEX Corps adviser, the ROIC sat as chair of a committee consisting of the Corps G-2 (intelligence), Corps G-2 adviser, Corps G-3 adviser (operations). Americans only played an advisory role to the ARVN, so the GVN counterpart was also included in the committee, and other U.S. personnel involved in anti-infrastructure operations, such as AID. The ROIC was also the point of contact between Corps and Saigon.[25]

From an operational standpoint, the ROIC recommended missions against the VCI and it was his responsibility to interest and involve the Vietnamese in ICEX. These two tasks showed that the CIA still ran ICEX although it was watched over by CORDS and ultimately MACV. This hierarchy did not mean the CIA held total sway over the fledgling anti-infrastructure program, but rather that there was a lack of personnel outside the CIA capable of handling the job. That situation would later change.

At the province level the CIA also picked up the slack. The province officer in charge chaired the Province Committee and monitored intelligence collection. The key to success here was timely collation and dissemination of information. Basically the province ICEX structure duplicated Corps and coordinated with the ICEX levels above and below.

Below province was the district-level ICEX structure. While this was the most important point in the anti-VCI chain, it was also the weakest. Komer realized the need for a strong district-level organization, but lack of time and personnel had made this the most difficult sector to build. The intelligence centers at the district level concentrated on rapid interpretation of intelligence and the planning of operations designed to exploit that intelligence. At this level there were not enough CIA personnel to go around. Instead, military province senior advisers (PSA) coordinated with the province ICEX staff and advised the Vietnamese district chiefs on the building and running of DIOCCs.

By the time ICEX became official in July 1967 most of the personnel were already in place. The selection of additional personnel from the military, CIA, AID, and USIA had begun. The CIA did not have as pervasive a presence as the ICEX organizational chart would at first indicate. According to a CORDS document titled "Action Program for Attack on VC Infrastructure, 1967–1968," the ratio of CIA to MACV personnel was one to sixty. By mid-1968 this ratio would increase as more and more military advisers filled the slots to replace those held by the CIA.[26]

By the end of 1967 CORDS had formalized financial and logistical support for the DIOCCs. A total of $517,000 was authorized to support 115 DIOCCs all over South Vietnam. Funds would be allocated to pay indigenous employees, purchase office equipment, and provide transportation in support of the DIOCCs. This money was not used for operational assets that aided ICEX, such as the PRU, NPFF, or any other military unit that might participate in targeting the VCI. These funds were most important in providing files and other supplies needed to set up a joint targeting capability.[27]

Problems in the Interrogation Pipeline

As can be expected, ICEX had its shortcomings. Most important was the inability of the new program to absorb Viet Cong suspects into the legal system. Nelson Brickham had foreseen the problem in his November 1966 memo to Komer, which noted that new problems such as "disposal of VC after they are captured" would have to be dealt with. It was the intent of the United States that any program to eliminate the enemy infrastructure be based within the legal system, which, in the case of South Vietnam, was unable to handle the increase in suspects. A key study was undertaken in December 1967 that outlined the shortcomings of the system. They were many.[28]

The most serious problem, as far as ICEX was concerned, was the breakdown in the interrogation process as VCI suspects went through the legal pipeline. Specific guidelines existed for the handling of prisoners of war, but VCI were technically civilians, and so fell outside those parameters.

Upon capture a suspect was interrogated by the detaining unit in the field for any information that might be of immediate tactical use. The process could last from one to twelve hours. If the suspect was considered to be an innocent civilian, he or she was released. If not, the suspect went to the next highest headquarters, usually the district.

At this point the process broke down. If an American unit had captured the prisoner, he went directly to division headquarters, bypassing both district and province. He then went to Saigon (if captured by an Army unit; to III MAF Combined Interrogation Center at Danang if captured by a Marine Corps unit) where he might remain for two months. During this time any information regarding the VCI obtained from the prisoner was unlikely to make its way into the ICEX intelligence files.

If captured by an ARVN unit the suspect might go to the province interrogation center—or he might not, going instead to ARVN division headquarters, or even higher, to the corps level. Only if the suspect was captured by a PRU or perhaps the National Police would he proceed to the province interrogation center, where the intelligence extracted could be processed into the ICEX system for use against other VCI.

In an ideal situation these problems would not affect ICEX because neutralization of the VCI would be handled almost exclusively by the National Police or the PRU. But the reality was that while a bulk of the targeting and elimination of the VCI fell on the shoulders of ICEX, the job was important enough that at least a portion of the efforts of the entire GVN should have been directed toward it. Phoenix would later suffer from the same shirking of responsibility by the military, who continued to regard elimination of the VCI as the "other war."

Corruption at the province level also had to be taken into account. Because of generally poor supervision in Saigon, officials at the province level often operated independently and there were many instances in which the province chief was little more than an extortion-ring boss who charged his captives a ransom for their freedom, even if the prisoner was obviously a high-ranking member of the VCI. A sweep operation carried out by the 4th U.S. Infantry Division in Pleiku Province between 1 January and 1 April 1967 netted 165 VCI suspects. Of these, only seven were retained by the GVN.

Operation Dragnet in Binh Dinh Province captured seventeen hundred suspects, many of whom were considered low-level VCI. Fifteen hundred were released, even though the ARVN had initially categorized thirteen hundred of them as VCI, giving each of them specific titles, such as "VC hamlet chief, VC subhamlet chief, tax collector, village guard...."[29]

According to a report on the handling of VCI prisoners, "the suspects who were released apparently were members of an organization with the means to effect reprisals or to buy the release of captured members of sufficient importance." [The problem lay not in the false arrest of innocent civilians as VCI—although that undoubtedly occurred—but rather in that it was more important to the district chief that he play it safe and at the same time make some money.[30]

Prison facilities for those VCI captured and convicted also were inadequate. In 1967 the problem was security rather than space. Prisoners were beginning to fill to capacity because of the new emphasis on anti-infrastructure operations, and although some were overcrowded, most were still at the recommended levels by late 1967.

Viet Cong and NVA attacks on prisons all over South Vietnam prompted General Westmoreland to write a letter to General Cao Van Vien, chief of the Joint General Staff. Westmoreland noted that "more VC, many of them key infrastructure cadre, are released in the space of a few minutes than we can pick up in three months of painstaking police and military operations."[31]

A spate of attacks on prisons in I Corps prompted a study that revealed shortcomings in the five major prisons in the region. The report concluded that all the prisons in I Corps had serious security problems and were beginning to suffer from overcrowding and poor conditions.[32]

Of all the problems that plagued ICEX and later Phoenix, the most understated and most often ignored was that of prisons. Hardcore VC cadre often were allowed to run loose among common criminals, giving them an ideal opportunity to recruit new members. But the problem was never solved and critics would later attack the detention system as inhumane.

Fledgling Phoenix

How effective was ICEX? It is practically impossible to judge the program independent of Phoenix because the two melded into one, as had been the plan from the beginning. Most ICEX reports pointed out the infancy of the program and dwelt on how much ground was left to cover. By the end of November 1967 ICEX were perceived as progressing "vigorously" at the "corps, province, and district level." Noting that the GVN was still reluctant to accept the ICEX concept because of a "preoccupation with elections and formation [of a] new government," the program could boast a structure in place in all forty-four provinces, with at least a skeleton administration in most of South Vietnam's districts. By November 1967 there were fifty-three operating DIOCCs at the district level, up from ten in July of the same year.[33]

Some were more effective than others. Quang Tri Province in I Corps and Binh Dinh Province in II Corps were "examples of aggressive implementation of [the] ICEX concept."[34] Again, the success of an ICEX program in a given province was directly proportional to the amount of support tendered by the GVN. On the national level official GVN attitudes toward ICEX slowly changed. The II Corps commander, General Vinh Loc, endorsed the ICEX concept and even provided direct support for DIOCCs in his region. Hau Nghia Province experienced support by key GVN officials because of its strategic position and importance to the survival of Saigon. This resulted in the appointment of quality people as DIOCC chiefs. In Saigon, General Loan, chief of the National Police, reversed his previous position of distrust for ICEX and embraced the concept after being convinced that the power base of his police would not be threatened and his intelligence operations and sources would not be compromised. Probably the most important reason for General Loan's reversal was the realization that participation in the DIOCC could only enhance police intelligence-gathering capabilities and therefore its prestige.[35]

ICEX was Phoenix without the name. In 1968 the program would be transferred almost unchanged to the Phoenix program, but in 1967 ICEX moved throughout South Vietnam as the first step toward making destruction of the enemy infrastructure a primary goal. ICEX probably did not seriously cripple the VCI, but it did put in place the apparatus needed to do the job.

Why and how did ICEX and Phoenix come to be? It was more than just a simple evolution of ideas culminating in the Phoenix program. The birth of the institution that formalized American commitment to the destruction of the Viet Cong infrastructure as a primary goal of the war was at the root of both the transformation of the military's philosophy on how the war was to be won and the final act in which the tangle of civilian pacification programs became simplified with the formation of CORDS. From a historical point of view the move represented a mixed beginning of good and bad. On the positive side, anti-infrastructure operations began to play an important part in the military's war planning. At the same time the fledgling Phoenix program would begin to fall victim to a system of paper chasing and number crunching that measured success in terms of raw data coughed up to Saigon at the end of each month.

How could that have happened? It seemed logical to assume that a program considered to be so important by the Americans would have been at the cutting edge of planning, logistics, and operations capabilities. Yet that was not the case for two reasons. First, as has been discussed, the Vietnamese often were less than enthusiastic over the concept. Second, although pacification had been given new life under CORDS, it had become a part of the massive war effort that demanded numbers as evidence of progress. For better or for worse, the Phoenix program had become an integral part of MACV's military machine.

4

From the Ashes of Tet: 1968

ICEX placed anti-infrastructure efforts within the matrix of American military operations. During 1967 virtually all successes or failures could be traced directly to the American advisory effort; the Vietnamese had shown little interest in such an alien concept. When the program came to be called Phoenix in late 1967, the emphasis was placed on getting Vietnamese support from the highest levels and improving the intelligence-gathering capabilities of all assets under the Phoenix umbrella. These assets were to be aimed at targeting specific members of the VCI. Reports were fond of calling it a "rifle-shot" rather than a "shotgun" approach to combating the communist political underground.

1968 was to be a year of development and growth, but such hopes were dashed on the wave of the Tet Offensive, which swept over South Vietnam in late January 1968. Viet Cong guerrillas and North Vietnamese soldiers attacked most of South Vietnam's cities throwing the country into chaos and calling into question American claims that there was light at the end of the tunnel. Besides fueling arguments about whether the war was being won or lost, the Tet Offensive affected the Phoenix program in two major ways. First, it interrupted and in many cases destroyed the gains made in pacification during the past year. Second, and on a more positive note, it jolted South Vietnamese President Nguyen Van Thieu into realizing that it had been the existence of the Viet Cong infrastructure that had allowed the

Tet Offensive to occur. Thieu quickly gave his approval for the Phoenix program and ordered his subordinates to do the same. The enemy had accomplished what Robert Komer, the CIA, and the American ambassador could not: convince the Vietnamese leadership that Phoenix was a necessary step in winning the war. But there was much still to be done.

During the first six months of 1968 the newborn Phoenix program licked its wounds and slowly rebuilt. In July 1968 the GVN officially endorsed the Phoenix program with a presidential decree and work began in earnest. But not everything went so smoothly. During 1968 many of the problems that would plague Phoenix developed, leading to immediate criticism from many of those in opposition to the war.

What's in a Name?

The Phoenix program was officially born on 20 December 1967, when the South Vietnamese prime minister issued a decree calling for the coordination of all services in a program aimed at the VCI. This differed from ICEX only in the official South Vietnamese support for the program. Anti-infrastructure operations became a top priority at the highest level.

The name Phoenix appeared rather suddenly in the press at the beginning of 1968, and there was nothing malevolent about it. But the mere word seemed to attract attention much more than what was actually going on. When Phoenix was ICEX few in the press paid it much attention. Somehow Phoenix sounded more mysterious. Nor was the press uncovering the story of a covert operation. Almost since its inception the Phoenix program was basically an aboveboard effort using American military advisers.[1]

Using the phoenix as its symbolic mascot may have been a mistake, however. Although the mythological phoenix was not evil, it did conjure images of the supernatural; the ability to rise from death and defeat into the glory of rebirth and victory. But there was no real intention by CORDS to attach deep meaning to the name. Phoenix was the best English approximation of the

Vietnamese mythical bird Phung Hoang. And there the similarity ended.

The Phung Hoang was one of four sacred animals in Vietnamese mythology and it represented grace, virtue, peace, and concord. It was also the symbol of womanhood and female virtue and was used for centuries as the symbol of queens and empresses. The emperor was usually represented by the dragon. The Phung Hoang was an amalgamation of many of the symbols held dear by traditional Vietnamese society. Its song represented the five notes of the Vietnamese musical scale and its feathers came from the five basic colors. Physically, it was also a creature with borrowed characteristics. It had the neck of a snake, breast of a swallow, back of a tortoise, and tail of a fish. The Phung Hoang appeared only during times of peace and prosperity, scurrying into hiding when danger and bad times approached.[2]

The Vietnamese name Phung Hoang, too, was somewhat unfortunate. While it was supposed to symbolize the coming of peace and prosperity, or from the American perspective a rising from the ashes, some U.S. advisers joked that Phung Hoang better represented many of the South Vietnamese soldiers and territorial forces who ran at the first sign of trouble.

Robert Komer did not delve into the classics searching for a double entendre that could be a source of philosophical satisfaction for those in Vietnam with classical educations. He simply chose a name already in use. In late 1966 an experimental anti-infrastructure program had been started in I Corps. It was staffed and run by the Vietnamese with the guidance of a CIA adviser. Komer was pleased both with the concept and the name.[3]

While many used the names Phoenix and Phung Hoang as simplistic handles for criticism, the basic lines of the new emphasis on anti-infrastructure operations had not changed much from ICEX. Had the Tet Offensive not occurred ICEX would have slid smoothly into the Phoenix program with no discernible break in transition. But history is rarely so cooperative.

The communists failed in their offensive and although their reasons for launching it in the first place are still open to debate, it seems clear that Hanoi hoped to influence the Americans into backing away from wholehearted support of South Vietnam. Militarily, the Tet Offensive was a disaster for the communists. Many VC political and military cadres were wiped out as they rose to guide the masses in a popular revolt that never materialized. While the U.S. Army fared well during the offensive, the pacification effort suffered some problems. Instead of joining the communists, most of the people fled from them, generating some six hundred thousand refugees. In addition, word of the massacre of civilians in the ancient imperial capital of Hue spread throughout South Vietnam, providing a glimpse of what life might be like if the communists were to win the war. Some twenty-eight hundred civilians accused by the communists of being counterrevolutionaries were methodically rounded up, shot, and buried in mass graves.

The GVN responded to the Tet Offensive with Operation Recovery, a program designed to give relief to the rising refugee population. CORDS supervised the undertaking. Temporary refugee centers were built by U.S. engineers to house the victims of Tet, and CORDS saw to it that stockpiles of building materials were on hand to rebuild many of the villages. CORDS also provided massive quantities of rice to feed the refugees and to break the black market.[4]

The effort by CORDS to handle the refugee problem put the Phoenix program into the background for the first six months of 1968. But the VCI had its own problems to handle. Many of the cadre had been killed during the offensive and the ones who survived or who had remained behind devoted their time to rebuilding. Although Saigon did not have the time or resources to devote to anti-infrastructure operations in the wake of the Tet Offensive, the cooperation achieved between the GVN and CORDS during Operation Recovery carried over into the planning phase of the Phoenix program beginning in the summer of 1968.

While the pacification effort concentrated on refugees, the task of keeping pressure on the VCI continued to fall on the military. The creation of CORDS and ICEX had shown that the highest levels of MACV were willing to make anti-infrastructure operations top priority. But with the Phoenix program on hold conventional military operations had to fill in for specific targeting. During troop sweeps the Army attempted to accomplish two talks: destroy main-force units and capture VCI. From the point of view of those in CORDS the results were rarely satisfactory.

Seal-and-Search Operation in Ben Cui Village[5]

In early January 1968 there were indications that the communists were planning something big. Intelligence sources told the 3rd Brigade of the 1st Infantry Division of a VC/NVA buildup in the area around Ben Cui Village in Ben Cat District, Binh Duong Province (situated in III Corps). For the past three or four weeks the VC had been seen moving in groups of anywhere from squad size to 120 men. Most disturbing was the impression that they seemed unconcerned that the Americans might detect them. The VC would move into a village at night, organize propaganda meetings, and spend the night. In the morning they would take money, round up some extra supplies and leave. Agents in these villages were able to identify some of the units and they reported that NVA soldiers often came along. When NVA were present the villagers were required to turn out all lights. GVN agents also reported that the villagers were not allowed to keep dogs because the barking might alert ARVN and RF/PF soldiers stationed just across the river at Ben Cat.

By the end of the first week in January there were enough independent reports to indicate that this was not an isolated event. On the night of 6 January GVN troops at Ben Cat, Ben Cui, and Lai Khe came under attack. Lai Khe was mortared, but Ben Cat and Ben Cui were hit hardest. The Viet Cong penetrated the district chief's compound, momentarily paralyzing GVN reaction capabilities. In Ben Cui, Viet Cong assassination teams killed two village officials and kidnapped others. News of this latest development convinced the Americans to seal off Ben Cui with a major sweep operation.

The plan was to seal off the village from the east and west and then close the north approach to the village with three rifle companies. The ARVN would then move in from the south and the trap would be closed. Two LRRP (long-range reconnaissance patrol) ambush teams were positioned on the east flank, the area from which any Viet Cong or NVA reinforcements were expected to come.

The whole array of American firepower was available for the operation. An artillery battery was standing by with preset coordinates in case fire support was needed. A Spooky gunship was to be on station beginning at 3:00 A.M. (the time when the moon would go down) to provide illumination rounds to light up the scene and to pepper the area with its considerable firepower, should that be required. A helicopter mounted with high-powered Xenon searchlights also would be making its rounds.

By 9:30 A.M. the units began closing around the village and the search elements took over. This group consisted of eighteen PRUs, twenty-one Popular Force troops and ten National Policemen. The PFs came from an outpost to the north of Ben Cui and were accompanied by an American NCO. It was his job to make sure the PFs used good fire control (they tended to fire up all their ammunition in the first few minutes of a fight) and to keep them from stumbling on to the LRRP ambush parties. The PRUs were along because of their professional, no-nonsense reputation. The American 3rd Brigade S-2, Major Eugene D. Tapscott, noted that the National Police were virtually worthless without the presence of the PRUs. "If you have only the National Police," he observed, "they are somewhat reluctant to conduct a really thorough and strong search, but if you mix the National Police with the RF/PF and the PRU, who are the real tough guys, then you get the best results out of the search."

The Americans controlled the entire operation. In fact, the district chief was not informed about the seal and search until 2:00 A.M. on 11 January. That gave him just enough time to round up the search party and get them ready by daybreak. At 7:00 A.M. the search element was in position at the north end of Ben Cui.

The operation went off without a hitch. No one in the village knew the area was surrounded until a PSYOPS helicopter with blaring loudspeakers heralded the coming sweep force in the early morning hours. All males were segregated and placed into one collection point. Their identification cards were collected by the National Police and all VC prisoners who had been rounded up by the security elements on the village outskirts were brought in for interrogation. A total of 235 males were screened, seventeen of whom were detained as communist suspects. Nine Viet Cong soldiers were killed and thirteen more were captured.

In many ways the operation was a success. The village was an enemy-controlled area in which the VC operated with virtual impunity. In the months leading up to Tet, U.S. troops had not operated in the area at night and the ARVN did not have the inclination or the ability to clean out the Viet Cong. The long months of danger-free existence seemed to lull the communists into a false sense of security.

Although the Phoenix program had nothing to do with the operation, there was a sense of the importance of eliminating the VCI from the area even though the main objective was to catch Viet Cong main-force units napping. When the Tet Offensive exploded across South Vietnam a few short weeks later, much of the GVN presence that was so necessary to pacification was pushed out of the way. Without that presence the GVN could not hope to maintain the intelligence resources needed to conduct an effective anti-infrastructure campaign. The result was a continuation of cordon-and-sweep tactics that could be used by the Army to illustrate that it was emphasizing elimination of the enemy's political infrastructure.

Unfortunately, the Army did not make the connection between the twin needs for pacification and providing security by destroying main-force units. It really only wanted to concentrate on the latter. In after-action reports it is clear that most units only went through the motions of civic action and developing intelligence specifically designed to ferret out the VCI.

By March 1968 the shock of the Tet Offensive had worn off (except for a few places in I Corps, such as Hue) and the Army continued to perform the dual missions of chasing main-force units and rounding up VCI. The Phoenix program continued to build DIOCCs and begin developing dossiers on suspected VCI, but for the most part it was having little impact on the communist infrastructure. Despite the military setback suffered by the communists during Tet, there were still plenty of political cadre in the villages. The Army and ARVN continued to counterattack, keeping pressure on the Viet Cong and NVA, and pacification remained in the background. Attacking the VCI, too, remained an afterthought.

Armor against the VCI[6]

Chanh Luu Village in Ben Cat District, Binh Duong Province, long had been controlled by the Viet Cong. During the Tet Offensive the village had served as a supply base for VC and NVA forces as they prepared for the big attack. By midsummer, intelligence sources and aerial observation indicated that Chanh Luu was still a rest area for main-force units as well as a supply base containing large caches of supplies and munitions. The C-61, C-62, and C-301 Local Force Companies were permanently stationed in the village and the K-1, K-2, K-3, and K-4 Battalions of the Dong Nai Regiment generally operated within ten to twelve kilometers from Binh My Village, also in Ben Cat District. By early August 1968 it was clear that U.S. forces had to do something about the village because it was a gathering point for main-force cadre. While not specifically political infrastructure, the main-force cadre were important to the operations and intelligence of the Viet Cong military apparatus.

The mission order was simple: "To conduct a cordon and search of Chanh Luu Village and to pacify any resistance by enemy elements in the area and to render the enemy inoperative." The task went to the 11th ACR (Armored Cavalry Regiment), commanded by Colonel George S. Patton. The plan was a three-phase affair that would begin by deceiving the enemy and end with a cordon-and-search of the village.

The first phase was to mislead the enemy into believing the U.S. forces were converging on the village of Bien My, also a well-known VC supply point. The 11th ACR sent decoy radio transmissions, made visual aerial recons, and sent troops toward Bien My. In an unbelievable display of gullibility, the VC also were fooled by phony maps dropped on trails in the eastern part of the area of operation. The maps contained illustrated routes of movement by U.S. and ARVN troops, times of entry into the target areas, and map coordinates. Sure enough, aerial recon indicated that the decoy maps were being picked up by enemy troops in the area.

On the morning of 3 August, 3rd Squadron, 11th ACR began moving north of Chanh Luu toward the village of Bien My. Five days of maneuvering ended on the evening of 8 August when the 3rd Squadron was met by infantry units that had been stationed some ten thousand meters east of Chanh Luu at a firebase called Normandy II. Everything was in position for the actual operation against Chanh Luu.

At 11:00 P.M. on 8 August, 3rd Squadron and its three supporting infantry companies turned around and headed for their real objective, Chanh Luu Village. Because the units could not converge on the village simultaneously, 4.2-inch mortar fire was used to fill in the gaps until U.S. troops could arrive on the scene. When the units were all in place the mortars and artillery switched over to firing illumination rounds, which lit up the sky for the rest of the night.

The Viet Cong were caught off guard by the ruse. Most of the guerrillas in the area were scattered throughout the jungle outside the villages and upon seeing the armor moving on Chanh Luu fired two volleys meant to warn other VC. The Americans expected a counterattack, but nothing materialized. Intelligence personnel with the 541st Military Intelligence Detachment later reported that the VC could not get enough of their scattered forces together for a counterattack.

At 7:00 A.M. on 9 August the final phase of the operation was launched. The Vietnamese element of the operation, the 5th ARVN Battalion, had been held at a position southeast of Chanh Luu waiting for the moment when helicopters could airlift it directly into the village. The ARVN landed in the village and began a systematic search that lasted for two days.

Viet Cong trapped in the village immediately opened fire on the ARVN. The Vietnamese interpreter for 3rd Squadron later recalled that "the confused enemy were running up and down the village carrying AK-47s and small arms."

The search of Chanh Luu was "efficient and systematic." The ARVN captured one small group of Viet Cong almost immediately upon entering the village. After questioning, the prisoners led the way to another group of hiding guerrillas and to a cache of ammunition and supplies. The search mushroomed until the entire village had been covered. When it was all over eighteen Viet Cong had been killed and 125 captured. On the civilian side, ten suspects thought to be infrastructure were detained along with 225 other detainees.

As was standard procedure in these types of searches, a MEDCAP (medical civil action program) mission was sent into the village to care for any people who might need medical attention. In this case the program was not popular and most of the villagers did not react to it. According to one soldier interviewed after the operation, "the people were afraid; it was the first MEDCAP they had ever seen. They were also afraid that if they went to the MEDCAP, they might be accused of something; fear, I think, was behind it all."

The village appeared clean and well-ordered, but MEDCAP personnel reported people with "cuts, rotten teeth, and sores." In spite of the fact that the Vietnamese did not react to the MEDCAP, the officer in charge later wrote:

> I think we accomplished our mission [acceptance of the MEDCAP by the villagers] very well. After continued urging by the interpreter in telling them they would not be harmed, and after the first two or three that came to our medical team and were treated went back and told others, people began to make use of the MEDCAP. I think they [the villagers] believed the Americans showed them they really wanted to help and we were not as bad as the VC had depicted us.

The after-action report concerning the MEDCAP was clearly only lip service to a primitive form of pacification practiced by Army units largely concerned with sweeping enemy units away with fire and movement. In the case of Chanh Luu Village this was partially justified. The village was firmly under communist control and most of the infrastructure had no need to hide. The 11th ACR captured a few members of the infrastructure, but the after-action report made it clear they were really after main-force and local-force members.

Getting Down to Business

Despite the problems arising from the use of conventional troops in an anti-infrastructure role, the Tet Offensive proved to be an important watershed for pacification in South Vietnam for at least four reasons. First, the communists' ability to drive the poorly armed Territorial Forces out of their bases like tumbleweeds before the wind convinced the GVN of something CORDS had been pushing for some time: President Thieu decided to arm the population for self-defense. Thieu had always feared that to do so would only mean providing the VC with a ready supply of easy-to-capture weapons. Tet showed him he had no choice but to change his mind. The result was the People's Self-Defense Force (PSDF), a nationwide system of local militias.[7]

Second, although the fledgling Phoenix program had been forced to flee from the countryside, as the GVN slowly returned it became clear that the damage was not as extensive as had first been thought. Most importantly, the VCI had surfaced for the offensive and, failing in their attempt, lay exposed like bats caught in the coming daylight. So although the Phoenix program suffered a setback during Tet it was also handed an opportunity: Phoenix got the respite it needed to grow while the VCI crawled away and concentrated on rebuilding.

Third, the GVN National Assembly enacted the National Mobilization Decree, which instituted the draft for young men eighteen and nineteen years old. This allowed the GVN—under MACV's guidance—to shuffle military priorities. The new PSDF was responsible for village defense, which freed the RF/PF to concentrate on area security. Part of the ARVN became a province and district (mostly province) reaction force, and the U.S. military concentrated on chasing the enemy. CORDS now had the rough outline of a security force that could protect the relatively defenseless pacification program—including Phoenix. For the first time South Vietnam was on a true war footing.[8]

Finally, Tet forced the Viet Cong to change its political and military structure. The People's Liberation Army Forces, the military arm of the National Liberation Front, continued to exist, but in a new form. No longer could the Viet Cong claim that theirs was an indigenous revolution born of dissatisfaction with the GVN and its "colonial" roots. The VCI as it had been known in the days before Tet ceased to exist. There simply were not enough cadre left alive to infiltrate the entire countryside. To take up the slack, Hanoi sent troops and cadre from North Vietnam, dropping the facade of the people's war. From 1968 until the fall of Saigon in 1975, the war became indisputably controlled by Hanoi.

But this did not mean that the VCI assumed a lesser importance (although much of the native southern cadre was destroyed, the infrastructure continued to be called VCI because they were still Viet Cong, as distinguished from the NVA). The argument put forth by the Viet Cong that they represented the nationalist interests of the Vietnamese people began to lose weight. In the villages the winning side was the one that provided the peasants with the best physical security and personal stability.

MACV understood this point. Emphasis on Phoenix and pacification in general remained paramount, in many ways even more important than before. The enemy faced by U.S. troops and the ARVN was now the NVA, an invading and basically foreign army that needed supplies, support bases, and rest areas. Materiel coming down the Ho Chi Minh Trail could only provide a portion of what the NVA needed to carry on the war. The VCI made sure they could infiltrate easily into South Vietnam's porous border, providing networks of hideouts, food caches, and friendly villages where communist troops could regroup on the way to the "front." Even if U.S. and GVN forces managed to decisively defeat the NVA, the VCI could always remain underground and revert to guerrilla warfare. The reverse was not true. If the VCI were wiped out the NVA would have to return north or remain in the south and die.

Presidential Decree

When President Thieu recovered from the shock of the Tet Offensive he realized that the massive U.S. troop buildup had been an illusory cure for South Vietnam's woes. Although American might had defeated the communists on the field of battle at almost every turn, the enemy had still managed to launch a major offensive. Thieu began taking a personal interest in what he realized was his best hope of preventing a recurrence of Tet—intelligence collection and operations. He was deeply shaken by the number of unsuspected Viet Cong agents who had uncloaked themselves during the Tet attacks. The CIA had always been aware of the VCI's strength and abilities, as witnessed by the long history of VC assassinations of GVN rural officials, but no one really knew their numbers. CIA estimates put the number at more than one hundred thousand (MACV estimated about seventy-thousand VCI; the discrepancy became a source of contention for years) and after the Tet attacks, Thieu could no longer ignore the figure.[9]

Although all of Thieu's motives for quickly throwing his support behind the Phoenix program have not been fully explained, two other factors were put forward by some of his subordinates. First, the chairman of the new Phung Hoang national committee, Premier Tran Van Khiem, had strong support within the army and therefore might become a potential rival to Thieu. Second, the Phung Hoang's national apparatus could become an alternate source of political power should Thieu choose to disregard it. Thieu realized the Americans fully backed the Phoenix concept and it would be implemented in some form with or without his approval. Better to endorse Phoenix and keep a watch over it than reject it and always wonder what it was up to.[10]

At any rate, President Thieu, with the help of William Colby, Komer's deputy for CORDS, drafted a decree that officially sanctioned the existence of Phoenix/Phung Hoang on 1 July 1968. It was distributed to U.S. and GVN officials on 8 July. Presidential Decree No. 280-a/TT/SL established the Phung Hoang plan to control and coordinate all GVN efforts aimed at destroying the VCI. Articles 1 and 2 defined Phung Hoang as a national program designed to incorporate all military and civilian agencies and aim them specifically at the VCI.

Article 3 was of paramount importance to the Americans. It defined who was or was not a member of the VCI. This was

Program had often defined as communist infrastructure anyone who was in any way connected with the Viet Cong, failing to take into account the degree of involvement. It was hoped that Phoenix/Phung Hoang would be much more discerning.

> Article 3—Definitions: The Viet Cong Infrastructure is all Viet Cong, political and administrative organizations established by the Communist Party which goes under the name People's Revolutionary Party, from the cities to the countryside. The Central Office of South Vietnam (COSVN) is the highest level steering organ of the Viet Cong in South Vietnam, which directs these political and administrative organizations through the various echelons of the People's Revolutionary Party of South Vietnam, and the Front for the Liberation of South Vietnam (NLFSVN), from central level down to the hamlets.
>
> In addition the communists plant a number of cadres to direct and control other parties and organizations, such as the Progressive Socialist Party, the Southern Democratic Party, the Alliance of National Democratic and Peace Forces or other similar organizations in the future. Only these communist cadres are regarded as part of the Viet Cong Infrastructure.
>
> Viet Cong military units, members of mass organizations established by the Viet Cong, citizens forced to perform as laborers, or civilians living in areas temporarily controlled by the Viet Cong, are not classified as belonging to the Viet Cong Infrastructure.[11]

Although these definitions had to be redefined in later years, they marked a good starting point for PIOCC and DIOCC organizations. Article 3 specified that since VC military units were not included in the definition of infrastructure, those VCI captured were not entitled to be treated as prisoners of war under the Geneva Convention. Instead they could be processed under the GVN legal system.

The decree set forth the organization of Phung Hoang Committees from the national or central level down to district. While these definitions and organizations held little real meaning to the success or failure of the program, part of Article 5 did. Paragraph three stated that "the principal operational element within the Phung Hoang organization is the National Police. . . ."[12] In

1968 the National Police did not have personnel capable of handling the responsibility of anti-infrastructure operations, in particular the sophistication necessary to target and capture specific VCI. William Colby, Komer's assistant for CORDS, recognized this problem and had a provision written into the decree that charged the military with temporarily helping fill the void:

> The military forces are responsible for providing support to the National Police until the latter have sufficient capability to perform their missions. The Special Police Branch and the Police Field Force are the two components charged with eliminating the Viet Cong Infrastructure, and when necessary, may receive support from other forces and resources.[13]

This preoccupation with using the police as the Phoenix program's action arm stemmed from the need to distinguish anti-infrastructure operations from strictly military operations. If the police were handling the VCI it was easier to work within the existing legal system. Part of the reason also stemmed from the British experience in Malaya. Because the British had been successful in their counterinsurgency effort there was a tendency to adopt their programs and place them in the Vietnamese context with little or no attempt to adapt them to Vietnamese realities. The Strategic Hamlet program was an example of this mentality and so were the National Police in the role of anti-infrastructure operatives. But the police had worked in Malaya, so it seemed logical that they would work in Vietnam. As will be discussed later, this theory was doomed to failure from the start, although on the surface it made perfect sense.

Question of Emphasis

The Phoenix program was later criticized for failing to neutralize high-ranking cadre, turning its attention instead on an easier prey, the lowest-level infrastructure. Part of this trend lay in the original decree's failure to establish target priorities, allowing Phung Hoang Committees to target hamlet and village cadre rather than province, region, or COSVN infrastructure. The

Phung Hoang Committees to target hamlet and village cadre rather than province, region, or COSVN infrastructure. The problem was recognized almost immediately and was partially rectified on 27 July with a CORDS Standard Operating Procedure (SOP), the first of three (a fourth was in process before the American withdrawal from Vietnam, but was never instituted) such clarifying documents that outlined specific procedures to be followed by all Phung Hoang Committees. Article 7 of SOP 1 called on the Phung Hoang organization to ". . . direct commanders of all Corps Tactical Zones, according to the local situation, to give priority to the effort to eliminate the Viet Cong Infrastructure."[14] This took away from GVN Corps commanders any flexibility they might have thought they had in carrying out the Phung Hoang mission.

But from the beginning the philosophy that only neutralization of high-ranking VCI could ultimately destroy the Viet Cong was misguided. In fact, critics who noted that Phoenix didn't really do an adequate job because it neutralized only low-level cadre were missing the point. Province advisers frequently observed in their monthly reports that although Phoenix more than met its quota, the program was not effective because it failed to neutralize enough high-ranking VCI.

But the reality of the way the VCI operated actually made it more important to go after low- and middle-level cadre, the communists on the ground in the villages. High-ranking VCI at the province level rarely stayed in contested or GVN-controlled villages. Rather, they lived in secure areas such as remote outposts on the Cambodian border or in "liberated" hamlets and villages. Therefore, they were inhabiting areas already out of reach of government forces and exerting pressure on a segment of the population already in their grasp. Standard big-unit operations often were better suited for rooting them out of their strongholds. The ability of COSVN, regional, and even province VCI to affect those people in contested or government-controlled areas lay in their contact with the cadre in the villages. If Phoenix could neutralize the mid-level VCI in the contested and government-controlled areas they effectively severed the link between them and the high-level VCI, rendering them virtually powerless. Without ever actually coming in contact with the very high-ranking officials they were supposed to target, the Phoenix program could neutralize their effectiveness. Without realizing it, Phoenix seriously injured—and in some cases disabled—the Viet Cong infrastructure in a number of districts and provinces.[15]

Phoenix/Phung Hoang Administrative Structure

Decree 280-a/TT/SL made it clear that Phung Hoang was to be the priority for every GVN official in South Vietnam. At the top, the Central Phung Hoang Committee was chaired by the minister of the interior, with the director general of the National Police sitting in as vice-chairman. The minister of defense, military J-2 and J-3 of the GVN Joint General Staff (JGS), and representatives from the Chieu Hoi Ministry, Revolutionary Development (RD) Ministry, Police Special Branch (PSB), and National Police Field Force (NPFF) rounded out the committee. It was their job to act as liaison between the lower Phung Hoang committees and the prime minister as well as guide and coordinate activities in South Vietnam's four military regions.

At the regional level the ARVN Corps commander chaired the committee, effectively melding anti-infrastructure activities with military objectives. The Corps police commander was vice-chair of the Regional Phung Hoang Committee, while the other members roughly paralleled the Central Committee. The Regional Phung Hoang Committee supervised, inspected, and supported operations for the Province Phung Hoang Committee, the next rung down the Phoenix ladder.

At the province level the Phung Hoang responsibilities began to differ. The central and regional levels were mainly administrative and oversight bodies, but it was recognized that the highest level for effective targeting and operations was the province. The Province Phung Hoang Committee was chaired by the province chief, who was usually an ARVN colonel. The province police chief served as vice-chairman and representatives from G-2, G-3, RD Cadre, Chieu Hoi, Census/Grievance, PSB, and NPFF made up the main body. In addition, intelligence officers from all military units in the province were attached to the province committee.

Most importantly, from an operational point of view, the province committee was to use its intelligence sources to "uncover all Viet Cong organizations in the province and find ways to destroy those organizations, if possible, in the shortest possible time."[16] This was a tall order that was rarely met, but in an attempt to live up to the spirit of Thieu's interest in the Phoenix program, the Province Phung Hoang Committee was required to meet at least once a week to discuss intelligence, targeting, and operations. It also traced VCI neutralization results and maintained files, charts, and statistics showing progress against the VCI. The permanent center of the Province Phung Hoang Committee was to operate twenty-four hours a day to meet the intelligence needs of the DIOCCs, the operational nerve center of the Phoenix program.

The district had a DIOCC that was effectively a district-level Phung Hoang Committee, but because it served as an intelligence and operations center it was able to forego the administrative role that theoretically was fulfilled at the province level. The DIOCC was staffed with an administrative unit almost identical to the Province Phung Hoang Committee and was also to operate on a continuous basis. In addition to collating intelligence of the VCI and carrying out operations, the DIOCC was supposed to serve as a secondary source of intelligence for U.S., ARVN, RF/PF, and other military and civilian units stationed in the district.

Each DIOCC was divided into four sections: administrative, military intelligence (designed to supplement order of battle intelligence on enemy main-force units), police intelligence (directed at the VCI), and operations. Clearly, the guidelines set forth in the presidential decree were overoptimistic. Most DIOCCs had a difficult time generating intelligence on their primary target—the VCI—let alone helping with military intelligence.

While the DIOCC's role was almost identical to the Province Phung Hoang Committee, it was also subservient. This was another oversight that was quickly seen and addressed in SOP 1, but in the meantime district and province often fought over which had the authority to plan and launch operations. Did the DIOCC need approval from the province first? It was impractical for the DIOCC to wait for orders from the province committee, but it took a specific reference in SOP 1 to convince the hierarchy-conscious Vietnamese.[17]

The far-reaching nature of Decree 280-a/TT/SL transcended its obvious overoptimism. Few believed the Phung Hoang committees were capable of anything approaching the level of coordination specified by the decree. But part of CORDS's satisfaction over the move stemmed from the knowledge that American advisers would be present at every level down to the district. This was the real essence of the Phoenix program—an American advisory effort to the Vietnamese Phung Hoang.

American Reaction

The American anti-infrastructure apparatus was largely in place from the ICEX program. Virtually all advances made against the VCI through ICEX were a result of direct American action. The presidential decree shifted the American role from one of trying to convince the GVN to implement an anti-infrastructure program to one of advice and guidance, a much better position as far as CORDS officials were concerned. The official U.S. response to the decree was that it was "a major milestone in the stepped-up attack against the VCI," which, of course, it was.[18]

On 9 July CORDS Directive 381-41 defined the U.S. role in the Phung Hoang program. The new U.S. role emphasized advice rather than direct action. The purpose of American support was:

> To prescribe policies, establish responsibilities and command relationships, and outline procedures for a joint U.S. civil/military action program [Phoenix] . . . to complement and support the Vietnamese Phung Hoang (PH) program for intelligence coordination and exploitation for elimination of the Viet Cong Infrastructure.[19]

The U.S. directive put all responsibility for gathering intelligence and carrying out operations squarely on the GVN, noting that the police were best suited to deal with the VCI:

> The elimination of the VCI is fundamentally a Vietnamese responsibility employing essentially police type techniques and special resources.[20]

The emphasis on police operations diverged from ICEX, which had named the PRU as the "rifle shot" aimed at the VCI. The new directive eliminated mention of the PRU, implying that the police were the best instrument. The PRU was still linked with the CIA and CORDS wanted a more mainstream organization involved in what had come to be regarded as an internal legal matter.

The American ICEX advisory structure remained in place down to the district level, where there was a subtle but surprising addition. American Phoenix advisers were given the authority to participate in raids. It was widely known that American officers led PRU or RF/PF operations against the Viet Cong, but it had never been sanctioned in an official directive. But until Phung Hoang found its stride American guidance would be necessary.[21]

Finally, the Phoenix program was stated in the directive to be unclassified, at least the name and acknowledgment that the program was aimed at the VCI. Actual operations were "classified Confidential, and [the] details were not to be discussed with unauthorized persons." Considering the nature of the program and that the Viet Cong were expected to react violently to the Phoenix program, the low classification level was unusual.[22]

Despite the official documents heralding the rise of the Phoenix program, there was a long distance between putting the concept on paper and putting it into action. While the new apparatus was planned from national down to district level, anti-infrastructure operations remained much the same as before the Tet Offensive. As the Viet Cong and NVA were pushed out of the cities in February 1968, they maintained pockets of influence in the countryside. American and ARVN conventional units threw their weight at them, often destroying entire villages, and with them the pacification effort up to that point. However, when troops in a particular province took the business of pacification as seriously as it did the purely military aspects of seeking out and destroying enemy main-force units, there existed the potential for efficient, well-coordinated, and effective operations against the VCI.

During a six-month period beginning in May and ending in

October 1968, American and Vietnamese forces waged a campaign that virtually eliminated VC influence in Quang Dien District, Thua Thien Province (I Corps).

An Integrated Pacification Campaign[23]

Quang Dien was an area of rich rice-producing land lying on the coastal plain only a few short miles east of the ancient capital of Hue. In the early days of 1968, during the Tet Offensive, communist troops completely occupied Quang Dien. Only three beleaguered ARVN posts were able to hold out against the onslaught and these appeared to be deemed unimportant by the NVA and Viet Cong forces, which simply bypassed and isolated them.

In May 1968 the GVN began the slow process of cleaning out communist control in Quang Dien. The eventual success of the effort, wrote Lieutenant Colonel Leslie D. Carter, commander of 1st Battalion, 502d Infantry, 101st Airborne Division, "was achieved not by contacts between major forces or by large-scale cordon operations, but rather by the less dramatic day-to-day execution of a harmonious and well-integrated U.S./Vietnamese campaign."

When the NVA and Viet Cong were finally thrown out of Hue in early March of 1968, the Army and Marines were assigned to clean up communist pockets of control in I Corps, a process that went on for the rest of the year. In April, the 1st Battalion, 502d Infantry (1/502d) were deployed to Quang Dien. A period of bitter and bloody fighting against a tenacious enemy followed, culminating in a four-day cordon of Phuoc Yen. During the operation 429 NVA were killed and 107 were captured—the district was cleared of major organized resistance and the stage was set to secure the area and press on with the business of pacification.

From the start, Lieutenant Colonel Carter recognized that any pacification program needed to be two-pronged.

> This task of pacifying the district required the elimination of both the local VC fighting forces and the infrastructure which constituted the local VC government and controlled and di-

rected VC political, economic, and psychological activities. A key component in digging out these locally based, deep-rooted, and elusive VC elements, and in establishing a permanent GVN presence to deter their return, was the effective utilization and exploitation of the potential of the RF/PF in all operations.

There was a recognition that American fighting men could not carry out pacification. The brunt of the work must be shouldered by local Vietnamese forces. However, the RF/PF in Quang Dien had many of the problems endemic to local forces all across South Vietnam. Foremost on the list of complaints Americans had about the RF/PF was their complete disregard for deadlines and timetables. To accomplish a task by noon rather than 4:00 P.M., or even to do it today rather than tomorrow, was not very important. All that mattered to most RF/PF troopers was that it be accomplished sometime. The three months of military training that each trooper went through did little to alter this attitude. Because of this, unit and individual discipline was not generally highly developed. Instead of concentrating on finding the enemy, RF/PF troops often foraged for food, turning backpacks into temporary homes for small pigs and stray chickens. Fire discipline also was poor and the RF/PF tended to use up all its ammunition quickly, shooting at the slightest movement in nearby bushes. This tactic was called *recon by fire* and was frowned upon by American advisers for obvious reasons.

On the other hand, the RF/PF troops possessed an intimate knowledge of their surroundings, which gave them an advantage U.S. and ARVN troops could never match. They knew who lived where and were intimately familiar with the villagers' patterns of activity. Events that would pass unnoticed by the Americans usually were picked up by the RF/PF, who might quickly take under fire some individual or group that had gone unchallenged by U.S. soldiers.

The close contact between American soldiers and the RF/PF during pacification operations between May and October 1968 caused a dramatic improvement in the morale, aggressiveness, and proficiency of the district forces. By mid-October they were capable of providing adequate security throughout the district.

When the 1/502d was deployed to Quang Dien it immediately set up a "collocation of command posts," meaning that the headquarters of both the 1/502d and the district chief—who commanded the RF/PF in the area—occupied the same compound. The compound contained the district chief's office and his administrative and military staff, the district TOC (tactical operations center), the S-2 and his staff and interrogation facilities, the district police headquarters, communication facilities, and the MACV advisory staff. All the machinery needed to plan and execute an attack against the Viet Cong was in the same area. This threw both staffs into constant contact, forcing them to work together. By the end of the operation the U.S. forces and RF/PF came to be regarded as a single force.

During the first stage of operations in Quang Dien enemy resistance was still formidable. RF/PF elements usually linked up with troops from the 1/502d early each morning in preparation for the day's sweep. The linkups usually took place in a secure area with the RF/PF moving to the rendezvous on foot. On occasion American helicopters were dispatched to ferry them into position. RF/PF troopers were deployed with the forward elements of the U.S. forces, where their knowledge of terrain, villages, villagers, booby traps, and hidden bunkers was most useful. While on operations with American troops, RF/PF soldiers received the same support: hot meals or packaged rations, medical support, fire support, and ammunition.

Unfortunately, the RF/PF had to divide its attention between two missions throughout the operation. Local forces primarily were tasked with providing security for pacified villages and since Viet Cong attacks often occurred at night, the RF/PF soldiers operating with the Americans had to break off and return to their compounds at night. The U.S. troops stayed in the field continuously, waiting for the RF/PF to return each morning.

When VC units were found the Americans would act as a blocking force while the RF/PF landed in helicopters as a combat assault force and maneuvered toward the Americans, catching the enemy in a deadly crossfire. RF/PF soldiers were especially good at air assault because their light weight and smaller supply load allowed nine or ten of them aboard each transport helicopter, rather than six American troops. By the end of this first phase of the operation the RF/PF became quite proficient at helicopter operations.

As the Viet Cong military structure in Quang Dien weakened, attention turned to the political infrastructure. By this time the RF/PF had become efficient enough that it often operated alone with only American helicopter support. By October the RF/PF provided virtually all security in Quang Dien District and the 1/502d moved outside the district, leaving only a platoon of American troops to keep a watch over the situation.

As the Viet Cong local-force units were gradually destroyed, the VCI became more exposed. By September 1968 the situation deteriorated rapidly for the communists. The inability of the military units to protect the infrastructure led to an erosion of the general population's support. Conversely, confidence in the GVN grew as more and more people came forward to point out local VCI in the district.

In a way, hunting the VCI in Viet Cong–controlled areas was easier than it was in contested or secure regions. In hostile areas the main task was to strip away military protection for the political infrastructure, few of whom had secret identities. Their control was out in the open. In contested villages the VCI usually were clandestine and many villagers did not know who they were. Quang Dien had a well-defined infrastructure and everyone in the villages knew who the communist leaders were. With the removal of the Viet Cong military threat and the insertion of a benevolent GVN presence that demonstrated its ability to protect the people, the VCI became little more than sitting ducks.

As more and more communist political and economic cadres were identified and captured, Viet Cong morale in general began to fall. By early October the rate of ralliers coming in to the Chieu Hoi program increased. Wives, parents, and other relatives of known VCI were urged to persuade them to take advantage of the Chieu Hoi program and give themselves up. Both prisoners and Hoi Chanh told GVN officials that because of the constant pressure, province-level VCI had instructed cadres in Quang Dien to withdraw from the district and move to safer areas in the southwest.

From 1 June to 1 November 1968, combined U.S./RF/PF forces had killed 215 NVA/VC, captured 102, and received 167

Hoi Chanhs, a substantial portion of them VCI. Only four RF/PF troopers were killed; no Americans died. As October came to a close Quang Dien District could be regarded as pacified—by anyone's standards. Lieutenant Colonel Carter summed up in his after-action report:

> Attention and energies could be turned from combat operations to ... reconstitution of effective rice-roots government and civil authority—with the RF/PF concurrently remaining assuming primary responsibility for maintaining requisite security and remaining alert for the return of VC influence.

The commander of a unit involved in the pacification of a district is expected to put a good face on his operation in the after-action report. But what did the Viet Cong feel were the results of operations in Quang Dien District? Perhaps the best testimony to the destruction of Quang Dien's VCI came from a communist staff member of the Thua Thien-Hue military region who had been operating in Quang Dien District. He was killed during a routine U.S. night ambush on 12 October. On his body was a long letter to his superiors complaining of the deteriorating situation in his area.

> As we are facing many difficulties caused by the enemy actions, I send this report again today for your consideration and suggestion. Truly speaking, you do not understand the real problem and difficulty of our area, and perhaps even Mr. Nam [a high-ranking province cadre] could not give you the real situation of this area when he came to your meeting, because he does not stay in this area.... At Ninh Dai no village military action cadres are left, all of them were killed or captured a long time ago. You might ask why we do not recruit to fill in, but actually we no longer have the capability; there are only the Secretary General and about 3 fellow comrades left in the area.
>   In using sweep and occupy tactics, the enemy has attempted to intentionally round up and annihilate all our cadres and local guerrillas in order to create a secure area of their own.... After organizing the hamlets, they push the communist denunciation movement, keep pressure and watch closely our infrastructure. As a result, some of them already defected

or were pointed out by ralliers. This caused much trouble among the people; the people now lose confidence in the final victory of the people's revolution. . . .

The captured letter pointed out the desperate situation the VCI was in following operations in Quang Dien District. It also illustrated the relationship between province cadre and the grassroots infrastructure in the villages. The higher-ranking cadre had little contact with the villages and often were unaware of the realities of day-to-day affairs. The highest levels of the Phoenix program would later ignore this chink in the relationship between province and village and push for "higher quality neutralizations," forgetting evidence that indicated that simply severing this tenuous link often was more effective than attempting to eliminate the high-level cadre.

Although there was no organized Phoenix program in much of I Corps immediately after the Tet Offensive of 1968, the actions of the 1/502d and the Quang Dien District RF/PF units illustrated that any and all American and GVN forces could perform anti-infrastructure operations effectively. The most important ingredient was the will to emphasize pacification. The ability to do so was always present.

Time to Regroup

The move toward the Phoenix program as an umbrella organization for intelligence and operations against the communist political infrastructure was formal recognition that the capability to target the VCI on a specific and individual basis worked better than rounding them up in standard military sweep operations. It also meant that the Army would make this part of pacification a primary goal. Unfortunately, it was always easier to cordon-and-search villages in an attempt to net VCI than it was to develop a network of intelligence and build dossiers on specific cadre members. Yet cordon-and-searches were the least-desirable Phoenix operations from a theoretical standpoint, because they inconvenienced villagers, causing them to resent the GVN, and because they often picked up innocent people. Usually the innocent people would be released, but the experience left a bad impression with those caught up in the net. In a hostile village there were no "innocent" people; they were all treated as unfriendly because they had been controlled by the Viet Cong. Once the village was pacified, or at least contested, anti-VCI operations required a more delicate touch to prevent renewed alienation of the people from the government.

As 1968 came to a close the effects of the Tet Offensive were wearing off and the enemy was pushed back into more remote areas. The VCI had fewer villages that could be considered completely communist controlled and had to rely more and more on an underground cadre to maintain influence in the countryside. This did not mean that the communists were in serious trouble, but they did have to revise their plans for a final victory in South Vietnam.

For the Phoenix program, increased GVN presence throughout the countryside brought mixed benefits. On the positive side it allowed the building and maintenance of DIOCCs in virtually every one of South Vietnam's districts. A negative aspect was the new makeup of the VCI. It was made up more and more of northerners who remained underground, appearing rarely, but often enough to remain an omnipresent part of a villager's life. They oversaw the collection of taxes, conducted propaganda meetings, and directed raids on GVN outposts.

The communists' return to small underground cells meant the Phoenix program could not rely on standard military operations to neutralize the VCI. As had been the goal of CORDS planners all along, Phoenix began to concentrate on specific targeting operations—the rifle shot aimed at the heart of the VCI. It would be a frustrating undertaking.

5

Three Operations: A Study in Contrasts

STANDARDIZATION was a concept the Phoenix program pursued from beginning to end, but the sheer size and scope of the anti-infrastructure effort made it an elusive task. Operations against the VCI were ideally specifically targeted affairs that snatched a known cadre from the midst of his comrades. More often, Phoenix netted VCI in cordon-and-sweep operations. In between lay an array of imaginative scenarios thought up by American and South Vietnamese Phoenix personnel to fit whatever special circumstances plagued their respective districts.

During late 1968 and throughout 1969 many operations evolved that illustrated the myriad possibilities within the Phoenix program. All successful efforts had one thing in common—they were presided over by enthusiastic South Vietnamese officers who deeply believed in the Phoenix concept and were advised by equally devoted and competent U.S. advisers. Without both ingredients the program was doomed to almost certain failure.

Three provinces, all in III Corps, provide good examples of the Phoenix program's operational diversity, although many others existed. Their uniquely tailored anti-infrastructure missions showed what could be done with a little imagination. These operations range from poor (a cordon-and-search operation relying on excessive firepower) to better (the creative use of limited resources to pursue the VCI) to best (an integrated program using sound intelligence to track and capture specifically targeted cadre).

Counterguerrilla Operation

Three villages in Gia Dinh Province were going through the cordon-and-search routine, a procedure they had endured many times before. It was the morning of Christmas Eve, 24 December 1969, and the villages of Thanh Loc, An Nhon, and An Phu Dong in Go Vap District had been awakened by the blare of loudspeakers and the sound of combat boots on the gravel roads. The villagers milled around outside their houses, the National Police checked identification at a table in the village square, and the People's Self-Defense Force (PSDF) blocked off designated areas.[1]

It was about 8:30 A.M. when the PSDF ran into gunfire coming from a sugar cane field near the village. Unsure about how many Viet Cong they were up against, the PSDF leader sent one man running to tell the American Phoenix adviser of the firefight. The adviser, his interpreter, and the Vietnamese S-2 for the district immediately drove toward the commotion. As they reached the area they were joined by a PF squad that was moving into position to drive the Viet Cong from the cane field.

The PFs poured small-arms fire and grenades into the Viet Cong position. One guerrilla raised his AK over his head in surrender and walked out of the field into the open. He quickly told the PFs that three of his comrades were still in the field.

By this time the 148th RF Company, under the command of Captain Khanh, arrived on the scene. The American Phoenix adviser suggested that a helicopter gunship be brought in for fire support; everyone readily agreed. A call to the district chief, Lieutenant Colonel Tan, got quick approval and a second call was made to summon air support.

As the RF company, the PF squad, the Phoenix adviser and the various other South Vietnamese military units sat around, the helicopters sped to the battleground. Within twenty minutes they were over the cane field: one carpeted the area with M60 machine-gun fire and rocket barrages while the other landed and picked up the district's ARVN S-2 and the interpreter. The American Phoenix adviser remained on the ground and directed the helicopter attack. Both choppers made two passes over the field, saturating it with weapons fire.

As the growling helicopters rotored back toward their base the RF company made a sweep through the cane field to see what damage had been done. The RFs came across the body of one Viet Cong. Another guerrilla surrendered, having somehow survived the firestorm, and told his captors that the commander, Nguyen Van Chot, had managed to escape into a nearby rice field. The prisoner said that only Chot was still on the loose.

The RFs moved off to the rice field and set about searching the area for the lone Viet Cong. They found footprints in the mud, but rather than search onward, Captain Khanh ordered a recon by fire, meaning to spray the area with bullets until everything dies. Not surprisingly, the ploy failed. No more Viet Cong bodies turned up. Captain Khanh ordered an ambush set for the next twenty-four hours, but it yielded nothing. The Viet Cong commander had escaped.

The RFs had two POWs. Both were taken to the DIOCC for interrogation. One of the prisoners, the one captured after the helicopter attack, was a seventeen-year-old boy who proved to be "quite informative." He revealed the location of a weapons cache the RFs quickly found.

Early the next day the prisoners were transferred "to higher headquarters for further exploitation." It was there that more details came to light. The POWs had operated in the Go Vap area for the past eleven months and were well-acquainted with the district VCI. Because the American Phoenix adviser had been present during the operation, he knew of the capture and was able to follow up on the intelligence. Often, South Vietnamese district and province officials did not bother to inform the DIOCC about current intelligence on the VCI. This time, however, the DIOCC was able to round up eleven suspects, eight of whom "proved to be members of the Viet Cong infrastructure."

There was another spinoff for the Phoenix program. The ARVN S-2 in Go Vap District drafted a leaflet that was sent through channels for "mass reproduction." There was an expected waiting period of fifteen to twenty days, but the Phoenix adviser "arranged for the leaflets to be produced in two days."

On 22 January, almost a month after the capture of the two Viet Cong, thirty-eight thousand leaflets were dropped over the villages of Thanh Loc, An Phu Dong, and Thanh My Tay. The appeal was simple:

> Dear Cham, Hiep, So, Chat, Hghia, Ho, Chau, Chan, Co, Chai, Dan, Den, Hum, Hai, Men, Trong, Nghia, Tien, Tuong, Tinh, Tuyet, Bon, Cau, Dua, Kip, Kiet, Man, Nghia, Tu, Thang, Vien, tu Chung, Tho, Tam, Sau, who are guerrilla members of the NLFSVN [National Liberation Front, South Vietnam], what have you done for your family, or your village and hamlet? Or have you just broken up the happiness of many families and destroyed houses and land?
>
> Some among you have awakened recently, they deserted the Communist ranks and they were received by the GVN and the people with open arms in a family affection.
>
> You should be ready for the end if you remain in the Communist ranks. You will be dealing with difficulties bigger from day to day and you will suffer serious failure when the ARVN expand strongly.
>
> You had better return to your family where you will be guaranteed security and helped to establish a new life.

The Phoenix adviser who wrote the report on the combined action seemed very proud of the results. In one month the operation netted eight VCI, and the original two prisoners provided information on other Viet Cong in the district. However, this operation was not what Phoenix was all about. The DIOCC had only stumbled onto the intelligence and had used the same massive firepower characteristic of traditional military operations; and it was all used on a mere four guerrillas. The RF commander knew there were only four men in the cane field, but he chose to call in helicopter gunships rather than go after the enemy with his own troops. Worst of all, it was yet another in a long line of cordon-and-search operations that yielded little considering the strain placed on the villagers.

But from a Phoenix adviser's point of view, this was all a step in the right direction. While cordon-and-search operations were a nuisance for everyone involved, they often led to good intelligence, which in turn led to VCI. This mundane work doggedly sought to make life difficult for the Viet Cong and were in many cases the bread and butter of the Phoenix program. With a little imagination and good intelligence Phoenix could take the next step toward sound targeting.

Such was the case in Long Khanh Province.

Operations in Long Khanh Province

Phoenix was designed to use many sources of intelligence to provide data for the neutralization of the VCI. The same diversity was supposed to apply to operations. Unfortunately, the various operational arms were often reluctant to cooperate and the Phoenix program found itself relying on one particular action arm for operations. In some areas it was the PRU, in others the NPFF if it was up to muster. In some circumstances Phoenix created operations specifically designed to bring various resources together in a single effort.

Beginning 1 June 1969 the Long Khanh PIOCC devised an operation designed to cut off food supplies to various district-level VCI within the province.[2] The National Police had previously had the mission of setting up checkpoints and providing some sort of plan to stop the movement of supplies to the VCI, but they had bungled the job. The police had made their checkpoints stationary and had established them along existing lines of communication, mostly on National Highways 1 and 20. Viet Cong supply teams did not normally move along major highways, especially when they knew the police would always be in their little guardhouses along the route. Instead, they made their way around the checkpoints, secure in the knowledge that the police would never move.

To make matters worse, the checkpoints were manned daily from 8:00 A.M. to 5:00 P.M. The Viet Cong felt more comfortable moving at night anyway, so the regular business hours of the police were very convenient. But even if the Viet Cong had chosen to risk the checkpoints they probably would have made it through because the police were not conducting thorough searches of vehicles passing through.

In April 1969 the Long Khanh province chief assigned the Phoenix program the additional task of coordinating operations to cut the Viet Cong supply system. The province chief reasoned that by using the existing intelligence and operational capabilities of the Phoenix program the job could be done without creating a new task force.

District Phoenix and Phung Hoang officials received their instructions by mid-May. The PIOCC came up with a Resource Control Program designed to coordinate efforts to cut off supplies to the VCI and at the same time identify communist cadre. The program lasted from 1 June to 31 July 1969 and was made up of three specific operations.

Operation Mobile I

As the name implied, Mobile I was designed to get the police out of their static checkpoints and attempt to fool the Viet Cong by establishing a series of moving roadblocks.[3] So as not to offend the police in too direct a manner, the operation left the static checkpoints in place, creating new ones on top of the old.

Three mobile teams were created, each made up of two National Policemen, two members of the NPFF, and two members of the PRU. Each day the PIOCC assigned several locations for the teams to set up checkpoints. The police provided two half-ton trucks for each team and the PIOCC sent along lists of known or suspected VCI to aid the teams in making arrests.

At 8:00 A.M. every day each team would move out to its assigned location. Instead of static guardposts, the teams set up roadblocks by parking their trucks in the middle of the road, usually in places where it would be difficult for the Viet Cong to simply move off the road and skirt by the roadblocks. All pedestrians and vehicles were stopped and checked. A police team member checked IDs while the PRU and the remaining policemen searched cars and trucks. The NPFF were responsible for security, setting up machine gun positions to protect the team from trouble. Suspects netted in the roadblocks were sent to the PIOCC for interrogation.

The only really useful aspect of Operation Mobile I, besides changing the routine of the static guardposts, was that it provided the PIOCC with a stream of suspects who might provide timely information for future VCI targeting. In theory, a team was always standing by at the PIOCC to launch immediate operations should any valuable intelligence come in from the checkpoints.

Operation Cutoff I

Another variation on the cordon-and-search theme was Operation Cutoff I.[4] Meant to use intelligence gathered at the various Phoenix centers, Cutoff I was really only set apart from standard cordon-and-search operations by reliance on Phoenix-generated intelligence as its primary impetus, and by its attempt to bring together as many intelligence and combat elements as possible into a single operation. Both aspects were used primarily to cultivate the spirit of the Phoenix program by bringing divergent organizations under one banner.

In most cases cordon elements were made up of the RF/PF, troopers from the 18th ARVN Division, and American soldiers from the 199th Battalion. However, occasionally the RF/PF had the entire responsibility for the cordon. Search elements were composed of National Police, NPFF, and PRU and were divided into four teams of eight men each. Each team was assigned an area of operation within the hamlet that was to be cordoned.

In practice, operations began early in the morning; the cordon was to be in place by 4:00 A.M. At first light the start of the search phase was heralded by blaring loudspeakers operated by PSYOPS teams telling the villagers to stay in their houses and remain calm. The search elements then moved into action, going from building to building. Standing orders stated that "where possible, the search was [to be] conducted in the presence of the owner or occupant of the building." This was not done so much to be considerate to the villagers, but rather to prevent later claims that the soldiers had looted homes and stores.

As the search of each home was completed the occupants were told to move out into the market square for "final processing." Identification cards were confiscated, they would be returned to all those categorized as "innocent civilians" after the processing was complete. The processing itself was conducted by Police Special Branch personnel and consisted simply of matching ID cards to lists of known VCI, called "communist offenders" in the operation reports.

As the search and processing phases were going on, the PSYOPS teams put on a little show. All the villagers who had their papers in order were moved to the village square, where Culture/Drama teams acted out patriotic skits, hoi chanhs pointed out the lies behind the communists' claims, and American MEDCAP teams examined the sick and dispensed medicine.

The whole affair was a step toward a benevolent government presence in the countryside, but these shows were really only pale imitations of communist propaganda teams that regularly exhorted the villagers to rally to the revolutionary cause. The big difference between the communists' propaganda and that of the PSYOPS teams would become clear in the evening: as the day came to a close the cordon-and-search elements would be gone. Communist cadres could not be uprooted so easily.

Anyone whose ID card came up on the list of VCI suspects held by the PSB, or whose documentation was lacking, was moved to an interrogation area. Like the other elements of the cordon-and-search operation, interrogation personnel were combined from many intelligence branches. The PSB, Military Security Service (MSS), and U.S. military intelligence personnel were all represented in the field interrogation process. Based on the results of the initial interrogation, suspects were either released or sent to the PIC for further questioning. In some cases suspects immediately cooperated with their captors and gave information about VCI in the area. These people were generally sent on to Chieu Hoi centers.

After about three hours the cordon-and-search operation would close down and the troops would go home.[5] Operations such as this rarely produced valuable information concerning the VCI and even if they did, the inconvenience, sporadic brutality, and inevitable destruction of property that resulted from such large operations offset any gains that might come at the expense of the VCI.

Operation SARC X

SARC X was not a standard Phoenix operation in that it did not gather intelligence on VCI for the purpose of neutralization. Instead, the operation swept large areas of territory seeking targets of opportunity. But unlike the infamous search-and-destroy or cordon-and-search operations, SARC X sought to cut down on the time used in patrolling jungle trails by going to the air.

The mission was to "establish and utilize a special airmobile resources control (SARC) team in order to interdict the movement of illegal/unauthorized comodities intended for enemy use."[6] Phoenix assets were used because it was felt that interdicting supplies was a prime way of getting to the VCI. At one end of the supply chain was the Viet Cong or NVA soldier who waited in the bush for food and equipment. That was strictly the military side. But on the other end of the chain were the people who arranged and controlled the process of supplying the troops in the field—the VCI. It was felt that SARC X was a way for Phoenix to pull itself up the side of the chain leading to the VCI. By going after the chain itself, SARC X could net intelligence on how and where the VCI operated and use other assets to target them.

Initially, one SARC team was established using three elements. The command element contained the PIOCC secretary acting as the operational commander, the Phoenix coordinator, one interpreter, and an American adviser. Providing security below the searching helicopters was a ground element made up of two squads from the Aerorifle Platoon, C Troop, 1/17 Cavalry (U.S.). The concept was simple. The cavalry provided air support in the form of one command and control ship and one hunter–killer team. The helicopter carrying the command element, usually a UH-1, circled above the operation area watching and instructing the rest of the team. The hunter–killer team ran as a pack of two helicopters, an AH-1 Cobra gunship and a light observation helicopter (LOH, pronounced "loach") flying over the operational area providing cover and weapon support for the team. The hunter–killer team was a formidable threat as it darted in the air over suspected Viet Cong supply runners.

Intelligence from the PIOCC was analyzed for possible operation areas and when one was decided upon the SARC team skimmed over the countryside scanning roads and jungle for targets. When one was located—usually a lone vehicle on a seldom-used trail—the hunter–killer team dropped red smoke and hovered menacingly as the ground element was inserted to inspect the target. After the Americans had secured the area, making certain that no Viet Cong guerrillas were skulking about, the search element was unloaded. Vehicles were searched, drivers and passengers were questioned, and any "contraband items" were confiscated. If the SARC team found such items, the people became suspects and were taken to the nearest DIOCC for interrogation, after which they were classified as "innocent civilians," "insurgency supporters," or VCI. Innocent civilians were immediately released, while those less fortunate were sent to the PIC for further "processing."

The goal was quick use of intelligence garnered from the SARC teams so other Phoenix elements could follow up with more operations aimed at the VCI. If all went well, the advantage created by the speed of operations using helicopters could catch the enemy off guard, sometimes netting other VCI before they realized they had been compromised by the SARC teams.

The operations were partially successful. In combination, Mobile I, Cutoff I, and SARC X all contributed to a rise in VCI neutralizations for Long Khanh Province in the third quarter of 1969. However, they were all reactive in nature because they lacked the intelligence needed for specific targeting of known VCI. In a best-case scenario the Phoenix program would not have to rely on such gimmicks or on standard cordon-and-search operations. Such was the case in another part of III Corps.

Bandits and the Tropic Lightning

The VCI in Hau Nghia and parts of Binh Duong had been recognized as a serious threat to any possible GVN gains in III Corps ever since elements of the 25th U.S. Infantry Division (Tropic Lightning) arrived in the area in 1966. The emphasis on pacification by the GVN following the Tet Offensive also combined to encourage military intelligence personnel within the 25th Division to design an anti-infrastructure program to augment the DIOCCs in Hau Nghia and Binh Duong.

The concept that evolved was the brainchild of Captain William E. Phelps, a military intelligence officer with the Counterintelligence (CI) Section, 25th Military Intelligence Detachment (MID). By September 1968 the idea had grown into reality. A team of men whose sole mission was the identification and elimination of the VCI in the region was formed using American CI personnel, Hoi Chanhs, and Kit Carson Scouts from the My Hanh Village area in Duc Hoa District, Hau Nghia Province. My Hanh was chosen as the place to begin operations for two reasons. First, the VCI was well-entrenched in the area, and second, they could count on support from 2nd Battalion, 14th Infantry (2/14th), which operated in Duc Hoa from Fire Support Base Keene.[7]

The team began operations in My Hanh on 28 September 1968, using two Hoi Chanhs who had been active within the area during their days with the Viet Cong. As time passed the group grew to seven Kit Carson Scouts, most of whom had originally come from the area. Within a month they had earned a nickname—the Bandits. Although the seven operated in Cu Chi and Duc Hoa Districts over a seven-month period, they were able to return to the area on personal business and intelligence-gathering forays even though their identities soon became well-known to the Viet Cong.

The Viet Cong did attempt to neutralize the Bandits, but were unsuccessful. There were several assassination attempts and one of the Bandits was captured, but within hours he escaped. One night the local guerrillas came into the village and kidnapped the family of one Bandit, hoping they could work out some sort of deal. In no mood to negotiate, the Bandits immediately "counterabducted" the family of a well-known, high-ranking VC from the province. The Bandit's family was released immediately.

The 2/14th controlled most anti-VCI operations in the area because it possessed the necessary resources to "exploit targets."

For its part of the operations the 25th MID ran agent sources, usually the Bandits themselves, who reported information gained from their various contacts and from visits to the villages. As in other operations of this type, the Bandits relied heavily on Hoi Chanh and on U.S. Army and ARVN prisoner interrogation reports.

If hard intelligence on the location of VCI or equipment and arms caches was received, 25th MID would work on developing a plan for exploitation of the target. If the target was deemed important the MID prepared a plan for an operation called, innocuously enough, a "formal target analysis." This report included "a description of the terrain; the exact nature of the target (who or what); an estimate of enemy security (booby traps and security forces); and a recommended plan of action." The final phase went into full swing when the unit commander gave a personal briefing. On all operations final authority rested with the 2/14th commander, not with MID.

Operations were designed to include whatever units were appropriate to the situation. In almost all instances the Bandits were involved, but never did they go on operations without accompanying MID personnel. Because of their familiarity with the area the Bandits often could locate hiding places and booby traps that other soldiers would pass over.

Because the Bandits were known to the local Viet Cong there was little attempt to keep their movements secret. However, when a new source was used, perhaps a Hoi Chanh or some village citizen, every attempt was made to keep his or her identity secret. Usually a team would go to the area of operation, where the source would point out VCI and VC sympathizers. Obviously, there was an inherent problem here, one that plagued the Phoenix program throughout its existence. The Bandits were relying on the testimony of a single person to accuse another villager of being a VCI. The propensity for graft was astronomical and in some cases district officials abused their powers. However, in Duc Hoa District there was little of this sort of abuse because the district chief was an able and honest man, well-respected by Vietnamese and Americans alike. In addition, a properly run Phoenix program weeded out most of the innocent people caught up by corrupt or incompetent officials once the suspects made it into the legal system. If the evidence against any individual was insufficient the court released the person and the capture would not be counted in the monthly quota.

Because a source lost his usefulness to the GVN once his identity was discovered by the Viet Cong, various plans were devised to keep his presence secret, many of them bordering on imbecilic. After-action reports noted that, "if the source was needed out in the open, he was disguised with sunglasses, an ARVN uniform, or some other method and mingled with the Bandits." Of course, when the Bandits were the source no such "precautions" were necessary.

The Vietnam War saw the helicopter rise to such a position of prominence within the military that it became a virtual symbol of the conflict. The Phoenix program, too, came to regard helicopters as indispensible, using them on many insertions. In Cu Chi and Duc Hoa helicopters were often used on operations. The most common mission configuration was one VCI team— the Bandits—and two rifle platoons from the 2/14th flown into the objective (usually a hut or cluster of huts) by air elements of the 25th Division. The rifle platoons cordoned off the target and the Bandits searched the area. When an operation went according to plan the VCI would be found cowering in huts or hiding in tunnels carved out beneath dirt floors. Sometimes the VCI tried to escape through the tunnels, coming up fifty to one hundred meters from the huts. But the Bandits usually did their homework and were aware of such tunnel escapes.

When a captured VCI matched the blacklist, the Bandits performed a field interrogation "for information that could be immediately exploited." In most cases the Bandits were looking for locations of nearby weapons caches or other VCI in the area. The American troops maintained the cordon throughout the field interrogation, holding any other civilians whether or not they were considered innocent. There could be no risk that someone would run off and sound the alarm to any other Viet Cong in the area. Captured VCI were often offered Chieu Hoi status in return for immediate cooperation. If the offer garnered any information the Bandits and accompanying rifle platoons surged back into the helicopters and streaked off after the new target, bringing their source along just in case his information was less than honest. The same process was repeated until the Bandits came up empty.

Anyone detained during Bandit operations was evacuated to Cu Chi for more "detailed interrogation." If this finally pointed toward another appropriate target, as it often did, a new target development phase was initiated. It was at Cu Chí that officials decided whether captives who had helped the Bandits were to be given Hoi Chanh status. In some cases these prisoners were so helpful that they were allowed to join the Bandit ranks.

As was usually the case with Phoenix operations all over South Vietnam, the key ingredient to any successful mission was timeliness. Frequently, the Bandits would receive perishable intelligence that demanded an immediate response, such as a VCI meeting nearby. In those cases there was no time for the detailed process of target development that was standard procedure with MID. On those occasions the Bandits had the authority to act on the intelligence without the usual string of approvals, but even then American MID personnel were required on the mission.

Bandit operations in Duc Hoa District had many successes between 29 September 1968 and 27 April 1969. They also had some failures. Just as conventional troop sweeps often came up empty, so, too, did anti-infrastructure operations miss the target. And while Bandit operations largely were responsible for the decline of Viet Cong influence in Duc Hoa District it must be remembered that Hau Nghia Province as a whole had significant problems with the VCI throughout 1969 and into 1970.[8] It is sometimes easy to look at successful operations in isolation and come to the conclusion that the VCI must have always been against the ropes. That was not the case. But the Bandits did have enough successes that it is instructive to examine their operational methods.

Letters from the Bandits

When Captain Phelps formed the Bandit program in September 1968, the VCI in Duc Hoa District were a prevalent presence among the population. Many of them were well-known to both the Americans and to the Bandits. The trick was to track them down and catch them. One common denominator possessed by most VCI, one that tied them to the district and village, was family. The Bandits knew who they were and where they lived. No one, neither the Americans nor the GVN, considered the families of Viet Cong legitimate targets as long as they were not involved in subversive activities themselves. But the families provided the Bandits with a handle for bringing some of the VCI out into the open.

On 29 September 1968 five notes were delivered in My Hanh Village, one to each of five wives known to have husbands who were VCI. Each note contained a simple message telling the wives that the Bandits knew the names, location, habits, and position within the VCI of each husband. The note concluded with information on the Chieu Hoi program and said that if "he [the husband] felt it was unsafe to Chieu Hoi, an arranged capture could be negotiated."[9]

It was assumed that some of the VCI would be closely watched by their comrades and it might be difficult to simply walk to the nearest Chieu Hoi center. Worse, the Viet Cong might take revenge on the families. The Viet Cong were not a trusting or forgiving lot. From the Bandits' point of view, though, it was preferable for the VCI to Chieu Hoi. Any arranged capture could easily be turned into a trap. Each note concluded with the prediction that any VCI who did not give up his communist ways—one way or another—would find himself dead.

Many VCI were willing to desert the Viet Cong, especially when they found that the GVN knew exactly who they were and what they were up to. In any war, on any side, it is difficult to find people who continue to show unswerving devotion to their cause when they know they will die for their beliefs. Most have sympathies and political leanings that fall somewhere along the proverbial fence. The VCI were no exception. Despite many popular portrayals the VCI were not all hardcore communists willing to die for Ho Chi Minh. Many of them, particularly the middle- and low-level cadre, were in their positions either because they felt it was the safest way to live through the war or because they had been coerced into the position.

The notes were successful. Four of the five VCI did Chieu

Hoi by 14 October. The after-action report credited "the fact that the recipients [of the notes] lost their protective anonymity and faced a personal threat" for the success of the Bandit notes. It was certainly true that any unmasked VCI living within a contested area was of little use to the communists. It was better to Chieu Hoi.

Operation Undertaker

The Bandits didn't spend all their time passing out notes to the wives of VCI in My Hanh. They had gathered enough intelligence on other VCI operating in the area to begin planning operations against them. On 15 October the Bandits, supported by Companies B and C, 2/14th, rounded up twenty-three VCI, including one important district-level cadre and two village cadre. Two days later the same force captured nine VCI, including the My Hanh finance chief. On the next two days, 18 and 19 October, the operation produced eighteen Viet Cong guerrillas and eight Hoi Chanhs.[10]

One of the Hoi Chanhs, a female named Ling, led the Bandits and a force from the 1/27th on an operation on 24 October that "resulted in the capture of thirty-six assorted VC supply cadre, guerrillas and laborers" in an area south of the Michelin Rubber Plantation in Binh Duong Province.

The next month the Bandits were back operating in the My Hanh area, where they netted the chief of the Giang Son Hamlet Farmer's Association and two Viet Cong communications and liaison agents on 18 November. On 1 December a Duc Hoa District liaison agent and a VC penetration agent were apprehended in the same area. The penetration agent's mission was to join ARVN ranks and "breed discontent among ARVN soldiers with the U.S. presence, and to report on ARVN and U.S. activities in Duc Hoa District."

A most unusual operation developed on 2 December when an old woman appeared at a 2/14th infantry position and requested permission to bury a relative in the area. One of the Bandits immediately recognized her as a relative of a female Viet

Cong security agent who operated in the area. The 25th MID quickly dubbed the upcoming mission as Operation Undertaker. The Viet Cong were not going to be impressed by the Bandits' humor.

On the assumption that the female agent would be at the funeral of her dead relative, permission was given for the Bandits to infiltrate the funeral procession and keep their eyes open for the target. Sure enough, she showed up and the Bandits quietly escorted her away from the group of mourners.

Operation Draw String

On 23 March 1969, 3rd Battalion, 525th Military Intelligence Group interrogated a captured Viet Cong agent who informed his captors of the names and locations of eight VCI operating in Cu Chi District, Hau Nghia Province. The information was passed on to the 25th MID, whereupon they began forming an intelligence target analysis.[11]

The captured agent was Nguyen Ngoc Van, a boy of fifteen years who seemed only too glad that his war was over. Rather than play the hardcore communist—which he was not—Van quickly described and named the eight VCI and said he was willing to lead U.S. troops to their homes in Cay Trom, a densely populated hamlet on Highway 1 about four kilometers northwest of Cu Chi. The area was considered pacified by the GVN, but a more accurate description would have been "contested," because the Viet Cong had a number of sympathizers who managed the collection of rice and other forms of taxation on a yearly basis. All these people, including the eight VCI named by Van, had official identification cards and could pass freely throughout the district.

Van was interrogated for three days. He told the Americans he had last seen the communist tax collectors come through his village in May of 1968. There were four armed men and he said "three of the men were light-skinned and spoke a language that he could not understand."[12] The fourth man acted as an interpreter. All wore "yellow uniforms, boots, and steel helmets." Rice was collected according to a family's ability to pay and since Van's family was very poor they were only required to "contribute" one bag of rice.

The four armed foreign-speaking soldiers were never seen again, but Van often saw the people who organized each tax collection. These were the eight that the 25th MID was targeting. They were all young—about twenty years old—and all worked together as a sort of loosely knit cell. Nguyen Van Ria was the leader. He was twenty-two years old and seemed to make no attempt to blend into the population. He wore his hair long, was blind in his right eye, and had a gold tooth. His primary mission was gathering data on U.S. and ARVN outposts, which he fed to the local Viet Cong guerrillas so they could plan mortar attacks.

Danh, a nondescript farmer who lived with his parents in Cay Trom, was a VC counterintelligence agent. It was his job to locate GVN intelligence agents and report their whereabouts to the Viet Cong assassination squads for elimination.

Four of the eight targets were female. One of them, a "very attractive" girl named Hyunh Thi Noi, was called "Mata Hari" by intelligence analysts with the 25th MID. In the intelligence report made from the interrogation of Nguyen Ngoc Van, Noi's mission was described as "befriending GVN intelligence agents who had come into Cay Trom through the use of her feminine charms. After winning their confidence, she turns them over to the VC for elimination." The remaining five were of lesser importance in the Viet Cong hierarchy, being mostly informers, explosives couriers, and commo-liaison agents. But all were targeted by the 25th MID for neutralization.

Carrying out an approach to each house without warning the others required a plan. To begin with, a visual reconnaissance mission was flown over the target area on 29 March. The photographs were shown to Van, who easily identified the houses of each of the eight VCI. The target analysis was then complete and the operation was named "Draw String."

The mission date was to be 30 March. Operation Draw String was planned as a night snatch mission, but since the eight targets were fairly widely dispersed throughout Cay Trom Hamlet, the mission force needed to be fairly large. But at the same time it could not be so large that it would alert VC agents that something was afoot. The original plan was to use the 1/5th CRIP (combined reconnaissance and intelligence platoon) so it would look as if the unit were heading out on a standard ambush mission. This would be accomplished by travelling to an ARVN outpost near the target at 6:00 P.M. and then moving on to a preplanned ambush site at 8:00 P.M. When they arrived at the ambush site the CRIP would split into two teams and move from one house to another, scooping up each target and returning to the outpost. A small team of National Police would also come along to formally arrest the suspects. At 9:30 P.M. the 25th Division "Ready Ship," a helicopter set aside for special missions, would move in and extract the prisoners and the MI team.

The mission did not go as planned. Viet Cong movement was spotted outside the ARVN outpost and a small firefight broke out, forcing the team to remain within the outpost until things were sorted out. A few minutes after midnight (the mission should have been over by then if all had gone according to plan) the VC opened up with a mortar attack. It wasn't until 5:30 A.M. on 31 March that the CRIP moved out of the ARVN compound and began picking up the targets. Forty-five minutes later the mission was over and the CRIP had five of the eight VCI back at the outpost. Among them were Ria, the leader, and Noi, the "Mata Hari."

At the Cu Chi DIOCC the ARVN S-2 decided his people would do the initial interrogation of the prisoners, not an unusual event because the presence of the National Police on any mission meant that the GVN was officially arresting the suspects on suspicion of crimes against the state. The Americans readily agreed and the five VCI were turned over to the Vietnamese. It quickly became clear that the Vietnamese S-2 was having no luck getting information out of the prisoners. The Americans had seen this before. If the prisoners didn't talk, they often would be released for lack of evidence because the Vietnamese didn't want to admit they had simply come up empty-handed during the interrogation.

Hoping to head off the possible release of the VCI suspects, the 25th MID personnel drew up a compilation of the information in the initial intelligence target analysis, had it translated into Vietnamese, and gave it to the ARVN S-2 to aid him in his interrogation. When that failed to get cooperation from the prisoners, the Americans requested that they be turned over to the U.S. Army for transfer to the Cu Chi POW compound. The district chief agreed and the prisoners were moved.

Captain Phelps and his anti-VCI Bandit team were notified on the morning of 1 April that the newest VCI prisoners were a tough bunch and that American interrogators were likely to come up empty, just as the Vietnamese had. Unconventional methods were needed to get any useful information out of them. Two of the Bandits dressed up in Viet Cong black pajamas, made up cover stories, and were thrown into the cell with the five prisoners. Since the Bandits had not participated in Operation Draw String there was little danger the prisoners would recognize them, although there was some risk, since the Bandits and their exploits were well-known by this time.

After a few hours to let the new "prisoners" work their way into the confidence of the silent VCI, the two Bandits were taken out of the cell for "interrogation." The ruse had worked. The five had talked freely about their activities with the Viet Cong and the Americans decided to inform the Vietnamese S-2 so that he, too, could insert a phony prisoner into the cell. With the evidence gathered in this manner by both the Americans and the Vietnamese it seemed that there was enough evidence to prosecute the prisoners as VCI. The next morning the prisoners would be transferred back to ARVN control, unaware that they had already sealed their fate.

On 2 April Ria and one of the other prisoners, Nguyen Van Cu, signed confessions about their activities with the Viet Cong. Noi and the other two did not, but Ria implicated Noi in his confession by saying she had been involved in a plan to capture a member of the Bandit team six weeks earlier. All five were then turned over to the Police Special Branch in Cu Chi for further interrogation. Since Ria and Cu had signed written confessions they were tried as VCI, but Noi and the other two were released for lack of evidence, even though the two Bandits who had posed as fellow VCI had heard verbal confessions from all of them.

The Americans were not really surprised—this was a common occurrence. For some unexplainable reason, the Vietnamese often were unwilling to try captured VCI suspects unless they had confessions. The 25th MID agent who had planned Operation Draw String attempted to put a good face on the entire legal proceedings in his after-action report.

> Even though Cao, Noi and Chiep [one of the other VCI arrested] were released, it is felt ... that their apprehension and subsequent interrogation by both U.S. and ARVN agencies had neutralized them as intelligence agents for the Viet Cong. Even though they have been found "innocent" the National Police will have agents keeping tabs on their activities, and if contact is made again with the VC they will be apprehended.

The report seemed like wishful thinking, considering that the National Police had been unwilling to accept the verbal confessions given by the VCI suspects to the Bandits. Why, then, would the police be able or willing to keep tabs on the VCI after they had been released? Americans all over South Vietnam had many days of frustration during their dealings with the National Police.

The Bandits' part was not yet played out. While playing decoy in the prisoner holding cell they had heard more than just the confessions of five part-time VCI. They also confirmed that there was treason within their own ranks. A chance statement by Nguyen Van Ria cleared up an event that had seemed strange when it happened. It had all begun about two weeks before, on 15 March.

On that day one of the Bandits, Tran Van Noh, was captured by three Viet Cong as he rode his Honda motorcycle through Phuoc Hiep Village. They had been waiting specifically for him, which seemed strange because Noh was one of the least-known of the Bandits. How did the Viet Cong know where he would be? Was there a plant within Bandit ranks? Noh managed to escape after a few hours, but he was forced to flee without his motorcycle, his most prized possession. The matter was placed on hold until the Bandits heard the whole story in the prisoner cell.

The Viet Cong had learned Noh was a GVN intelligence agent from another Bandit, Tam Thanh, who had told a VC assassination squad where Noh was likely to be and when, and agreed to lure him to Cay Trom. Tam Thanh had recently become one of the Bandits after going through the Chieu Hoi program, but he was uncomfortable with the arrangement and longed to return to the Viet Cong fold. GVN intelligence reports later noted that Tam Thanh had been a bad risk all along; he had a history of switching sides, depending on who seemed to be winning at the time, and from the beginning of Tam Thanh's association with the Bandits there had been reason to suspect he was a communist plant purposely sent through the Chieu Hoi program to infiltrate the Bandits. Whatever the reason, Tam Thanh's betrayal had failed to net Noh. In return for his help the Viet Cong had promised Tam Thanh he could return to a safe communist area outside My Hanh Village. As a bonus Tam Thanh could have Noh's motorcycle.

The Bandits by this time were suspicious of Tam Thanh and they became more sure of his treachery when he went to My Hanh Village, ostensibly on leave. But Tam Thanh was in trouble from both sides. Bandit intelligence sources within the Viet Cong ranks stated that the VC were closely watching Tam Thanh and would not give him even the most inconsequential of tasks to perform for the revolution. Noh's escape had made the Viet Cong suspicious of Tam Thanh's loyalties and they soon became convinced he was really a U.S. agent. Reports to the Bandits also indicated that if these suspicions continued, the VC security chief, Nam Xay, would have Tam Thanh executed.

The plot thickened. The Bandits' knowledge of the behavioral patterns and social relationships in the area again came into play. Although the communists sought to divorce themselves from much of the old Vietnamese culture, there was little they could really do to eradicate it. Tam Thanh was the eldest son in his family and the brother-in-law of a high-ranking district VCI named Sau Chanh. Therefore, if Tam Thanh were killed by the VC assassination squads, it would fall upon the security chief, Nam Xay, to assume the responsibility for the family's welfare. By that reasoning the Bandits assumed that Nam Xay could be expected to drop in periodically on Tam Thanh's family.

Tam Thanh had dropped from sight and the Bandits assumed he was dead, killed by the Viet Cong. They staked out Tam Thanh's home, hoping to catch Nam Xay fulfilling his filial responsibilities. At 5:00 P.M. on 10 April Nam Xay showed up and was taken off before he even got in the front door. Back at the interrogation center Nam Xay told of Tam Thanh's execution, confirming all the guesswork by the Bandits. They had been correct about Tam Thanh's treachery and about the way in which he had met his end. The Viet Cong were not a trusting lot.

At the end of April 1969 the Bandits could claim an impressive score against the VCI in the Duc Hoa and Cu Chi Districts of Hau Nghia Province. Their small number (the exact number was not revealed in any reports) accounted for 291 enemy neutralizations between September 1968 and May 1969, 259 of those through capture and the Chieu Hoi program. Only thirty-two Viet Cong were killed, most of them guerrillas. Ninety-nine of the total were VCI, most of whom were sentenced. Other parts of the 25th MID anti-infrastructure program also accounted for numerous VCI. A detailed after-action report dated 28 August 1969 concluded that the Bandit operations were successful in largely destroying the VCI in the region, but provided the caveat that final success or failure must be weighed against the total enemy situation.

> All operations directed against the enemy are related and complimentary to their effects, therefore, the success of the Counter VCI Operations must be assessed by an examination of the entire enemy situation. The Viet Cong Infrastructure in Hau Nghia Province has suffered serious damage, and the enemy's ability to plan, direct and control operations has been greatly impaired.[13]

Captured enemy documents seemed to back up the 25th MID claim that the VCI was on the run. Yet in the total picture of Hau Nghia Province, the Phoenix program did not seem to be faring well during 1969. The case of Duc Hoa and Cu Chi Districts seemed to confirm that the Phoenix program could only be judged accurately on the district level. If province reports showed that Phoenix was largely unsuccessful—as they did in Hau Nghia Province during most of 1969—they had to be judged against separate district reports on anti-infrastructure results. This didn't mean purely numbers of VCI neutralized, but a total examination of the Viet Cong's ability to operate after a reduction in the ranks of their infrastructure. And since the Viet Cong ability to operate varied from district to district, it followed that the Phoenix program would be most effective if it got down on the hamlet and village level where the Viet Cong were closely intertwined with the population.

Military attitudes toward the anti-infrastructure campaign played a major role in whether the Phoenix program was effective. If American and ARVN units were willing to support anti-infrastructure efforts, such as that run by the 25th MID and the Bandits in Hau Nghia Province, there was a better chance for success. Unfortunately, there was often a tendency to emphasize cordon-and-search operations simply because they were easier to execute.

The vast diversity of Phoenix operations beginning in 1969 made it clear that the program had the inherent flexibility to adapt to any situation found in Vietnam. But that was only at the district and province level. On the national level Phoenix still had to contend with stonewalling by the GVN and an unwillingness to give the anti-infrastructure effort the prestige and power necessary to survive in Saigon's asphyxiating bureaucracy.

All three of these operations had strong U.S. support; without it they might not have ever taken place. The continuing problem for American Phoenix advisers remained how to get their Vietnamese counterparts to do the job themselves, preferably relying on specific targeting. In 1969 major steps were taken to enhance the effectiveness of local Phoenix efforts and to improve support at the national level. The results were mixed.

6

Coming of Age: 1969–1970

IF THE last half of 1968 was a time of regrouping and rebuilding, then 1969 and 1970 were years of growth. They were years to gather strength by staffing the provinces and districts with personnel whose sole task was to advise and run the program. In 1969 there was less reliance on the CIA and more on military advisers. The number of DIOCCs targeting the VCI rose, as did the number of VCI neutralized. In 1970 CORDS emphasized programs designed to overcome many of the weaknesses and shortcomings of the Phoenix program that had come to light during the previous years.

Quotas became more unrealistic and it became clear they were a source of records falsification, double counting, and outright corruption. Phoenix began to rely more and more on statistics, generating complex monthly reports that quantified neutralized VCI into every conceivable category. The Phoenix program's growing pains attracted criticism—both from sources within MACV and CORDS and from the press and antiwar activists—and set in motion a series of revisions and additions that improved anti-infrastructure efforts.

Phoenix remained afflicted by South Vietnamese apathy. Although some provinces and districts were fortunate to have officials who were enthusiastic about the program, many still did not. And where Phoenix was widely used, it sometimes was plagued by brutality and torture. CORDS attempted to address the problem by calling on Phoenix advisers to report all such incidents, and in many instances they did. Although Americans were only advisers to the program, CORDS often had the power to see to it the offending officials lost all financial support or were transferred out.

But despite a general honing of the Phoenix program's abilities and a rethinking of the practices and procedures that had led to instances of abuses and corruption, the anti-infrastructure effort remained less than adequate. Although there was a rise in the number of neutralizations, there was a corresponding climb in the number of communist cadre U.S. intelligence estimated were in South Vietnam. Differing points of view designed to explain this apparent contradiction arose and the paper battle was on. On one side were those who believed the neutralization statistics were nonsense and that in reality the Phoenix program was having little measurable impact on the VCI. Those on the other side argued that the figures only indicated that the communists were being forced to replace VCI losses with less-skilled personnel or with cadre from North Vietnam.

Throughout the rest of its existence the Phoenix program would be scrutinized from a central perspective that ignored much of the damage done to the VCI on the local level. Despite the fact that captured documents indicated serious VCI losses in many parts of South Vietnam, the only real barometer continued to be the neutralization quota figures. As in most of the rest of the war, results were tallied and sent to Saigon, where the verdict of success or failure was based on numbers.

While Phoenix officials in Saigon succeeded in answering many of the problems that had come to the surface during the program's short life, translating those directives into action in the field was a different matter. Anti-infrastructure methods did not always keep pace with the concepts.

View from Above

During 1969 CORDS and GVN officials went to great lengths to ensure that the Phoenix program remained a high priority all the way down the line to the districts. For his part, President Thieu promoted the program both by example and decree.

Most of the numerous publicity appearances made by high-ranking GVN officials in 1969 contained at least some mention of the Phoenix program. On field trips and television presentations President Thieu and Prime Minister Khiem emphasized the importance of the program to the future and continued freedom of South Vietnam.

More substantial than trips down the publicity trail were a series of decrees and official documents issued by the Office of the President and the Ministry of Interior (MOI), under which authority for Phoenix/Phung Hoang existed. On 21 March 1969, Ministry of Interior Circular 757 set forth guidelines for "processing," classifying, and sentencing VCI suspects. This was an important step, because up until then whichever agency captured a VCI suspect decided how to interrogate the suspect and use the intelligence. When they were finished, the unfortunate prisoners were dumped into the legal system for sentencing and then into an overcrowded and understaffed prison. MOI Circular 2212, published on 20 August 1969, refined Circular 757, providing more specific guidelines for the evidence required to prosecute captured VCI.[1]

The big picture began to look even better when the GVN appointed a senior colonel to supervise the Central Phung Hoang Permanent Office (CPHPO). A lieutenant colonel with extensive military intelligence experience became second-in-command. Assigning a colonel to head the CPHPO lent Phoenix more prestige within the hierarchy-conscious South Vietnamese military.

Although the CPHPO had existed since 1968, it had little power and less respect. With the new appointments, however, the CPHPO began to produce high-level intelligence directives for dissemination down to the PIOCCs and DIOCCs. Previously, the CPHPO had simply translated American Phoenix directives and passed them down the line. According to some American observers, "there was an immediate upswing in the tempo of the operations and work at the CPHPO, and the result was felt throughout the Phung Hoang program."[2]

CPHPO was successful in producing several directives and guidance documents that carried extra weight because they were signed by both the president and the prime minister. Most importantly, these directives carefully defined the responsibilities of the province chiefs, forcing them to become increasingly involved in planning and operations.

The directives were more than just words on paper. An inspection system was instituted in mid-1969 that allowed in-depth evaluations to be performed by Phung Hoang inspectors from Saigon at any echelon of the program. This inspection focused on operations rather than statistics and briefings. In tandem with inspections, the CPHPO issued an Operational Planning Guide that deemphasized the numbers game and concentrated on operational security, more effective targeting, specific dossier preparation techniques, and the conduct of effective operations.[3]

In 1969 it was becoming clear that the concept of a loose umbrella organization was not sufficient to hold all intelligence agencies together. Some other existing organization should bring Phung Hoang under its wing and nurture it to adulthood. Unfortunately, there existed no entity that could really do the job. It had to be a South Vietnamese effort; any program under American auspices was doomed to failure. And it had to be a powerful part of the Saigon political hierarchy. The CPHPO published a study recommending that Phung Hoang be integrated into the National Police. This plan had been suggested by others, most notably Sir Robert Thompson, the British adviser to the GVN who had made his name helping to defeat the insurgency in Malaya.

The study was approved by the prime minister, who prepared to integrate Phung Hoang into the National Police. The CPHPO concluded that the integration would solve five weaknesses within the anti-infrastructure program. First, Phung Hoang would become part of an official and long-standing GVN agency, allowing proper budgeting, support, and seniority. Second, the National Police facilities would be available for immediate use. Third, existing police command and communications channels would be made available. Fourth, the existing police structure would provide a single focal point for the American advisory effort. Finally, supervision of Phung Hoang would be conducted at the highest level.[4]

Instituted in concert with the move to integrate Phung

Hoang into the National Police was a publicity blitz intended both to alert the South Vietnamese people to the extent of the GVN commitment to destroying the VCI and to offset negative publicity in the press. In August and September a publicity plan was written up that required participation by all GVN agencies. On 1 October Prime Minister Khiem launched the campaign at the national level, calling for the Vietnamese people to get involved in the attack on the VCI. Pictures of the Vietnamese mythological Phung Hoang could be seen on television screens and official news releases all over South Vietnam and hundreds of thousands of Phung Hoang leaflets were distributed in the countryside. For the next two years the program was expanded to include independent publicity bureaus in all of South Vietnam's forty-four provinces. According to officials in Saigon, "the effect was dramatic and the initial results most gratifying at the village and hamlet level."[5]

Mixed Results

The year 1969 provided evidence of enough improvements in Phoenix that CORDS could consider the program at least marginally successful. Between January and September 12,156 VCI were reported neutralized (the final total for 1969 was 19,534), an attrition rate of 14.8 percent of the average total estimated VCI strength over the eight-month period. Planners had expected a better performance, but January and February had started out slowly. All GVN military and paramilitary forces spent the first two months of 1969 preparing for Tet, which, according to intelligence reports, would see the communists attempting to recreate their 1968 offensive. So GVN forces dug in and were "literally welded into a defensive posture."[6]

When March came around and no large-scale Viet Cong military offensive materialized, ARVN officers and GVN officials took it as vindication of their defensive posture, reasoning that the communists had decided not to attack such strong defenses. This attitude made it difficult for U.S. advisers to pry GVN personnel from their shells and get back to working with Phung Hoang.[7]

In II Corps, emphasis was placed on expanding Phoenix training facilities. A regional school was nearing completion in Nha Trang that would house the National Police Directorate and the Phung Hoang Directorate in a single area. Coordination at the top would be simplified as a result of the move. Training at the new school would concentrate on PIOCC and DIOCC management, a weak point within Phoenix that hindered specific targeting operations. Early graduates of the school (some students were being trained even though the school would not be completed until late 1969) had improved the Phoenix program in Binh Thuan and Lam Dong Provinces. This statistic was made more meaningful because Vietnamese-generated neutralizations (those VCI arrested without the aid of U.S. intelligence or troops) in three of II Corps' twelve provinces equaled those credited to American units. Nationwide, only four provinces could claim the same distinction.[8]

Improvements in GVN participation also were recorded in III Corps. In August the commanding general of the region toured the eleven provinces in III Corps, calling on all GVN personnel to make an all-out effort to make Phung Hoang work. Early in the year province officials had gone back to paying only lip service to the program, maintaining that it was an American program and did not really affect them. By September, U.S. Phoenix officials were reporting that attitudes in III Corps had again picked up and the program was improving. Even so, only Dinh Tuy, Long An, Long Khanh, and Phuoc Long Provinces turned in performances that exceeded the monthly quotas.[9]

The office of the U.S. Phoenix director in Saigon reported that the second half of 1969 showed a marked improvement all over South Vietnam. After the slow start at the beginning of the year statistics picked up an increase in Phoenix performance. September neutralizations were the highest to date, with 2,005 VCI captured, killed, or rallied nationwide (the monthly goal was 1,200). Third quarter neutralizations provided 39 percent of the yearly total and 23 percent of those VCI neutralized were reported to hold positions at the district level or higher.[10]

Why the sudden upswing? According to the Phoenix Directorate in Saigon it was because the program had overcome most of the factors that previously had been holding Phoenix back.

Reports listed increased emphasis by GVN officials, increased use of specific targeting, improvement in training and motivation of personnel, better coordination, and more accurate reporting from the field.[11]

In the eyes of those watching the Phoenix program from Saigon it seemed that 1969 was indeed a year of vast improvement, however slow. Statistics, the opiate that soothed Saigon, seemed to bear this out. Adjusted neutralization totals for 1969 showed that the Phoenix program had eliminated 19,534 VCI. The total broke down to 4,832 rallied, 6,187 killed, and 8,515 captured.[12] Critics immediately pointed to the relative closeness in totals for VCI captured and killed. What they ignored (or simply didn't know) was that beginning in 1969 only those VCI convicted and sentenced to a minimum one-year sentence were counted as neutralized. This had been done to prevent falsification of statistics by overzealous Phung Hoang officials. In 1969 only about 25 percent of the VCI captured fit this guideline; therefore about four times the number shown in the statistics had actually been captured. This was a substantially greater number than the total of VCI killed, a fact that should have laid to rest charges that Phoenix was an assassination program.

View from Below

While CORDS had reason to rejoice over the new efficiency and enthusiasm within the top levels of the GVN, it was often a different story down at the province and district levels. Although Saigon did in theory have ultimate control over the fate of the province chiefs, it often was able to ignore directives at will. It was unlikely that any province chief who had disliked the Phoenix program before the MOI directives would change his opinions after them.

For the American Phoenix adviser on the ground, Saigon's decrees were only window dressing. The program's success or failure still depended on a competent DIOCC, which in turn relied on the province headquarters. The most crucial aspect of the adviser's performance was his relationship with his counterpart. If he was unable to adapt to the ways of South Vietnam's rural life, he was doomed from the onset. Examples of success and failure abounded.

During much of 1969 Di An District in Bien Hoa Province (III Corps) had a better-than-average Phoenix program that was fortunate to have a competent and enthusiastic major as district chief. But even so, improvement in intelligence-gathering and operations often came only because the Americans were willing to play a complex game of give and take with their Phung Hoang counterparts. An American Phoenix adviser wrote that he had suggested that a more efficient way to monitor local VCI would be to separate files on suspects from those who had been positively identified. His counterpart agreed and pointed out that the DIOCC had only one file cabinet and it was full. Where could they get another? The simple act of agreement meant that the ball was back in the American court. The price for accepting advice was a new file cabinet, but it was a small price to pay to take a new step forward, even a small one.[13]

Most Phoenix advisers could only evaluate the program in their district, or at most, their province. At least one district Phoenix adviser was able to view the program from the perspective of two separate districts in Quang Tri Province in I Corps. The first half of his tour was spent in Trieu Phong District and the second half in Gio Linh, a district sitting just below the DMZ in northern I Corps. He observed that in Trieu Phong and Phung Hoang Committees held fortnightly intelligence and operations meetings at the DIOCC that included district and village officials. In Gio Linh there were no such meetings at all. Worse, the adviser was not allowed to play any role in Phung Hoang. In four months of duty he never met the district National Police chief or any of the people who supposedly worked in the DIOCC.[14]

Gio Linh District was able to ignore Phoenix despite decrees from Saigon stressing the program's importance. In many ways, the burden of pushing the program toward efficiency remained on the U.S. Phoenix adviser. Unfortunately, that was all an adviser could do—push. The very nature of the Phoenix program required that the Vietnamese lead the way while the Americans watched and advised. Even if they had wanted to take over the program it could not have worked without active GVN participation. In this respect American military officers could not lead by example as they had been trained to do.

In Quang Nam Province—also in I Corps—1969 proved to be a good year. The province had one of the highest neutralization rates (883 VCI neutralized) in all of South Vietnam. Initial criticism that such a high rate could be attributed only to quota-fixing or high kill rates were quickly proven incorrect. The province senior adviser reported that at the beginning of 1969 Quang Nam had an estimated ten thousand VCI in the province. Of those, sixty-five hundred had dossiers on file at the PIOCC. That meant that rather than devote most of its time to developing intelligence on VCI in the province, the PIOCC could concentrate on tracking down those who were already known.[15]

In a way, the huge number of VCI in the province made them an easier target. (The average number of VCI in provinces outside of I Corps was usually between one thousand and five thousand. Because of the heavy concentration of enemy military units in I Corps, there was more of an opportunity for political agitation by the VCI.) In addition, the intelligence units attached to the many American units in I Corps often worked closely with the Phoenix program, passing on vital information that the PIOCC may not have had the capability to pick up. Finally, in 1969 Quang Nam had an effective and energetic province chief who emphasized the Phoenix program.[16]

Few would argue that the Phoenix program had come a long way by the end of 1969. But everyone also agreed it had a long way to go. Most encouraging were statistics illustrating a dramatic rise in the number of district and higher VCI neutralized. Beginning in June the number began to rise and between July and October 23 percent of all VCI neutralized nationwide had held positions at the district level or higher. During the first half of 1969 the percentage had been 19 percent.[17]

Criticism that the Vietnamese were not devoting enough energy to specific targeting remained true, but the number of such operations rose significantly during 1969.[18] Performance remained spotty from province to province, but reports of soundly planned operations were more numerous than in the previous year.

Quick Reaction

Even when a PIOCC had extensive dossiers on local VCI, nothing could be done if they could not be located. The key to success was good informants. In this respect the Chieu Hoi program was often the single largest producer of Phoenix intelligence. Other important sources were reports from the local villagers themselves. Unfortunately, this sort of intelligence was not always forthcoming. The villagers feared Viet Cong retribution, but just as often they saw no reason to trust the government. So they simply sat back, watched, and waited.

When civilians did come out and report VCI, Phoenix officials had cause to congratulate themselves. After all, the whole point was to make the GVN presence in the countryside a benevolent one. Such was the case in Go Cong Province.[19]

A man walked through a rice field late in the afternoon of 26 December 1969. Nothing unusual about that; people passed through that particular rice field every day. And every day a small boy, about twelve years old, watched their passing as he tended his rice plants. The man who walked briskly by today was one of the communist cadre who often came to the village of Tan Nien Tay where the boy lived. As he passed by he paid no heed to the boy who watched him.

The moment the man passed out of sight into the trees beyond the rice paddy, the boy ran to tell the chief of Xom Chua Hamlet what he had seen.

The hamlet chief listened to the description and suspected that this was one of the important VCI on the DIOCC blacklist. Leaping onto his little Honda motor scooter the chief rode off to Tan Nien Tay Village headquarters to inform the deputy for security. It was 4:30 P.M.

The deputy agreed that the description sounded like one of the cadre they had placed on the local blacklist, so he quickly assembled a reaction force of seven Popular Force soldiers and eight members of the local People's Self Defense Force. As the reaction force prepared for action the deputy ordered a nearby PF outpost to block the suspect's avenue of escape. If he managed to break away from the reaction force he would certainly run toward the dense forest near the field where he had been sighted by the boy.

The reaction force piled on Hondas and scurried to head off the suspect along the route the boy had reported. After going three kilometers or so the men left their scooters and moved on foot. Another four hundred meters and someone spotted the man. The reaction team hurriedly flanked the target and called for him to surrender. No reply. The reaction team opened fire, wounding the man in the groin. In no condition to continue the fight, he surrendered. It was now 5:00 P.M. only thirty minutes since the boy had reported the sighting to the hamlet chief.

Back at district headquarters the suspect was matched to the dossier of a key Eastern District-level VCI. If the match was not proof enough of the man's status within the Party, he was also carrying one kilo of documents and a hand-sketched map of Tan Nien Tay Village.

Immediate reaction to perishable intelligence, combined with the timely report by the boy, had netted one valuable VCI. For his quick thinking, the boy was given a reward of five thousand piasters ($50 U.S.).

Exit the CIA

One of the criticisms of Phoenix was the covert control of the program by the CIA. Despite the influx of military advisers at the province and district level, the CIA still controlled the chain of command and the purse strings. William Colby, the top man in CORDS in 1969, had been with the CIA. The American directors of the Phoenix program at the national level were all with the CIA. At the regional level the CIA officer in charge generally called the shots.

Only at the province and district level was the chain of command open to question. Some military and civilian province senior advisers believed they were in that chain, but often that was not the case. The CIA case officer in the province had a separate chain of command and often told the PSA only what the agency wanted him to know. The province chief usually bought into this deception, because the CIA officer controlled the money that went into rural development, particularly the PRU. In some cases the PSA had no idea this was going on.[20]

The duplicitous and ineffective system came to an end on 1 July 1969:

> ... Management and support responsibilities for the Phoenix program were officially transferred from the Office of the Special Assistant to the Ambassador (OSA) [a euphemism for the CIA] to MACV, who assumed full responsibility for providing or arranging monetary and logistical support through American channels.[21]

Before July 1969 one-third of the financial and administrative support to the Phoenix program had come from the CIA, with the remaining two-thirds from MACV. The elimination of the CIA from the financial picture also removed the hidden chain of command that had plagued CORDS advisers at the province level. From July 1969 on, the CIA made up only a small part of the program, and, for the most part, they functioned within the system.[22]

Over the Top: 1970

According to the Phung Hoang Directorate's annual plan, 1970 would see the Phoenix program (on 28 December 1970 the decision was made to withdraw the distinction between U.S. advisers [Phoenix] and Vietnamese personnel [Phung Hoang], and consider them all now part of the Phung Hoang program) advance "both quantitatively and qualitatively toward its goal to eliminate the Viet Cong infrastructure." Compared to previous years, the promise was fulfilled.[23]

According to intelligence estimates on the total number of VCI in South Vietnam, in 1970 Phung Hoang took a sizable bite out of the communist infrastructure. In June 1970 MACV estimated there were about sixty-seven thousand VCI in South Vietnam. This was down 18 percent from 1967, indicating that

Phung Hoang was neutralizing VCI faster than they could be replaced.[24] This was the same philosophy as the attrition strategy in the "conventional" side of the war and the accuracy and importance of the figures should be viewed with caution. Also throwing doubt into the calculation was the discrepancy between MACV's VCI figures and those of the CIA. Back in October 1968 the CIA had placed VCI strength at 111,000 while MACV estimated it at 84,900.[25]

Less questionable were the statistics on "quality" neutralizations. Of the 22,341 VCI neutralized in 1970, 31 percent were members of the People's Revolutionary Party (PRP), one of the qualifications of an 'A' category VCI. This was up from 10.7 percent in 1968. Critics who had argued that Phung Hoang did not neutralize enough high-level VCI were simply not paying attention to their own statistics. It is unlikely that 31 percent of the VCI in South Vietnam were in high-level positions, which points to the probability that key VCI were being neutralized at a faster rate during 1970 than were lower-level cadre. The point is still arguable, but when coupled with the increased movement of key VCI out of the villages and into Viet Cong strongholds, it would seem that the Phung Hoang program's claim is based in reality. Whatever the case, by any standard, the Phung Hoang program had improved considerably.[26]

Part of the reason behind the improvement was a strong push by U.S. advisers. After two years of basic work on the program, many advisers could emphasize the specific targeting capabilities of the DIOCCs. One innovation was the development of the VCI target folder, a simple prepared set of biographical, operational, and administrative questions sent down to the districts. This standardized intelligence dossiers nationwide and solved many of the paperwork headaches at the DIOCC level. By the end of the year one hundred thousand copies had been printed and distributed to all Phung Hoang Centers.[27]

Another time-saving convenience was the implementation of a sophisticated computerized collation program called the Phung Hoang Management Information System (PHMIS). This program combined the National Police criminal tracking system with VCI information in an effort to gear up the police for handling both. The PHMIS was manned by Vietnamese from the start, using only a few American advisers as programming trainers.[28]

Phung Hoang Operational Capability

By any standard the war of big units was winding down in South Vietnam by 1970. American and ARVN commanders who had previously been loath to give up their forces to aid in pacification and territorial security found few excuses once the NVA and Viet Cong main-force units had slipped away to lick their wounds. Most commanders agreed that the attack on the VCI could never be successful without local security resulting from military operations. On the other hand, the war against NVA and Viet Cong military units would not produce lasting results unless the VCI were first contained.

In 1970 local security in support of pacification was a primary task for American and ARVN units, as outlined in the Combined Campaign Plan. The plan called for tactical units to participate in cordon operations as sweep-and-blocking forces in conjunction with the police. Tactical units were to exchange intelligence with Phung Hoang Centers at the regional and province levels, but this did not always occur. Although examples of outstanding cooperation were reported, the military Tactical Operations Centers (TOC) generally took command of joint operations and relegated the Phung Hoang Centers to subordinate tasks. In this respect military participation in anti-infrastructure operations was a setback, but in some areas it measurably improved neutralization counts.[29]

When it became clear that some of the enemy killed by military units during the course of patrols and ambushes were later identified as VCI, local ARVN and American commanders took steps to coordinate more closely with the PIOCCs. In many cases previous coordination would have resulted in targeted operations that would have boosted the figures on specifically targeted VCI. As it was, however, tactical units accounted for only 11.8 percent of all VCI neutralizations in 1970. This was a far cry from the charge that a majority of Phoenix neutralizations came from standard military units.[30]

The largest number of neutralizations came from the RF/PF: 39.3 percent. Most of these neutralizations were the result of active patrols and ambushes, but in many provinces this was not arbitrary. Rather, the effectiveness of the RF/PF was due to rough intelligence from the PIOCCs concerning reports of VCI movement. It was not exactly specific targeting, but it was better than cordon-and-search operations. Generally, strong Phung Hoang programs and the effective use of RF/PF went hand in hand. In areas where the province chief was unsupportive of Phung Hoang, RF/PF performance was also lacking. In many cases, such as in Kien Giang Province in IV Corps, the RF/PF were either practically nonexistent or were used in a garrison role.[31]

The largely ignored People's Self-Defense Force (PSDF), an unpaid militia made up of 1.5 million armed men and women and 2.5 million support forces, was charged with an increasing role in Phung Hoang, particularly after the threat of enemy main-force units had died down. These militiamen were strictly locals who knew the area better than most VCI. They were a formidable threat to the communists, not so much as an armed force, but as a source of information to Phung Hoang. Beginning in 1970 the PSDF was specifically included in pacification planning; its role would be greater still in 1971.[32]

The PRU continued its steady performance throughout 1970. At thirty-five hundred strong by the end of the year, they accounted for about fifteen hundred VCI, or 6.7 percent of the total neutralizations. Although it was man-for-man the most effective anti-infrastructure arm, the PRU never managed to make a serious dent in the VCI. Most of its reputation came from its early association with the CIA. But by 1970 it was part of the Ministry of Interior and was commanded by the local province chief.[33]

Coordination between the PRUs and the DIOCCs was less than ideal in most provinces because the PRUs were critical of security practices by the less-professional Phung Hoang personnel. As a result the PRU often was reluctant to share intelligence with the DIOCC for fear that it had been penetrated by the Viet Cong. In some cases this was true. The PRUs were coming under National Police control in 1970, but to maintain their high operational standard, Saigon let the PRUs continue to operate outside the police. Within the context of emphasis on the DIOCC and increasing reliance on the police, however, the PRUs were becoming even less of a factor in Phung Hoang than before.

The final aspect of neutralizations for Phung Hoang was the Chieu Hoi program. In 1970, 7,745 VCI rallied through the program, or just under one-third of total neutralizations. This was a 60 percent increase over the 4,832 who rallied in 1969. Part of the reason for the jump was the increasing pressure placed on the VCI by GVN pacification. Those Viet Cong cadre who were less ideologically devout decided to give up the fight. The rise and fall of Chieu Hoi figures generally reflected the status of Viet Cong fortunes in the countryside.

During the last two months of 1970 greater emphasis was placed on inducing specific VCI to rally through the Chieu Hoi program. To foster this VCI inducement program, a concept called Armed Propaganda Teams (APT) was initiated. These were seven-man teams placed under the operational control of the DIOCCs that would visit the families of known VCI in an effort to convince them to rally. The APTs were primarily proselyting cadre, but they also were heavily armed to defend themselves against attack. Every day the APTs responded to new intelligence in their attempt to gather Viet Cong converts.[34]

Vietnamization

Since its inception, the Phoenix program was beset by a lack of experienced advisers. After years of building the ARVN into a conventional fighting force, diverting advisers to something as alien as anti-infrastructure operations was difficult. Besides, nothing in the American military experience had prepared the Army for something like Phoenix.

Because Phung Hoang was primarily an intelligence program, it required skilled personnel who were also good teachers.

Ideally they also would be language qualified. Beginning in mid-1969 the primary source of DIOCC advisers was newly commissioned second lieutenants from the Military Intelligence (MI) Branch. The problem was that they were inexperienced and of too low rank to operate successfully within the image-conscious Vietnamese military hierarchy. However, this lack of status was often overcome by the ingenuity and enthusiasm of junior officers assigned to Phoenix and despite the shortcomings, the program continued to grow.

Beginning in 1968, all new Phoenix advisers passed through the two-week Phoenix Coordinator Orientation Course (PCOC) before heading to their respective assignments. By the end of 1970, 1,675 advisers had graduated, all but 548 of whom had been assigned to DIOCCs.[35] Although the numbers were adequate, the system could not alleviate the status problem of having fresh second lieutenants working side by side with seasoned Vietnamese Phung Hoang counterparts.

By early 1970 the problem received serious attention from the Department of the Army, which conducted a study. The Army broke Phung Hoang advisers into four categories: district senior advisers, unit advisers (such as PRU or police advisers), intelligence advisers, and mobile training advisers. Each was prioritized, with the district adviser program, including Phung Hoang advisers, receiving top billing. First, the Army recommended that all Phung Hoang advisers serve eighteen-month tours rather than the usual twelve months. This was not a popular idea with officers serving in a war that was already winding down and the idea was never adopted.[36]

The secretary of the Army gave Phung Hoang advisers some preferential treatment to give the duty slot more prestige and attract better officers. The new program differed from that of the traditional province adviser because it fell within one career branch—military intelligence. Province senior advisers generally came from all branches of the combat arms, particularly infantry. Incentive to enter the Phung Hoang adviser program included choice of assignment location within South Vietnam, two R&Rs, priority consideration for next assignment, and assurance that the promotion board would take into account the significance of duty with the Phung Hoang program.[37]

By August 1970 the program called for 393 military slots; majors at the PIOCC level and captains at the DIOCC. But there was still an overwhelming number of lieutenants filling the billets. A plan to bring higher-ranking officers into Phung Hoang was instituted on 21 September 1970. It was a new training program developed at Ft. Bragg, North Carolina, called the Military Assistance Security Adviser (MASA) course. The initial class was made up of twenty-eight students: twenty-four lieutenants, three captains, and one major. That was a disappointingly low-ranking group of officers.[38] Despite the promise of better promotion potential and perks, attracting higher-ranking officers would remain a far-off goal; most captains and majors wanted a unit command, not a pacification advisory slot.

While MASA was gearing up for higher-ranking officers, someone was needed to teach the actual process of day-to-day intelligence work. In response to requests from MACV, the Army approved the addition of 227 enlisted intelligence specialist slots. It would be their job to train the Vietnamese in proper dossier preparation and specific targeting techniques. Because of ongoing U.S. troop reductions, sixty specialists, many with Vietnamese language skills, were immediately available. As of 31 December 1970, 218 of the 227 specialists had been assigned to the Phung Hoang program.[39]

1970 was the high-water mark for the number of American Phung Hoang advisers in Vietnam. By the end of the year there were 704 military advisers and two civilians working with the program. The CIA retained a handful of advisers who devoted all their time to anti-infrastructure operations and a majority of these remained with the PRU or the Police Special Branch.[40]

Integration into the National Police

Perhaps the most important change within the Phung Hoang program during 1970 was the gradual shift from a military emphasis to police primacy. The National Police had always been the weak sister in Vietnam's anti-infrastructure organization and as a result were not fully prepared, even as late as 1970, to take over Phung Hoang.

On 29 May 1970 the Central Phung Hoang Permanent Office (CPHPO) was incorporated into the Directorate General of National Police (DGNP), forming a separate bloc. In the countryside more emphasis was placed on using the police in major roles within PIOCC and DIOCC operations, but in many cases the police simply were not up to the task. As a result, leadership of the police continued to remain in the hands of the military.

The ratio of military to police personnel in the Phung Hoang program illustrates both the changing nature of police involvement and the continuing military dominance. At the province level, police leadership had begun to outstrip the military, while at the district level it lagged far behind. In I Corps command of the five PIOCCs was almost evenly split; three police and two military. Of the forty DIOCCs, six were police and thirty-four were military. II Corps was even at six and six in the PIOCCs, but one and fifty-one at the district level. III Corps split the PIOCCs four and seven, DIOCCs three and fifty. In IV Corps the police were dominant at the province level with twelve PIOCCs under their control to the military's four. The ratio at the district level was closer, too, at twenty-four to sixty-five. On the national level, that broke down to twenty-five PIOCCs controlled by the police to nineteen controlled by the military; thirty-four DIOCCs controlled by the police to two hundred controlled by the military.[41]

In some areas, particularly metropolitan areas such as Saigon, the police assumed almost complete responsibility for the program, handling it within the Police Special Branch (PSB). Curiously, the PRU also did its best work in the cities, particularly Saigon, accounting for 13.9 percent of its total neutralizations for 1970. This was by far the largest single PRU percentage anywhere in South Vietnam.[42]

Efforts were made during 1970 to exhort the PSB to fulfill their responsibilities in the political intelligence portion of the Phung Hoang Centers and thereby assume the leadership role in the attack on the VCI. By the end of 1970 this was true in the cities, but there were never enough well-trained PSB personnel to extend down to the district level.

The NPFF also was emphasized during 1970. It was not uniformly capable throughout South Vietnam, but in many provinces the NPFF performed well. The consensus of U.S. advisers was that the NPFF continued to be underused throughout 1970, and that continuous prodding of Vietnamese officials to use these troops more often would be needed for years to come. However, as Vietnamization marched on, CORDS officials realized the need to train the NPFF to take the lead in the Phung Hoang program.

The inability of the Phung Hoang program to extend police primacy down to the district level was simply caused by a lack of trained personnel. There were enough minimally qualified police officials to operate the PIOCCs, but at the district level many of the police were scraped from the bottom of the barrel. It was the low quality of police that had the greatest effect on operations. But as with everything in Phung Hoang, results were mixed throughout the country.

An important step was taken in December 1970 to strengthen the National Police and their role in Phung Hoang. A total of two thousand ARVN officers and twenty-five thousand ARVN soldiers were to be transferred from the army to the police as part of this new program. Training would begin in early 1971 at the National Police Academy in Thu Duc. At the end of the training period these new policemen would take their military experience and disperse to PIOCCs and DIOCCs all over South Vietnam. In the meantime, however, U.S. advisers had to concentrate on dealing with the police they had on hand.[43]

Phung Hoang Effectiveness

Aside from neutralization figures, it was difficult to gauge what sort of effect Phung Hoang was having on the VCI. Some indication came from advisers who sent in memos and reports to CORDS in Saigon. But this provided only a spotty picture. As part of the attempt to make Phung Hoang an integral and open part of people's daily lives, and at the same time provide another statistic to supplement neutralization figures, CORDS instituted a public awareness survey to measure the effect of Phung Hoang on the population. Far from being the pervasive and intrusive

Viet Cong casualties are taken to the Chau Doc Province hospital in Chau Phu following an NPFF paramilitary operation in 1969.

PRUs from Quang Tin Province in full battle dress await the arrival of Prime Minister Nguyen Cao Ky before the 1967 elections. In the field the PRU rarely wore uniforms.

An American Phoenix adviser in Tri Ton District (Chau Doc Province) with his reaction team. These men were called Kit Carson Scouts and were recruited from the ranks of Viet Cong defectors. *(Photo: F.C. Brown)*

A U.S. Phoenix adviser with a group of Kit Carson Scouts disguised as Khmer Rouge guerrillas set out on an operation along the Cambodian border in 1971. *(Photo: F.C. Brown)*

A prominantly placed Phoenix "wanted" poster lists names of VCI in Tri Ton District, Chau Doc Province. *(Photo: F.C. Brown)*

Navy SEALs were among the few Americans who were personally involved in missions against the VCI. They were also among the most effective. *(Photo: U.S. Navy)*

Following a successful "snatch" mission a Navy SEAL marches a VCI suspect off for interrogation. *(Photo: U.S. Navy)*

Posters identifying known VCI were often nailed up around villages in an attempt to compromise key communist officials. *(Photo: U.S. Army)*

Three teenage girls, members of a rural pacification team, were murdered in Long Khanh Province in April 1967 by the Viet Cong. Because of pacification's increasing effectiveness, the communists consistently targeted pacification personnel for assassination. *(Photo: U.S. Army)*

Female VCI suspect awaits interrogation. The Viet Cong political underground was extensive and included Vietnamese from all walks of life. *(Photo: F.C. Brown)*

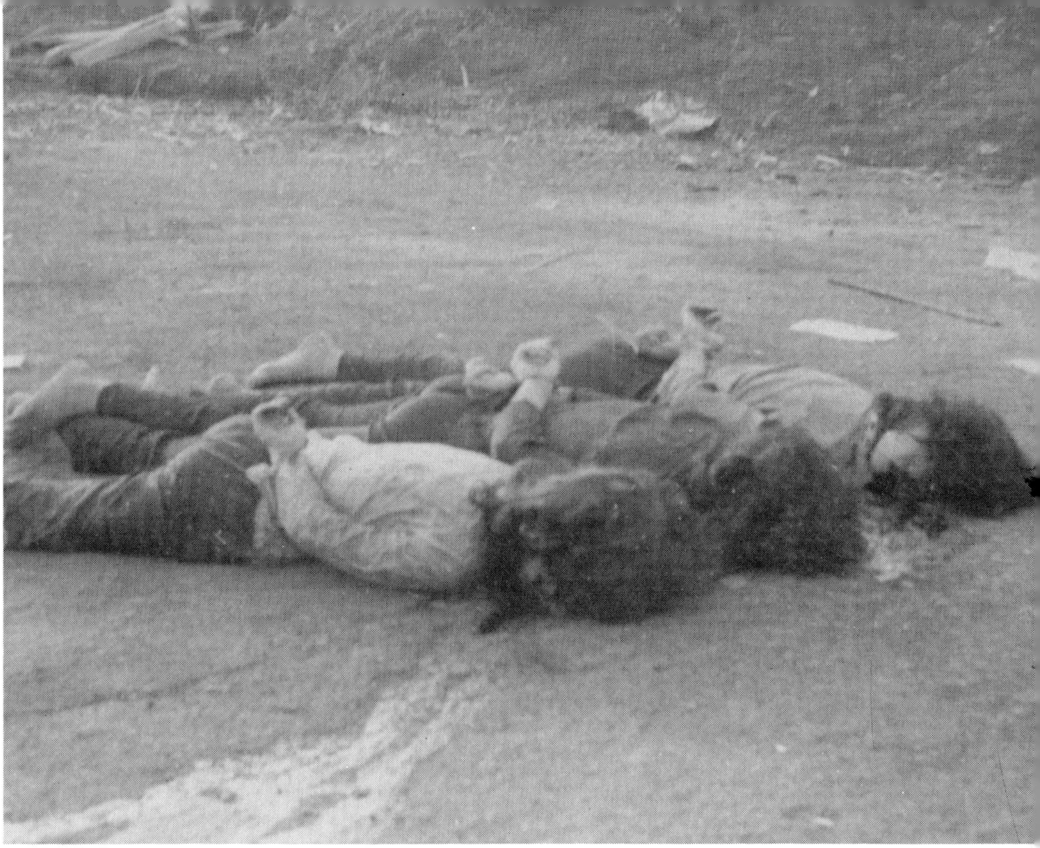

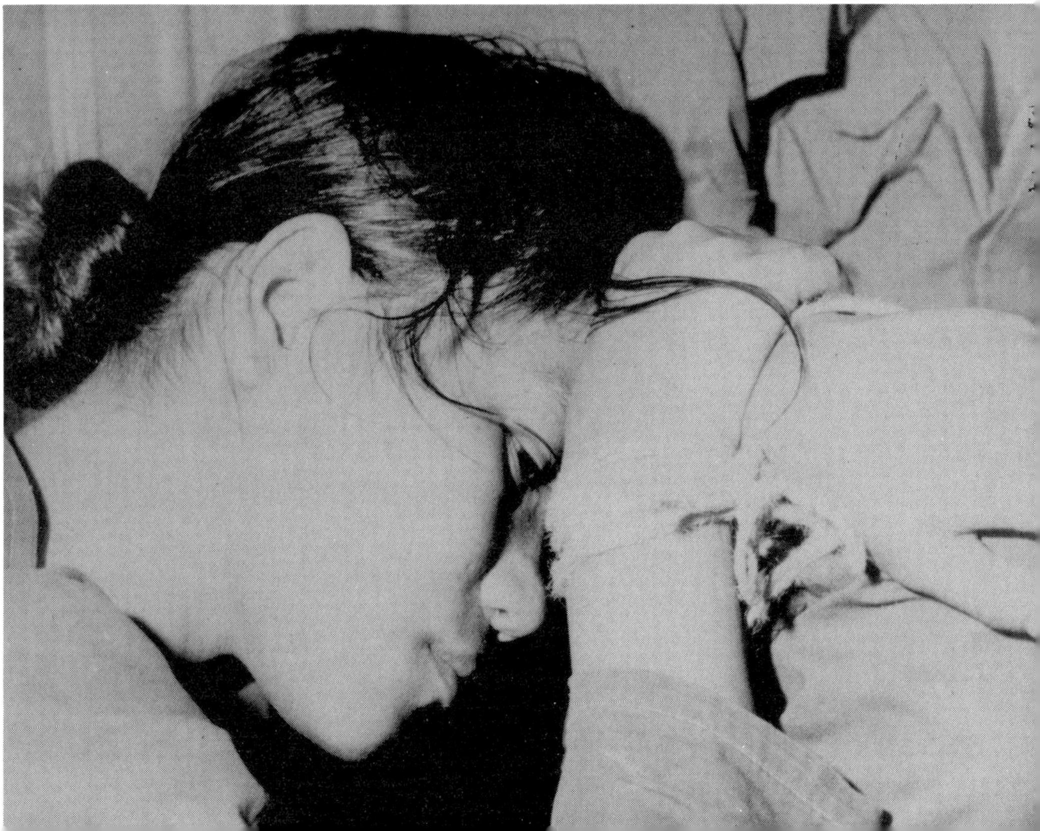

Phoenix program insignia showing the mythical Vietnamese Phung Hoang was never authorized for wear by U.S. Army personnel, but many Phoenix advisers chose to wear it. *(Photo: F.C. Brown)*

Three American advisers pose with weapons prior to leading a team of Kit Carson Scouts on ambush operations in March 1970. *(Photo: F.C. Brown)*

Young Cambodians living in the Delta provinces often served with irregular forces involved with the Phoenix program. This 16-year-old youth was an assistant to a U.S. intelligence unit in Chau Doc Province. *(Photo: F.C. Brown)*

A PRU team leader from Quang Tin Province. The PRU developed a reputation as the best anti-VCI force in South Vietnam. *(Photo: Militaria Asiatica)*

Cordon and search operations made up a majority of anti-infrastructure operations in Vietnam. Two NPFF (in uniform) question a villager. Other villagers patiently await their turn. *(Photo: U.S. Army)*

presence characterized by critics in the United States, most people did not even know there was such a thing as the Phung Hoang program.

As late as November 1970, a GVN study showed that 51.1 percent of the 1,134 respondents interviewed in 234 hamlets countrywide said they had never heard of Phung Hoang. Of the remainder, only 30.3 percent knew it was a program to eliminate the VCI; 13 percent were aware it was an "anti-Viet Cong" program of some sort and the remaining 5.6 percent answered that Phung Hoang was "a program for fighting the Viet Cong."

Of those aware of Phung Hoang, 497 were asked their opinions as to the program's effectiveness. Just over 85 percent of them thought Phung Hoang was effective. The largest group—31.7 percent—felt the program was "successfully eliminating [the] Viet Cong infrastructure." Another 15.4 percent felt Phung Hoang was having some success in eliminating Viet Cong forces, while only 11.4 percent indicated Phung Hoang had little or no success.[44]

The results of the survey were in some ways better indicators of success than simple neutralization statistics, but they were still open to question. Those surveyed were often either avowedly pro-GVN, or simply saying what they thought the interviewer wanted to hear. Still, it is interesting that fully half those surveyed did not even know what Phung Hoang was, and a majority of those who did felt it was effective.

As usual, there was a wild variation in effectiveness from province to province. In IV Corps this was particularly evident. During March 1970 a survey of all sixteen provinces in the Delta showed remarkable variation. In An Xuyen, South Vietnam's southernmost province, Phung Hoang was very effective:

> The Phung Hoang program in An Xuyen continues to make inroads into the VC infrastructure. The bulk of all neutralizations continue to be at hamlet and village level.... Greatest damage during the reporting period was inflicted upon Tan Loc Village, Quan Long District where pressure exerted by District and Village officials resulted in the rallying of 12 VCI members.[45]

All but two of An Xuyen Province's DIOCCs were reported to be strong producers of sound intelligence. The province chief was a strong supporter of Phung Hoang and he closely monitored the performance of the police in his province. Both the PRUs and the NPFF were reportedly "react[ing] well to Phung Hoang targeting and specific targeting techniques are improving."[46]

In addition, An Xuyen Province turned in a high percentage of maximum sentences on convicted VCI. Recalling that such sentences could only be handed down if there was a dossier on the suspect that included three separate accusing sources, this becomes a significant statistic. Of the forty-eight cases tried in the province during March, thirty-seven received maximum An Tri sentences of two years. Five others were released for lack of evidence. In the rest of IV Corps during the same month the average sentence was less than one year. An Xuyen's high sentencing rate came about because the DIOCCs used specific targeting to compile accurate dossiers that would stand up in court.[47]

Chau Doc Province also had a strong Phung Hoang program. Viet Cong ralliers reported that effective anti-infrastructure operations had curtailed overt VCI activity and had driven all high-level cadres across the border into Cambodia. Most importantly, the VCI neutralized during March were arrested mostly by operations directed against specific village-level VCI.[48]

In the center of IV Corps, in Phong Dinh Province, U.S. Phung Hoang advisers reported that the program had had a "stunning impact" on the VCI. Several district-level VCI had been neutralized in February, but the advisers tempered their optimism by noting that most of them had been captured through "general targeting" rather than specific targeting; the PIOCC had learned of the district cadres' approximate whereabouts from lower-level VCI captured earlier and had ambushed them. Some of the DIOCCs still did not receive adequate support from all intelligence agencies in the province and intelligence collation was less than adequate. Yet the Phong Dinh Phung Hoang program was able to respond quickly to perishable information and that capability had led to a strong neutralization effort in March 1970.[49]

Next door in Sadec Province, the situation was not so bright. Neutralizations dropped off during March, largely because the province Phung Hoang program was unable to adapt to the Viet Cong's increasingly sophisticated covert system. Communist extortion of money and goods continued unhindered throughout the province. By the end of the month only six VCI had been convicted.[50]

For the most part, however, the Phung Hoang program in IV Corps turned in a strong performance throughout 1970. One regional adviser noted that Phung Hoang had "definitely placed a large dent in the VCI armor." Neutralizations were high, most of the DIOCCs were functioning adequately, and there was support for the program from a majority of the province chiefs. But most advisers also noted that specific targeting was still inadequate. This became a common characteristic in Phung Hoang reports. Americans were pleased by the progress in many of the provinces, but PIOCC and DIOCC performance was never ideal. The obvious impact of Phung Hoang on the VCI often became secondary to meeting strict criteria for intelligence gathering and VCI dossier preparation.[51]

In the rest of South Vietnam, Phung Hoang was not as uniformly successful as it was in IV Corps. Both the CIA and MACV had concluded that approximately 50 percent of all identified VCI in the country resided in just eight provinces: Quang Nam, Quang Tin, and Quang Ngai in I Corps; Binh Dinh in II Corps; and Dinh Tuong, Kien Hoa, Vinh Long, and An Xuyen in IV Corps. The four provinces in IV Corps had their VCI problem well in hand. The remaining four provinces, however, found themselves operating with Phung Hoang staffs no larger than those in areas with virtually no identified VCI. Steps were taken to divert funds and manpower to those problem areas. By the end of 1970 National Police activity was increased, particularly in I Corps.[52]

Overall, 1970 was a good year for the Phung Hoang program. The VCI was on the run in many provinces and PIOCC and DIOCC efficiency was growing. At the same time, U.S. advisory commitment to the program was winding down. In many ways the timing was poor. Despite advances, Phung Hoang needed American guidance and input more than ever. But Vietnamization was the order of the day and the United States wanted out of Vietnam. Attention turned to the National Police, which would be forced to carry most of the anti-infrastructure burden. However, even as late as 1970 the police were not up to the job.

7

Police Work: The National Police Field Force and the Police Special Branch

As CORDS officials were always quick to point out, the Phoenix program was not in itself a mechanism that could hunt down the VCI. That task was left to existing action arms that were "best suited" to neutralizing the VCI. Phoenix was merely a central clearinghouse for intelligence collation and targeting information. The main organizations geared toward anti-infrastructure operations were the National Police (NP)—specifically the paramilitary National Police Field Force (NPFF) and the intelligence-gathering Police Special Branch (PSB)—and the PRU. The uniformed NP and the NPFF were advised through U.S.AID, which acted through the Public Safety Directorate. The PSB and the PRU had been established by the CIA, which continued to advise them until the end of the war.

Aside from the police and the PRU, Phoenix often pointed the Territorial Forces—the RF/PF—in the direction of the VCI. More commonly, the RF/PF were on the scene during cordon-and-search operations, which netted VCI in large dragnets. Because of their participation in this type of operations, the RF/PF accounted for more VCI neutralized than any other single force.

On the American side very few troops actually participated in Phoenix operations. The Army sometimes set up special teams that exploited intelligence on the VCI, in I Corps the Marines ran anti-infrastructure operations, and in IV Corps the

Navy ran small teams against the VCI. But, for the most part, the actual troops who pursued the VCI were South Vietnamese.

From the beginning, the Phoenix program was intended to be separate from military operations. Because the VCI represented an internal security problem, cleaning it up was seen as a police matter. Unfortunately, the police were not up to the task. When Ngo Dinh Diem ruled South Vietnam almost all the police were garrisoned in the major urban areas; there were at most one thousand stationed in a few key rural districts. In addition, very few police had any training in intelligence or paramilitary operations. In short, the police were seen as another instrument to buttress the president's seat of power in Saigon.

The British experience in Malaya had shown that good solid police work could turn the tide against the insurgent underground. Although there were vast differences between Malaya and Vietnam, some of the lessons learned by the British were applicable against the VCI. The CIA understood that. Agency involvement in anti-infrastructure operations since the early days of the war had been the sole concentrated attempt to deal with the VCI. As Phoenix became a high priority, emphasis was shifted from the PRU to the police, a logical move considering that the NPFF outnumbered the PRU by about ten to one. When it came to providing full-time security to South Vietnam's villages, quantity often outweighed quality. The NP would simply have to evolve the skills to take over the job.

The problem was always how to make the police proficient enough to do the kind of job the PRUs had been doing all along. The police lacked the resources and experienced personnel needed to become a strong fighting force. MACV was largely to blame. By teaching the ARVN conventional war strategy, the Americans relegated the police to second-class status. ARVN got most of the money, most of the talented manpower—particularly the officer corps—and all the prestige. Only the dregs went into the police.

The NPFF was created to provide a paramilitary arm of the police that could be used specifically to attack the VCI. But it relied heavily on the ARVN and whatever U.S. forces were in the area. In many instances the NPFF was used as static guards for the province chief or some other official. When it did go on operations it was overshadowed by the conventional units, which had all the firepower. In many cases the police were simply brought along on operations to give the appearance that the VCI were the main quarry.

Raid on Giang Ca Loc Pagoda

Army units operating in Vinh Binh Province (IV Corps) were always on the lookout for VC and NVA main-force units prowling the deltatic swamps and mangrove forests. On 31 January 1970 they found what they were looking for. Intelligence sources had located the 501st VC Main Force Battalion in the tangled mangrove south of Quan Chanh canal in the southern part of the province. Many of the VC were in the village of Giang Ca Loc rounding up supplies.[1]

On the morning of the 31st RF forces from the Vinh Binh sector, supported by elements of the 191st Cavalry, conducted a sweep through the village. Before the RF was airlifted into Giang Ca Loc, the VC got wind of the operation and scattered into the swamp. Platoons of RF were placed at several sites along the canal hoping to ambush the VC as they scurried for safety. No luck. On the sixth insertion one of the gunship escorts spotted three armed men running into a house just north of the landing zone. Rather than engage the target with rockets, the gunship pilots hovered, watching to make sure their quarry didn't escape, and called in ground troops to move in from the south to capture the VC.

For some reason the RF soldiers did not surround the building. They simply walked in the front door. Hovering above, the helicopter pilots watched as the RF barged in, followed immediately by the three VC scurrying out the back. The RF couldn't get them, but the gunships did. All three were cut down by the door gunners before they could escape to the safety of the mangrove.

Further along the canal several more individuals were spotted running across the rice paddies north of the village. Ground troops fired on the fleeing enemy "with unknown results." A ground sweep turned up one body. The 191st made two more insertions, but no more VC turned up. The results of the entire operation were four VC killed; one M60 machine gun, one .38 caliber revolver, and ten kilos of documents captured.

The communists in Vietnam churned out documents and tons of them were captured by U.S. and ARVN troops. During this operation the documents proved to have immediate intelligence value. That same day Army intelligence units had the documents translated and discovered that the Viet Cong had an important political meeting at which both local and province-level VCI would be present. The meeting was scheduled for 3:15 P.M. the next day—1 February—at the temple in Giang Ca Loc Village. They were to be guarded by a platoon from the 501st Main Force Battalion.

The information was passed on to the DIOCC, which in turn notified the NPFF commander at Tra Vinh. Since there was no doubt this latest intelligence provided an opportunity to capture key VCI, it was decided to raid the meeting. The only worry was that the Viet Cong might call it off because of the fighting the previous day. This was the perfect opportunity to use the NPFF the way it was supposed to be used—to surround, surprise, and capture the VCI. Instead, the Americans decided to apply as much firepower as could be mustered. The NPFF presence seemed only a necessary formality.

The 191st would fly the NPFF into the area. Additional backup assets included an armored cavalry troop and artillery support from a fire base in Giang Ca Le. It was their job to provide blocking fire to the north of the village, while a helicopter-mounted light fire team from the 191st—called the Bounty Hunters—patrolled the open areas to the south of the temple. The NPFF would pull off the actual strike at the VCI meeting.

After a short briefing of the helicopter crews the soldiers took off. The troop transports and gunships flew in a wide circle north and west of the temple, which stood out clearly above the flat terrain. A few kilometers from the target half the helicopters broke off and attacked from the northeast. The transports landed while the gunships laid down heavy suppressing fire.

The Viet Cong were caught off guard, but they recovered in time to fire their rifles at the helicopters coming in from the north. One VC fell dead outside the door of the temple, killed by a door gunner in one of the helicopters.

The NPFF quickly piled out of the helicopters and moved in on the temple from the northeast. The short delay in the unloading of the troop transports caused by enemy small-arms fire had allowed the Viet Cong to gather their wits and direct their attention toward the advancing NPFF. The police dived for cover in the face of the Viet Cong fire, but their commander was able to rally them and continue the attack.

During the delay, as the NPFF lay pinned down, the Bounty Hunters tore into the temple and the nearby houses with miniguns and rockets. A helicopter gunner later added that "they also employed white phosphorous grenades on the structures with great effect." The VC were driven from the houses by the onslaught and a few moments later the NPFF stormed into the pagoda, driving the VCI and their bodyguards into the street. Caught in the open, the Viet Cong had no time to organize any sort of defense and they broke and ran.

The gunship operators smelled blood and the desire to capture the VCI was quickly forgotten. As some of the Viet Cong fled headlong across the rice paddies south of the temple, the gunships screamed down on them raining lead until only a few were left alive. Most of the surviving Viet Cong made for a small canal about two hundred meters west of the temple. The canal ran south toward the undeveloped edge of the village and disappeared into the tangled mangrove swamp. It was the safety of the swamp the VC sought, but few of them made it. The gunships squatted in the air in front of the mangrove and gunned down the running VC as they made for the canal.

There was some return fire from a few Viet Cong soldiers on the banks, but most were in panicked flight. One American sergeant recalled that "they were mostly just running and throwing off every bit of gear they had, trying to get into the grass, into the canal. A few of them were running from hooches to bunkers, bunkers to hooches, and back out of there into the water and mangroves."

Many of the Viet Cong thought they reached safety when they dived into the canal water. A U.S. Army captain who was in the helicopters as they chased down the hapless Viet Cong observed their reaction upon reaching the water. "They think once they get in the water that they're immune, but if you're in the air you can see the outline of the body and throw grenades on them. The gunships use a lot of grenades, especially around a water environment, because they blow them up on top."

The gunships, working in tandem, accounted for most of the VC killed in the canal. Flying at treetop level, the lead gunship skimmed the water, dropping grenades on top of the swimming shapes. The wing ship then worked over the area with the minigun while the lead ship circled around for another pass. On one of the first passes by a tandem gunship team a Viet Cong was blown completely out of the water by a grenade that landed next to him in the canal. The second ship swung into action with miniguns blazing and the stunned and wounded communist soldier died in a hail of bullets. The gunner on that particular helicopter got official credit for killing fourteen Viet Cong.

After about twenty minutes the killing was over. Artillery fire was called in to seal the fate of any Viet Cong who happened to deceive the watchful eyes of the helicopter crews. The gunships headed back to Tra Vinh, returning forty-five minutes later with more transport helicopters filled with about fifty RF troops. They would secure the area and replace the NPFF who jumped into the empty helicopters and returned to base. The RF "policed up the battlefield, securing bodies and equipment."

The entire operation took only two hours from the time the NPFF were inserted until 5:00 P.M., when they were extracted. The actual fighting had lasted about twenty minutes. According to everyone who played a part in the operation it was a success. The NPFF had performed well and twenty-three Viet Cong were killed against the loss of only one friendly soldier who was mistakenly shot by one of his own comrades. The after-action report noted that certain lessons were learned.

> That the enemy was there at all indicates the inflexibility or foolishness of the VC, who held their meeting at the temple despite the strong possibility that it had been compromised by the operation on 31 January. The success of the operation on

1 February points to the value of the airmobile raid in responding to certain types of perishable intelligence.

Conspicuously absent from the after-action report was any mention of the original plan to capture the VCI at the temple using the NPFF. In fact, the targeted VCI, who were certainly killed in the attack, were lost somewhere on the casualty list. Worst of all, the NPFF really did nothing during the operation. The helicopters dispatched the enemy from the air. The report is unclear on exactly what happened when the NPFF reached the temple, but certainly it did not perform its mission properly since it allowed the VCI to escape through the back. But to the U.S. Army the operation was still a success, and by normal military standards it was; the VCI and a number of other Viet Cong were killed. Yet the after-action report concerned itself only with the traditional military aspects of the operation, ignoring the intelligence value that was lost when the VCI died. For the Phoenix program, the operation could only be considered an intelligence loss.

National Police

The NPFF was only a small part of a large police organization—the National Police. Originally created in June 1962—eight years after South Vietnam became a nation—the National Police represented a halfhearted move by Ngo Dinh Diem to bring the myriad police organizations under one banner. Diem feared any strong power base other than his own and so considered a strong national police organization a threat to his authority. Instead, he kept the police fragmented into small and ineffective organizations, among them the Sûreté, the Saigon Municipal Police, and the Combat Police.

The only police force based in the countryside, where the Viet Cong operated, was the Civil Guard, a small constabulary that confined itself to small, fortified bases. Because the Civil Guard was ineffective, it was largely ignored by the Viet Cong.

In 1962 these elements were combined into a single National Police force that numbered about seventeen thousand.[2]

Diem was finally forced to bring the police together under a single directorate because of the rising Viet Cong threat. But true to his suspicious nature, Diem also feared a coup and wanted as many diverse power bases as possible around him. Rather than concentrate on making the new police force into a viable action arm, Diem used it as a counterweight to the army. He also placed most of his police manpower in the cities rather than the countryside in the belief that the most serious threat to his regime came from within rather than from the Viet Cong. Only a small rural police contingent, the Civil Guard remained among the villagers and was no threat to the growing Viet Cong. Diem further stripped the Civil Guard of any possible usefulness by taking it out of the Saigon chain of command and placing it under the directorship of the minister of defense. Thus isolated, the Civil Guard withered and virtually disappeared.

As reorganized in 1962, the NP included all branches normally found in a police force—marine police to patrol the waterways, women police, and uniformed police for traffic and street patrol duties. Only a small percentage of the NP was actually aimed at the VCI.

Not until the Tet Offensive in January 1968 showed Saigon the seriousness of the communist threat did the National Police receive the attention it deserved. Increases in funds and manpower began to improve, but President Thieu still was unwilling to give the NP high status within the GVN.

As the police continued to grow steadily, only a part of its strength was aimed at the VCI. This was the National Police Field Force, the paramilitary arm designed to operate at the province and district level on a day-to-day basis.

National Police Field Force: Structure

The NPFF was created in January 1965 from the remnants of a program begun under Ngo Dinh Diem called the Combat Police. Diem had envisioned his police as a paramilitary organization geared toward quick reaction to riot situations, and as a lightly armed, highly mobile unit that could attack the Viet Cong in the villages, the same basic mission it retained under the Phoenix umbrella. As a paramilitary force, the NPFF was pointed directly at the VCI by intelligence agencies, particularly the Police Special Branch.[3]

NPFF personnel received both military and civil training—military for their role within the Phoenix program as an anti-infrastructure force, and civil because they were to remain permanently in villages they swept clean of VCI and prevent any resurgence of communist influence. While the theory was a sound one, it was often overoptimistic.

The NPFF was divided into companies of lightly armed, mobile foot units that could operate against the VCI and guerrilla units in an area previously cleared of enemy main-force units by ARVN or U.S. troops. Basically, the NPFF took over where the conventional troops left off: U.S. and ARVN troops fought the big-unit war to clean out the Viet Cong and NVA, and the NPFF took over to hunt the VCI and maintain a level of pacification once the troops left. If all went smoothly, the NPFF would clear out the VCI, maintain security, and then replace the paramilitary units with uniformed elements. The NPFF would then remain in the district as a security force to bolster the RF/PF and protect the uniformed police.

At the national level the NPFF was commanded by an assistant director general who headed up the Armed Support Bloc. Directly down the chain of command was the commanding officer of the NPFF and under him the chief of staff. A reserve battalion of six NPFF companies remained at the national headquarters. At the regional level another battalion was placed at the disposal of each of the four military regions under the command of the regional director general. The assistant regional director also served as the NPFF regional battalion commander. At the province level at least one NPFF company (usually more) was stationed in the provincial capital. When only one company was present the command structure was simple—the NPFF company commander was also the assistant province chief of police for the NPFF. When more than one NPFF company was garrisoned in the province, rivalries and personal jealousies often became a problem. Generally, the senior NPFF company commander also held the post of assistant province chief of police for the NPFF.[4]

The NPFF commander—the assistant director general for armed support—was responsible for assigning all NPFF units to their various regions and provinces. It was his responsibility to recruit, train, equip, and transport all NPFF units. Perhaps most importantly, the NPFF commander was to see to it that NPFF units in the field were used properly. Inspections were scheduled to insure that regional and provincial police officials kept in line.

The regional commander in some instances became little more than a jumpoff point between the national level and the provinces. This was a predictable outcome because the province was the operational base, while Saigon provided high-level management and financial support. Regional NPFF commands became little more than a stopping-off point for communications between the province and the capital. The regional NPFF commander's main responsibility was to insure that provincial NPFF units were not used improperly, such as in static garrison duties.

As the planners of the Phoenix program had quickly realized, the province was seen as the best operational level—for both intelligence-gathering and for NPFF operations. The district would have been even better, but it was impractical and unwieldy to have NPFF companies stationed in all of South Vietnam's more than 250 districts. The province chief was the ultimate commander of the NPFF in his province, but the assistant province chief of police for the NPFF had day-to-day command. It was his responsibility to recruit manpower from within the province, and set the ground rules for deployment of his units. Most importantly, the province NPFF commander established direct relations with the provincial PSB. The relation was symbiotic and its success or failure rested largely with the personalities and professionalism of the NPFF and PSB commanders. The PSB—stationed in the PIOCC—furnished the NPFF with intelligence and targets for operations against the VCI.

In return, the NPFF provided whatever intelligence it could gather during combat patrols and operations. The PSB used the new intelligence to target other VCI and the cycle began again. Although the PSB and the NPFF were roughly equal in theory, in reality the PSB was the brain that told the NPFF where to go and what to do. However, the PSB could not call upon the NPFF to perform duties contrary to its mission—such as guard duty at the PIOCC. Nor could NPFF elements be attached permanently to the PSB.[5]

The police were not equipped or trained to counter enemy main-force units—that was the responsibility of the armed forces, particularly the ARVN. Generally, in contested areas where VC and NVA units were still roaming around, the NPFF accompanied U.S. or ARVN troops, acting in a support role. Because the NPFF was an anti-infrastructure force, it gave the regular forces an excuse to disregard their own responsibilities in capturing VCI by allowing them to claim that the NPFF was along to do that. But without specific targeting intelligence, the NPFF could only play a role in cordon-and-search operations, where it checked ID cards against blacklists of known VCI. Any people whose names matched the lists were arrested, as was anyone who did not possess an ID card.

Recruitment and Training

Under normal circumstances provincial NPFF companies were recruited from the province in which they would serve. At the regional level battalion manpower was filled from the particular region in which the battalion was assigned. Only when the regional and provincial commands could not fill all their manpower slots from local recruits would the National Armed Support Bloc step in and assign personnel from areas with surplus manpower.

The province police chief was directly responsible for recruitment and training within his province. When a recruit was selected he was sent to the NPFF Training Center (usually at the regional capital) for coursework and practical training in paramilitary and standard police methods. Emphasis was on cooperation with the PSB and techniques of intelligence gathering. Upon completion of training the new recruit was considered a fully trained National Policeman with the added paramilitary skills needed to hunt the VCI.[6]

All that sounded good in theory. But recruitment and manpower remained the single biggest obstacle in turning the NPFF into an effective force. Because conventional military tactics had become the backbone of the South Vietnamese strategy to win the war, the ARVN received preferential treatment in recruitment, training, and pay. The single most limiting factor throughout the NP structure was lack of high-quality manpower and leadership. The NPFF in particular was denied access to any reasonably well-educated personnel—those with a high school education were automatically taken into the army's ranks. In 1969, the average new policeman had fewer than seven years of formal education. And because of the new emphasis placed on VCI neutralization by the Phoenix program, the NP expanded rapidly between 1968 and 1971. Twenty-six percent of the NPFF had less than one year of experience as a policeman. The lack of experience combined with a lack of education often added up to incompetence and inefficiency in the field.[7]

The problem was recognized in early 1969 and steps were taken to remedy the situation. In January 1969 the assigned strength of the NPFF nationwide was 11,068. On 31 December that number had risen to eighteen thousand. More men were being allocated to the NPFF, an important gesture considering the NPFF's prestige vis-à-vis the ARVN. But that was only on paper; the actual number was a little more than fourteen thousand. To make matters worse, Saigon did not provide enough funds to pay for the increase in NPFF manpower. What they did do was transfer en masse all uniformed National Policemen aged eighteen through twenty (approximately four thousand men) to the NPFF.[8] These men lacked any form of paramilitary training and although they would be on the manpower rosters for the NPFF, it would be months before they were capable of operating in the field.

While 1969 was a key year for the Phoenix program in general, it was one of building and training for the NPFF. The four thousand men dumped by the NP onto the NPFF, plus an additional backlog of about twenty-four hundred untrained recruits, became a nightmare for AID advisers. Yet by December 1969 much of the problem had been solved and the men had been assigned to units in the field.[9]

As more and more responsibility for anti-infrastructure operations was placed on the police, the NPFF began to receive a greater share of the recruit pool. But although manpower quotas were being met by the end of 1970, the quality of many of the recruits was barely passable. Part of the problem was motivation. Many NPFF recruits were joining the police for the wrong reasons.

In early 1971 some U.S. police advisers noticed that few of the students understood the mission of the NPFF. Many joined up because they felt it was a lesser evil than the military. When asked why they enlisted, some recruits answered that the "National Police served the people in the villages and hamlets and helped provide for their security." When told that the Popular Forces also did that, a more candid recruit replied that he had heard that the Popular Forces were going to replace the ARVN in a wider combat role, so the National Police seemed the safest alternative. Another recruit told his instructors that he joined the police because he liked their uniforms better than those of the Popular Forces.[10]

After all the problems of command, control, manpower, and mission were answered, there still remained the question of performance. Was the NPFF capable of eliminating the VCI in the countryside?

Performance

Problems with the NPFF began early and were never adequately solved, although CORDS was well aware of NPFF shortcomings and took steps to address them. During his days as chief of CORDS, Robert Komer sent evaluation teams from province to province in an attempt to keep the NPFF program honest. He found the task difficult.

During 1968 in Tuyen Duc Province the battle to upgrade the NPFF was ongoing. The province chief and the police chief refused to use the NPFF in an anti-infrastructure role, preferring instead to arm it with the oldest weapons and use it in static guard duties. Komer was outraged and used his power within the Saigon hierarchy to threaten to cut off all U.S. support to Tuyen Duc Province.[11]

An evaluation team reported that the NPFF detachments in

Tuyen Duc and Dalat, the 211th and 212th NPFF Companies respectively, had little ammunition, poor housing, and insufficient rations. Worse, the 211th had been assigned by the province chief to occupy two garrison positions around Dalat in direct violation of the NPFF operational rules. The 212th, on the other hand, went out on plenty of operations—between four and six a week—but neutralized few VCI on their walks in the sun.[12]

The 212th NPFF Company was doing all it could. During cordon-and-search operations the police were to be accompanied by a PSB detachment that would use blacklists to apprehend VCI suspects. However, in most cases the PSB remained at home and the NPFF dutifully went out on its own with no idea of whom or what they were looking for. The evaluation teams could easily see the problem, noting that, "The [VCI] yield is very low, which indicates low quality targeting as the primary cause of the poor results."[13] But little could be done as long as the NPFF remained such a low priority within the Saigon hierarchy.

By November, however, the situation in Tuyen Duc Province began to turn around. Two other units, the 209/1 and 209/2 NPFF Companies, began to respond to prodding by American advisers. Eight incompetent NPFF company commanders were relieved of command or replaced and NPFF units were moved out of the population centers and into the rural districts. The province chief moved more than 50 percent of the NPFF out of the province capital and began coordinating actions between the NPFF and PSB. The results were immediately apparent, though U.S. advisers were only cautiously optimistic. One adviser noted that, "The ball appears to be rolling and if results are not forthcoming, then we had better go back to the drawing board or start pointing fingers elsewhere."[14]

In Thua Thien Province in I Corps the 106th NPFF Company, stationed in Hue, also was misused. One platoon provided security for the province headquarters and the home of the province NP chief. Another platoon was graciously supplied to the U.S. 1st Cavalry Division to assist in cordon-and-search operations. A third platoon guarded the Hue Treasury Service Building, while the fourth platoon performed maintenance duties at the NPFF compound.

Worse still, these men were underarmed. For the 210-man company there were ninety-six M1 carbines (the authorized weapon was the M2, an automatic version of the M1 carbine) and an assortment of captured weapons. That left 114 men unarmed. Even if these sedentary guards were attacked at their posts by the enemy, they would have been unable to defend themselves. The other NPFF companies throughout the province were equally poorly armed and misused.[15]

If NPFF companies had been properly used, there would have been no time for guard duty in the province's major cities. The police should have remained in the villages and hamlets after a cordon-and-search operation to ensure that the Viet Cong did not return after the government presence left. This was rarely the case, however. One U.S. Army officer with the 501st Infantry, 101st Airborne Division, operating in Thua Thien Province, noted that whenever an NPFF platoon joined his unit for an operation it never remained behind after a village was secured. Instead, it returned to its garrisons in the cities. "Once we depart this hamlet there is nothing left to prevent the return of the VC," he observed.[16]

Incensed by these reports, Komer immediately called for the withdrawal of U.S. support for the 106th and 111th NPFF Companies until they were no longer employed in "housekeeping duties." His wish was granted a few weeks later, but it represented only one small drop in a very large bucket.[17]

Just south of Thua Thien Province, in Quang Nam Province, things were just as bad. Two units, the 104-1 and 104-2 NPFF Companies, spent most of their time guarding the province police chief's compound or garrisoning the provincial capital of Hoi An. But in this case part of the NPFF was deployed in its proper role. Two squads were assigned to the U.S. 196th Infantry Brigade, Americal Division. These two squads remained with the U.S. brigade for fifteen to thirty days, after which they would be replaced by two other squads from one of the two NPFF companies. While this was a step in the right direction, the use of NPFF units smaller than platoon size was specifically forbidden by the NPFF SOP of January 1968. Even more disappointing was that the NPFF mission in Quang Nam rarely included anti-infrastructure operations. For the most part the NPFF squads aided the Americans in military police duties, or in attempting to stem the flow of contraband into the province.[18]

Official GVN unwillingness to use the NPFF in its proper role was most clear in III Corps. In a number of cases province chiefs defied the spirit of the NPFF SOP by exploiting a loophole in the language. The NPFF was designed for security work in the countryside and was specifically prohibited from garrison duty in the cities. However, no specific rule prohibited using NPFF companies as perimeter security forces around those cities, even though the meaning of SOP was clear—the NPFF was to be used in the districts. Out of eleven provinces in III Corps, only Hau Nghia, Gia Dinh, and Bien Hoa made any attempt to deploy the NPFF in the districts, and then only as paramilitary units attached to U.S. and ARVN units rather than as reaction forces acting on DIOCC intelligence.[19]

When the NPFF in III Corps was used for anti-infrastructure operations, it was always at the request of an American adviser who had personally designed an operation. Even then they were usually U.S. or ARVN cordon-and-search operations, with the NPFF coming along mostly as a symbol of legality. An operation in Tay Ninh Province was typical. After cordoning the village in the early morning hours, U.S. and ARVN troops filtered about eight hundred villagers through four tables of PSB agents who checked ID cards and matched names against blacklists. Meanwhile, the NPFF milled around searching houses and looking for anything suspicious. A mere twelve VCI suspects were detained.[20]

Although the police were misused in III Corps, the region still managed to produce high VCI neutralization levels throughout 1968. As far as Saigon was concerned that meant good progress. Not so in IV Corps, however. Komer quickly became concerned when he saw the numbers going from average to poor. During the first six months of 1968, NPFF performance in the densely populated southern section of South Vietnam was on a par with the rest of the country. After 15 June it took a nosedive, an especially troublesome development considering that IV Corps had the largest NPFF force in all South Vietnam. Komer wanted to know why.[21]

The answer, according to the deputy for CORDS in IV

Corps, was because of an increase in the number of joint operations performed by the NPFF since 1 June 1968. Also, a thorough housecleaning in the region had seen twelve incompetent NPFF chiefs lose their jobs. NPFF performance was back on the rise in October, an apparent vindication of Komer's get-tough policy. Komer would not learn of the results in IV Corps, however, because he left Vietnam in November, leaving the new CORDS chief, William Colby, to learn of the news.[22]

American advisers were frustrated by the lack of cooperation from province officials in making good use of the NPFF. But they had only their own government to thank for the problem. Early training of the ARVN had instilled a conventional mindset about warfare on both military officers and politicians that overshadowed all attempts at shifting to a more police-oriented strategy. Yet, despite the misuse of the NPFF by province chiefs all over South Vietnam, progress was made. 1969 saw a slow but sure change in the way the police were used in the provinces. By 1970 there was some positive change, both as a result of pressure by CORDS to replace province officials who were unwilling to use the NPFF correctly and because the police had been given overall command of the Phung Hoang program. This increase in funds, authority, and prestige had a profound effect on performance.

NPFF operations increased substantially in 1970 and although the quality of NPFF forces nationwide was not always up to the task, many provinces did begin to use them effectively. American advisers continued to complain that the NPFF was underemployed and that it took constant prodding of province officials to keep the NPFF pointed in the right direction.

But there were important bright spots. Creative use of combined forces in Phoenix operations gave the NPFF useful experience for the future. During September 1970 the Quang Tin Province chief (I Corps) centralized the various Phoenix operational assets into a single Phoenix reaction force. This simple move streamlined the program and at the same time gave the NPFF hands-on experience with the best anti-infrastructure team in the country—the PRU. The reaction force consisted of 180 members of the NPFF, sixty PRUs, and thirty Armed Propaganda Team (APT) members from the province Phung

Hoang center. This 270-man force was further broken down into platoons that could operate independently or with U.S. or ARVN troops. The reaction force was praised by U.S. advisers and performed well throughout 1970.[23]

Another combined operation was launched in Dinh Tuong Province (IV Corps) during mid-November 1970. It was an operation run from the PIOCC, which had targeted 173 VCI. Forces committed to the operation included one RF battalion—plus forty-three additional RF companies—163 PF platoons, seven NPFF platoons, and elements of the province PSB. Also participating were Hoi Chanhs who manned screening stations in villages and pointed out VCI on the list. At the close of the operation 128 VCI had been killed, fifteen had been captured, and fifty-one had rallied to the Chieu Hoi program.[24]

Gains came to a halt when the United States stepped up its pullout of troops from Vietnam. After only three years of improvement and guidance, the NPFF was being left to its own devices. The prospects for the future were not bright, especially considering the reputation it had been given for poor performance. Yet in those three short years the NPFF had shown remarkable progress. If it had been groomed since the early 1960s things might have been different. The problem had been one of guidance; if the NPFF was not pointed in the right direction it could not be expected to produce results. Guidance should have come in the form of sound intelligence. The group responsible for that aspect of police anti-infrastructure operations was the Police Special Branch. Had the PSB passed on good intelligence the NPFF undoubtedly would have come out looking much better.

Police Special Branch: Manpower and Training

The Police Special Branch had been advised by the CIA since 1954. From the beginning PSB was to be an intelligence-gathering arm aimed at political aspects of the insurgency the

ARVN and their U.S. advisers were unable and unwilling to concentrate upon.

The first PSB school was built inside the National Police training compound in Saigon in 1955. For the next eight years the PSB received little attention and was overshadowed by the larger National Police training program, which was itself insignificant next to the ARVN. Then, in 1963, PSB training was standardized and placed under the NP Personnel and Training Bloc. This move seemed to be a positive step, but in reality many of the PSB graduates were allowed to serve for only a short time before being absorbed into the uniformed NP and other non-intelligence duties. Although the problem was recognized, nothing was done until late 1968 when the DGNP, at the urging of CORDS, gave the PSB control of its own training and personnel assignments.[25]

Although the CIA meant to train the PSB as the political intelligence arm of the GVN, it made little headway until late 1968. Even then it lacked the resources and manpower to improve the PSB. Part of the problem lay in a lack of training facilities. In I Corps a single classroom had been graciously allocated by the regional NP command. This did not include housing or mess facilities; students slept on the classroom floor and begged food from the policemen. In II Corps it was even worse. Again, PSB recruits received no food and slept wherever they could find an empty space on the floor, and they were given only a rickety prefabricated structure considered uninhabitable by the NP. Things looked better in III Corps because the PSB had a classroom and dormitory building, but the NP planned to take it over in early 1969. In IV Corps the PSB training center was a tin building that was to be torn down to make room for a new dock facility.[26]

Even though 1969 promised to see more support for the PSB, all arrangements for building facilities and land continued to rest in the hands of the NP. The police had no incentive to provide the PSB with good facilities because they, too, received little from Saigon. CORDS had managed to convince the GVN that action against the VCI was of paramount importance, but it would be a slow road between realization and action.

Some headway was made in training, however. Before 1968 figures showed that of the thirteen thousand men and women employed by PSB, fewer than one out of four had any kind of intelligence training. American advisers could not go back and find trained recruits who had been absorbed into NP ranks over the years because recordkeeping had been nonexistent. Plans in late 1968 called for 17,500 individuals to be recruited and trained by the end of 1970. But considering the pitiful proportion of personnel with even rudimentary training in intelligence work, it would take that long just to teach basics to PSB recruits and "old hands" alike. No one in CORDS realistically felt that the PBS would be an effective organization before 1972.

For the foreseeable future, PSB would expand and practice the basics of intelligence work. CORDS understood this and William Colby approved a plan that aimed for quantity rather than quality, the understanding being that the PSB would concentrate on basic training rather than the finer points of sophisticated intelligence-gathering. To help get the program off the ground, CORDS approved the spending of VN$93.6 million in November 1968 to upgrade PSB training and facilities.[27]

To help streamline the expansion process, CORDS took a direct part in the training, establishing new schools in all four military regions and in Saigon. But they were still small. Only 240 students in all four military regions could be accommodated in each four-week course. Funds earmarked for PSB training would go toward raising the total to four hundred students, but that was not expected for at least six months.[28]

The PSB training center in Saigon did better. During 1967, thirteen hundred students went through training; about fifteen hundred graduated in 1968. The expanded PSB training program expected to push through twenty-five hundred graduates in 1969. Each session included mandatory courses in how to be an effective case officer, interrogation, surveillance, and reporting. Advanced training was given to senior officers and a new section was created for female PSB personnel, called "Swans." About 250 Swans went through the first course in mid-1968 and many went on to be effective interrogators.[29]

Incredibly, PSB did not have a counterintelligence (CI) section until 1969. The first class in CI was scheduled for mid-1968, but was given only to senior PSB officers and then only as a familiarization course. There was no CI section within PSB until 1970, and even then it was of questionable effectiveness, given CIA reports of widespread communist infiltration of all levels of the GVN political and military apparatus.[30]

Although plans to increase PSB training were modest, they still outstripped GVN and CORDS ability to staff the schools with instructors. In Saigon, only eleven full-time and seven part-time teachers lectured some two thousand students. And the shortage of instructors was not just caused by a lack of qualified personnel—little was done to train new instructors. For example, in 1969 only twenty-seven instructor slots were approved by the GVN.

Police Special Branch schools in all four military regions also suffered from understaffing. In early 1969 I Corps had three instructors, II Corps had two (plus three interrogation specialists), III Corps had three, and IV Corps eleven part-time teachers borrowed from the operations branch of the NPFF. At the beginning of 1969 only twenty-four officers were being trained to become instructors and only an additional thirty were scheduled for training during the remainder of the year.[31]

Where were all the U.S. advisers to the PSB? For all practical purposes they were nonexistent. Only two American civilians, assisted by a third during the first half of 1969, were attached to the PSB training program in Saigon. Additionally, each military region had one American adviser to assist with PSB instruction.

The quantity of personnel going through PSB training was clearly insufficient to meet GVN intelligence needs. The quality was even worse. An experimental aptitude test administered in late 1968 showed that 25 to 30 percent of the four thousand students tested failed. The GVN agreed to keep these students out of the mainstream of intelligence activities, relegating them instead to administrative chores. This statistic is startling because it indicates that of the approximately two thousand PSB graduates coming out of each PSB class in both Saigon and the four military regions, at least five hundred of them were unfit for intelligence work.[32]

Performance

The Phoenix program has been criticized because most VCI put out of action were neutralized as a result of "conventional" military sweep operations rather than specific targeting. Naturally, blame was quickly fixed on the NPFF because it was involved in the military sweeps. But the real weak link in the anti-infrastructure chain was the PSB. It simply failed to generate the intelligence necessary to target individual VCI.

Why not directly criticize the PSB instead of blaming the NPFF? Simply put, critics could blame only what they could see and for the most part that was the NPFF, not the PSB. The NPFF was basically an aboveboard operation advised and monitored by U.S.AID. The PSB, on the other hand, was administered closely by the CIA. That meant many layers of secrecy, most of which were never penetrated. But those who were involved in training the NPFF were well aware of the problem—intelligence was not generated by the PSB, leaving the NPFF sitting on its hands while critics accused it of incompetence.

A few reports did criticize the PSB, though without naming the CIA. An NPFF end-of-year report for 1969 noted that the NPFF needed to be pointed in the right direction before it could do its job:

> Solution of the problems of intelligence and operations [within the NPFF] unfortunately are almost 100% dependent upon improvements in other areas (PSB and Phoenix/Phung Hoang).[33]

The conclusion was logical. The NPFF could do absolutely nothing without sound targeting from the PSB. But it also raised another question. If the CIA had been concentrating on anti-infrastructure operations in Vietnam for so long, then why was the PSB progressing at such a slow pace? Other CIA programs, such as the PRU were considered very successful. The answer lay within the CIA itself.

There was a simmering rivalry within Agency ranks between the foreign intelligence officers and the paramilitary operators.

Foreign intelligence officers were the cloak-and-dagger men. They ran agent nets, recruited agents to spy for them, and helped generate the human sources that produced hard intelligence—the bread and butter of the CIA. The paramilitary operators ran the covert programs, such as the PRU and other operations, like the secret war in Laos. These men were the mysterious and controversial part of the Agency. Both factions played a part in the Phoenix program. Unfortunately, the rivalry often only kept the two sides from cooperating in the overall fight against the VCI.

According to some CIA operatives involved with paramilitary operations in Vietnam, the primary reason the PSB failed to perform adequately was a lack of proper emphasis. For the most part, the PSB was run by foreign intelligence types who concentrated on agent penetrations and neglected the need to coordinate PSB intelligence with paramilitary operations such as the PRU. The result was that the PRUs and their CIA mentors generated their own intelligence on the VCI. The NPFF, however, lacked the resources to follow suit. Instead, it sat around waiting for the PSB to give it something to do.

There were exceptions. In some provinces the CIA officer in charge of advising the PSB came from a paramilitary background. When that was the case, the PSB tended to be more action-oriented. In one case a CIA officer with a paramilitary background became regional PSB adviser for III Corps. He was surprised by the lack of understanding about the nature of anti-infrastructure operations within the PSB. He was even more surprised to discover that most of them were useless:

> There were probably thirty or forty other PSB people at the province level and you always had some at the district, but the number that were worth anything at the province level would probably be a dozen. Plus two or three at the district, at the most.[34]

This was not a strong endorsement, especially coming from someone within the CIA. Perhaps most importantly, such comments were evidence of the rivalry between foreign intelligence officers and their paramilitary siblings.

In the end, the PSB did little to change the nature of anti-infrastructure operations in South Vietnam. The CIA had envisioned the PSB as a sort of central intelligence clearinghouse for the Phoenix program, a central nerve center for the PIOCCs and DIOCCs. It didn't turn out that way. Some DIOCCs responded to a lack of intelligence by creating their own network, while others sat back and did nothing. Like almost everything else within the Phoenix program, the quality of individual foresight and initiative became very important. Good advisers and their Vietnamese counterparts came up with their own solutions.

Only one program within Phoenix managed to rise above the problems of poor intelligence and create its own. It, too, was a CIA creation—the Provincial Reconnaissance Units, the crux of criticism regarding the Phoenix program.

8

Dirty Work: PRUs and SEALs

Two small groups of unconventional warriors wreaked havoc on the VCI throughout South Vietnam. Their names and reputations became legendary: Provincial Reconnaissance Units, the bad boys of unconventional warfare in Vietnam, and the U.S. Navy SEALs (Sea, Air, and Land teams). The PRUs were indigenous troops recruited and trained for paramilitary small-unit action and the SEALs were American forces designed to strike at enemy strongholds deep in communist-controlled territory. In short, both units took the fight to the Viet Cong.

PRUs and SEALs often worked together. Both had many of the same characteristics: small numbers, high morale, and specialized training. These factors led to a large degree of success in anti-infrastructure operations. But their effectiveness was a double-edged sword. Both PRUs and SEALs came to symbolize sneak attacks in the dead of night on unsuspecting victims. Assassination became the catchword, a label that clung to the Phoenix program. The charge was inaccurate. Both SEALs and PRUs killed many VCI and Viet Cong guerrillas—that was war. They also inevitably killed innocent civilians—that was regrettable, but inevitable when fighting an enemy that wrapped itself in the population.

Small numbers also limited overall effectiveness. PRUs and SEALs together amounted to fewer than six thousand men in all of South Vietnam, not enough to seriously damage the VCI on their own. Yet on a per capita basis, PRUs and SEALs accounted for more VCI neutralized than all other anti-infrastructure units combined. Aside from specialized training and esprit de corps, another factor helped PRU and SEAL effectiveness—intelligence. PRUs and SEALs had access to the best intelligence, often coming straight from the CIA. Its timeliness and accuracy directly resulted in the neutralization of high-ranking VCI on many occasions.

Provincial Reconnaissance Units

If any single organization came to be synonymous with assassination it was the PRU. When critics recited examples of how the Phoenix program dealt in murder and terror they inevitably used examples of the PRU. Some of the stories were true—PRUs were brutal and did hate their enemy. But they also were effective anti-infrastructure operatives, man for man the best the Phoenix program ever had. Yet they never numbered much more than five thousand in all of South Vietnam and their mission included more than just anti-infrastructure operations for Phoenix. A majority of their work was guerrilla-type, behind-the-lines, hit-and-run operations designed to harass the Viet Cong.

The PRU had its roots in the Counterterror Teams of the early 1960s. William Colby, who was at that time the CIA Far East Division chief, saw that the name and reputation of the CTT had to be changed for it to transcend its killer image. In 1966 the CTT became the PRU, but the mission remained the same. As anti-infrastructure operations became viewed as more important to the war effort, the PRU also became more important. The CIA remained in control of the PRU and in 1967 Robert Komer saw it as an available asset that could be used as the pointed end of his new anti-infrastructure apparatus.

PRU Structure

If a strict chain of command, a rank structure, and rigid rules make up military structure and discipline, then the PRU definitely was not part of the military. But that was not the point of the PRU. CIA reasoning behind the creation of the PRU was that an unconventional enemy called for unconventional methods. The PRU needed to fight like the Viet Cong and most importantly they needed to hate the Viet Cong. That was where recruitment came in.

Within each province, the CIA looked for men who would do well in the ranks of the PRU. One CIA official in I Corps recalled what he looked for in his men:

> They were recruited locally and it was pretty much by word of mouth. It was strictly friends of friends and hoi chanhs and that sort of thing.... These were hard-bitten guys who were really ticked off by the communists. They had lost families and they wanted revenge.[1]

The CIA did not often have to actively search for men to become PRUs. Potential recruits tended to gather in each province, linked by their hatred of the communists. There was very little "overrecruiting" to be done; few recruits were weeded out of the original batch. The CIA knew who they wanted:

> The people who were of like mind and like ability automatically gravitated to that sort of thing. Roughnecks tended to stick together. That's the kind of guys who went into the PRU. It was very clannish. You really had to be a tough nut to get into the PRU and stay in.[2]

Only a small number of men were made of the right stuff for the PRU. For that reason, and because a large PRU force would have been unwieldy, PRU operated in small groups. Each province had at its disposal three squads—one platoon—of PRUs for anti-infrastructure operations. Another reason for their small number was security. Sensitive intelligence would surely have been compromised if too many operatives were in on operations planning. The PRU managed to consistently surprise the VCI, largely because tight security kept Viet Cong infiltrators out of their ranks. Other branches, such as the National Police, were not so careful and often were riddled with communist informers.

Alone among South Vietnamese forces, PRUs took anti-infrastructure operations seriously. To these men, playing cat and mouse with the VCI was not something to be attended to only when the Americans were looking, it was their entire existence. Much of the reason for their continued success as anti-infrastructure forces was the effective use of intelligence. For the most part these men did not rely on the PSB, which tended to have a difficult time generating enough hard intelligence to keep the police busy. CIA intelligence played a large part in PRU operations, but unlike other Vietnamese anti-infrastructure forces, PRUs often created and acted upon their own intelligence. After an operation PRUs and their American advisers put together reports based on visual information during the raid, field interrogations, informer reports, and information provided by hoi chanhs. The result was more operations.

The DIOCC also played an important role. Although the PRU was a province-based force, it operated in all the districts depending on where intelligence pointed it. Each DIOCC made it a top priority to take PRU operation reports and combine them with other local intelligence, feeding it back to the PRU if additional targets could be identified. The combination of self-generating intelligence and special attention from the DIOCCs contributed heavily to PRU successes.

After intelligence pointed out a target, PRUs went to work. Operations were small affairs—two squads was generally the upper limit—that struck swiftly at the VCI. PRUs usually worked during the late night or early morning, when their targets were sleeping. PRU operations rarely lasted more than a single day; they were not out in the field vainly chasing an elusive enemy as conventional forces often did. Good intelligence did the chasing for the PRU. It simply went in and picked up the pieces.

Charges of Brutality and Torture

Capture of the enemy was important because the PRU needed additional intelligence gathered from interrogations to continue its success. However, the PRU was not reluctant to kill its intended targets, and it often did. Many Americans back in the United States could never understand this, preferring to view it as cold-blooded murder. But the result of what PRUs did was not much different than body counts from search-and-destroy missions, aerial bombings, and artillery strikes. Both resulted in death to the enemy, but PRU operations were much more discerning than the massive affairs launched by conventional U.S. and ARVN forces. That fact was often lost in the rhetoric of assassination and murder. For the Vietnamese—particularly the PRU—this was total war. There was no time for the niceties of rules of engagement. Americans could afford that; they were going home. But whoever lost in Vietnam was sure to pay the price to the victors, so the PRU fought with all its heart, and sometimes that heart was blackened by years of bitter fighting that no American could ever comprehend.

Even though brutal death was part of the war, American advisers did not generally condone what they considered excesses by the PRU. When an adviser saw excessive brutality it was generally reported through official channels. In December 1969, the PRU in Quang Tri Province captured eight VCI after killing seven others; a number of the captives were district-level cadre. Without bothering to interrogate the prisoners, the PRUs calmly shot five of them, each with a single pistol bullet to the head.[3]

Americans were particularly angered when potential intelligence died with prisoners. But they also learned to use the PRU reputation for violence as a threat to hold over recalcitrant VCI. One CIA province adviser stationed in the Mekong Delta between 1973 and 1975 had the good fortune to capture a regional-level VCI. The VC official was on his way by boat to a cadre meeting when he got lost and ran into a remote RF outpost at the edge of the U Minh forest. He was brought back and turned over to the PIC.

The CIA had known of this man for some time and he was a real prize. The CIA adviser interrogated him, but the VCI was hardcore and would volunteer nothing, saying that he was a simple mechanic on his way to Saigon to visit his daughter. The CIA adviser threatened to turn the prisoner over to the Vietnamese at the regional interrogation center (he was obligated to do so anyway) where he would be away from any Americans. But the VCI continued to resist. He was sent on up to the regional center where the Vietnamese cut out his tongue and finally hanged him. They cared nothing about the intelligence they were losing.[4]

U.S. Advisers and the PRU

American advisers to the ARVN were seen as carrying on the tradition of the combat soldier. They trained their Vietnamese charges to fight the enemy in battle; fire and maneuver—shoot and scoot in grunt parlance—were the basics of warfare. Americans had fought that way because it was the right thing to do. But part of the advisory effort in Vietnam was aimed at training guerrilla soldiers in the ways of the revolutionary battlefield. It was an up-close-and-personal style of warfare, one that could not always make a clear distinction between armed enemy soldier and underground political cadre. American advisers with the PRU fit the second category. They taught—and often fought with—this small group of aggressive unconventional warriors in combat aimed at the VCI.

Although the roots of the PRU dated back to the early 1960s, its role within the Phoenix framework began in 1967. In May of that year NSAM 341 made the PRU part of CORDS under the special assistant to the ambassador (in reality the CIA chief of station), John Hart. The memo only formalized the presence of the PRU within CORDS; the CIA had been using the PRU in the same role for over a year. A letter from John Hart to General Westmoreland in June 1967 resulted in an agreement on the role the PRU and the CIA would play in anti-infrastructure operations. The CIA would be responsible for:

> ... policy guidance, technical direction, support and coordination of the program. The CIA Regional Officer in Charge (ROIC) was to be the next in the chain of command with the CIA Province Officer handling PRU field operations. Therefore, military assigned to PRU would fall under CIA OPCON [operational control] at each level.[5]

At this stage the CIA was to remain firmly in control of the PRU, even though it lacked the manpower to advise PRUs in each and every province. Military advisers were to be assigned to the PRU, under the direction of each ROIC. They were to assist in operational coordination, administration, and training. At the province level their duties were the same except that there would be more hands-on participation. Instructions to advisers stated that "under direction of the CIA province representative . . . [advisers] *will participate,* as appropriate, in operational missions" (emphasis in original).[6]

Compared with American involvement in the Phoenix program as a whole, the number of U.S. military advisers involved in the PRU program was small from beginning to end. In 1967 the CIA requested four officers and forty-nine enlisted men; the request was approved by Westmoreland on 1 July 1967 and was to remain in effect until 30 June 1968. MACV had always felt uncomfortable with this type of unconventional warfare and wanted to reserve the right to withdraw from the PRU program.[7]

Although MACV seemed to be in the perfect position to control its options with the PRU, another factor creeped in to upset the symmetry. Like many problems, this one came from the GVN, although the Americans brought it down on their own shoulders.

By emphasizing the conventional side of the military out of all proportion to the actual situation in South Vietnam, high-level U.S. advisers convinced the GVN to give ARVN manpower preference. All able-bodied males were subject to the draft, even if they were in the NP or the PRU. In many instances, members of the PRU would be drafted out of their units, even if they were clearly best-suited for anti-infrastructure operations. Steps were taken to change the draft laws so that service in the NP, RF/PF, and PRU counted as military service. In the case of the PRU, General Westmoreland personally appealed to the GVN to consider time in the PRU as military service:

> Looking forward to 1968, it seems clear that the PRU should be maintained at peak effectiveness. Presently, however, PRU members are not given credit for military service. Under the new mobilization law a substantial number stand to be inducted

within a very short time. This can only result in seriously compromising the effectiveness of this highly-trained force.[8]

The problem of manpower preference for ARVN continued throughout the war and as Vietnamization took hold, a compromise was worked out that allowed a sufficient pool of qualified draftees for the ARVN as well as the police. The solution was far from perfect, but both the PRU and the police were allowed partial draft exemptions for service in the paramilitary forces.

Despite bureaucratic interference by the GVN, MACV continued its support of the PRU. On 18 November 1968 MACV conducted a review of the PRU advisory program and concluded that "there was a continuing need on an expanded basis for military advisers." The decision was based on the significant contribution made by the PRU in anti-infrastructure operations. MACV forwarded the request for more military PRU adviser slots to JCS, which approved an increase in April 1969. The new number of military advisers with the PRU was thirty-nine officers and sixty-nine enlisted men.[9]

By early 1969 MACV was still sufficiently comfortable with the PRU to continue the military advisory effort. In October 1969 there were 104 military advisers participating in the PRU program throughout South Vietnam. The number of advisers assigned to each region roughly followed the degree of threat posed by the VCI in those areas: the greater the control over the population by the VCI, the more military PRU advisers. Most MACV PRU advisers were from the Army, but three of the military branches were represented. In I Corps there were six Army and five Marine advisers; in II Corps twenty-three Army; III Corps had twenty-five Army and four Marines; and IV Corps had six Army and twenty-four Navy advisers. At the PRU Headquarter and Training Center there were eight Army, two Marine, and one Navy adviser.[10]

As MACV became fond of noting, the 104 military advisers represented a small manpower investment for the large returns of the PRU program. Numerically this was true, but in its totality the PRU program represented the largest per capita advisory program within the pacification effort. Besides the military advisers there were between fifteen and thirty (the CIA has not revealed total figures) CIA advisers who dealt exclusively with the PRU. This represented a total of roughly 125 American PRU advisers. Against a maximum total of five thousand PRUs nationwide the ratio of Americans to PRUs was 2.5 percent. Considering that in 1969 twelve thousand NPFF had only thirty American (U.S.AID) advisers the reason for the PRU program's effectiveness becomes clearer.[11]

As we have seen, the GVN only grudgingly gave priority to anti-infrastructure operations and in the first year or so of CORDS existence, gains against the VCI were almost exclusively because of the American advisory effort. The continued success of the PRU throughout the war was directly because of American participation. Americans remained intimately involved on a broad scale with operations, logistics, training, and financing of the PRU until 1973. The CIA itself fully funded the PRU, providing an average of $7 million a year through 1972. Even after MACV left Vietnam in March 1973, CIA financial and advisory support for the PRU continued right up until the fall of Saigon.[12]

Despite the clear connection between American support of the PRU and its dramatic success against the VCI, MACV began to realize that benefits were outweighed by problems. Reaction on the home front to charges that PRU operatives were CIA assassins forced a reappraisal of American military involvement.

Reexamining the System

The specific motive behind MACV's uneasiness with continued involvement in the PRU program stemmed from bad publicity. Continuing allegations of atrocities both inside the PRU program and within standard military operations focused more attention on an old target—the Phoenix program. The military was already reeling from the November 1969 revelation of the My Lai massacre that had actually occurred on 16 March 1968. The coverage was particularly awkward since it came just as MACV was contemplating what should be done with the PRU and perhaps helped force a premature decision.

Another problem stemmed from unanswered questions regarding the legal status of the PRU. Although it was unquestionably effective against the VCI, there was some controversy about its place within Vietnamese society and law. Under Vietnamese law, former members of the VCI were not permitted to serve in the armed forces. The PRU often was made up of former VCI or guerrillas who had rallied through the Chieu Hoi program. The law remained on the books until Saigon fell. Technically, the PRU existed and operated outside the GVN legal system. The solution would have been to change the law, but circumstances made it simpler to phase the PRU into the National Police.

The problem of a legal framework for the PRU went back to the beginning of Phoenix. As early as October 1968 high-ranking Phoenix officials were pointing out that the PRU organization presented a problem with both the status of U.S. advisers and with who had the authority to command them. William Colby, who would take over the helm of CORDS in less than one month, observed that:

> From time to time a problem arises as to the authority of the Province Chief over the PRU, as distinct from American authority. The PRU has no legal base, but operates under a cover arrangement with JGS [Vietnamese Joint General Staff]....
> [There needs to be] some legal base within the GVN so that the force [PRU] is included within the GVN structure, and so its operations can be given a legal and constitutional character and avoid the danger of extra-legal activity.[13]

This legal question also spilled over to the American advisory effort. As civilians, CIA personnel were not governed by the UCMJ. Nor was the PRU since it was made up of foreign nationals. But the one hundred or so U.S. military advisers were subject to the UCMJ and the lack of legal status held by the PRU provided a chink the arrows of critics were sure to eventually penetrate.

Serious efforts to address the PRU problem always seemed to come back to integration into the National Police. No other practical solution was at hand. Colby and CIA advisers tended to disapprove of integration because such a move would dilute PRU effectiveness. Some PRU advisers even went so far as to turn their displeasure into action: on a number of occasions CIA advisers refused to permit the NPFF to participate in joint operations with the PRU.[14]

Control of the PRU began gradually shifting to the NP in the spring of 1969. A decree by the prime minister on 31 March placed the management of the PRU directly under the Directorate General for National Police (DGNP) and entrusted PRU operational guidelines to the minister of interior and the minister of defense. In principal, the decree placed the PRU within the same framework as the Phoenix program. PRU structure and mission would remain unchanged, but the reins would pass from CORDS and the CIA to the GVN.[15]

While the transfer to the National Police was official the long process of U.S. disengagement from the PRU remained. In the field, both American advisers and Vietnamese province and district chiefs remained unclear as to their command status within the PRU. As usual, official proclamations issued in Saigon were not always easily implemented out in the countryside. Both GVN province officials and U.S. advisers continued to vie for control; the Americans felt that to give control of the PRU to the province chief would result in an end to its effectiveness. To clarify the fact that the PRU was now part of the police, the new PRU director within the DGNP, Major Nguyen Van Lang, gave a series of briefings at the PRU training center at Vung Tau. All PRU leaders and American advisers were required to attend in the hopes that all points of confusion would be clarified.[16]

The easiest way for MACV to solve the management confusion and at the same time remove the military from the rising PRU controversy was to pull out of the program. The first step was taken on 30 September 1969, when MACV reversed itself and issued instructions that PRU advisers no longer would participate in PRU combat operations:

> They will act only in strict advisory capacity, remaining at command posts, at launch sites, in command ships on helicopter insertions and/or at fire support bases; they will, however, participate fully with PRU chiefs in operational planning and ensure that proper mission coordination is effected, and that air, fire, other support properly laid on.[17]

Two factors combined to make MACV reverse its 1967 decision to require U.S. advisers to accompany PRUs on operations. First, press attention on the Phoenix program prevented MACV from keeping in close operational touch with the PRU. Somehow the military thought that if it kept at arms-length from the PRU it would not be tainted by allegations of brutality. In many cases it simply didn't realize that critics were out to tar both Americans and Vietnamese with the same atrocity brush.

Second, as Vietnamization took hold, MACV correctly saw that one of the primary areas that demanded immediate South Vietnamese self-sufficiency was the Phoenix program. If the GVN couldn't control the VCI without help from the Americans it was lost. Because there were so few military advisers involved in the PRU program it was one of the easiest from which to disengage.

General Creighton Abrams felt the pressure to disengage the military from continued participation in the PRU program. In fact, he wanted the Army out immediately. The 104 military advisers with the PRU were to be pulled out by the end of October 1970. The CIA did not appreciate the sudden change of heart and resented being left holding the bag. A CIA counterproposal suggested that MACV scale down the number of military advisers to sixty by the end of FY 1971.[18]

MACV would have none of it. Abrams was adamant about immediate withdrawal and stopped filling PRU adviser vacancies created by end-of-tour departures. At that rate, military participation in the PRU program would end as planned in October 1970.[19]

Confusion regarding the PRU, as well as reluctance to continue military involvement in the program, was not confined only to U.S. officials in Vietnam. Objections made their way directly to the office of the secretary of defense in Washington. A report by Secretary of the Army Stanley R. Resor questioned both the PRU program and Phoenix in general:

> In my view, one of the serious problems attending the Phoenix program is the danger that we may make the program more "efficient," without due regard to the social and moral costs which that might entail. I believe that we should review the

program to determine if its emphasis should shift from the present dragnet system to a more selective attack on the [VCI] leadership.[20]

Of course, the secretary of the army was reporting not on what the Phoenix program was designed to do—selectively target VCI—but rather on the method used in most provinces to neutralize VCI—cordon and search. But his point was well made: the existence of the PRU outside the legal framework of the National Police could not continue.

More briefing papers from Vietnam found their way up the bureaucratic ladder in Washington. They were read and reaction made its way back down. American reassessment of its involvement with the PRU soon came from the highest levels. In November 1969 Secretary of Defense Melvin Laird called for a reevaluation of involvement with the PRU:

> I would like to outline my concern over Department of Defense involvement in the Provincial Reconnaissance Unit Program. My concern is accentuated by the mounting publicity that has recently been directed toward isolated incidents involving U.S. personnel in the Republic of Vietnam. . . . I believe the U.S. military involvement in advisory functions other than those concerning RVN military units and pacification should be reviewed. One such function is the PRU Program. . . . I believe we should divest ourselves of this mission as early and as completely as possible. . . .[21]

In his memo about rethinking U.S. involvement with the PRU, Secretary of Defense Melvin Laird had fallen victim to the notion that pacification was purely peaceful; he did not regard anti-infrastructure operations as an integral part of pacification. But part of his argument was valid. There would be charges of American complicity in atrocities as long as U.S. advisers remained with the PRU.

Yet in one form or another American advisers remained with the PRU until the end of the war. The only difference lay in the chain of command. After mid-1969 the PRU fell under the command of the province chief, who was to use it in an anti-infrastructure role. But as was the case with the NPFF, GVN province officials often did not follow the guidelines and PRUs became virtual palace guards or, worse, armed thugs used to extort the population by ruthless province officials. This was not always the case, but it happened often enough late in the war to cause concern within CORDS.[22]

Military involvement in the PRU program had been a bargain for MACV. Aside from the salaries of the military advisers involved, funding for the PRU came entirely out of the CIA's pocket. For that small investment MACV received intelligence from one of the best indigenous sources in South Vietnam and it could claim partial credit for a highly successful anti-infrastructure effort. During the final ten months of U.S. military involvement, the PRU conducted 50,770 missions, reporting 7,408 Viet Cong and VCI captured and 4,406 killed. One hundred-seventy-nine PRUs were killed during the same period. For a force of fewer than five thousand men, those were tremendous results.[23]

But at this late stage in the war, image was more important than results. Following the dramatic surge in anti-war sentiment back in the States after the Cambodian incursion in the spring of 1970, MACV could not afford any more public relations black eyes. In the opinion of the Joint Chiefs of Staff and Secretary of Defense Melvin Laird, the PRU was another potential embarrassment. Yet the Defense Department recognized the importance of the program to the Phoenix effort; the military just wanted someone else to run it. The chairman of the Joint Chiefs of Staff wrote that ". . . the importance of the PRU program in neutralizing the VCI is fully appreciated [but the JCS] concurs in the desirability of withdrawing U.S. military advisers." The JCS simply wanted someone else to do the dirty work.[24]

And so it was. The CIA took over the job of advising and managing the PRU, as it had in the years before 1968. The numbers of PRU personnel and operations remained fairly constant throughout the rest of the war, but the CIA lacked the manpower to fill in all the gaps left by MACV. Whether the shifting advisory situation noticeably affected PRU performance is difficult to judge. However, most observers agreed that the PRU remained a formidable force.

PRU Effectiveness against the VCI

The PRU was called the most effective action arm within the Phoenix program. The reputation was largely true. Despite complaints that PRUs were brutal, few American advisers could find fault with their courage, combat ability, or competence. On the whole, the PRUs were the best fighters in each and every province. Advisers reported that PRUs were the only forces that could be consistently relied upon to perform their anti-infrastructure task. But like the rest of the Phoenix program, PRU effectiveness varied from province to province and over time. In 1967, at what was perhaps the height of PRU operational independence and effectiveness, U.S. officials in Gia Dinh Province reported that the province chief had destroyed PRU effectiveness by dividing its twenty-one men into sections, a few to each district. In Binh Chanh District there were only seven PRUs. Worse still, the few PRUs in each district often were unavailable for operations. An adviser reported that in May 1967 all the province's PRU agents were in jail for a drunken brawl they had started with a local Revolutionary Development team.[25]

Late in the war PRU effectiveness was also spotty, mostly because the new structure that placed the PRU within the National Police resulted in a corresponding decrease in U.S. advisory and financial input. It can be said that PRU effectiveness was directly proportional to American control. As long as the PRUs were paid and controlled by the Americans they worked well; when they became part of the GVN's unwieldy and often corrupt and incompetent system, performance suffered. The GVN did not emphasize anti-infrastructure operations, even near the end of the war. For example, in Kien Giang Province during the final two years of the war, the PRU had degenerated into bands of armed thugs who extorted money from the local population at will. Because the GVN was losing control of the country, the PRU sometimes became a haven for criminals and ARVN defectors looking to make some easy money.[26]

Despite the inevitable problems from area to area, PRUs were man for man the best anti-infrastructure arm available to the Phoenix program. However, their small numbers doomed their efforts to insignificance in the big picture.

In mid-1968 the PRU was getting rave reviews at CORDS headquarters in Saigon. At the end of May there were 4,205 PRU agents in South Vietnam, an increase of 532 since the beginning of the year. Fifty-eight percent of these were in III and IV Corps, the areas with the most serious VCI problem. Anti-infrastructure operations made up 65 percent of all PRU missions in 1968, with the biggest increase coming in May. By the end of May 1968 the PRU had conducted 1,730 anti-infrastructure operations (out of 2,650 operations of all types), as opposed to a monthly average of 1,300 (out of an average total of 2,200 operations) during February, March, and April. The PRU killed or captured 968 Viet Cong in May 1968, a decline from February's total of 1,165. The PRU managed to score these totals while suffering few casualties of their own. That presented a kill ratio of 25:1—twenty-five VC killed for every one PRU operative. When captured VCI were included in the ratio—a majority of PRU neutralizations—the figure jumped to 75:1. But this total included VC regulars as well as VCI. In May, PRUs accounted for sixty-nine VCI captured or killed, or 20 percent of all PRU neutralizations. The rest were VC guerrillas. During February, March, and April of 1968 PRUs had 188 VCI neutralizations, or 12.5 percent of the total number of VC captured and killed. These figures did not include apprehensions made by the PRU during joint operations with the NPFF or RF/PF.[27]

The figures looked good to CORDS. And they were. By the middle of 1970 PRU effectiveness continued to climb. Between January and July the PRU had killed 285 VCI, captured 553, and had been responsible with rallying twenty-four. This represented 862 VCI neutralized, or 7 percent of the total by all GVN and American forces. That was the problem: the PRU was such a small organization that, despite its tremendous effectiveness, it could only manage to account for 7 percent of total VCI neutralizations. The neutralization rates for 1970 were higher than in 1969 despite a numerically smaller PRU—in mid-1970 its strength had fallen to some thirty-five hundred members nationwide because of the restructuring of the National Police.[28]

Throughout the war operational appraisals consistently

spoke highly of the PRU. On 22 December 1968, William Colby passed along a cable to the CIA office in Saigon noting that the PRU was wracking up dramatic successes against the VCI:

> At 1600 Hours 17 Dec. a 60-man PRU unit supported by six troop helicopters, 1 C&C [command and control] and four gunships inserted . . . approximately 9 kilometers south of Can Tho. The action caught the VC in the process of assembling. The action lasted until 1730 hours and resulted in 23 VC KIA [killed in action], 4 VCC [VC captured], 3 weapons captured and 10 kilos of documents. Two PRU were wounded.[29]

Praise for the PRU continued and the figures seemed to back it up. By 1971 the PRU accounted for 422 VCI neutralized per 1,000 PRU strength, or almost one VCI neutralized by every two PRU operatives. This was astronomically high, especially when placed beside the second-highest man-for-man neutralization rate—the National Police (including the NPFF), which accounted for a paltry 36 VCI for every 1,000 NP.[30]

Clearly the PRU was a very efficient VCI hunter, easily living up to its reputation as the best anti-infrastructure unit in Vietnam. No one could have disputed the Phoenix program's effectiveness if everyone had performed as well as the PRU. But when the final count came in PRUs accounted for only a small portion of all VCI neutralizations.

The PRU did hurt the VCI, but MACV was using a double standard when judging them. Saigon criticized Phoenix because it did not eliminate a high percentage of the total estimated VCI strength nationwide, yet it praised the PRU based solely on man-to-man ratios that ignored the total VCI picture. Saigon might have done better to find a middle ground, some method that credited overall statistics and individual unit performance. In the end all that counted was how the communists' ability to continue functioning in South Vietnam was affected, not total numbers.

Most importantly, the real benefit of examining PRU effectiveness was not to prove that it was the best in the anti-infrastructure business, but to see why it was. PRU operational professionalism and the use of intelligence were the two main reasons. One "typical" operation provides some insight into why the PRU became known as the best.

A PRU Operation in Ben Cat[31]

PRU operations were not all gunfire and bloodshed. In fact, if the intelligence was good VCI targets would be surprised and would have no chance to put up a fight. Most operations went off without a hitch; they could almost be called mundane. And in many cases good intelligence began with the Chieu Hoi program. Communist ralliers provided Phoenix with the initial intelligence for operations that led to the capture of important VCI throughout South Vietnam. In Ben Cat District the Phoenix program netted enough intelligence through Chieu Hoi to capture Nguyen Van Dang. Dang was the assistant party secretary to the Chau Thanh VC District Committee. But his capture was only the first cast of a widening net.

The Ben Cat DIOCC had compiled information on Dang from the interrogation of a Hoi Chanh and, using the intelligence, targeted Dang for neutralization. On 13 August 1969 the PRU team assigned to Ben Cat prepared for another routine operation. Information from the hoi chanh indicated that Dang was holed up in a tunnel used as a safe location for various VCI. Far from being safe, however, the tunnel served as a trap for Dang as the unit moved in for the capture.

A field interrogation produced quick results; Dang was in no mood to anger his captors, so he quickly revealed the location of another tunnel that held Dang Van Mai, a former assistant party secretary, and Vo Van Banh, the Viet Cong security section chief for the district. The PRU wasted no time in reacting.

A team moved quickly to the tunnel pointed out by Dang and called on the two VCI to surrender. But these two were not as willing to surrender as Dang had been. After a short, sharp firefight the PRU had its prisoners. Banh was wounded and evacuated by helicopter before he could be interrogated, but Mai and a large stack of captured documents were taken immediately to the Province Interrogation Center (PIC). Mai and the documents provided the intelligence for the next step in the operation.

The province PRU chief and his American counterpart conducted the interrogation using the captured documents both to jog Mai's memory and to trip him up if tried to lie. Mai had nothing to gain by concealing information; he revealed the names of five additional Party members as well as their usual haunts and probable routines. The district party chairman, Nguyen Van Kia, became the main target.

Kia was a real prize because he was a "legal," a communist operating within the legal system of South Vietnam. He had the required ID card and worked as a horse cart driver, using his legal status and mobility as a driver to maintain contact with other members of the infrastructure. Without the intelligence gathered during the interrogation of Mai, Phoenix would have had a difficult time tracking down Kia.

Since Kia was a special case the PRU used special methods for his capture. A few days after the interrogation a PRU team divided into four- and five-man cells prepared to snatch Kia. They all dressed in civilian clothes and carried only pistols. Since no one could predict exactly when and where Kia would show up, the PRU was positioned at the main traffic intersections within the target's suspected area of operation. Kia showed up driving his cart and the PRU picked him up without incident.

The remaining four VCI named by Mai were even easier to capture. Like Kia, all four were legal residents of Mai's village in Ben Cat District and all held jobs that allowed them to fit into the society around them so as not to arouse suspicion. Although the arrest of Dang Van Mai was quiet and had aroused little attention, it was a sure bet his comrades would hear of his capture before long. The PRU had only hours before its targets would disappear from the district.

The captured documents did most of the work for the PRU by providing addresses of the four VCI. By early evening, only an hour or so after the capture of Mai, another PRU team closed in on the remaining four VCI. The operation was a success. All four were captured in their homes. The PRU had netted the chairman of the PRP executive committee, the civilian proselyting section chief, liaison section chief, and a district security cadre. All four were quickly sent to the DIOCC where they fingered the five remaining district committee-level cadre. Once these five were arrested, the VCI in Ben Cat District would be completely wiped out.

One of the remaining VCI was Phan Van Mua, chief of the supply and transportation section in the district. By day Mua watched over his small herd of water buffalo (purchased by the Viet Cong to provide him with a cover); by night he used his livestock to transport rice to a Viet Cong pickup point across a nearby river. Early the next morning, as Mua sat in the shade watching his buffalo, the PRU appeared and carried him off to the DIOCC. The Viet Cong had to find another way to get their rice that night.

Nguyen Thi Bah was the VC message section chief for the district. It was her job to coordinate the clandestine communications network by which the VCI passed messages. Her job was especially dangerous because it required her to move around the district frequently as she carried messages back and forth between various cadre. The PRU did not know her exact location, so it set up ambush teams along the routes revealed during the interrogation of the previously captured VCI. On the second evening of the watch Bah was captured.

A few days later the remaining three VCI were captured and Ben Cat District was rid of the VCI, for the time being. The Viet Cong would attempt to reintroduce a political infrastructure to the district, but would be at a disadvantage because the new cadre would lack familiarity with the people and the surroundings. As long as the Phoenix program continued along the same effective lines, the GVN would have the initiative.

This Phoenix operation ranks high on the list of effectiveness and many Phoenix advisers only dreamed of such spectacular results. Everything went right for the PRU and the DIOCC. First, a valuable Hoi Chanh provided timely information that led to a key cadre who in turn revealed information on other VCI. The documents captured allowed the DIOCC to add details that probably would have been unavailable with interrogation alone. Perhaps most importantly, it is clear from the after-action report that the American adviser at the PIC and the PRU chief had the ability to quickly translate the captured documents into useful intelligence. The result was information that could be acted upon immediately. And while captured documents were a common commodity during the Vietnam War, the PRU in Ben Cat District was particularly lucky with the stack it recovered from the tunnel. All factors clearly combined to make a successful Phoenix operation.

The PRU could never have become the effective anti-infrastructure force it did without massive American help. The CIA trained the operatives, paid them, and in the beginning, fought with them. Because the PRU was a small force, it received a greater degree of individualized training from the American advisers. The National Police and the RF/PF were not so fortunate. They had to substitute quantity for quality, spreading scarce resources and advisers throughout the ranks. The PRU had the benefit of CIA and military advisers, as well as better pay, an important consideration in the underpaid South Vietnamese military and paramilitary. With all the benefits of being in the PRU it is small wonder that it became the best in the business.

Besides the CIA and the Army, another group of American advisers trained and fought with the PRU, honing it into a cohesive and effective fighting force. But these Americans weren't soldiers, they were sailors.

United States Navy SEALs

The legend that grew up around the U.S. Navy's SEALs (sea, air, and land were the three elements SEALs are trained to operate in) did not die when United States forces left Vietnam in 1973. To this day SEALs are larger-than-life covert warriors with a reputation for fierceness and efficiency. But whatever they have become today, the SEALs were born and bred in Vietnam.

When American involvement in Vietnam was in its infancy, President John F. Kennedy brought to public attention the warfare technique that came to be called counterinsurgency. His most famous creation was the Green Berets, the U.S. Army Special Forces. But he also authorized the Navy SEALs. At an NSC meeting in January 1962 Kennedy asked about counterinsurgency capabilities in all the services. He knew that the Special Forces were already operational, but what about the Navy? "We have our SEALs," replied the Navy's NSC representative, knowing full well the SEALs were barely off the drawing board.[32]

Back in June 1961 the chief of Naval Operations had ordered a study on the "development of an improved guerrilla/counterguerrilla capability." By December the general outline for SEAL Teams 1 and 2 had taken shape, waiting only for final approval.[33] Now there was no more time for planning. On the same day Kennedy asked about the Navy's counterinsurgency capability, word went out to activate SEAL Team 1 at Coronado, California and SEAL Team 2 at Little Creek, Virginia. SEAL Team 1 consisted of five officers and fifty enlisted men drawn from the ranks of UDT 11 and 12 (Underwater Demolition Team), and SEAL Team 2 had ten officers and fifty enlisted men, mostly from UDT 21. The history of UDTs went back to WWII, when Navy swimmers scouted beaches in both the Atlantic and Pacific Theaters, gathering valuable intelligence on beach conditions and enemy defenses. Their forays paved the way for landings such as Anzio, Normandy, and Okinawa. Although many SEAL operations in Vietnam were in support of the Phoenix program, a majority of them were reconnaissance missions such as those in WWII, or small-unit strike missions aimed at the heart of enemy territory.

The SEALs understood their mission from day one:

> To develop a specialized capability for sabotage, demolition and other clandestine activities conducted in and from restricted waters, rivers, and canals, and to conduct training for selected U.S. and indigenous personnel in a wide variety of skills for use in naval clandestine operations.

The SEALs were destined for Vietnam.[34]

In July 1962 the first SEALs arrived in Vietnam. Their mission was to train Biet Hai (Junk Force Commando Platoon) and Lien Doi Nguoi Nhai (LDNN—South Vietnamese SEAL equivalents) personnel in special tactics. SEALs also found themselves on the cutting edge of the war in the early days. SEALs on duty with training teams were sent to Danang, where they worked with elements of MACV SOG (Special Operations Group) preparing LDNN to run operations in North Vietnam.

In 1966 SEAL activity expanded rapidly. In February SEAL Team 1 deployed Detachment Golf to Nha Be for duty in the Rung Sat Special Zone (RSSZ)—also known as the Forest of Assassins. The RSSZ was a tangled area of jungle and villages stretching from just east of Saigon to the South China Sea. Both the GVN and the Viet Cong considered it strategic ground because control of the RSSZ meant control of the vital link between Saigon and the sea.

In January 1967 SEAL Team 2 sent Detachment Alfa to the Mekong Delta, with some platoons going to Nha Be and My Tho, others to Binh Thuy. A second unit, Detachment Bravo, was made up of specially trained SEALs whose mission was to advise PRUs in anti-infrastructure operations, sometimes in support of the Phoenix program. SEAL Team 1 tasked Detachments Bravo and Echo with serving as advisers to the PRU program on highly classified missions. Unlike the SEAL detachments in the RSSZ, which were under the command of COMNAVFORV (Commander Naval Forces, Vietnam), Detachments Bravo and Echo came directly under MACV.[35]

These SEALs were not simple advisers and planners; they also actively led most of the combat missions. Anti-infrastructure operations were generally "snatches," nighttime raids into enemy territory with the express purpose of bringing back a live prisoner, the essence of the Phoenix program. After a successful raid in September 1967 a SEAL lieutenant told a reporter, "We like to grab people. That's of real value. Killing them does no good. Any time we make a hit we're there to take them alive. But once we're seen, we're compromised. Our primary mission ceases and we turn to our secondary mission—killing VC."[36]

A combination of superb training, special weapons, and a hands-off attitude from the Navy and MACV got results for the SEALs. Small teams of SEALs working with PRUs would slip ashore in enemy territory night or day to ambush enemy guerrilla units, kidnap an unwary political cadre, or destroy a weapons cache. The Viet Cong in the Delta never knew when or where the SEALs would strike. It was a fitting role reversal for Vietnam's guerrilla war.

Because SEAL duty in Vietnam was extraordinarily strenuous and dangerous, members served only six-month tours instead of the normal twelve- and thirteen-month stints pulled by the Army and Marines. Yet many SEALs returned to Vietnam after rotating stateside, extending for three and sometimes four tours. In 1968 through 1970, the height of SEAL participation in Vietnam, SEAL personnel numbered around 250 in-country at one time, a small number for the results produced.[37]

SEALs generally operated apart from the everyday grind of the Army's search-and-destroy strategy, though on a few occasions SEALs participated in the cordon-and-search operations that often characterized U.S. military participation in pacification. They were not well-suited for the role. On the morning of 6 September 1968 a platoon from Alfa Detachment, SEAL Team 1, was inserted by boat into a VC-controlled village in Go Cong Province. Along on the mission were one hundred PRU and one hundred fifty uniformed NPFF. After patrolling several thousand meters around the village, the force surrounded and searched the villages, hoping to snare important members of the VCI. After four hours and several "house calls" at the residences of suspected VCI, the mission was terminated. The SEALs were not enthusiastic about their role. An after-action summary observed: "Do not recommend SEALs operate with this large a group. Creates havoc."[38]

SEALs definitely operated best in small teams. That was the way they were trained. Before leaving their base in the States SEAL teams trained for the type of warfare they would encounter in Vietnam. Besides exercises in mobile operations, counterinsurgency, specialized weapons training, and heavy doses of physical endurance training, SEALs spent time in the classroom learning about the enemy they would face. Both officers and enlisted men learned about the communist political infrastructure to understand its importance to the Viet Cong war effort. Because the SEALs emphasized anti-infrastructure operations, they could boast of dislodging the communists' hold on many parts of the Mekong Delta. SEAL advisers to the PRU operated in twelve of fourteen Delta provinces and by the end of 1968 netted an average of eight hundred VCI captured or killed per month.[39]

SEALs against the VCI

There was no such thing as a typical SEAL anti-infrastructure operation. But the successful ones did have one thing in common—they used timely intelligence. Some intelligence came through the PSB or other Phoenix assets, though much of it came straight from the CIA. But the SEALs often found it was more convenient to run their own intelligence nets. These nets generally were made up of specially trained PRUs and were designed to penetrate the VCI. Sometimes things went awry. On 15 November 1968, 3rd Platoon, Detachment Alfa, SEAL Team 2 received word that one of its PRU agents was in trouble. He had been posing as a minor VC official and had been uncovered and captured. The SEALs went in to get him out of the fire. The agent was rescued and the SEALs nabbed three VC security cadre, who in turn led the SEALs to a large cache of weapons.[40]

More conventional "snatch" operations were the hallmark of SEAL participation in the Phoenix program. They went deep into hostile territory the Viet Cong called home and captured cadre, bringing them back for interrogation. But because the SEALs operated in the midst of heavy concentrations of VC security forces, they often lacked time for the niceties of capturing an enemy. SEALs and their PRU teams often killed as many VCI as they captured. This was mainly because VCI neutralized by the SEALs did not include defectors through the Chieu Hoi program or the numbers of cadre who were rounded up in cordon-and-search operations. Only those VCI captured or killed by the SEALs and their PRUs were counted. Obviously, in the heat of battle many VCI were going to be killed; that was war. And because SEALs and PRUs operated deep in enemy territory they often lacked the luxury of taking time to capture a prisoner and drag him back to safety. When bullets flew and the enemy threatened to surround them, SEALs and PRUs shot first and took prisoners second.

During the early stages of the Phoenix program, American anti-infrastructure operatives, such as the SEALs, CIA PRU advisers, and U.S. Army Phoenix advisers, bore the brunt of operations as CORDS tried to get the police geared to handle most of the work. But the police sometimes were involved as the SEALs tried to use intelligence from whatever source they could. On 12 May 1968 the Dinh Tuong Province National Police gave a prisoner to the local SEALs for interrogation. The prisoner agreed to lead the SEALs into a village that had long been controlled by the VCI and point out the main cadre. Six suspects were arrested by the National Police. Interrogations yielded the names and locations of thirteen more "Viet Cong espionage/intelligence agents," all of whom were rounded up by the SEALs. The after-action report said intelligence gathered from the operation led to the "arrest of over 100 other Viet Cong agents operating in and near the provincial capital of My Tho." These agents had penetrated "every U.S. and allied agency and military unit in the city and their removal completely blocked the enemy from knowledge of U.S. and allied intentions within Dinh Tuong Province."[41]

As the SEALs became more proficient at "snatch" operations, the VCI could not consider themselves safe even in the most secure areas. On at least two operations in June 1968, SEALs in Vinh Long Province captured communist cadre from under the noses of their security guards in Viet Cong-controlled areas. On 9 June, reacting to intelligence, SEALs were inserted into their mission area by boat and quickly captured thirteen VCI as they attended a political rally (because SEAL operational reports are still highly classified, many do not include the mission location). On 30 June a SEAL platoon pursued one particularly troublesome and clever VC tax collector. Because the insert zone was near an area of heavy river boat traffic, the SEALs made their landing in a Vietnamese junk. On foot, they moved to the prearranged ambush site: a dense grove of banana trees. They found more than they had bargained for. Besides the VC tax collector, four other black-clad cadre, a platoon of security guerrillas, and eight "cargo handlers" from two VC sampans were pulled up to the bank. Rather than risk being overwhelmed, the SEALs opened fire, killing all eight of the VC boatmen as they ran for their sampans, as well as three of the VC security guards. Two VCI were captured, although the tax collector managed to escape.[42]

SEALs also tried to work with other Vietnamese units that sometimes operated against the VCI, particularly the RF/PF. Unfortunately, the RF/PF was not always very good at it. During a two-day operation on 6 and 7 November 1968, four SEALs, a platoon of PRUs, and one platoon from a local RF company were assigned to conduct ambushes on known VC trails. Since there were no American advisers operating with the RF, they soon lost interest in their jobs. In fact, they did absolutely nothing. Not once did the RF leave the main road, nor did it bother to make radio contact with the SEALs. One RF trooper had an epileptic seizure. Despite the RF's lack of involvement, the SEALs and their PRUs managed to pick up one known VCI.[43]

Of course, the highest priority went to high-level VCI. When the SEALs got intelligence on one of the big fish they moved quickly. On 22 February 1969 seven men from 5th Platoon, Alfa Detachment, SEAL Team 2 set an ambush based on intelligence handed down from the PSB. The report said some high-ranking VCI were on their way toward a meeting near the My Tho River. The SEALs and their PRUs reached the outskirts of a village at last light and set a hasty ambush. Almost immediately eight apparently unarmed men walked through the killing zone—the SEALs let them pass. Within a few more minutes seven men—this time heavily armed—walked down the trail and the SEALs opened fire. Five were killed and two captured. Intelligence reports said three of the Viet Cong were "very high-ranking Viet Cong officials."[44]

During another specifically targeted operation, on 1 July 1969, G Platoon, Golf Detachment, SEAL Team 1 set out to capture four important VCI, including Bui Ngoc Tan, the Viet Cong Party chief for Long An Province. All four VCI were known to be meeting in Ben Luc District near the Vam Co Dong River. The SEALs were inserted by Boston Whaler. As they crept over the side of the boat, they made their way upstream to where the VCI were to meet. The heavy security net set out by the VC spotted the SEALs and a sharp firefight erupted. The SEALs got the best of it, but all four targets were killed during the action. Besides the province Party chief, the SEALs neutralized Nguyen Thanh Tuan, a squad leader in the VC military intelligence section for SR-3; Huyen Tan Cong, the assistant squad leader; and Pham Van Hiep, chief commo-liaison cadre for SR-3. Later the SEALs found out they had also killed the assistant Party secretary for Long An Province.[45]

At first glance it may seem as though the SEALs could never fail. In reality, many of their missions turned up empty. Faulty intelligence, early warnings to the Viet Cong of impending SEAL operations, and lack of adequate support from the Vietnamese combined to let hundreds of VCI escape death or capture at the hands of the SEALs and their PRUs. The SEALs' operational independence and penchant for secrecy also combined to inflate the image of their exploits. Journalists rarely saw them in action and their figures were not subject to the same scrutiny as other Phoenix statistics. In some cases SEALs were privately reported to have been dismal failures at selectively neutralizing the VCI, although none of them could be accused of lacking in warlike qualities.[46]

Like all other aspects of American involvement in the Phoenix program, the SEALs found themselves more and more constrained as the date for U.S. withdrawal from Vietnam drew closer. By 1970 problems and restrictions that were tightening around the Army also began to constrict the SEALs. Popular condemnation of the war at home and revelations of the brutal massacre of civilians at My Lai led to a redefinition of the rules of engagement. Rumors that the Phoenix program was assassinating innocent civilians raised questions about the SEALs' legal status while operating against the Viet Cong infrastructure.

Although congressional inquiries did not turn up any hard evidence to back the charges against Phoenix, the SEALs became caught up in the swirl of discontent. Public knowledge of SEAL operations was limited, but all units involved with Phoenix were affected by the furor. In June 1971 SEALs cut back on anti-infrastructure operations because MACV was uncomfortable with the charge that "civilians" were the target of Phoenix and the SEALs. In mid-July, all SEAL operations except for Bright Light (operations aimed at freeing American and ARVN POWs in Viet Cong prison camps within South Vietnam) were put on hold until a team from Navy headquarters visited SEAL personnel and tested them on their understanding of the rules of engagement.[47]

The SEALs had ceased most operations on their own initiative because, in the words of one SEAL member, "the rules were so strict we had to even announce that we were coming before we could shoot, and then we could shoot only when we were shot at."[48] Things had changed drastically since the early days of SEAL operations in the Delta. Even the PRU training mission which had been so successful was altered. New standing orders written in late 1970 specifically said SEALs were "not permitted to actively participate in combat missions."[49]

As Vietnamization released advisers, soldiers, and sailors from duty in Vietnam, so, too, did the SEALs begin to trickle home. By June 1971 most SEALs had returned to Little Creek and Coronado, leaving behind a small contingent of advisers with the Vietnamese Navy.

Rough totals for SEAL involvement in Vietnam were impressive. By the end of 1970 SEALs and their South Vietnamese allies had killed more than two thousand Viet Cong and captured about twenty-seven hundred, many of them important members of the political infrastructure. All this had been accomplished relatively cheaply in terms of SEAL casualties. Only three dozen or so were killed during nine years of involvement in Vietnam.[50]

In the overall conduct of the war, SEALs did not change the tide of battle. But they did illustrate that a few well-trained men using counterinsurgency tactics and specially trained allies could devastate a guerrilla enemy, particularly the political infrastructure. General William Westmoreland was quick to sum up their contribution when he said, "I would like to have a thousand more like them."[51]

9

Long Arm of the Law: Courts and Detention Systems

Much of American outrage over the war in Vietnam was directed at what was viewed as South Vietnam's lack of regard for democracy and human rights. The Phoenix program in particular bore the brunt of much of the criticism because it was seen as the leading edge of a system that disregarded individual rights and threw noncombatants and victims of hearsay into an inhuman prison system. Like many of the accusations against the Phoenix program some of these charges were true, some not. All were exaggerated.

South Vietnam was at war and was forced to take special steps to protect itself from an enemy that struck from within as well as from North Vietnam. These steps had no precedence in Vietnamese history and culture, which had relied on tradition and religion to solve its legal woes. What laws it did have were introduced first by the Chinese and then by the French. Both were considered oppressors. Although the Americans were not imperialists and South Vietnam was a sovereign state that instituted its own laws, Vietnamese peasants were suspicious and never learned to trust or accept this new concept of law.

The emergence of the Phoenix program put a strain on an already overloaded legal and detention system and throughout the war this problem was never adequately redressed. However, steps were taken that improved prison conditions, diminished abuses of arrest and interrogation, and strengthened due process under the law.

The laws that empowered the police and the Phoenix program to arrest and try members of the VCI were well-founded in the South Vietnamese legal system. National Security Laws had been passed to cope with the internal rebellion and Saigon saw itself as protecting the young nation from destruction by the communists. In addition, infrastructure neutralization was well within the parameters of the Geneva Convention concerning treatment of prisoners. Torture during interrogation and abuse within the prison system were not standard procedure and steps were taken to correct them.

Perhaps the greatest shortcoming of the Phoenix program was its inability to cope with the flood of VCI suspects into the detention system. Innocent people swept up in the dragnet sat in jail for weeks and sometimes months before they were interrogated and either charged or released. Many were eventually released for lack of evidence, but the damage was already done; the GVN had provided a willing pool of converts to the Viet Cong cause. On the other hand, the average sentence given to proven VCI was less than one year. To the average citizen, it often seemed that the Phoenix program treated innocent suspects worse than it did convicted VCI. In many cases they were correct.

Sitting and Waiting

In 1970 the war was quiet over most of South Vietnam. At least as far as wars go it was quiet. The Tet Offensive had given way to guerrilla actions, isolated terrorism and, of course, the pacification battle in the countryside. Phoenix advisers who had served in Vietnam in 1968 and 1969 agreed that the countryside was quiet compared to the old days. And they used the driving rule to prove it. The driving rule said that if you could drive a Jeep across the district without getting shot at, mortared, or generally harassed by the Viet Cong then it was pacified. Hardly a scientific methodology for determining pacification, but in many ways it was an accurate reflection of reality.

The Phoenix program was in high gear, bringing in more VCI than in the previous two years. Most importantly, the program was attempting to work out the flaws and shortcomings that had plagued it since its inception. The biggest problem had been what to do with the hundreds and sometimes thousands of VCI arrested nationwide each month. Many innocent suspects sat for weeks or months in province jails waiting for the Province Security Committee to convene, review the evidence, and release the suspects on grounds of insufficient evidence. Throughout the war, Phoenix was unable to correct the injustice of holding suspects for long periods without bringing them to trial. In many cases the Phoenix program had extensive dossiers or blacklists as evidence of the suspect's association with the VCI. But in many other cases there was no evidence at all.

On 14 March 1970, seven women sat in a small, bare cell, absentmindedly brushing at the flies buzzing around their faces. They were being held in the Kien Phong Province Interrogation Center in Cao Lanh, which doubled as a detention center for accused VCI waiting for a hearing. They were all suspected of being VCI.[1] The rules were strict and simple. The suspects were not allowed to speak to one another and no unauthorized visitors were permitted in the PIC.

The cell was about ten feet by twelve feet with a concrete floor where the women sat, ate, and slept. Although there was no room to walk around, the women did not seem to mind sleeping on the floor, although they complained of the cold that seeped through their thin sleeping mats and into their frail bodies at night. The PIC provided no blankets to keep them warm.

Meals were sent to the women and the guards allowed their families to bring extra food and clothes. But these women seemed to be lost in the system and it was unlikely that their families even knew where they were. During the day the seven women worked in the PIC cleaning offices or outside in the compound doing various jobs.

By Third World standards the PIC was not a horrible place. No stories of torture and brutality came from behind the barbed wire walls, the prisoners got two meals a day, and none languished for endless days in cells. All prisoners worked on the grounds or were allowed out of their cells daily for exercise.

None of the seven women complained of maltreatment and none looked the worse for their confinement.

But none of them knew what their eventual fate would be either. One small woman, Nguyen Thi Hon, had been arrested one month before and was afraid she might never again see her family. She said all she did was give rice to some local guerrillas who came through her village one night. The local police heard about this from a neighbor and Hon was arrested a few days later. She clearly was not a VCI, and the Province Security Committee probably would agree, but it had already been a month and Hon was still in the PIC. Only one of the women, Thuong Thi Dung, had been cleared by the Province Security Committee for release.

None of the women knew their rights under South Vietnamese National Security law. Theoretically the Province Security Committee had three months to decide their cases, and although none of them had been in prison that long, it was a serious inconvenience for them if they were deemed innocent by the committee. The inability of the GVN legal system to quickly handle suspects was contrary to the stated goal of the Phoenix program to protect the people from terrorism. While it might be argued that Phoenix was putting away legitimate VCI and preventing them from carrying out their terrorism, it was also holding many innocent people for months without charge or trial.

Only one of the women had been tried and found guilty. Nguyen Thi Ranh was convicted of being a minor member of the VCI and sentenced to one year, half the maximum sentence. She probably had been coerced into joining the communists. Ranh did not seem to have any deep ideological commitment to the Viet Cong and because of her good behavior the province officials sent her back to the detention center as a sort of supervisor for the other women who had not yet been tried.

If any of the other women were found guilty they would be sentenced commensurate with the importance of their role within the Viet Cong political infrastructure. The more important their status within the VCI the more severe the sentence.

The women had been interrogated separately by the National Police stationed at the PIC. Each had endured the same questions over and over for an entire day. "What is your name, who are your parents, where is your village, who are the other VCI in the area?" The lack of direction or specific questions during the interrogations indicated that the police had little or no evidence on the women and were simply probing, hoping to come up with something that might incriminate other VCI in the area.

All the women were scared, uncertain of what the future held. All except one, a self-assured young woman who gave her name as Tran Kim Dinh. She told the interrogators she was married and had a four-month-old baby who was cared for by her mother-in-law. Dinh had been arrested six weeks earlier and still had not been formally charged. It was her husband the National Police really wanted; they were not sure what part Tran Kim Dinh played in the local VCI, if any. But Dinh was proud of her husband's role with the Viet Cong, telling anyone who was interested that he was a VC propaganda cadre. She also seemed proud that her husband's activities had kept them apart for over a year, and that she did not really know if he was dead or alive.

Dinh had told her interrogators that she was from a farming family, but everyone noticed that she had smooth skin on her hands and feet, very different from the rough, calloused leather that covered the other women's hands and feet. Dinh was also aloof from her six cellmates, and they all seemed to act as if she was not one of them. But none would talk about Dinh to the interrogators.

A group of American reporters received special permission to talk with some of the prisoners in the PIC and Dinh and her six companions were among them. While photographers snapped pictures of the women only Dinh seemed to mind. She turned her head, moved into the corner, and simply walked away whenever a photographer pointed a lens at her. The other women didn't seem to notice the cameras. Dinh was very aware of what some of the photos might be used for. The police often took pictures from press clippings and used them on wanted posters. In case she was released, Dinh did not want her face showing up later on some Phoenix poster.

If the journalists had not talked with the seven prisoners no one outside the PIC might have ever known about their predicament. As it was, the seven women faded from sight after the journalists left and it was impossible to determine their fates. If other civilian prisons throughout South Vietnam were any indication, the women probably remained in jail for another month or so waiting patiently for the Province Security Committee to review their cases.

The detention centers often became breeding grounds for Viet Cong sympathies. Ideologically committed VCI often were mixed with low-level suspects who, after a month or so of exposure to the haranguing of their communist cellmates, were sure to leave with Viet Cong sympathies. On the other hand, innocent people rounded up on slim or nonexistent evidence and dumped in a detention center for months before being released for lack of evidence were also a ready source of converts to the communist cause. They were unlikely to understand the logistical problems within the legal system that landed them in jail, or sympathize with the predicament of the province chief who was too busy with other tasks to pay immediate attention to the fate of those in the detention center.

In many ways the legal apparatus behind the Phoenix program was much too sophisticated for rural South Vietnam. The rules called for detailed dossiers to be put together on each suspected VCI to bring the case to trial. But most peasants did not lead the sort of life that left a paper trail by which to build a dossier. They were simple folk, trained by years of war to bend with the tide of battle and cooperate with whatever side had the power to affect their lives on any particular day. The people of rural South Vietnam simply did not care about the twists and turns of the Phoenix program's evolution toward efficiency and fairness. All they knew was that many of their friends and relatives ended up in a province detention center simply because someone suspected them of being VCI.

Concept of Law and War in Vietnam

Arrest, trial, and detention under special laws designed for wartime have always attracted criticism from Americans. Vietnam, like many other Third World nations emerging from colonialism onto the untested ground of independence, faced legal problems in mixing colonial and traditional customs into a system of law that addressed the demands of a newborn state. Only time would allow them to experiment and develop their own legal system.

South Vietnam had these problems, but to them were added a burgeoning war that strained the legal system and the state itself. Vietnam under the French had had two systems of justice: one traditional, based on Confucian ideals and a rural lifestyle, the other imposed by the French and aimed largely at the urban population. French law was widely regarded as a tool of oppression used by a foreign government to control rather than protect. When South Vietnam became a sovereign state in 1954, South Vietnamese citizens had no perspective from which to trust and respect the new laws.

Because President Diem was faced with the competing forces of nation building and fighting a civil war, he relied on the use of decrees to control the population and maintain order. Although many of Diem's decrees were based on some previous law, some were not.

In 1962 Diem's sister-in-law, the infamous Madame Ngo Dinh Nhu, felt that South Vietnam did not possess the appropriate ethics and morals befitting a Christian nation. Of course, the majority of citizens in South Vietnam were Buddhists, but Diem, a celibate Catholic, approved of the measure and signed into law a decree prohibiting abortion, sorcery, smoking by anyone under eighteen, and "voluptuous activities," defined as dancing, prostitution, and beauty contests. The decree was vague and could not be enforced. Such laws only reinforced the notion that the new government was not acting in the interests of the people.[2]

Although laws dealing with the Viet Cong—the threat from within—directly affected the security of the new nation, they too, were often vague and unenforceable. Diem recognized the need to strike at the communist infrastructure, but he was unsure of how to do so. Instead, he decreed that the VCI was a threat to state security and membership in it was defined as a subversive act. The prescribed penalty for this "hooliganism" was death.[3]

Two decrees set forth after Diem's death established a national emergency. The first, in August 1964, declared South Vietnam to be in a state of emergency, and another in June 1965 defined the situation as a state of war. Both statutes gave the government power to take appropriate measures for maintaining security.

Early Prison System

Any law, whether capricious or just, cannot have an impact upon society unless there exists an effective enforcement mechanism. The two chief mechanisms are the police and the court and detention systems, neither of which were effective in Vietnam during the early 1960s.

In 1965 there were only 160 lawyers and about the same number of judges in all of South Vietnam. In 1967 there were 193 lawyers, 150 of whom practiced in Saigon. Only fourteen out of forty-four provinces had even a single lawyer. This handful of men was expected to handle a caseload that increased astronomically between 1965 and 1970.[4]

Between January and December 1965 the number of political prisoners jumped almost 100 percent, from 9,885 to 18,788. This number did not include common criminals or prisoners of war. The total capacity of all civilian jails and prisons in South Vietnam was 21,400. Most of the political prisoners were VCI, but because an organized anti-infrastructure system was virtually nonexistent, many of the prisoners were merely minor supporters or collaborators.[5]

By 1966 there was no more room for additional prisoners. The most practical measure to alleviate overcrowding was to release old prisoners when new ones came in. The average time of imprisonment for offenders, including VCI, was six months. Even the most hardcore VC was often sent back to his old haunts through this revolving door of justice.[6]

Prisoners of war fell under a separate system created and maintained by MACV. The Americans constructed camps and prisons, all within the guidelines of the Geneva Convention. The International Red Cross agreed. In 1966 a Red Cross report stated that "the MACV instruction [regarding facilities and treatment of POWs] . . . is a brilliant expression of liberal and realistic attitude . . . [and] goes far beyond the requirements of the Geneva Convention." Regular Red Cross inspections continued to report American compliance with international law.[7]

Unfortunately, the emphasis on POW facilities and the total disregard for civilian prisons to house convicted VCI was another indication of the military's misunderstanding of the nature of the war. MACV was content to watch political prisoners swell provincial jails, never admitting that although they had the problem of POWs well in hand, the most important enemy—the VCI—was not being adequately handled within the detention system. Worse, by allowing local prisons to handle VCI, MACV set the stage for allegations of human rights abuse. Provincial prisons lacked funds, space, and quality personnel, and abuse was common. The courts dealt with the problem by simply releasing excess prisoners. Even if a prisoner was only a collaborator, he was almost sure to join the VC after a little time in a local jail.

Against this setting of misplaced priorities the VCI continued to grow. Because MACV regarded the infrastructure as a civilian problem, the court and detention system was unprepared to handle the influx of prisoners once anti-infrastructure operations became a priority in late 1967.

Interrogation: American Involvement

As had been the case with early anti-infrastructure operations in general, responsibility for interrogation and detention of VCI fell on the CIA. The most important consideration was to separate VCI suspects from common criminals and Viet Cong civil detainees, who already filled the national and provincial prisons. The CIA also hoped that by designing and maintaining separate facilities for VCI, they could ensure rapid exploitation of intelligence extracted during interrogation. Separate facilities also would make screening of suspects easier and provide rapid release for the innocent. Responsibility for the operation of these new facilities would fall on the province chief.[8]

It had been recommended that interrogation facilities be built down to the district level to get the most out of intelligence gathered through interrogations. This was impossible because the CIA lacked the manpower and resources to extend its presence down to the district level. Instead, it settled for facilities in all forty-four of South Vietnam's provinces. These were the Province Interrogation Centers (PIC) and by 1968 most had been completed. They were designed to employ the highest standards of interrogation techniques on captured VCI before they went to trial. Unfortunately, by not having a district equivalent of the PIC, intelligence gathered from interrogations was sometimes old by the time it could be acted upon.

Each PIC had at least one American adviser, usually a CIA officer, who taught the South Vietnamese professional interrogation techniques. This was not to include torture, although many CIA advisers reported encountering the use of torture by Vietnamese interrogators. Torture was regarded by both the GVN and the communists as a time-honored and valid method of gathering information and it was often a difficult habit to break. It was the job of the American adviser to convince his counterpart and other PIC officials that torture produced unreliable intelligence. William Colby, who in 1968 was Komer's deputy for CORDS, noted that intelligence extracted under torture was often worse than having no intelligence at all. If accepted as fact, erroneous information painted a skewed picture of the VCI situation and could only play into the communists' hands.[9]

Though Americans often were reluctant to admit it, torture was just a way of war. Captured enemies were routinely mistreated, intelligence value be damned, and there was nothing the Americans could do about it. Agency personnel at the PICs reported that when they were around to watch, the Vietnamese followed American interrogation guidelines. When the Vietnamese were alone, anything could happen.

One CIA regional officer in charge in III Corps took weekly trips to inspect the PICs in the eleven provinces under his direction, and to keep in personal touch with the Vietnamese and their American advisers. In one year of duty, he saw only one piece of evidence to indicate that the Vietnamese were torturing their prisoners. In one interrogation room he came upon an electrical telephone crankset and some wires that could be hooked up to an unfortunate victim. The incident was reported and the Vietnamese dismantled the device.[10]

Did they put it up again after the American left? Probably. The incident proved little: either the Vietnamese did not practice torture regularly in III Corps, or they were clever enough to do it away from American eyes. But American advisers could do only so much to stop the problem. After all, as many Americans opposed to U.S. involvement in Vietnam were fond of saying, it was their war.

Although the Americans objected to the use of torture for practical and humanitarian reasons, MACV did not specifically address the problem in a written memorandum forbidding advisers from participating in torture, nor did MACV require them to report incidents whenever they occurred. Only after protests from antiwar groups and the press did MACV act.

On 18 May 1970 a directive was issued that specifically set guidelines for American Phoenix advisers and their conduct during interrogation of VCI suspects. They were not to participate and they were instructed to make their objections known to the Vietnamese interrogators. Finally, they were required to report their observations to "the next higher U.S. authority for decision as to action to be taken with the GVN."[11] This is not to say that CORDS or MACV condoned torture before the directive was issued; they did not. The directive was only a written recognition of a policy that had long been in place.

While the directive was partly in response to criticism Phoenix was receiving, it also directly stemmed from an embarrassing incident that helped feed anti-Phoenix fires within the United States. On 14 February 1969, ACLU attorney William H. Zinman filed a proffer on behalf of a U.S. Army intelligence officer, Lieutenant Francis T. Reitemeyer.

The proffer stated that Lieutenant Reitemeyer had been assigned as an adviser to the Phoenix program, and that he was to command a band of PRUs whose job was to capture or kill as many Viet Cong sympathizers within a given area as possible. There was nothing horrible in that statement, but Reitemeyer went on to claim that he would be required to maintain a "kill quota of fifty bodies a month."

Critics of the Phoenix program seemed to be vindicated in their belief that Phoenix was a program of assassination and torture. The only problem was that Lieutenant Reitemeyer had never been to Vietnam; he had no personal experience on which to base his charge. Reitemeyer was only passing along war stories he said were told by instructors at the Army's intelligence school.[12]

In fact, Lieutenant Reitemeyer had had a strange career before joining the Army. He had been born in Clark, New Jersey and held a degree in classical languages from Seton Hall University. In 1967, when he joined the Army, Reitemeyer was studying for the priesthood at Immaculate Conception Seminary. After receiving a commission he was assigned to the Army Intelligence School at Ft. Holabird, Maryland, where he completed his training as a Phoenix adviser on 6 December 1968.

Reitemeyer decided the Phoenix program was not for him and he asked for release from the Army as a conscientious objector. Another student at Ft. Holabird, Lieutenant Michael J. Cohn, also took the same legal action to get out of the Army. The two were never called upon to testify on the allegations in the proffer, but the judge in the case ruled on 14 July 1969 that the two men were entitled to release from the Army as conscientious objectors. The Army appealed the decision, but abruptly withdrew the appeal in October. The case was closed.[13]

When the proffer became public in February 1969 hardly any notice was taken. Then in November 1969 the massacre of Vietnamese civilians at My Lai came to public attention. Journalists scurried to find other stories of American atrocities and someone remembered the Reitemeyer case. The Army was besieged by questions. A Pentagon spokesman told reporters that Reitemeyer and Cohn had been dismissed from the intelligence school for academic failure, hinting that perhaps they had made up the story to cover their failure. More damaging to the two officers' allegations was a sworn statement given to the Army by Reitemeyer on 6 December 1968—almost three months before the proffer had been filed. In the statement Reitemeyer denied that he had received "assassination training."

Why had the Army required such a statement? It had come

to the attention of instructors at Ft. Holabird that Reitemeyer had told a girlfriend he was being trained to murder. Reitemeyer willingly stated for the record that he had not told his girlfriend any such thing, and that he was not being trained in assassination.[14]

Half-truths and innuendo plagued the Phoenix program from its inception, but the My Lai massacre and the Reitemeyer affair focused full attention on charges of assassination. And because the CIA had begun the program and continued to run many of the PICs, it caught most of the fire. But by 1969 Phoenix had expanded into a bird too big for the CIA's limited manpower to handle. The problem only got worse. By August 1971 the CIA would spare only twenty-six advisers to work in the PICs, providing interrogation advice.[15]

At the district level the CIA had no responsibility; MACV provided the personnel. These were the Phoenix advisers, the men who were supposed to keep the district level interrogation and operations facilities—the DIOCCs—functioning. At the DIOCCs, Phoenix advisers and their Phung Hoang counterparts conducted an initial screening and interrogation of VCI suspects, releasing those deemed innocent and passing important detainees on up to the PIC for further interrogation.

At the end of 1968 DIOCC performance was sketchy. Success or failure was generally dependent upon the quality of Vietnamese leadership and intelligence-gathering capabilities. And throughout South Vietnam, intelligence personnel assigned to track and neutralize the VCI were generally poor. The Police Special Branch and the Military Security Service (MSS) did not have the training and background for this type of work, despite the presence of their CIA advisers. At the district level many GVN personnel could barely read and write and had only a basic understanding of the mission they were involved with.[16]

Only at the province level was there any talent in intelligence gathering, but even there success or failure depended largely upon competent leadership. In Vinh Binh Province, for example, local authorities prohibited a planned operation against known VCI because the communists were reported to have connections high in the GVN.[17]

Power of Arrest

Almost since its inception, the Phoenix program was plagued by accusations that it sidestepped due process and wrongfully arrested suspected VCI. In 1970 the GVN, at the prodding of CORDS, set forth a system for processing those accused and arrested as VCI. On the surface the system was fair, fast, and efficient. Sheer numbers, however, and the nature of the myriad resources that made up the Phoenix program, combined to prevent the system from remaining workable. Anyone suspected of an offense against the "National Security" could be taken into custody and held up to twenty-four hours for interrogation by an "apprehending agency" (PRU, ARVN, RF/PF, etc.) before being turned over to the National Police. All arrests had to be preceded by a warrant issued by a "competent judicial authority," which usually included the province chief, mayor, district chief, or police chief from the area in which the suspect resided. In case the Vietnamese became too exuberant and arrested a suspect without obtaining the proper papers, there was a provision by which a warrant could be issued after the fact by any proper official.[18]

Proper arresting officials were members of the uniformed National Police, the National Police Field Forces, Judicial Police, Military Police, Military Security Service, and any civilian witnessing a crime. Although regular army units were careful to take members of the National Police along as arresting officials on any operations where VCI might be encountered, the law provided the twenty-four-hour interrogation period before suspects must be turned over to the police.

Once a suspect was in police custody, the authorities had two days to complete the preliminary inquiry and identification process and turn over the evidence to a screening committee, which decided whether there was enough evidence to prosecute the suspect. If the evidence was sufficient the police had a maximum of three more days to transfer the suspect to the PIC, where yet another investigation was begun, this one for up to thirty days. The province chief and the public prosecutor could spend up to three days reviewing the suspect's dossier before it was required to be forwarded to the Province Security Committee (PSC—this body was created within Vietnamese law in 1957), which then had to sentence or release the suspect, or, if it was decided that the suspect was part of the military rather than the political infrastructure, the case was referred to a military court. The Province Security Committee had seven days to act. Any deviation from this rigid timetable required authorization from the minister of interior.[19]

This process also sought to address the problem of rapidly screening legitimate suspects from among innocent civilians caught up in troop sweep operations. Because the Phoenix program had intended to use intelligence gathering and specific targeting as its means of neutralizing VCI, it was unprepared to handle the scores of civilians rounded up in troop sweeps. Many of these innocent civilians were held for days, and in some cases for months, before the legal machinery got around to letting them go. Oversights such as these did nothing to win the confidence of the people for the GVN. In an attempt to rectify the problem, Phoenix legal guidelines called for screening committees to meet at either the district or province headquarters. They were made up of the province or district chief, his deputy, representatives from the National Police, PSB, MSS, personnel from the PIOCC or DIOCC, and various military intelligence personnel. In particular, the screening committees were to use assets in a position to know who was innocent and who was not. Members of local Chieu Hoi bureaus, village and hamlet officials in particular, often were familiar with the population and could clear some detainees on sight. But to prevent these officials from using the power of release from arrest for corrupt purposes, they were not allowed to order any releases. They could only request that the screening committee do so.[20]

Screening committees made clear-cut decisions that fell into one of three categories. One, they could be found innocent and released. If this was the case they would be returned to the place where they had been arrested. Two, suspects could be determined to be members of an "enemy military organization," either NVA regulars, or VC soldiers. If this was the case, they were classified as prisoners of war and turned over to military custody. Three, the suspect could be classified as a national security offender. These were the VCI and they were not considered part of the enemy military. Anyone placed in this category was a civil detainee and was placed in police custody.

Any village cordon-and-search operation was required to bring along a village screening committee. This committee was to consist of the village chief and his deputy, chief of the Revolutionary Development Cadre, and a village National Police representative. The most important aspect of the screening committee was the inclusion of hamlet and village officials in the release process. This represented a departure from the standard overcentralization of authority within the GVN system and it came about largely because CORDS pressured Saigon into accepting the change. Also important was the inclusion of local village officials into the legal system, a major step in the attempt to make Phoenix a popular program within the general population.

Evidence and the Accused

Anyone accused of being a member of the VCI was subject to an emergency detention procedure called *an tri*. The an tri laws were special powers that allowed the state to sentence "command echelon VCI and Communist Party members" to a two-year minimum sentence, and "cadre-level VCI" a minimum of one- to two-year sentences. In contrast to normal democratic procedures of due process, including the right to face one's accuser, an tri made it possible to try and convict VCI suspects based on dossiers. The Provincial Security Committee had the authority to impose detention on anyone deemed to be a threat to national security.

In principal, this was not as capricious as it might seem. The committees were not bound by any rigid rules, but the burden of proof did rest upon the prosecution, not the accused. The prosecution had to prove that the defendant was in fact a member of the VCI by presenting evidence in the form of captured documents, eyewitnesses (at least three witnesses were required), intelligence reports, and confessions. No suspect could be convicted solely on a confession or on the results of an interrogation.[21]

Part of the problem behind sentencing lay in the definition of VCI categories. The basic categories A, B, and C had been defined in 1968, but Saigon felt that a more precise system of definition would insure more effective prosecution and sentencing. On 21 March 1969 the Ministry of Interior issued a circular on classification and rehabilitation of VCI offenders.[22]

The circular emphasized capture of VCI members and proposed that a lenient rehabilitation program was the best policy. From a national perspective the new guidelines represented a uniform procedure for moving the VCI through the legal system. In practice they were not always workable, nor did they address the problems that would plague the Phoenix program throughout its existence: failure to sentence VCI properly, overcrowding of detention centers, and lengthy detention time before trial.

The reality of the situation on the ground tended to negate any gains made in neutralizing the VCI. Although the legal minds behind the Phoenix program had tried to think out every conceivable way to keep the sentencing process fair and fast, the situation immediately bogged down. After becoming DEPCORDS in November 1968, William Colby quickly brought up the lack of speed in sentencing and addressed the crux of the problem.

> One reason that the local National Police and Special Police have a difficult task in constructing good dossiers is because it is unclear what amount of evidence is sufficient to guarantee an an tri sentence from the Security Committees.[23]

This problem was never solved. The administrative capacity of the GVN to handle the influx of arrested VCI could not keep up with the flow of prisoners. Roughly 50 percent of the prisoners in jail at any given time were there awaiting sentencing rather than serving sentences. This was not fair to those held on little or no evidence, but the GVN often responded to the problem by simply releasing prisoners when the administrative load became too heavy.

Another method of coping with the overload was to declare a general amnesty, generally applied to low-level VCI. On 1 November 1968, National Day in South Vietnam, the GVN released 782 convicted VCI as a propaganda ploy. In addition, another 5,043 prisoners were released during numerous other amnesties during 1968 alone.[24]

Problems within the Legal System

Like so much else within the Phoenix program, the well-thought-out arrest and detention plans that seemed to address every possible problem gave way to the realities of everyday operations in South Vietnam. Foremost was the tendency of province officials to falsify reports or outright ignore instructions from Saigon. In August 1969 Deputy Undersecretary of the Army James V. Siena took a trip to Vietnam and recorded his observations of the Phoenix program in a memorandum to his boss, Secretary of Defense Melvin Laird. Siena gave the example of one highly regarded province chief who refused to back the Phoenix program and made no secret of his reasons for doing so. In his view the program "exacts too high a price in social stability for the returns it yields." He pointed out that most of the VCI neutralized by Phoenix were not ideologically committed to communism and they were not regarded as "bad men" by their fellow citizens. Delving into the sociological roots of the war in Vietnam, the province chief noted that becoming "a VC or an ARVN soldier depends on who was in control when you became old enough to bear arms."[25]

Another problem that stood in the way of American plans to craft an efficient legal machine lay in the unpredictability of the future. For Americans the future was certain—one day they would all go home. For the South Vietnamese it was not so simple. The ongoing Paris Peace Talks hinted of a political settlement some time in the future. Today's VCI might become tomorrow's political leaders and there was a reluctance on the part of many provincial GVN officials to "make life miserable now for someone who might be a legitimate political power in the future."[26]

Corruption was a serious problem within the legal framework of the Phoenix program. A district official might use his power to extort money or favors from wealthy, but innocent, members of the community by threatening them with prosecution as VCI if they did not cooperate. In other cases the Viet Cong would sometimes buy the dossier on an important VCI so that he could not be prosecuted, or pay outright for the release of a key VCI being held in a local detention facility.

Most disturbing from the point of view of Phoenix advisers was the tendency of detention officials to release VCI or to give them lenient sentences. Most critics at the time completely ignored this disturbing aspect of Phoenix in favor of overblowing the charges of assassination. It made better copy. But in reality the inefficiency and outright incompetence of the detention system was the real failure within the Phoenix program. The VCI classification and sentencing guidelines set forth by the MOI were routinely ignored in the field and reports by Phoenix observers noted a uniform "pattern of lenient sentencing and early release."[27]

According to official observers, the processing and detention system was like a revolving door. Although many arrests of VCI were made daily, few of them remained in jail for long. An estimated sixty thousand to one-hundred thousand persons were arrested yearly (on all charges, not simply those accused of being VCI) between 1968 and 1972 but the total prison population increased by only several thousand a year. The problem lay in the lack of detention facilities, combined with local GVN attitudes toward the VCI. To be on the safe side, VCI were being released rather than imprisoned.

The Ministry of Interior often overruled the decisions of Province Security Committee, ignoring its own classification sentencing guidelines, which called for a minimum two-year sentence for class A VCI offenders. An estimated 75 to 90 percent of VCI arrested in 1968 and through April 1969 were released between six and twelve months after capture. A majority of those were actually set free soon after capture.[28]

These are not the actions of a bloodthirsty government bent

on murdering all suspected VCI. [In fact, given the figures of VCI arrested and then released, it becomes impossible to make a case that Phoenix was simply an assassination program.

VCI in Prison: Facts and Figures

The statistics on VCI held in jails throughout South Vietnam clearly illustrate the situation faced by the Phoenix program. Between January and November 1968, 75 percent of the prisoners held in civilian prisons either escaped or were released. In January 1968 the GVN prison system held 34,000 prisoners. By October, the number had grown to only 37,515. This net increase of 3,515 prisoners was offset by 2,665 prisoners set free during Viet Cong attacks on the prisons, 5,825 prisoners released in a series of general amnesties, and 8,389 prisoners released when their sentences were up. The total number of prisoners released—16,879—and the net increase in the prison population—3,515—added up to 20,394, more than the number of VCI arrested from January to November 1968. Therefore, while Phoenix neutralized some 15,000 VCI during 1968, a trend toward releasing a majority of them made their efforts practically useless.[29]

The situation did not get any better as time went on. Although in late 1969 the Phoenix program began requiring that a suspected VCI be sentenced before being counted as neutralized, the new criteria only succeeded in building up the backlog of prisoners awaiting a decision on their fates from the Province Security Committees. While people could no longer be arbitrarily labeled as VCI to satisfy the quota, the new rule did nothing to help the thousands of innocent victims sitting in jail awaiting their fate.

II Corps had the worst record for PSC performance. At the end of May 1970, 1,009 VCI suspects were awaiting action on their cases. None could be counted as neutralized until a decision was made by the PSCs, so the reputation of the Phoenix program in II Corps suffered in the monthly province reports, which generally failed to point out that the reason for the low neutralization figure was the PSC's lack of action and not the Phoenix program's ability to get out and round up suspects. Binh Dinh Province turned in the worst performance, with 779 suspects waiting in jail cells for a decision.[30]

Even as late as 1972 the PSCs had not worked out a system that quickly released those detainees deemed innocent. In III Corps the Vietnamese public prosecutor pointed out to American CORDS officials that conditions varied from province to province. In Long An the average pretrial detention period was ten days—not an unreasonable wait. In Hau Nghia the waiting period was twenty days. The difference resulted directly from a lack of strong leadership. In Long An the province chief took an active interest in the PSC and attended all meetings. The province chief of Hau Nghia was more interested in tactical operations against enemy main-force units, so he paid little attention to the Phoenix program and the legal system.[31]

In many cases the PSCs were overwhelmed by the backlog of cases waiting to be heard. But the real problem lay in their unwillingness to follow MOI guidelines and meet at least once a week. In cases where the province chief felt the case load was especially heavy he called for the PSC to meet more than once a week. In general, such instructions were ignored. Again, II Corps provided the worst example. During the first half of 1970 the twelve PSCs met in the entire Corps seventy-six times. If they had followed the rule of one meeting a week they would have met at least 240 times during the five-month period.[32]

The impact on detainees awaiting their fate in the PIC was obvious: those who were finally found innocent went away bitter at the GVN for making them endure such hardship. The Viet Cong couldn't have had a better recruiting service. Those sentenced as members of the VCI went on to serve their sentences in the province prison. But while the PSC was often callous in its lack of concern for those awaiting a preliminary hearing, they were just as often lax in sentencing real offenders to long jail terms. Although the maximum sentence was two years for category A offenders (with extra time added at the end of the sentence if the convicted VCI was considered especially dangerous), few received it. II Corps again provided a good example of the problem. The average sentence for all VCI imprisoned in II Corps during the first five months of 1970 was 9.17 months. The province with the longest average sentence was Darlac with 18 months. The shortest was Binh Thuan, with a mere 5.25 months.[33]

Because the average sentence was less than one year, a majority of those VCI imprisoned were not counted as neutralized by the Phoenix program. So while the number-watchers in Saigon criticized Phoenix for failing to meet its quota, other critics lambasted the program for failing to cope with the detention problem. Phoenix got it coming and going.

Crowd Control: National Registration

In Vietnam, the communists knew many things that were never understood by the GVN or the Americans. Perhaps the foremost lesson came from deep within Leninist teachings on revolution: control of the population is paramount to the consolidation of power. Since WWII Hanoi had concentrated on controlling the population of North Vietnam, while in the South, President Diem paid attention only to his power base in the urban areas. Not until 1966 did the GVN seek to undertake a program of population registration, and then only at the prodding of the United States. The plan was called the National Identity Registration Program (NIRP).

The original planning would be based on population figures for South Vietnam, but the GVN soon discovered there were no population figures; registration would have to proceed based on an estimated census. The last complete census had been taken in 1935, so all figures were suspect, but American advisers (under the auspices of U.S.AID) set out to guess at the percentage of the population that should be registered.

The registrable population was arrived at by assuming that 65 percent of the total population was fifteen years of age or older and 35 percent was under fifteen years of age. These figures were based on computations from the 1935 census, data from the National Institute of Statistics, and U.S.AID and public health figures. In 1967 the registrable population was estimated at 9.35 million, often rounded off in tables and charts to 9.5 million.[34]

An ID card system had been instituted in the early 1960s and seven hundred thousand cards had been issued. But because the population had not been fingerprinted and a record of the ID cards entered into a central system, the program had become virtually worthless. On 1 October 1968 NIRP began traveling from village to village, registering and fingerprinting all members of the population over the age of fifteen. The program went slowly and the National Police, who were assigned to implement NIRP in the countryside, did not take the job seriously. Very few ID cards were issued during 1968. Record-keeping was shoddy and the program faltered. To make matters worse, in October 1969, at the urging of the United States, Saigon revised the population estimate upward to 11.3 million, based on new pacification figures. The number still reflected the assumption that 65 percent of the population was over the age of fifteen.[35]

But the NIRP still lacked the essential GVN motivating factor—deadlines and quotas. Beginning in 1969 and into 1970 the prime minister requested that the NIRP be accelerated and completed in July 1971. The "request" got the National Police into action, but, like many other American-brokered GVN programs, the goal was unrealistic. It was simply impossible to issue more than 11 million ID cards in one year, even if the National Police had been geared to perform the task.

By December 1970 many provinces were far behind schedule. In Quang Ngai, police officials reported 63,631 unprocessed persons and 13,988 unissued ID cards. Since figures were only based on a population estimate, the GVN measured progress by averaging the number of registrations made per day by the various NIRP teams in each province. Kien Giang Province turned in the best average, with 466 registrations per day. The next best province total came from An Giang Province, with 285.5 ID cards issued a day. But those were the best examples: "Long Khanh Province failed to report the required information and twenty other provinces reported incorrectly."[36]

As the July deadline approached and it became clear the NIRP was not going to issue all the required ID cards, the National Police Command was allowed to revise the total downward. This was done in three steps—to 10.9 million in April; to 9.2 million in May; and finally to 9.1 million in June. The registrable population was still believed to be around 11.5 million, but only a little more than 9 million would have cards issued to them by July 1971.[37]

The deadline came and went. As of September 1971 NIRP teams were still roaming South Vietnam, but they had almost reached the total number of ID cards that were to have been issued by July. On 31 September the NIRP reported it had registered 9.3 million persons nationwide. Of those registered, 8.3 million had received ID cards.[38]

As of January 1972 the National Police had entered the 9 million registered names into a central computer in Saigon called Big Mack. Information on arrested suspects could be cross-checked against the records on the computer, making the building of dossiers much simpler. At the end of January 1972 300,000 "offenders" had been identified, including 225,333 ARVN deserters, 2,053 "subversive criminals" (mostly VCI), 36,725 draft evaders, 19,954 "miscellaneous criminals," and 38,194 "registration irregularities." The computer system worked best for identifying deserters; relatively few VCI were identified.[39]

As far as Saigon was concerned, this was good progress, and NIRP quotas were quietly done away with as the police slipped back into their former registration pace. Even if the goal had been reached, MACV estimated that about three-hundred thousand Vietnamese would turn fifteen each year.[40] Given the previous pace of NIRP, it was unlikely the National Police were capable of handling the yearly quota. But the question was moot. By the spring of 1972 about 1 million Vietnamese had still not been issued ID cards, and with the communist Easter Offensive in April and May 1972, the NIRP faded away.

Like much else within the war effort, opportunities for corruption and personal politics arose in the NIRP. Because the general population was required to possess identification, some police saw an opportunity to make money on the side. There were cases of ID cards withheld when the unfortunate individual refused to pay a fee to the policeman on duty. In one case, two policemen in Bac Lieu Province were accused of fraud when it was reported that they had been charging three hundred to four hundred piasters ($3 U.S.) for ID cards. Some villagers reported that they had spent more than ten thousand piasters ($45 U.S.) and had spent days in line at the local police station just to get a receipt so they would not be charged again. They said they never did get the ID cards.[41]

Local police administration officials often were selective in the attention they devoted to the NIRP. In Kien Phong Province the police chief did nothing to smooth the registration procedure as it became more and more tangled in inefficiency. The American PSA reported that "[the] official seems helpless to correct the unbelievable confusion in the NIRP which fosters an ever-growing backlog compounded of inefficiency, inadequate film-processing, noxious work conditions and woefully inept direction."[42]

Why issue ID cards to all South Vietnamese citizens over the age of fifteen? Simply because it was thought that a system of national registration would make it impossible for VCI living underground to mingle with the population. In Malaya the British had succeeded in virtually starving the insurgents with a system of ID and ration cards. In Vietnam it would not be so simple. The Viet Cong quickly realized they could actually make their lives easier by flouting the NIRP system. In many cases local VCI were able to get ID cards, either through bribery, stealth, or by infiltrating the Chieu Hoi program. With an ID card a member of the VCI became a "legal," a communist agent making his way through society with the appropriate paperwork.[43]

The NIRP was supposed to make VCI targeting easier for the Phoenix program. It allowed police to build dossiers and check suspects' legal status against registration statistics. In reality the NIRP made it easier for the police to rely on cordon-and-search operations. Whenever an Army unit went into a village to search for Viet Cong and weapons caches, they took along police, who would set up a check station and run every villager through. Any person not holding an ID card was immediately suspected of being VC. The police also matched ID cards of known VCI "legals" against lists drawn up in the DIOCC. This method produced some VCI, but it did the Viet Cong little irreparable damage.

Phoenix and the Geneva Convention

The American public often was led to believe that VCI caught and convicted under the Phoenix program represented a new high in undemocratic methods. In reality, such special powers had been used for centuries by beleaguered nations to cope with insurgencies and civil wars. The United States suspended the writ of habeas corpus during the Civil War in an effort to control spies and Confederate sympathizers in the North. More recently, the United States interned Americans of Japanese descent under the pretext of preventing espionage and sabotage. Without addressing the morality of such measures, it is easy to see how desperate circumstances can cause a nation to resort to special laws.

Following the American and ARVN incursion into Cambodia in April 1970, public opinion in the United States swung dramatically against the war and called for U.S. troops to leave Vietnam at once. The Phoenix program had been under fire since its inception, but new attention was drawn to it in the wake of Cambodian incursion. In keeping with the general mood within the United States, Congress held hearings on the war that included an examination of the legality of the Phoenix program.

On 19 July 1971, during hearings by the House Committee on Government Operations on U.S. Assistance Programs in Vietnam, Congressman Paul N. McCloskey questioned William Colby on whether U.S. and GVN actions within the Phoenix program were in keeping with the Hague Regulations of 1907 and Geneva Conventions of 1949. The conventions of 1949 updated the 1907 Regulations to reflect world experience in World Wars I and II. In particular, the 1949 conventions addressed the issues of insurgents and irregular forces, which had not been a serious part of WWI, but had become prevalent during WWII.

But even these additions failed to address the realities of the Vietnam War. For example, the conventions do not cover the role of a subversive political infrastructure within the types of people's war that rose to prominence after 1945. In Colby's opinion the Phoenix program fell within the guidelines of the conventions where they applied, although there were some "individual failures in its implementation."[44] It was those failures

Congress harped on, but the failures were minor and did not violate the conventions as a whole.

Article 4 of the Third Geneva Convention of 1949 sets standards for what constitutes a prisoner of war and how he is to be treated. Any "member of the armed forces of a party to the conflict as well as militias or volunteer corps forming part of such armed forces" were to be treated as POWs. The most important characteristics that placed a captive in the POW category were a "fixed distinctive insignia recognizable at a distance" and openly carrying arms. The VCI did not fall into these categories, as they were dressed in civilian clothes and they carried concealed weapons when they carried them at all.

Article 3 called for humane treatment of "persons taking no active part in the hostilities." Clearly, these two articles did not cover a member of a subversive political infrastructure that directed and supported the war, but took no "active" part in it. On the one hand the VCI did not fall within the definition of a POW; on the other hand they were much more than persons taking no active part in the hostilities. The United States and the GVN were under no legal obligation to treat the VCI as anything other than common criminals, but they accepted a general obligation of humanitarianism under Article 13.[45]

Articles 42 and 43 of the convention allow for internment if certain conditions are met. The an tri procedure sought to meet those conditions. According to the conventions, persons sentenced under Articles 42 and 43 were to have their sentences reviewed every six months. The an tri laws called for review after a maximum of two years, so if there was a clear violation of the Geneva Conventions it was here. But as we have seen, only some 30 percent of VCI convicted received a two-year an tri sentence, so any violation fell far short of the criticism leveled at the Phoenix program and the detention system.

Tangle of Legalities

The Phoenix program sought to make itself a legitimate part of the war effort by building around it a system of laws, sentencing procedures, prisons, and secondary programs designed to involve the population in hunting down the VCI. It did not—as the critics charged—build these programs as a false front to cover up a pointed and deliberate program of assassination and torture. Unfortunately, the system turned into a net that tangled both the GVN and the U.S. pacification advisory effort in complex legal directives and confusing subprograms.

The NIRP was one example. It was designed to aid the Phoenix program and at the same time protect the rights of the population. Of course, many examples of corruption and infringement on personal rights muddied the waters, but, at the behest of the Americans, the GVN was trying to institute a system that reached into the countryside in an attempt to tear the population away from the Viet Cong. It was largely unsuccessful because the programs were begun too late. The Americans were leaving Vietnam and the GVN was neither willing nor able to take up the slack.

10

Return to Ashes: 1971–1972

AMERICA's headlong rush to exit Vietnam played havoc with attempts to prepare the Vietnamese to fight the war themselves. Since 1965 MACV's willingness to shoulder the lion's share of the fighting had settled the ARVN into a secondary role, which they seemed neither willing nor able to change. For the Phoenix program this presented a problem: Phung Hoang was supposed to be a purely Vietnamese program, yet only since 1970 had it made real strides toward breaking the bond with its American parent—Phoenix. Just as anti-infrastructure operations were taking a real toll on the VCI, American advisers were on their way home. The timing could not have been worse.

From 1971 through the final U.S. troop withdrawal from Vietnam in March 1973 many changes occurred in the Phoenix program, most of them for the better. The police were given a greater role, the courts were streamlined, less emphasis was placed on quotas, and the entire program was made more public. Instead of operating behind secrecy and misunderstanding, the "new" Phoenix sought to involve the population with reward programs and public presentations.

Public opinion in the United States also dealt a heavy blow to the Phoenix program. Although reporters periodically filed stories on the Phoenix program—usually about PRU raids rather than the day-in–day-out grind of intelligence collation—it wasn't until 1971 that Phoenix became a big story. Congressional hearings on U.S. aid to South Vietnam provided a showcase for testimony both pro and con on the Phoenix program, and the press stationed in South Vietnam went off in pursuit of more copy. Once again, the timing couldn't have been worse. Advances made by Phung Hoang were ignored, and rather than risk a public backlash during the final year of the troop withdrawal, American officials opted to recommend dissolution of the program in favor of placing an anti-infrastructure capability directly within the National Police. The attack on the VCI would remain, but the Phung Hoang program would come to an end.

Despite advances in the Phoenix program, the final verdict was failure. Although Phung Hoang had come to enjoy unqualified support from the highest levels of the Saigon government, only limited headway had been made with province- and district-level officials. In most provinces the departure of American advisers meant the certain collapse of the Phung Hoang program. There was less coordination between provinces and less connection with the central authority in Saigon.

Yet another blow came in the form of the North Vietnamese Army. Between 1970 and 1972 rural pacification had been the main task of both U.S. troops and the ARVN. The big-unit war had become the "other war." That all changed on 30 March 1972, when North Vietnam committed almost its entire army in a conventional thrust meant to snuff out South Vietnam's existence. With the bulk of American troops gone, Hanoi felt the time was right to deliver a *coup de grâce* to the ARVN. Although the conventional aspects of the invasion received most of the press attention, pacification also was dealt a stunning blow. Phung Hoang fled before the North Vietnamese tanks like snow before the springtime sun. Without a strong security presence to guard pacification gains, lurking enemy main-force units easily could overrun and smash fragile intelligence structures such as Phung Hoang. Perhaps one of the marvels of the Phung Hoang program in Vietnam was that it could function as well as it did in the face of threats from enemy conventional units hiding in sanctuaries in Cambodia, Laos, and North Vietnam. Ideally, anti-infrastructure programs should be put into operation during the early stages of an insurgency, not after the threat has escalated to conventional warfare.

Despite the NVA's offensive, the greatest blow to the Phung Hoang program came from a continued lack of understanding by the public and Congress. They were unwilling to accept the contention that anti-infrastructure operations were as much a part of counterinsurgency as troop sweeps and air raids. To many, it was more brutal to kill or capture an enemy in a stealthy night raid than to kill him during an ambush using conventional troops. The result was the same, but somehow Phoenix officials never adequately got that point across.

More difficult to distinguish was the fine line between guilty VCI and innocent suspect. The difference was not always clear, even when the evidence was finally sorted out.

Phoenix Excess or Just Another Neutralized VCI?

Nguyen Hong Dang died in the early morning hours of 18 November 1971. Not an unusual occurrence, except for two factors. First, he had died while in the custody of the An Giang Province Phung Hoang Center. Worse still, he was a local member of the Hoa Hao. Dang, an unassuming man, would never know that in death he would personify both the Phung Hoang program's shortcomings and its strengths. Dang had been fingered as a Viet Cong weapons merchant by a number of sources. American intelligence had no doubt of his guilt. But Dang had died in jail under questionable circumstances and the local community was angry, a particularly dangerous mood because they were Hoa Hao, a powerful anti-communist Buddhist sect that largely controlled local politics in the Mekong Delta.

The Hoa Hao was founded in 1939. One of many groups nominally involved in anti-French activities in the postwar years, the Hoa Hao found themselves victimized by Viet Minh attempts to destroy other nationalist groups that could threaten communist domination. In April 1947 the Viet Minh murdered Hoa Hao founder Huynh Phu So and the sect became virulently anti-communist. But they were not pro-Diem. In 1955 protests against the Diem regime were forcibly put down, but the Hoa Hao remained a powerful and tightly knit social and political organization.

Beginning in 1961 the CIA recruited Hoa Hao to serve in anti-communist militias sprinkled around the Mekong Delta. After several years of distrust by successive South Vietnamese regimes the Hoa Hao remained bitter foes of the Viet Cong. Their tightly knit social structure effectively kept the communists out of areas controlled by the Hoa Hao.

All this made the Phung Hoang Center's allegation that Dang was Viet Cong all the more difficult for the Hoa Hao to believe. Officials from Dang's village of My Phuoc in Chau Thanh District immediately protested. The facts were never sorted out satisfactorily, but in the end the entire Phung Hoang program was tainted by the acts of a few.

In this case three men were involved in the arrest and interrogation of Nguyen Hong Dang. Nguyen Huu Lac, a maritime policeman detailed for duty to the Police Special Branch, and Master Sergeants Cao Van Duc and Le Van Tam, both from the An Giang Province intelligence office. On 17 November they were ordered to pick up Dang for questioning based on statements by two VCI captured the previous day. One of them, a woman who was a local deputy cell leader, revealed the names of several Viet Cong "agents," Dang among them.

According to the Hoa Hao, the officers arrived at Dang's house at 5:00 P.M. on 17 November. They did not knock. Barging in, they took a few moments to break lamps and tables, then bound and blindfolded Dang, "and started torturing him, paying no heed to the crying and supplication for mercy of the relatives of the victim." Dang was then marched off to the Phung Hoang Center where they "beat him to death."[1]

There was no doubt as to the cause of death. According to the death certificate, Dang died of a punctured lung that allowed blood to coagulate inside the lung. What was less clear was who should be blamed. The three policemen were acting on behalf of the Phung Hoang Committee, but no order for Dang's arrest had been issued. The policemen had only been told to "invite Mr. Dang to go to police headquarters for investigation."[2]

He died at 2:00 A.M. the next morning after detention personnel reported that he was "unconscious and seriously sick." The Phung Hoang Center chose to cover up Dang's death. Officials implied that he had died at the hands of other Viet Cong prisoners who believed Dang had fingered three important local VCI during the interrogation. The Phung Hoang Center made no attempt to arrest these three "new" VCI, however.

The Hoa Hao protested to the province chief, demanding redress. Among their demands were dissolution of the Phung Hoang Committees, punishment of the culprits, monetary compensation to Dang's family, public disclosure of the truth of the case, and reinstatement "of the honor of Mr. Dang, who is a true Hoa Hao follower and who has been arbitrarily accused as a Viet Cong."[3]

The province chief promptly responded, granting the Hoa Hao some of their demands, particularly money to Dang's widow, a review of arrest criteria, and an agreement to work more closely with the local Hoa Hao in Phung Hoang matters. The province chief could not reinstate Dang's good name because all evidence pointed to his guilt.

American intelligence personnel watched all this from afar. No U.S. advisers had been in any way involved in the incident, although intelligence on Dang's activities had also come to their attention: for some time, he had been running guns to the communists. From the American perspective Vietnamese handling of the affair was mixed. On the negative side the Phung Hoang Center employed brutal and poorly trained personnel who did indeed kill Dang. On the positive side intelligence on the Dang affair had been sound and there was no doubt he had been in close contact with the Viet Cong. However, American assessment of the motives behind Dang's activities differed from those of the Vietnamese. According to U.S. Phung Hoang advisers, Dang had been in the weapons business solely for the money.[4] As the Hoa Hao had correctly pointed out, Dang was a good Buddhist, not a communist. But for Dang, cold cash was more important than the spiritual or political world and selling guns was very profitable.

Nguyen Hong Dang was buried a few days later. Although the Hoa Hao still felt persecuted by the GVN, the settlement seemed satisfactory. The province chief had handled the situation quickly and efficiently. But the damage was done. Journalists had followed the well-publicized affair and their stories concentrated on the connection between the Phung Hoang Center and the beating death of Mr. Dang. They were correct to criticize the incident, but there were many more "lessons" left undiscussed. Perhaps most important was the speed with which the province chief responded to complaints. This was a vast improvement over the past few years.

Second, the Phung Hoang Committee took great strides to work with the local community to bring the Phung Hoang program closer to the people. Gone were the days when Phoenix was a secretive entity far removed from the people it sought to protect. This was in keeping with directives from the highest levels of the GVN, which for years had sought to cajole and coerce province and district officials into making Phung Hoang a priority.

Finally, the fact that Dang had been "specifically targeted" was lost in the shuffle. He was not caught up in a cordon-and-search dragnet and later found to be associated with the VCI, something for which the Phoenix program had long been criticized. One of the hallmarks of the year-and-a-half preceding the American withdrawal was an increased reliance on specifically targeted VCI. It was certainly too little too late and Dang's death illustrated that good intentions were not enough; a single mistake could set advances back to square one. Such are the travails of an unpopular war.

The incident symbolized the Phoenix program in the final two years of American involvement. There were clear improvements in methods and execution, but it was not enough. Dang's death was just one among hundreds all over South Vietnam in the final months of 1971. Yet perhaps more than any other his would be remembered. Dang was not an innocent victim, as were hundreds of civilians killed in the crossfire between communist and government troops. But Dang had died at the hands of the Phung Hoang program and somehow that was more sinister. After years of buffeting from all sides it came as no surprise that MACV wanted out of the Phoenix business. Success or failure of the program had nothing to do with the decision. But before they could retreat there were committees to be formed and studies to be conducted.

Phung Hoang Reexamination Study

As part of Vietnamization, Phoenix officials began a study to decide how best to reorganize the anti-infrastructure effort with minimum impact from the inevitable removal of U.S. advisers. Formulation of the plan began in mid-1971 and was approved on 23 September. The Phung Hoang Reexamination (PHREEX) study was the latest set of recommendations to the GVN on what needed to be done to strengthen the program during the years 1972 through 1975. Of course, time would run out before then.

PHREEX was a purely American project pushed onto the Vietnamese as a last-ditch effort to make Phung Hoang self-sufficient before MACV left Vietnam. And although Phung Hoang had taken large steps during 1971 toward becoming more independent, American pressure was still needed. As before, the highest levels of the Thieu government supported Phung Hoang, but some provinces and many districts did not always follow enthusiastically. The PHREEX study was prepared by CORDS, and by orders of the third and final CORDS chief, George D. Jacobson, was not to be discussed outside U.S. channels "until coordination is achieved at the national level."[5]

None of the PHREEX recommendations was really new, but in combination they were sound. Whether the Vietnamese would be willing or able to carry them out without American advisers constantly looking over their shoulders was a different matter, however.

Basically, there were three parts to PHREEX. First, firm new criteria for counting VCI as neutralized were to take effect. Between 1969 and 1971 a VCI was counted as neutralized if he rallied to the GVN, was sentenced to a minimum one-year an tri sentence, or was killed. That had been an improvement on older criteria, but there was still room for improvement. The new plan was much the same, but with a new twist. Rallied VCI and cadre sentenced to minimum one-year prison terms still counted, but for dead VCI suspects to be tallied as neutralized they must first have been on the PIOCC or DIOCC blacklist. This cut down considerably on the potential for corruption and double-counting.[6]

Second, PHREEX called for cleaning up the targeting and dossier system. All files on VCI suspects had to be approved at the province level with strict adherence to the three-source rule, which said suspects could be arrested only if there were three confirmed allegations of communist activity on a single individual. From a legal standpoint this was an improvement because it reined in those GVN officials who used the Phoenix program to eliminate political rivals. But it also tied the hands of special reaction forces, such as the PRU and NPFF, that often reacted to intelligence provided during field interrogations of prisoners. The new ruling made it much more difficult to act on perishable intelligence.[7]

Third, and most importantly, PHREEX called for elimination of monthly quotas. According to the study:

> Numerical gross quantitative goals will not be established. Numbers of VCI are not the goal—the goal is to neutralize each and all properly confirmed VCI. The qualitative goal is to measure the effectiveness of each Phung Hoang Center's specifically targeted operations against properly confirmed VCI.[8]

This was not to say that Saigon no longer cared whether the districts showed quantifiable progress against the VCI. The change simply meant a shift in priorities from numbers to trends. Each province was expected to make headway against the VCI based upon intelligence estimates of existing VCI within its boundaries. Each district was directed to prepare a list of known VCI (by name) selected for neutralization. The list was submitted to the province center, which approved or modified the goals. Quarterly progress reports then were used to determine headway made against the VCI based on the percentage of targeted VCI actually neutralized.

Any VCI listed as neutralized who were not on the original list would not be counted. At the end of each three-month period, provinces would be evaluated according to their ability to neutralize targeted VCI and new lists would be drawn up. In some cases a province might end up with many VCI who had not been on the list, but who had been shown to be bona fide communist political cadre. This was not ignored by Saigon, but the fact that province Phung Hoang officials had been unable to identify those individuals as VCI in the first place reflected on the intelligence-gathering capabilities of that province.[9]

American officials still had a few reservations about the new system, however. The old problem of targeting low-level VCI was not addressed and U.S. officials feared a return to the old ways of attacking supporters of the Viet Cong—who may have been coerced into aiding the communists—instead of Party members and administrative cadre. There was no real solution to this problem. Phung Hoang had to rely on the dedication and integrity of each province chief and the regional overseers who monitored VCI intelligence to see that this aspect of PHREEX was adhered to.

One problem that could be dealt with was an attempt by local VCI to thwart the new system. A favorite trick was to load a given region with "ringers," false VCI positions usually filled by low-level supporters or simply the names of local people. As often as not these people did not know they had been "elected" to their new positions and were in no way involved with the Viet Cong. Usually the Viet Cong would place these ringers in a position that had been emptied when some local VCI had been neutralized. Phung Hoang Committees would tend to place the name of whoever had filled the vacant cadre position back on the target list, thereby unknowingly taking pressure off the VCI.[10]

The solution seemed simple. CORDS officials suggested that neutralization target lists be drawn up only from known VCI who were in place at the beginning of each year. The suggestion was reasonable, but left loopholes. By ignoring the possibility that some of the refilled cadre positions might actually be legitimate VCI, Phung Hoang often gave the initiative to the communists. In some cases attempts to decide who was VCI and who was an imposter became an intelligence shell game.

On a more positive note, CORDS officials also inserted a provision into the PHREEX that took some of the pressure to neutralize the highest-level VCI off Phung Hoang. In the past Phoenix was criticized because it rarely neutralized the region, province, and district VCI. Most cadre in those categories were killed in ambushes or during military sweep operations, giving rise to criticism that Phoenix was incapable of neutralizing key communist officials and had to rely on conventional military units. Even MACV tended to go along with that assessment and Phoenix was viewed as largely ineffective by much of the "conventional" military.

But the reality was that the highest-level VCI tended to live in remote areas away from the general population, often across the border in Cambodia or Laos. If they did live among the people it was usually in areas controlled by the Viet Cong and guarded by large military units. These cadre were of little value to the revolution if they could not maintain contact with the general population by way of mid-level cadre living in the villages. CORDS began to realize this and saw that the highest-level VCI could be virtually ignored or left to ARVN troop sweeps if Phung Hoang could first control the mid-level cadre living in the villages.

CORDS suggested that those VCI living away from the general population not be included in the quarterly target lists.[11] Phung Hoang was not equipped to strike at these VCI because when they did emerge from their strongholds to mingle with the population it was usually at night, protected by guerrilla bodyguards. Capture was much more difficult than ambush, a fact borne out by past statistics. Most province and higher cadre were killed—not captured—because they were so heavily guarded. By removing the emphasis on the highest-level communist cadre, CORDS was at long last adjusting to a reality that had always existed.

Enemy Response

The readjustment of Phoenix priorities, beginning in early 1971 and culminating with the PHREEX, had an almost immediate effect on the VCI. Captured enemy documents and interrogation reports indicated an increasing emphasis on the part of the

VCI at all levels to warn their personnel of the new threat and singled out "Phung Hoang agents" as targets for assassination. More significant was the deterioration of the quality of cadre members filling various leadership positions. There was a steady increase throughout 1971 and 1972 in instances of doubling and even tripling of cadre responsibilities by single individuals. Captured VCI were increasingly younger and less educated, indicating a decrease in the pool of qualified cadre. This put more pressure on the district and province VCI to watch over the new and less reliable cadre. Worse—from the communist point of view—was that loss of any high-level VCI meant that their places would have to be taken by these lesser-quality cadre.[12]

The increased emphasis by the Viet Cong on assassinating Phung Hoang personnel was also used by CORDS as a way of shocking ineffective Phung Hoang officials into action. Intelligence gathered from interrogations and captured documents was compiled and distributed to show the threat of reprisals against GVN officials if the communists should ever come to power. Communist directives called for mass executions of those sympathetic to the Saigon government, but many officials refused to believe this, preferring to claim that such Viet Cong pronouncements were merely part of a communist program of intimidation and propaganda rather than absolute objectives. Indeed, such intimidation had long been part of the communists' political struggle. Rather than execute everyone involved with the GVN the Viet Cong had generally been selective in their killings, seeking to intimidate rather than liquidate. But U.S. officials pointed out that in some cases it would be in the communists' interest to totally eliminate the threat to their power. One of those cases was Phung Hoang personnel. And evidence indicated they intended to do just that when they came to power.

In June 1971 the Dinh Tuong Province PIOCC captured a low-level political officer from COSVN. The cadre readily admitted that the communists intended to liquidate entire categories of GVN personnel if North Vietnam won the protracted struggle. These categories included the ARVN officer corps, GVN civil servants, school teachers, and local community leaders. Also specifically mentioned were members of Phung Hoang.[13]

The warnings had little impact. The possibility of a communist victory seemed too remote. Complacency was as much an enemy as the Viet Cong.

Cracks in the System

Many of the basic problems that had plagued Phoenix since its inception remained unsolved in 1971 and 1972. Plans envisioned in Saigon often looked good on paper, but did not unfold as planned in the countryside.

In early 1971 some provinces had still not received the message that Phung Hoang had been placed under the control of the National Police. In Binh Tuy Province in III Corps there was still no directive from the GVN transferring control to the police. The result of this confusion was a lapse in targeting operations and a decline in VCI neutralizations during the first half of 1971.[14]

Quang Duc Province in II Corps was particularly ineffective; William Colby called it "unhealthy." The problem was a lack of intelligence expertise. As American advisers departed, their counterparts generally were unprepared to continue the work. According to U.S. advisers, the PIOCC staff was unqualified, the deputy police chief had neither the ambition nor the authority to get the program moving, and the province chief showed no interest in the VCI. The deputy for CORDS in II Corps wrote, "Quang Duc has never, to my knowledge, achieved a targeted neutralization." He proposed that all U.S. advisers be pulled out of the province rather than attempt to alter the situation.[15]

In May 1971 Vinh Long Province in IV Corps became the subject of a "pilot program" designed to bolster police participation in Vinh Long's Phung Hoang program. Vinh Long was selected for at least three reasons. First, the province was considered crucial to the pacification plans for IV Corps because of its population of more than half a million, the fifth-largest in the Delta. Second, Vinh Long had shown progress against Viet Cong guerrillas, but was less effective against the VCI. Intelligence estimated that Vinh Long Province had the second largest number of VCI in IV Corps. Third, the province had one of the weakest police programs in the Delta.[16]

The scope of the program was grand: "To neutralize 100 percent of the VCI over a six-month period through improved police techniques and procedures."[17] But big ideas were not enough. The proposal was presented to the province chief, who promptly killed the idea because he refused to give the police chief the authority necessary to implement the changes. Few province chiefs were willing to give up their total control of all assets in their province. Although the National Police Command in Saigon approved of the special program, it could not easily force province chiefs to cooperate, a glaring example of the lack of priority given to the National Police despite its increased prestige since 1969.

In the remainder of IV Corps, improvements were made in the Phung Hoang program, but many of the old problems remained. MACV continued to point out a lack of adequate specific targeting and an insufficient number of high-level VCI neutralized. But IV Corps continued to show gains in pacification and reduction in the influence of the VCI. Go Cong, Chau Doc, and Sa Dec Provinces had contained the VCI threat and continued to operate their own programs with little help from American advisers. The key to their success seemed to be full cooperation from their respective province chiefs.[18]

In an attempt to give one final nudge to province Phung Hoang programs in the Delta, American advisers went on a whirlwind inspection tour of all sixteen provinces in IV Corps, tallying strengths and weaknesses as they went. The advisers were critical of the overall program even though only five of the provinces had turned in less than 100 percent of their neutralization goals. Clearly, the emphasis on numbers had become secondary to other factors.[19]

Why were the Vietnamese "unprepared" to take over? Many had been involved in Phung Hoang since 1969, more time in the program than most Americans. The answer probably lay somewhere in the Vietnamese unwillingness and inability to decentralize authority. Despite official proclamations of support for Phoenix from President Thieu and his cabinet, the fact remained that personal power and influence became stronger closer to Saigon. By the time power was distributed at the district level there was little left to go around. The most competent people went to the regional and provincial headquarters; those who were left went to the district.

By 1971 this became particularly clear in IV Corps. At the regional level support and coordination for Phung Hoang couldn't have been better. The military commander, General Ngo Quang Truong, gave his unqualified support, issuing all the appropriate proclamations and directives. His support was a catalyst to most of the provinces, but it did not often reach down to the districts. Only one province, Chau Doc, had an efficient district intelligence coordination plan. Most districts throughout the Delta had inadequately trained intelligence officers, and by the summer of 1971 American Phung Hoang advisers were still frantically trying to set up short training courses designed to make the Vietnamese self-sufficient.[20]

New methods clearly were needed to supplement the flagging DIOCC system. One of the best ideas sought to tap a virtually unused source of intelligence—the rural population. For the most part Phoenix had never involved the people in uprooting the VCI. It wasn't until 1971 that such a program was seriously implemented.

Informant and Reward Programs

Official rewards designed to encourage people to turn in underground communist cadre gradually became an important part of GVN policy, although not until late in the war. The reason was twofold. First, the Phoenix program's intelligence coordination and plans for specifically targeting high-level VCI was not proceeding as hoped. Second, Vietnamization was well under way, American involvement was winding down and it was hoped that a reward program would generate more intelligence from the general public.

On the down side, the Americans had put off pushing a rewards program (rewards had been used by Phoenix from the beginning, but nothing on the scale of this new program) because they feared a backlash from the press and critics at home. Like much else about Phoenix, CORDS correctly predicted that a system of rewards would add to the Phoenix program's Wild West image and be seen as a system that encouraged bounty hunters. But when the program seriously began in the summer of 1971, there was only limited notice in the press. Vietnamization and the American pullout was the big story.

As was the case with most aspects of anti-infrastructure operations in Vietnam, there had been successful precedents to use as guidelines. In Malaya the British had used a system of rewards that decimated guerrilla ranks. During the Huk rebellion in the Philippines, rewards were also used effectively. In both cases the goal had been to rob the guerrillas of the glamour of political revolution by exposing the leaders as common criminals. The main objective was to drive a wedge between the insurgents and the population. In Vietnam the task was more difficult because the communists had been part of a national struggle to free Vietnam from imperialism and it was difficult for the Americans to disassociate themselves from the colonial image.

In Malaya and the Philippines, reward systems were part of the anti-infrastructure strategy from the beginning. In Vietnam the reward program came too late. But its implementation did illustrate an important trend: the GVN continued to emphasize anti-infrastructure operations even in the face of an imminent American troop withdrawal from South Vietnam. Saigon was willing to continue making anti-infrastructure operations a priority and took innovative steps—with American prodding and money—to supplement the Phoenix program's performance.

In the spring of 1971 CORDS put into place a reward program designed to encourage citizens to turn in VCI for money. Part of this system was called the Volunteer Informant Program (VIP) and it was designed to increase the number of Category A VCI specifically targeted for neutralization. Only the neutralization of district- or higher-level VCI qualified an informant for the reward.

The GVN and CORDS had used loose informant programs to supplement the Phoenix program in the past, including payments to Hoi Chanhs who turned in weapons or named other VCI. American Phoenix advisers had often had special funds at their disposal to use as payment for informant nets, but there was little management from the top and fraud was often reported. Only in 1971 did the program receive official approval from the highest levels. Saigon was serious about the VIP program and endorsed it fully.[21]

VIP was seen as a step toward educating the Vietnamese people about the dangers of VIC presence in the villages. Most importantly, VIP was another public program designed to show the people Phoenix was not a clandestine murder machine, but a program that wanted to work with the population toward a common goal of ridding South Vietnam of communism. In June 1971, Minister of Interior Tran Thien Khiem (who also served concurrently as prime minister) issued an official directive announcing a reward program in four trial provinces, one in each military region (Quang Nam, MR 1; Binh Dinh, MR 2; Bien Hoa, MR 3; and Vinh Binh, MR 4). The trial program was to begin in August.

The essential element was specific targeting. Only certain VCI were qualified as legitimate targets under the reward program. First, they had to be Class A VCI, or members of the People's Revolutionary Party. Second, all VCI on the list had to be considered a serious threat. Third, all those selected had to be "confirmed" VCI. In other words, they had to have dossiers on file that would assure an an tri conviction once they were arrested.[22]

The province chief selected the VCI considered to be the most important and passed along copies of their dossiers to the PSC for review. The Central Phung Hoang Committees gave final approval for all VCI selected for the rewards program. Whenever a VCI on the list was neutralized, the province chief selected another to be added. To keep reward payments from getting out of hand, rewards were to be offered for no more than ten VCI per province.

Rewards were from 1 to 3 million piasters ($3,600 to $10,900 in U.S. dollars) for information leading to the neutralization of any VCI on the list. An additional two hundred thousand piaster bonus ($900 U.S.) was given to any GVN unit that captured a VCI. The bonus was reduced by half if the VCI suspect was killed. A similar bonus could be given to Vietnamese Phung

Hoang center staff if they had contributed to compiling intelligence that led to the capture of an important VCI.[23]

In an attempt to curtail possible corruption within the program, the GVN decided that only certain people could be eligible for the rewards. They included civilians, rank-and-file GVN employees, enlisted men, and NCOs within the armed forces and paramilitary forces. Employees of the GVN in management positions and all officers in the armed forces were ineligible. Hoi Chanhs who provided information leading to the arrest of a VCI on the list could in some cases qualify for the reward, as could captured VCI or VC who voluntarily provided information on other VCI. No targeted VCI could surrender and collect the reward offered on himself.

But as usual, reality arose to confront the program and cause debilitating problems. The reward program plans were meticulously crafted to confront all possible problems, yet once implemented, the results were less than hoped for. First, both American and GVN officials found it difficult to suppress their penchant for secrecy. One proposal called for dummy vouchers to keep the amounts and sources of the rewards secret. CORDS director William Colby disagreed, noting that the entire point of the reward program was to involve the people in their own security:

> There is nothing covert or even really classified about this program after it gets going, and I think it would be unfortunate if . . . we felt that we have to try to keep it secret from everybody but the enemy.[24]

A second problem was one of finances. The American public was unwilling to spend more money on a war effort that was clearly winding down and an increase in funding for a program as controversial as Phung Hoang was especially unpopular. The timing was particularly poor. Congressional hearings on the war in Vietnam held during February 1970 and again in July and August 1971 had condemned Phung Hoang, despite William Colby's denial of charges that it was an assassination program.

MACV asked for $4.2 million in military support for the CORDS pacification program in FY 1972.[25] Estimates for the initial four-province experiment were broken down according to the perceived number of "dangerous" VCI in each province. IV Corps (the Mekong Delta) was considered the area with the greatest VCI threat, so it was allotted forty-eight separate reward funds totaling almost $2 million. II Corps received the second-largest amount at $750,000, followed by III Corps with $703,000, and I Corps with $372,900.[26] I Corps had the fewest VCI because the North Vietnamese overtly controlled the region with conventional troops, battling U.S. Marines and Army troops on the ground.

Did the informant and reward program work? It is difficult to say. A few American advisers noted that some of the rewards were collected when targeted VCI were neutralized on information provided by informers. Unfortunately, no records have been found that analyze the success or failure of the program. Record-keeping became more lax and the piles of documents and reports lessened as Americans awaited their turn to leave for home. The reward program was caught in the downshifting of priorities and it seems no one did a study of the program and its success or failure.

The question of the reward program's success or failure became moot when the United States suddenly decided to discontinue support. COMUSMACV Creighton Abrams and U.S. Ambassador Ellsworth Bunker reversed U.S. support for the program, ordering it discontinued on 28 October 1971. Their reasons were predictable: adverse publicity and the possibility that the program might have an unfavorable impact on negotiations. Most importantly, the ongoing Vietnamization of Phung Hoang made supervision of the reward program unwieldy. Besides, no one wanted to go out on a limb when all U.S. Phoenix advisers were scheduled to leave South Vietnam by 30 June 1972—a mere eight months away.[27]

The F-6 Program

Congressional scrutiny of the Phoenix program, beginning in 1970, focused on alleged excesses and incompetence. Testimony by critics of the program, most of whom had nothing to do with

Phoenix, painted a grim picture of anti-infrastructure operations. They alleged that documents calling for the capture of suspected VCI were only a cover under which the CIA assassinated all political opposition to the Thieu regime. After CORDS departed Vietnam in March 1973, according to these critics, the program continued with covert American direction under the cryptic name F-6. The reality of the F-6 program was neither so sinister or so permanent.[28]

The F-6 program was actually a defensive measure meant to bolster the Phung Hoang program following the NVA Easter Offensive, which began on 30 March 1972. This stopgap measure lasted from 21 April 1972 until 1 January 1973. It did indeed use some American advice and support, but that was perfectly "legal" because it occurred before the Paris Peace Talks finalized the U.S. pullout from South Vietnam.

As pressure from the NVA offensive rolled over parts of the ARVN in I, II, and III Corps, Saigon searched for some way to keep pacification from crumbling altogether. In IV Corps, NVA attacks were weak and disjointed compared to those to the north, but the increased infiltration of main-force units from over the border in Cambodia put heavy pressure on pacification there as well. Lieutenant General Ngo Quang Truong, commanding general of Military Region 4 (IV Corps), ordered a special Phung Hoang campaign designed to keep the VCI off balance despite their newfound power courtesy of the NVA. Truong did not remain in IV Corps to see the results of his initiative; he was transferred to I Corps in early May to take over command there following the collapse of ARVN units in the face of the communist offensive.

Basically, F-6 sought to increase pressure on the VCI by allowing province chiefs to move against suspected cadre on the strength of a single report of VCI activity rather than the three reports usually required. American and Vietnamese authorities were fully aware that the number of innocent citizens swept up would surely increase, but hard times demanded hard measures.

This was not a centralized program, but rather a broad-based set of powers given to each province chief to be used at his own initiative. Far from being a blank check, however, F-6 also instructed province chiefs to use caution when assembling cases against VCI suspects and to consider carefully each case according to its own merits.[29]

The first province to use these powers was Chau Doc, one of the hardest hit in IV Corps because of its strategic position on the Cambodian border. Intelligence indicated that NVA units were moving to staging areas just inside the province, led by VCI who knew the region. Phung Hoang Committees quickly ordered the roundup of all VCI suspects and within days 204 people had been arrested. By 25 April the number had climbed by an additional 239 and by the end of the first week in May the total was 761.[30]

Actually, these figures were not as dramatic as they might appear. Under "normal" circumstances, IV Corps listed an average of 550 VCI suspects under detention and awaiting trial at the end of each month. But no one in the American embassy or the GVN was willing to widen the margin for error. Ellsworth Bunker, U.S. ambassador to South Vietnam, advised that all Province Security Committees carefully screen all suspects before sentencing. The object of F-6 was to get all VCI suspects into detention centers so they could not help the NVA. Once in custody they were not a threat and care could be taken to weed out those innocent citizens caught up in the dragnet. Only those VCI suspects with evidence against them according to the standard an tri guidelines were to be sentenced. In other words, the special criteria set forth by F-6 were sufficient to arrest suspects, but not enough to convict them. For that the standard procedure of three separate charges and a complete intelligence dossier was needed.[31]

Special care also was taken to assure that F-6 would not go so far that adverse publicity might arise. These concerns were discussed by Ambassador Bunker with the National Police commander to ensure that "measures taken against the current threat do not degrade refinements of [the] Phung Hoang program for selective neutralization of confirmed VCI or increase public resentment of an tri procedures through misuse."[32]

After the initial three-week surge in arresting VCI suspects, the numbers tapered off. There are no final figures on the number of VCI suspects arrested during F-6 and no figures on those finally sentenced.

During the short life of the F-6 program a fundamental

change in the nature of the war led to a rapid change in American involvement in Phung Hoang. The escalated bombing of North Vietnam by President Nixon in response to the Easter Offensive and the mining of North Vietnamese harbors led to rapid progress in the Paris Peace Talks. This set limits on continued U.S. involvement in South Vietnam, including in the Phoenix program. As noted earlier, U.S. participation in Phoenix had been decreasing throughout the period of Vietnamization, and in the face of the Paris negotiations there was to be no muddying of the waters by Phoenix. On 1 December 1972 all American support for Phoenix was to end.

In an attempt to minimize some of the inevitable damage done to Phoenix by the coming Paris Accords, F-6 changed from prosecuting VCI suspects as threats to national security to sentencing them as criminals. This was done because those sentenced under criminal law would not be subject to release under any cease-fire agreement. President Thieu agreed and word was passed down to the province-level National Police. But as had been the case in all facets of Phoenix evolution, the police were hesitant to change. In this case they felt the new directive would make their jobs more difficult and slow down the processing of captured suspects.[33]

To antiwar critics back in the States, F-6 looked like a new and sinister program. True, F-6 was classified "confidential" and only a few details leaked to the general public, but there was absolutely no evidence to suggest that the program was "illegal." Only a few U.S. Phung Hoang advisers remained in the Delta by mid-1972, so in truth F-6 could claim to be purely a Vietnamese program.

Yet the continuing cry for a speedy American withdrawal from South Vietnam clouded reasonable judgment. Mention of the "mysterious" F-6 program in Congressional testimony prompted some congressmen to query administration officials. Senator Clifford P. Case wrote to Secretary of State William P. Rogers:

> I find particularly disturbing reports in the press about a new American-supported program, called "F-6", allegedly aimed at "neutralizing" the Viet Cong.
> I had assumed that with the discontinuation of the Phoenix

program in South Vietnam, the United States had foresworn the use of "dirty tricks," either directly by our representatives or by Vietnamese agencies supported by us.[34]

The senator's misunderstanding of the nature of the Viet Cong insurgency was profound and his thinking had been completely colored by news reports that the Phoenix program was predominantly "dirty tricks." William Colby had spent days on end since 1970 seated on Capitol Hill explaining the nuts and bolts of the Phoenix program. Judging by Senator Case's letter, no one was listening.

The State Department answered the senator's letter, explaining the nature of the F-6 program. The letter left little out despite the fact that the program was classified, explaining that F-6 was not an American program and that it was merely a temporary measure.[35] Senator Case may have been satisfied with the reply, but the press did not get the message. Stories continued to paint F-6 as a diabolical scheme to keep Phoenix alive.

End of the Line

With the culmination of the F-6 program early in 1973, the Phoenix program came to an end. Officially the American advisory effort had ended in December 1972 (although U.S. Phoenix advisers had left in July, some administrative and financial support for Phung Hoang remained in place), but since early 1972 only a few provinces retained U.S. advisers. Even the Vietnamese side of the program—Phung Hoang—had officially ceased to exist. In the spring of 1972 it was absorbed by the National Police. All personnel employed in the PIOCCs and DIOCCs were placed under the command of the National Police Directorate and given a new emphasis. Rather than simply targeting individual VCI for neutralization, the police aimed their efforts at "terrorism." In fact, the new name for the anti-infrastructure program reflected the shift in priorities. Called Protection of the People Against Terrorism (POPAT), the GVN sought to shift attention away from the neutralization numbers game and onto the broader and less personal "fight against terrorism."

POPAT began in September and continued through December 1972. It was meant to be a temporary campaign against the VCI, one that would gain maximum attention and show the people that the GVN could indeed protect the people against terrorism. But the escalating American withdrawal turned GVN thoughts away from anti-infrastructure operations and POPAT would become the end of what had been known as the Phoenix program.

Before it left the war for good, Phoenix made one last gasp toward centralization. In an attempt to consolidate the labor-intensive IOCC system, the intelligence centers were placed under police control beginning in April and called Police Operations Centers (POC). Unlike the old IOCCs, the POC did much more than coordinate intelligence. The POC was basically the police nerve center for each province. Operations were planned, policemen were garrisoned; anything having to do with police work was centered at the POC. This represented a shift from the decentralized Phoenix system back toward a more centralized effort such as the old ICEX system had been. Given the cutback in U.S. advisers and resources, the GVN had little choice.

During the final transfer of the trappings of Phoenix to the National Police, results against the VCI dropped. During the spring and summer of 1972 officials recorded fewer VCI neutralized and more incidents of terrorism against civilians in "secure" rural areas. According to the last U.S. pacification advisers, the downward trend did not last long, however. After a few months, "there was a subsequent recovery to previous levels or higher."[36] By December terrorist incidents had dropped to the lowest level since March 1972. No one, however, was willing to say that POPAT had much to do with the decrease.

The Paris Peace Accords signed on 27 January 1973 called for all U.S. troops and advisers to all military and paramilitary organizations, including the police, to withdraw from South Vietnam within sixty days. AID was allowed to continue supplying the police with material on a one-for-one replacement basis, and to train police outside South Vietnam. The rest was up to the Vietnamese.[37]

After MACV closed down and the last American troops left for home, most of South Vietnam was quiet. The Viet Cong was only a pale imitation of the formidable fighting force of the mid-1960s and the NVA had retreated across the border into Cambodia, Laos, and North Vietnam to recover from the beating it suffered during the Easter Offensive. The VCI was weak in most parts of South Vietnam and guerrilla warfare no longer occupied a place in communist strategy. The GVN, too, had been hurt during the offensive and there was little desire to step up Phung Hoang, although given the decrease in the enemy's conventional attacks the timing would have been perfect. The VCI that remained in South Vietnam was a matter of statistics rather than substance. Intelligence continued to churn out statistics on the total number of VCI in each province, using the central computer called Big Mack. Of questionable accuracy, Big Mack pronounced precise figures on the relative strengths and weaknesses of the VCI countrywide.

But the VCI numbers meant nothing. Most of the mid-level cadre remaining in the countryside were poor-quality draftees who had little loyalty to the communist cause. They were merely names on a roster. All evidence indicates that the effectiveness of the VCI had virtually ceased and the police were really chasing shadows. When Big Mack said that in April 1972 there was a "total of 67,017 VCI [in all of South Vietnam], compared with a January total of 76,398," it was a meaningless figure—meaningless because given the state of GVN intelligence such a precise figure was laughable, and meaningless because of those VCI in the countryside only a small percentage were of any value to the communists.[38]

One of the best examples of VCI impotence by 1972 was the situation in IV Corps. Most of the Delta had come to ignore both the GVN and the Viet Cong. Prosperity brought on partly by pacification advances and by increasing North Vietnamese military emphasis on the northern regions allowed Vietnamese peasants to exist relatively free of the life-and-death politics experienced by their fellow citizens to the north. Yet provinces such as An Giang and Go Cong had sizable VCI populations, according to Big Mack. During August and September 1972, An Giang Province recorded only three VCI neutralized, strong evidence that the local Phung Hoang program was ineffective. However, An Giang was considered one of the two most pacified provinces in IV Corps (Go Cong was the other) and Viet Cong cadre were not having much success getting close to the population. Big Mack simply could not distinguish between simple statistics and meaningful VCI strengths.[39]

The last American Phoenix advisers departed South Vietnam in December 1972. They left behind many of the same problems that had plagued Phoenix since its inception. No one could say the system was always fair, was always right in its accusations, or was completely effective. But, despite the shortcomings, Phoenix had undergone a tremendous evolution compacted into four years. More than any other aspect of the American advisory effort in South Vietman, the Phoenix program had learned from its mistakes and had taken step after step to correct them. In the end it all came to nothing, but U.S. advisers took some pride in that they had helped decimate the Viet Cong Infrastructure.

The Phoenix program could never be called successful because in the end South Vietnam fell. Many other factors besides the communist political infrastructure were responsible for that fall, but the VCI made it all possible. The communists held on through many setbacks, always allowing the NVA and VC mainforce units time to regroup following serious military setbacks. For its part, the Phoenix program had been one part of a very successful counterinsurgency program that, despite its shortcomings, slowly but surely decimated the Viet Cong.

After all praise and criticism was aired, the impact of the Phoenix program on the VCI remained unclear. Yet one source of evidence needed examination. Perhaps no better witness to the Phoenix program's success or failure would be the enemy himself, although few thought to ask.

11

Enemy Strikes Back: Communist Reaction to Phoenix

WHEN passing judgment on the success or failure of the Phoenix program, American planners generally relied on statistics and province reports. However, these sources only gave a partial picture. The total number of VCI neutralized often did not accurately reflect the damage done by Phoenix. In some provinces the number of high-ranking VCI neutralized was small, but at the village and hamlet level the political cadres' ability to function among the population had been severely hampered. By severing the link between these lower-ranking VCI and their bosses at the district and province level, the Phoenix program had succeeded in destroying the effectiveness of the VCI, even if the numbers did not reflect this.

Another important barometer of the Phoenix program's effectiveness was often ignored. What did the enemy think? In the final analysis it was the best judge.

The Phoenix program was honored often in the pages of North Vietnam's propaganda pamphlets and it became clear that the success of Phoenix was directly proportional to the amount of time and effort Hanoi and the Viet Cong spent on denouncing it.

Aside from documents and propaganda, the communists also took steps to minimize the effect the Phoenix program was having within its own ranks. By the middle of 1970 intelligence indicated that the Viet Cong had set up prison camps specifically for those accused by the Party of belonging to the Phoenix organization. But there was an ironic twist to some of these camps: the inmates were former communist political cadre and Viet Cong and North Vietnamese soldiers who were accused by the Party of having willfully fallen prey to the Phoenix and Chieu Hoi programs. Their fate was no better than that of American and South Vietnamese soldiers imprisoned in Viet Cong jungle camps.

Cage for the Phoenix

The full extent of the Viet Cong's concern for the effectiveness of the Phoenix program became evident in intelligence reports on these camps. From the evidence available to date it is impossible to estimate the number of such camps, but given their specialized nature it is unlikely there were more than a handful. Specific details on these "Phoenix prison camps" were rare, but at least one did come to the attention of American intelligence. The camp was called the "B-3 Thought Reform Camp" and was developed as a countermeasure to the Phoenix and Chieu Hoi programs conducted in Bien Hoa and Long Khanh Provinces.[1]

American forces became aware of the camp on 26 November 1970, when a joint U.S.–ARVN sweep through the area captured a "K-3 convalescent camp" containing a number of Viet Cong recovering from wounds or shell shock. Among them was one wretched ex-prisoner, Nguyen Van Chanh, who had been in the B-3 Thought Reform Camp long enough that the Party deemed him reeducated and free from the poison of his contact with Phoenix. Chanh was again considered a Party faithful, but he knew he would never be fully trusted. As a sort of reward for his reeducation, Chanh was sent to the convalescence camp to rest, or more likely, recover. It was his fate to be there when the Americans and South Vietnamese swept through. At least he would not have to live under a shadow of mistrust by his former comrades. The future of his comrades was not so bright. One of them was executed after he attempted to escape.

The B-3 Thought Reform Camp didn't sound like a sinister place. The name was more reminiscent of a political reorientation camp designed to nudge those who drifted from the Party back into line, a sterile place with white walls and bare bulbs. But this place was anything but sterile and these men had done more than simply question communism. According to the Viet Cong they had been tainted by the Phoenix program, an offense serious enough to warrant a special prison camp just for them, in this case six men. Not only were they punished for their transgressions, but the Party felt it could wring information about the Phoenix program from them—if they kept at it long enough.

The facilities were spartan. About forty bunkers had room for nearly seventy political staff and guards. Ten bunkers served as cages for the prisoners, indicating that there were never supposed to be more than a handful of men in the camp at one time.

Three raised guard towers surrounded the camp and acted as sentry posts to guard the prisoners and as lookouts for aircraft. Many planes did fly over—the camp was covered only by a light canopy, much different from the dense umbrella that loomed over the surrounding area, and the prisoners often could hear and see observation aircraft circling lazily overhead. They could only wonder whether the people in the planes cared about them, though at times it seemed the pilots suspected something was down there. An OV-1 Mohawk observation plane sometimes circled the area, but the prisoners soon learned its presence heralded only dread. Every time it appeared there would follow, a day or so later, a B-52 strike that rumbled in the valleys near the camp, sometimes close enough to shower the area with debris, the concussion from the explosions causing nosebleeds and earaches. And the guards could set their watches each morning by an AH-1 Cobra gunship that clattered over the canopy at 8:00 A.M. without fail.

Nor were the prisoners very far from GVN-held territory, though they could not have known that while in captivity. A rubber plantation was some miles away and the area surrounding it was held by the ARVN. It would have been a foot race between the ARVN and neighboring Viet Cong units if friendly forces had found out where the camp was: the nearest communist main-force battalion was a two- to four-hour march from the camp.

The Viet Cong did not seem too concerned about the possibility of an attack by the ARVN, which rarely ventured far from areas known to be safe, and the B-4 camp was not in one of those areas. The guards ran small patrols around the camp, but they seemed to rely mainly on warnings that came over a Chinese-made radio in the camp headquarters.

Chanh had been arrested by SR-4 security personnel in April of 1970 and sent immediately to the B-3 camp. The camp director, Bay Dung, a no-nonsense man with short-cropped hair, wasted no time in bringing Chanh to trial on charges of "falling prey to mistresses of the Phung Hoang program, which led them to make attempts at deserting the Viet Cong cause." The trial lasted a day and a half, and of the six prisoners, only two were considered guilty enough to be sent to North Vietnam for punishment. The rest would serve their terms in the camp.

Chanh had been told by another prisoner, Nguyen Van Long, who had already been at the B-3 camp for a few months before Chanh's arrival, that several prisoners had been sent North to face life sentences or execution in Hanoi. These men, Long said, had stolen top secret Viet Cong documents and had attempted to rally to the GVN. Long felt it was likely they all would be executed.

The rules in the camp were simple. All prisoners were to do exactly as they were told. The first attempt to escape would be punished by an oral reprimand, the second attempt would result in reduced rations, and the third attempt meant death. Escape was not easy at any rate, not because the security was tight, or the guards especially alert, but because the lack of protein in the prisoners' diet made them weak. Each man received 300 grams of rice a day. That was all. Seven times each month a large can of fish was given to the prisoners to be divided evenly among all six of them.

Chanh's newfound acquaintance, Nguyen Van Long, the man who had told him about the expected fate of the prisoners sent north to Hanoi, broke the rules once too often. In early August 1970, a few weeks before Chanh was captured by the

Americans, Long made a dash for freedom while the guards were taking off his leg irons. A guard chased him down and dragged him back to the camp. The chief of the security platoon, Muoi Chuyen, forced Long down on his stomach and calmly shot him with an AK-47. He told the remaining prisoners their fates would be the same if they did not follow instructions.

Before the execution of Nguyen Van Long, daily life in the prison camp went along smoothly and predictably. The daily routine was interrogation or sitting shackled and handcuffed in their cages. Chanh recalled that for the first three days after his imprisonment he was interrogated twice a day for about three hours each time. For the next four days he was interrogated in the morning only, spending the rest of the day in his cage. In the afternoon, the prisoners were escorted to the stream that ran through the camp and allowed to bathe.

On those mornings when he was to be interrogated, Chanh was marched into the back room of the headquarters bunker. The room was bare except for a table and two bamboo chairs. A flickering flame from a single oil lamp lit the proceedings. Muoi Chuyen, commander of the security platoon, and Bay Mach, head of the "Judicial Section," were always waiting, grim faces revealing nothing. They asked the questions.

Chanh knew what his interrogators were after. The unknown factor was whether they would accept Chanh's answers as truth. Since Chanh had been "exposed to Phoenix agents," the interrogators droned on about operational procedures. Did Chanh know who the agents in the Phoenix program were? How did they work? Was there anyone else in the Party whom they had infected?

One prisoner, Bay Dung, was especially unlucky. Chanh once witnessed his interrogation.

Muoi Chuyen held up a picture in the flickering light. It was the ID card of a girl reported to be a "Phoenix mistress," a woman recruited by the CIA to seduce members of the PRP and get them to either divulge information about the VCI in the area, or failing that, rally. The province-level cadre were very concerned; feminine wiles were considered more dangerous than a platoon of fierce PRUs.

"Now we have the picture of the girl, you must tell us the

true story about her." Muoi Chuyen played the tough cop while Bay Mach stood sternly in the background, ready to play an even tougher cop. Bay Dung didn't hesitate to tell what he knew. Why risk death over a few nights of lovemaking?

The trysts had occurred at the Ba Co Inn in Binh Son Hamlet, a well-known hangout for local VC in Bien Hoa Province. Bay Dung had met the woman one night while taking an evening off from his usual duties in the bush guarding local VCI as they moved under cover of the night. Bay Dung was the leader of an armed security platoon that operated all over SR-4, but for the most part remained in the vicinity of Long Thanh District, where Binh Son Hamlet was situated. Whenever he could get away from the war, Bay Dung went to the Ba Co Inn.

Like the prisoners who had come and gone through the B-3 camp, Bay Dung could add little to the story of the Phoenix mistresses. All he knew was that for a little money and a few secrets, he—and other VC in the hamlet—could get a long night filled with pleasure. The Party was concerned about the effectiveness of the Phoenix mistresses because they were plying their wares to the top echelons of the district-level infrastructure. Some men—both VC soldiers and cadre—were stealing money from their units, and too many other men were chronically short of cash. The Party believed this was because they had fallen under the spell of the seductive Phoenix women.

Orders had come down from the top levels of SR-4 outlining two courses of action to thwart this new Phoenix ploy. First, undercover agents were being sent to check on the activities of Viet Cong in the vicinity of the notorious Binh Son Hamlet. They were ordered to report any violations to the Political Staff Section of SR-4. Second, the Viet Cong sought to compromise the Phoenix mistresses at Ba Co Inn and at other places where such goings-on had been reported—Phuoc Tien Hamlet, and Phuoc My Village. A Viet Cong underground security agent living at Ba Co Inn snatched the ID card of the woman Bay Dung had slept with, and he also managed to acquire the cards of a few others. It was that agent who reported the midnight rendezvous of Chanh, Bay Dung, and most of the other indiscreet men who wound up as prisoners at the B-3 camp. Why the agent was unable to secure the capture of the Phoenix mistresses was unclear.

In addition to the interrogators, Chanh and his five fellow prisoners had to undergo indoctrination before they were considered cured. For months on end the prisoners were told the same thing over and over: never again make contact with the Phoenix mistresses. These women were put in the path of the revolution to demoralize the brave Viet Cong fighters and hinder their drive to liberate South Vietnam. The prisoners were told that three thousand women and girls had been recruited by the Phoenix program for these "immoral operations."

Interestingly, the prisoners were also told that the Viet Cong would have to set up their own seduction program, "unwantingly," to counterplot the Phoenix program. However, the Viet Cong had been using women as seductresses in their plans to assassinate GVN officials since the early 1960s.[2] That the GVN had turned the tables seemed to annoy the Viet Cong more than harm them.

The indoctrination cadre at the B-3 camp also admonished the prisoners to ignore all enemy propaganda leaflets, especially those distributed by Phoenix agents. If they were to come across any leaflets they were to leave them where they lay, or if they had the time, gather them up and burn them. Muoi Chuyen and Bay Mach constantly pointed out that the leaflets strewn about by the American and ARVN psyop units twisted the real meaning of the revolution into something disgusting, but anyone whose heart was really with the movement could see through the hoax.

Now, Nguyen Van Chanh's war was over. He was in the hands of the Americans and he seemed glad to be away from the Viet Cong. He was a cooperative prisoner, telling his newest interrogators all the details of his imprisonment. He did not know, however, what had become of the Phoenix mistresses, or whether they had even been part of the Phoenix program. The Viet Cong had been frightened of Phoenix since 1969, when the program had been seriously decimating much of the political cadre, especially in Chanh's area. Therefore, in the Party's eyes, Phoenix was responsible for every suspicious activity that upset the motion of the revolution.

There is no other documentary evidence yet uncovered that confirms the existence of the Phoenix mistresses. If they did exist they were very likely part of a plan cooked up by local South Vietnamese officials, perhaps with the aid of the CIA, which was constantly looking for new ways of developing intelligence networks and agent penetrations. Whether the Phoenix program in the area was even aware of the plan is unknown. But the existence of the B-3 Thought Reform Camp and its preoccupation with the Phoenix program was a backhanded compliment from the Viet Cong. Only a program that hurt them would be deemed worthy of such attention.

Long before the Phoenix program began stalking the VCI, the Viet Cong targeted the GVN presence in the countryside. There is little question that the Viet Cong performed their task well. They intimidated, assassinated, and kidnapped those who stood in their way and they did it without separating themselves from the peasants. Compared to the Viet Cong, the Phoenix program was feeble indeed. Yet back in the United States the argument over whether Phoenix was good or evil, effective or futile, continued. After the last U.S. combat troops climbed the stairs of a waiting freedom bird and turned their backs on the fighting that still raged behind them, the controversy remained.

But no one who had an opinion on the Phoenix program looked to the one source that could help them end their argument—the Viet Cong and the North Vietnamese. What did the enemy—those targeted by Phoenix—think of the program? Surely their response would indicate something one way or the other.

Indeed, it did. But hindsight has been helpful here. Proponents and critics did not have many of the captured documents that pertained to the Phoenix program at their disposal, nor could the span of propaganda statements issued from Hanoi and the Viet Cong in the South be viewed in unbroken perspective. Today it is much easier to look back and piece together a picture.

Evidence

One of the best indications of the Phoenix program's success or failure was the amount of ink it received in Viet Cong propaganda statements. Communist denouncements became increasingly shrill as the program became more effective. However, not everything reported by the Viet Cong regarding Phoenix was untrue. They pointed out specifics about Phoenix's excesses that the U.S. press, too, had observed. But, for the most part, Viet Cong propaganda concentrated on the pacification effort in general and, as the Phoenix program became public knowledge, on the purported policy of torture, intimidation, and assassination.

Captured enemy documents also pinpointed the communists' feelings about the effectiveness of pacification. As was the case with propaganda statements, Viet Cong concern over gains in the GVN program to reach into the countryside were directly proportional to the number of mentions made to the program in documents. In one way, however, captured documents were an even more important source of information on the enemy's concern for Phoenix than were propaganda statements: documents weren't designed to be captured, so they tended to represent the true nature of Viet Cong concerns in a more realistic fashion than did propaganda.

Before 1966 pacification did not receive the lion's share of attention in Viet Cong documents. No real surprise there; the GVN placed little emphasis on pacification, and of course, Phoenix was not yet in existence. In 1967, when pacification began in earnest, the Viet Cong paid it more attention. A document captured in September 1967 noted that the communists needed to "closely associate military activities with political activities and troop proselyting. Try to gain the greatest victory and frustrate all enemy plots, especially that of pacification."[3]

In the period up through the Strategic Hamlet program, the Viet Cong often ignored the efforts of the GVN to control the countryside, mostly because those efforts were feeble and ineffective. Although the Strategic Hamlets themselves and GVN troop outposts often were attacked by the Viet Cong, this early attempt at pacification did not receive the amount of attention in documents and propaganda that the later Phoenix program did.

After the Tet Offensive in early 1968, President Thieu began to emphasize pacification in his plans for prosecuting the war.

The Viet Cong sat up and took notice, recognizing that the GVN could deal them a serious blow if they did not prepare to fight the "other war."

Part of that preparation came in the form of increased propaganda. After Thieu's announcement of the Accelerated Pacification Plan in November 1968, the Viet Cong stepped up attacks on pacification teams throughout South Vietnam. Phoenix was also a primary target. Local communist cadres were ordered to "capture and annihilate" GVN personnel attached to the Phoenix program "at all costs. Our intent should be to individually destroy his [U.S. and GVN] important personnel, especially their commanders, or to seize [them] and then extract information on [the Phung Hoang] organization and networks . . . [and] punish them severely to foil their sabotage schemes."[4]

A Viet Cong document captured on 26 November 1968 exhorted communist cadres and main-force units to do everything possible to counter the GVN's pacification and Phoenix programs. Pacification was seen as a vehicle to gain "widespread control over the population in rural areas . . . particularly in areas under mixed control prior to a ceasefire."[5] Nothing surprising there; the GVN was indeed trying to exert control over the countryside—as the Viet Cong also had been trying to do for years. It was simply a matter of who could do it best.

Phoenix also came under fire in a document that called the program an attempt to "find every way to annihilate all underground cadres upon the declaration of a ceasefire."[6] Again, the Viet Cong used hyperbole in an attempt to attach a label of "assassination" to the Phoenix program.

Viet Cong Anti-Phoenix Measures

While Phoenix made attempts to capture infrastructure members and to target only those actually involved in the insurgency, the Viet Cong wanted to wipe out those officials and individuals who stood in their way. Communist cadres had orders "to kill without mercy" any GVN "agents" attempting to make their way into Viet Cong–controlled areas. And because the Viet Cong had no reason to trust the Vietnamese population under their control, they set up rules governing travel into those areas contested by the GVN. "All unauthorized contact with GVN persons, including relatives" was prohibited without permission from the cadre.[7]

At the same time, the Viet Cong postured as the legitimate representatives of the South Vietnamese people. Therefore, any action they took against the GVN—usually in the form of assassinating province, district, and hamlet officials—was justified, while the Phoenix program's operations to neutralize the VCI were "illegal."

In fact, the Viet Cong were much more brutal than Phoenix, assigning assassinations to special teams of armed reconnaissance units (ARU). These teams were given the responsibility of killing or kidnapping any GVN official rash enough to present them with the opportunity. Unlike the Phoenix program, which basically operated on a province and district level, the ARU was much more extensive, reportedly running operatives down to the village level. In 1965 individual ARU teams were made up of six members, but by 1970 they had apparently expanded that number, partially reflecting the need to counter the Phoenix program.[8]

Plans for each "hit" varied with the difficulty of the target. Easy marks were assigned to local thugs and sometimes children, while more difficult ones went to the specially trained ARU. Unlike Phoenix, the ARU made no attempt to capture the target. And also unlike Phoenix, the Viet Cong always knew who the GVN officials were, making their task easy.

The communist assassination apparatus was presided over by the An Ninh, a "security agency" run by the North Vietnamese Ministry of Public Security in Hanoi. The An Ninh had an estimated ten thousand to fifteen thousand agents in South Vietnam, from a five-hundred-man section at COSVN headquarters to three-man sections down at the village level. The An Ninh was basically a counterintelligence service, providing security for high-ranking VCI and targeting any GVN agents or officials seen as a threat. The Phoenix program was one of the biggest threats. An Ninh agents prepared blacklists of GVN officials for assassination and provided the latest intelligence on changes within the Phoenix program.[9]

Captured documents left little doubt that the Viet Cong meant to wipe out the GVN presence in the countryside and that their chosen method was assassination. These documents listed targets as "administrative machinery, regional force, pacification cadres, civilian spies, Chieu Hoi cadres, psywar cadres. . . ."[10] Individuals in these categories were placed on blacklists and they would be killed whenever the opportunity presented itself. A letter dated August 1968 ordered the villagers in a Viet Cong–controlled hamlet to submit rosters of local GVN officials. Some of these individuals would be warned of their "crimes" (presumably these were the lesser officials) and others would be assassinated. The letter also exhorted villagers to assassinate "some twenty-five GVN officials, including pacification cadres, in each village."[11]

Captured documents showed three types of scenarios for luring the victim in for assassination. "We can kill a person at his house or office. . . . We can kill him when he is going to work or on his way home from the office, when he is riding a bicycle or driving a car. We can lure him into a love trap or kill him during a party."[12] Certainly not a sophisticated system of neutralization, but a lot more effective than the Phoenix program, considering that the Viet Cong need not worry about hostile public opinion.

Anti-Phoenix Propaganda

Propaganda statements were much less specific about what the Viet Cong intended to do to those who stood in their way, but it was clear the Phoenix program was regarded as something to be reckoned with. There was also an element of opportunism in the statements, as the Viet Cong sought to capitalize on the adverse publicity that immediately sprang up in the United States when Phoenix was set in place. The communists hoped to portray Phoenix as a murderous and terrible yoke placed upon the people of South Vietnam as the last-gasp effort of a dying government in Saigon.

In October 1969 the Viet Cong characterized the Phoenix program by reporting that ". . . the Vietnamese . . . , refusing to admit defeat, announced that a 'Phoenix' campaign, which is in fact aimed at flagrantly killing or terrorizing our people, will be unleashed."[13] Of course, Phoenix had been "unleashed" over a year previously; presumably the Viet Cong were only then beginning to feel its effects.

Late in October the Phoenix program was made the subject of an entire program on Liberation Radio, the Viet Cong clandestine broadcast in South Vietnam. The report had all the earmarks of Viet Cong propaganda, pointing out that Phoenix was designed to "massacre, persecute, and torture people. . . ."[14]

The CIA also was brought into the picture with the statement that the "U.S. imperialists have poured dozens of million dollars for CIA to carry out the Phoenix plan: Sending spies and rangers to carry out espionage, assassination, and abduction operations, conducting long-term raids against small areas to investigate and terrorize every citizen, and massacring our compatriots en masse."[15]

Of course, the CIA was still involved in Phoenix at the province level, but by late 1968 it had been largely replaced in the administration of Phoenix by the military. Yet the CIA made the best bogeyman for propaganda purposes. In addition, the words "tortured" and "killed" had a better impact than "neutralized" or "captured," even though the latter terms were more accurate.

Phoenix rose to prominence in the communists' official news organs as well. An article in *Quan Doi Nhan Dan* outlined communist reaction to the pacification program in South Vietnam by noting that Phoenix "agents mingle with the people and operate clandestinely like a venomous snake." The pacification effort was to be stamped out by "annihilating the Phoenix intelligence agents and holding public tribunals to try them." The Viet Cong recognized the importance of Phoenix by regarding it as the "eyes and ears of the pacification effort" and that the destruction of the Phoenix program would "frustrate the U.S.-puppet pacification plan at its roots."[16]

The Viet Cong also chose to pretend that the Phoenix program was secret and had been revealed only after many people objected to the "killings." In reality the Phoenix program was not secret. American military advisers were openly assigned to the Phoenix program, and the PIOCCs and DIOCCs operated openly. The point was to make Phoenix a program that everyone was aware of, even if the intelligence-gathering methods and means remained secret.

Post-Tet Communist Reaction

A rash of captured documents and propaganda statements indicated that the Tet attacks of early 1968 had done little to stem Viet Cong apprehensions over Phoenix's continued successes. Even with the documents as evidence of the Phoenix program's rising success, the U.S. Army continued to emphasize order of battle intelligence.

But the record indicates that Phoenix was a priority with the Viet Cong, especially COSVN. In fact, 1969 marked an increase in specific attention paid to Phoenix by COSVN. COSVN Directive 136 specifically identified all members of the Phung Hoang organization as selected targets. At the Second Congress of the People's Revolutionary Party (PRP) in the middle of September 1969, the deputy party secretary said the "Phung Hoang program and the Accelerated Pacification Program (APP) were the greatest threats to VC activities." He also noted that the two programs were the most effective measures taken against the insurgency in the South and that countermeasures would be difficult to implement. The Second Congress also decided that unlimited infiltration of communist cadre into South Vietnam no longer would be feasible under Phoenix's watchful eye. Instead, the most effective way to resist the program would be to institute an intensive drive to recruit legally documented GVN citizens as Party members.[17] The old guard that constituted the hardcore cadre was no longer enough to fill the slots opened by the disastrous Tet Offensive and the increasingly effective Phoenix program.

Phoenix had risen in effectiveness quickly and the Viet Cong were often caught without a remedy. In Kien Hoa Province the Viet Cong cadre issued instructions in their July-to-December 1969 progress reports requiring "that local areas and units closely coordinate with security branch to search for and destroy Phung Hoang agents."[18]

In Dinh Tuong Province a captured enemy document revealed that the Viet Cong had published specific instructions for countering Phoenix; in this case the main task was to "annihilate and disintegrate enemy Phung Hoang operations, and put [the] main effort in investigating and studying the Phung Hoang organization in every village." The document also contained a detailed explanation of all aspects of the DIOCC.[19]

The year 1970 was considered by many within MACV the best year for the Phoenix program. Judging by reaction from the Viet Cong, there was more than a little truth to that opinion. In March 1970 a captured enemy document from Hau Nghia Province pointed out that late 1969 and early 1970 had been a failure for building up the province Communist Party. The document indicated that only two hundred new members had been recruited in SR-2 (Security Region 2, a VC administrative region that included Hau Nghia Province), while six hundred members had been arrested, had rallied, or had deserted.[20]

In June 1970 ralliers in Ba Xuyen and Bac Lieu Provinces reported that only about one hundred new Party members had been recruited in the past two years. In addition, the area had witnessed the loss of more than fifteen hundred PRP members for various reasons during the same two-year period.

A Central Phung Hoang Permanent Office (CPHPO) letter dated 1 July 1970 observed that enemy documents captured in Cambodia during the U.S.-ARVN invasion in May 1970 reflected the problems created by Phoenix, particularly those operations undertaken by village Phung Hoang committees. The communists distributed urgent information outlining four main points for combating the Phoenix program:

> Carefully study local Phung Hoang committees and inquire about the personnel so as to plan for their assassination or proselytizing.
>
> Mix your cadres with the population so as to penetrate village Phung Hoang committees.
>
> Take initiative to destroy village Phung Hoang committees before they operate and seize files.
>
> Strengthen security work to protect internal affairs.[21]

A captured document pertaining to VC Military Region 6 (the border area between eastern GVN II and III Corps), titled "On the Establishment of the Enemy [GVN] Phung Hoang Intelligence Organization in the Villages," outlined the Phoenix program in the region and noted that:

> At present, personnel of the Phung Hoang intelligence organization are the most dangerous enemies of the Revolution in suburban and rural areas. They have harassed us more than any other group and have caused us many difficulties.[22]

Even areas in South Vietnam that had long been under firm Viet Cong control, such as the Rung Sat Special Zone, were pressured by Phoenix. One captured document revealed that the assistant political officer of SR-4 had said Phoenix had been a great hindrance to Viet Cong activity in the Rung Sat because it had formed an "intelligence channel of the Phung Hoang activities which stay close to the people."[23]

VCI captured in Quang Nam Province revealed the extent of damage by the Phoenix program to the region's communist cadre. One captured district committee member said the NPFF, aided by village and hamlet informants, were the most effective force in eliminating the VCI. This was unusual in that the National Police generally were not an effective action arm of the Phoenix program. Other captured VCI reported that the VC in Quang Nam Province and Danang were in critical need of "qualified" cadre replacements. The province-level cadre had "advised subordinate units that replacements were not available from higher echelons but the units must recruit and train their own personnel."[24]

Fear of the Phoenix program even entered into negotiations between North Vietnam and the United States. Ha Van Lau, chief of the People's Army of Vietnam Liaison Mission to the International Control Commission and former deputy chief of the North Vietnamese delegation to the Paris Peace Talks, commented in late November 1970 that "the Phung Hoang program had done much harm by striking a hard blow against the VCI."[25]

Also in November 1970, a company-level Viet Cong rallier reported that a thirty-six-day training course had been held in early 1970 in Dinh Tuong Province to train VCI in countering the Phoenix program. He also said his own unit had been raided three times by Phoenix forces and that morale in the area had sagged because of these operations.[26]

Perhaps most crucial to the Phoenix program's attempt to neutralize the VCI was its ability to cut off financial resources going to the Viet Cong. In October 1970 a former Viet Cong tax collector reported that in Dinh Tuong Province, between 1968 and 1970, tax revenues going to the Viet Cong had been drastically reduced. In 1968 he claimed to have collected VN$700,000; in 1969, VN$300,000; and nothing in 1970. He said the decrease was caused by "increased Phung Hoang activity." VCI in his village often were reluctant to carry out their duties because "they were afraid they would be identified and then attacked." The former tax collector also noted that Viet Cong communications were hampered by Phoenix operations that tended to isolate individual cadres and units.[27]

A document captured in October 1970 in the area around Quang Ngai Province candidly noted some of the problems brought on by the Phoenix program in that region. Under a section titled "Weaknesses and Difficulties to be Overcome in the Near Future," the document observed that:

> The revolutionary forces have been worn down, particularly due to the loss of a number of key cadre at the district and village level and the slow recruitment of additional personnel. Therefore, many favorable opportunities exist, but we cannot gain major victories at this time.[28]

In many ways this passage summed up the essence of what the Phoenix program was *supposed* to be accomplishing, as opposed to what the bureaucrats *wanted* it to accomplish. The Phoenix program as it applied to this Viet Cong area was clearly not wiping out all, or even most, of the VCI, yet it was causing serious problems for the communists. Perhaps most importantly, the author of the document pointed out that serious losses in district- and village-level cadre were the problem, not higher-up VCI at the province, or even regional, level. It did not take total destruction of the VCI to seriously impede communist objectives in South Vietnam.

1970: VC Reaction to a Worsening Situation

Clearly, the Viet Cong had to somehow combat the problems Phoenix was heaping upon them. The suggested solutions were typical, though not specific. The communists had to "disrupt the [GVN] pacification effort, assassinate tyrants and enemy reconnaissance agents or spies, and break the oppressive enemy control."[29]

District and village officials were to be the targets of the Viet Cong as they sought to reassert control over the areas they lost in 1970. In addition to attacking pacification personnel and assassinating "tyrants" the VCI meant to return to the villages in the wake of proposed assassinations of GVN officials. In fact, the Viet Cong practiced the very thing for which they excoriated Phoenix—the imposition of "body" quotas in the neutralization program. However, the call for quotas by the communists was much more sinister; in this case there would be no attempt to "arrest" GVN officials. Instructions to VCI in Viet Cong Sub-Region 5 (the area on the coast of Southern I Corps and Northern II Corps) called on the Party faithful to "kill 1,400 persons (including 150 tyrants [GVN officials]) . . . and annihilate . . . four pacification groups."[30] One has to wonder what happened to the remaining 1,250 people who did not fall within the category of "tyrant."

Such naked violence seems shocking, particularly in the face of criticisms regarding the Phoenix program. Yet in reality this document revealed nothing new in the communists' method of establishing control of the Vietnamese countryside. But somehow the forces shouting opposition to the Phoenix program were silent in the face of these constant and strident calls for assassination by the communists. Even in the light of hindsight it is difficult to forgive them their hypocrisy.

As 1970 came to a close, the Viet Cong drew up high-level documents analyzing the progress of the revolution over the past year. Invariably there was a detailed mention of the Phoenix program. Although they all lamented the damage to the revolution by the Phoenix program, they also noted that in the final analysis, Phoenix was a failure. One document noted that "during the second quarter of 1970, Phung Hoang intelligence agents operated on a broad front . . . in order to support the accelerated pacification program and destroy revolutionary organizations at village and hamlet levels. They failed in this plan."[31]

It is not surprising that the Viet Cong would want to put the best face on a worsening situation. But as documents from 1970 showed, the VCI were wounded most deeply at the village and hamlet level, the very area intelligence specialists considered the least important to the communist political machine. Perhaps intelligence analysts would have served pacification better had they looked more closely at the captured documents.

1971: In Like a Lion, Out Like a Lamb

In 1971 the communists felt the full weight of the GVN's pacification program. MACV believed that 1970 had been a particularly effective year for the war in the villages and high-level communist documents lent credence to that claim. In early 1971, COSVN (Central Office in South Vietnam) passed Resolution 10, which admitted that the Americans and the GVN had achieved success with the pacification program, but noted that the success would be only temporary. The same factors that led Hanoi to believe that it would ultimately win the war—corruption, unpopularity of the Saigon regime, and the presence of "imperialist" U.S. troops—were still in place and so pacification, too, must ultimately fail.

COSVN Resolution 10 never fell into GVN hands, but an undated summary, believed to have been written at about the same time, did. The document was revealing in its admission that pacification was effective, but at the same time it was not surprising that the communists saw a final victory in the future.

> Pacification and counterpacification struggles by enemy [GVN and American] and friendly forces were and are being conducted under highly violent forms. The enemy has achieved

some temporary results, but is steadily failing in implementing his basic schemes. Meanwhile, we have fought courageously and persistently, surmounting all difficulties, and forging ahead, although some minor difficulties still exist in conducting fierce attacks against the enemy.

During the past two years, the U.S. and puppet focused their efforts on pacifying and encroaching upon rural areas, using the most barbarous schemes. . . . As a result, they caused many difficulties to and inflicted losses on friendly [VC/NVA] forces.[32]

In the final analysis, the document authors did not believe pacification was doing enough harm to the communist movement to make a difference in the end. By 1971 there was no question the United States was well on its way toward vacating South Vietnam for good, an occurrence Hanoi had been hoping for since the mid-1960s. In the face of such a decision from Washington, Phoenix could do little to prevent the final collapse of the GVN.

By the end of 1971, pacification was showing signs of weakening because the American drive to Vietnamize the war was happening too fast. American advisers were being withdrawn from the countryside at an alarming rate and there were few GVN personnel capable of stepping into the breach.

The Viet Cong seemed to sense the crumbling of the pacification program. Propaganda statements changed from a tone of indignation at Phoenix's alleged brutality to one of smug sarcasm. Conspicuous in their absence were "statistics" regarding assassination and torture perpetrated by Phoenix and in their place came a calm appraisal of specific failures within Phoenix and quotations from the American press regarding the program's inability to successfully neutralize the VCI. One commentary in *Quan Doi Nhan Dan* observed that:

> Through the Phoenix campaign, the U.S.–Thieu clique has arrested and detained 67,000 of our compatriots, among whom nearly 21,000 have been killed. Of course, these figures [from UPI] are far below reality. . . .
>
> [U.S. intelligence] sources reveal that the Viet Cong infra-

structure, that is, the number of cadres operating in the villages and hamlets, has increased by several thousand over the past year.... The enemy's pacification plan is being seriously shaken in many places. His Phoenix organizations are becoming more and more powerless.[33]

This was a far cry from the venomous rhetoric of only a year previously and it flew directly in the face of captured documents that outlined the difficulties the Viet Cong were having replacing lost cadre. The documents were certainly a more realistic barometer than communist propaganda and U.S. press reports.

Although Phoenix was faltering, it is difficult to believe the Viet Cong had simply bested it in the countryside—the shift from pessimism to optimism was simply too swift and dramatic. The real answer lay in the changing nature of the American commitment to South Vietnam and to the radical swing in the strategy and tactics of Hanoi.

The NVA Easter Offensive in April 1972 represented a conventional push to topple the Saigon government unprecedented in the history of the Vietnam War. Hanoi's ability to launch such an offensive was based on two major factors: a massive infusion of heavy weapons by the Soviet Union, and a dramatic reshuffling of revolutionary priorities, which included the subordination of winning hearts and minds in the countryside to winning military victories on the battlefield. The American pacification effort—and the Phoenix program specifically—could take much of the credit for the shift in strategy. The communists could see that even if they could win the "other war," the timetable needed to wrest the countryside from Saigon's control no longer was acceptable; Hanoi was losing its patience with guerrilla war. Political forces in Hanoi were becoming impatient and the time seemed right to win with a new set of rules—a conventional invasion.

Even so, the decision by Hanoi to openly invade the South with conventional forces must have been a difficult one, given that national reunification brought about on the points of North Vietnamese bayonets lacked the proper political trappings. It was still necessary for the Viet Cong in the South to retain an illusion of backing from the people of South Vietnam, even though the nature of the war had changed from battling for political loyalty to fighting for real estate.

Washington's inability or unwillingness to prevent NVA main-force units from getting stronger as they lay in their sanctuaries in North Vietnam, Laos, and Cambodia doomed pacification. It simply could not stand up to conventional armies. And it shouldn't have had to. That was why the Army, Marine Corps, and Strategic Air Command were in Vietnam, but they were not allowed to keep the enemy at bay.

So the war in the villages went on, although not in the same way as before the Easter Offensive. In Binh Dinh Province the Viet Cong were especially brutal, conducting "people's courts" that resulted in the execution of hundreds, perhaps thousands, of people in an attempt to purge the province of any vestiges of GVN control in case the ARVN and Americans succeeded in blunting the communist offensive, as they had during Tet in 1968.[34]

Even though the Viet Cong's ability to stave off the Phoenix program did not have as much effect on the faltering pacification effort as did the Easter Offensive, when communist propaganda pointed out that the pacification program was in danger, they were correct. But not from the Viet Cong—it had lost out to pacification.

Replacement of VCI Losses

By the end of 1972 the war in Vietnam was largely conventional. Part of this stemmed from Viet Cong losses to the Phoenix program and conventional troop sweeps, part to the inability of U.S. and GVN military and political planners to deal with the expanding role of Soviet aid to the NVA. All across South Vietnam the Viet Cong were unable to replace their cadre losses at a sufficient rate. Intelligence figures continued to maintain that the Phoenix program was not doing sufficient damage to the VCI, but they often ignored a new trend. The Viet Cong were relying more and more on abductions of villagers to fill the depleted ranks of low-level cadre. After the Tet Offensive in 1968, the

Viet Cong had relied on North Vietnamese communist cadres to fill the gap, but even those had become insufficient by 1972.

The Americans were aware of the new rise in kidnappings and some provinces conducted studies to track the new phenomenon. In Tuy Hoa District in Phu Yen Province (II Corps) there were 1,514 reported abductions between January and September 1972. Of those, 393 people returned home. GVN officials were aware that some returnees did not report their return and so were still counted as missing, but it was assumed that part of this discrepancy could be balanced against abductions that went unreported.[35]

A majority of the "abductees" spent their time in Viet Cong base areas undergoing indoctrination. Of the older victims—those over forty years of age—58 percent were returned to their villages, as compared to 19 percent of those under the age of forty. The reason for this, concluded the report, was that the Viet Cong kept the younger men and women as soldiers and laborers and returned the older people as new cadre.[36] Older people were deemed more mature and influential and hence more likely to strengthen the core of the village VCI. These people were not ideal recruits for the VCI, but the Party decided that if even a part of these abductees could be propagandized into working as cadre the effort was worthwhile.

Back into Ashes

We know very little about the GVN's attempts to keep pacification and Phoenix going in the two years preceding the fall of Saigon. One thing is certain though. Pacification teams in the countryside often had their backs against the wall as North Vietnamese troops and tanks rolled through various parts of South Vietnam. The facade of a national liberation movement was gradually dropped as it became clear that only power issuing from the barrel of Hanoi's gun was going to be sufficient to finish off the GVN. But after the departure of the Americans, proper political posturing was no longer as important as it had been when U.S. public opinion was at stake. True, the Viet Cong reputation as the leaders in the popular struggle to oust American "imperialism" was tarnished, but the real plum—Saigon—would be in Hanoi's pocket by the end of April 1975. By then, North Vietnam's communist leaders must have reasoned, the world would not care much about the political purity of a "people's movement" in far-away Vietnam. They were right.

Vietnamese Communists Look Back

The Vietnam War has been over for more than a decade now and many Americans are left with the final impression that the Phoenix program was at best an ineffective attempt to attack the VCI and at worst a calculated assassination program that was nothing less than cold-blooded murder. Neither assumption is true. Even today Vietnamese officials continue to maintain that Phoenix was the one program they truly feared, the one tool with which the GVN might have succeeded in breaking the back of the insurgency. And this remained true despite all the Phoenix program's shortcomings.

In his book *Vietnam: A History,* Stanley Karnow noted that his traditional perspective on the Phoenix program as an evil and corrupt killing machine changed after the war, when he had the opportunity to interview top Vietnamese communist officials. In a discussion with veteran Viet Cong official Madame Nguyen Thi Dinh, Karnow was told, "We never feared a division of troops, but the infiltration of a couple of guys into our ranks created tremendous difficulties for us." She concluded that Phoenix was "very dangerous."

Colonel Bui Tin, a senior military officer, called Phoenix "devious and cruel," and said the program cost "the loss of thousands of our cadres." Another communist commander in South Vietnam, General Tran Do, called Phoenix "extremely destructive." And no less a personality than Nguyen Co Thach, Vietnam's foreign minister since the fall of Saigon in 1975, admitted that the Phoenix program "wiped out many of our bases" and forced many high-ranking communists to retreat into Cambodia.[37]

Interviews of other Vietnamese government officials conducted by American and foreign journalists also have shed light on communist reaction to Phoenix. One Vietnamese official said

Phoenix cost "the loss of thousands of our cadre." Another said that "the grassroots party organization suffered heavy losses—hundreds of thousands of cadres and party members sacrificed their lives or went to prison."[38]

Yet another noted that "there were only two occasions when we were almost entirely wiped out. The first was in 1957–58, when Ngo Dinh Diem had much success in eliminating our infrastructure.... [The second was] your pacification program [which] was very successful, especially Phung Hoang. Your concepts were generally good. It was the implementation that often went wrong."[39]

It is not surprising that the Viet Cong would agree that the Phoenix plan of action was sound. After all, the basic concept of neutralizing the enemy's political infrastructure formed the roots of the Viet Cong method of destabilizing the GVN presence in the countryside. The difference between the communist and GVN efforts were twofold.

First, the Viet Cong emphasized anti-infrastructure operations from the beginning of the insurgency in 1959, while the GVN waited until mid-1968 to get the Phoenix program rolling.

Second, the Viet Cong made assassination the cornerstone of their program, while the Phoenix program sought to prosecute VCI through the criminal justice system. While there were many valid reasons to criticize Phoenix, accusing it of being an assassination program was not one of them. Accusing it of being wholly ineffective also fails to stand up to scrutiny, especially given the testimony of former guerrillas and political cadre still in power in Vietnam today. Perhaps most intriguing is that Phoenix was relatively effective in spite of all its shortcomings. Few programs or strategies can claim to have been so successful, yet Phoenix failed in the end. What might have happened if all the bugs had been worked out of the program early in the war? What if the South Vietnamese had emphasized anti-infrastructure operations from the beginning? For the future, what lessons are there for nations struggling to cope with insurgencies?

One conclusion is certain: in any outbreak of people's war, the political infrastructure cannot be ignored.

Epilogue

THE war in Vietnam ended much as the U.S. military had thought it would begin. Conventional North Vietnamese troops, spearheaded by blitzing armor, crashed into Saigon and erased the effects of two decades of American blood and treasure. It hadn't mattered that American soldiers had not lost on the battlefield; in the end they had gone home and Hanoi prevailed. Saigon's will to survive had failed in the final hour.

The beginning of the end had been the 1972 Easter Offensive which saw the North Vietnamese using massed conventional forces on a broad front for the first time. Contrary to South Vietnamese proclamations that the eventual blunting of the communist offensive had shown ARVN combat self-sufficiency, the offensive highlighted serious cracks in the army which had been so carefully crafted by the American advisory effort.

From the perspective of the pacification effort, the Easter Offensive and the final fall of Saigon illustrated a shift in communist military tactics from a creeping conflict in the countryside to the slash and thrust tactics of conventional war. The gradual success of pacification was partially behind that change in strategy. Final recognition by the Saigon government and MACV of the importance of the Viet Cong Infrastructure within the communist war effort had led to the decimation of the political underground in South Vietnam. But not everyone agreed with that assessment. Critics of the paramoucy of a pacification strategy cited the conventional outcome of the Vietnam War as proof that the war in the villages was always secondary to a conventional strategy.

In reality they were entirely separate. All insurgencies strive toward the use of conventional forces and tactics during the course of an armed revolution. Chairman Mao made that clear during the Chinese Revolution. As each stage of guerrilla war succeeds it evolves toward the final conventional phase which culminates in the downfall of the government. In Vietnam the communists were allowed to advance along Maoist lines despite the fact that they were losing in the countryside. According to historical precedent the Vietnamese communist insurgency should not have gotten to the conventional stage because they were losing the guerrilla war. But sacrosanct safe havens ensured that the NVA could grow in strength and experience despite repeated drubbings on the battlefield. The enemy simply retreated over the border, licked its wounds, and planned for the next attempt. During the Easter Offensive Hanoi committed virtually its entire army to the battlefield in the south, leaving only one division to defend the homeland. Past experience had shown that Hanoi could get away with such a move; the United States would not respond with an invasion of North Vietnam.

While the NVA experimented with conventional warfare the Viet Cong withered and died in South Vietnam. Search-and-destroy tactics, cordon-and-search operations, limited nation-building by the GVN, and the Phoenix program all combined to doom the Viet Cong. The insurgency was on the ropes by 1970.

Yet the Phoenix program ultimately failed. The concept was sound and in many parts of South Vietnam the VCI was crippled. But nationwide, implementation of the Phoenix program was poor. Guidelines from Saigon were often only loosely adhered to and in some cases ignored. Many province chiefs simply could not be convinced that the Phoenix program should be given top priority.

However, despite the combination of shortcomings and successes the Phoenix program was simply left behind by the changing nature of the war. By 1970 Hanoi had dropped the facade of internal insurrection and concentrated on building toward a conventional invasion of the South. In that respect the success of pacification had helped alter North Vietnamese strategy from insurgency to full-scale war.

The American experience in Vietnam is constantly used as a template for future conflicts and it is often difficult to discern important lessons from superficial ones. Foremost among the important lessons is the realization that anti-infrastructure operations are an indispensable part of counterinsurgency. If the enemy's political infrastructure is successfully targeted during the early stages of an insurgency, then half the battle is won. Without the infrastructure the guerrillas simply cannot operate.

Nor is attacking the infrastructure an impossible task. Far from being a ghostly apparition which is difficult to pin down, an insurgent infrastructure is easy to identify and eliminate. It is a stationary target. Unlike enemy guerrilla units the infrastructure must remain among the people in order to keep the revolution alive. Yet American and South Vietnamese units chased the guerrillas while the VCI was left virtually untouched during the early phases of American involvement in Vietnam. The political infrastructure must be the primary target from the onset of any counterinsurgency effort. In Vietnam both the GVN and the United States waited too long.

Public opinion also played a role in the demise of the Phoenix program. Stories—many of them distorted and unsubstantiated—made anti-infrastructure operations unpalatable to the general public. Charges of assassination created a false sense that the Phoenix program operated outside the rules of engagement. However, when operated according to procedure, the Phoenix program did not murder innocent civilians. Abuses certainly occurred, and American advisers were sometimes accused of doing nothing to stop it. But the charge carried the usual double standard. On one hand advisers were being held accountable for what their Vietnamese counterparts did, on the other they were only supposed to be teaching the Vietnamese to fight on their own. As anti-war critics were fond of saying, it was a Vietnamese war.

Perhaps the most misleading aspect of the Phoenix program was the word assassination. It became an emotional distinction which had little meaning during wartime. In an unconventional war much of the fighting and dying is done in the shadows. Ambushes and small-unit actions dominate the battlefield. When someone is killed in ambush he was not said to have been "assassinated." Yet that was the charge when a VCI suspect was killed during a Phoenix operation. The distinction seemed to be that if the attackers did not know the identity of those they killed it was war; if they did, it was assassination. The difference was arbitrary.

From a purely American point of view, the Phoenix advisory effort evolved quickly and efficiently. From its beginnings in 1967, Phoenix overcame shortcomings and weaknesses and by 1971 the program looked good on paper. At the top levels planners remolded Phoenix to compensate for past problems; in the field advisers strove to contribute what they could on the local level.

By 1973 the Phoenix returned to the ashes from whence it came. After five years of U.S. prodding the GVN had made advances in anti-infrastructure operations, but in the final analysis the Americans made the Phoenix program work. It was the American side of Phung Hoang which had evolved the program and attempted to deal with the problems as they arose. When the advisers left, the program began to decay. For American Phoenix advisers their job had been a frustrating one. They had been asked to participate in a program which was new to both Vietnamese and Americans and they had been told to produce results in a single year. When one adviser left another came in and began the sequence all over. The job of the Phoenix adviser was arguably the most thankless task the Vietnam War had to offer and as each adviser's tour ended he was generally glad to leave. Most departed with mixed feelings about the Phoenix program.

The last adviser to leave Vinh Long Province in 1972 put his feelings into verse:

> *When days were old and nights were bold*
> * and VCI were not invented,*
> *This mythical bird spoke only peaceful words*
> * and it seemingly was contented.*
>
> *Then came the war and they needed a claw*
> * that would snatch and grab Lao Dong*
> *They sent out a call to advisers and all,*
> * and some idiot gave birth to Phung Hoang.*

The bird swooped without flutter or frown
    and began to kill, pillage, and burn.
But before it was done, before the fight was won,
    its time had come to return.

And when like you ole bird I too shall pass
    amid the VCI dossiers scattered on the grass
May Zeus and Aphrodite both welcome us home.
    For our return signals the death of Phung Hoang.

—Final Phung Hoang Adviser
Vinh Long Province, IV Corps

Appendix

Table A-1
Phoenix/Phung Hoang Neutralization Results

Year	Rallied	Captured	Killed	Total
1968	2,229	11,288	2,259	15,776
1969	4,832	8,515*	6,187	19,534
1970	7,745	6,405	8,191	22,341
1971	5,621	5,012	7,057	17,690
1972 (end July)	1,586	2,138	2,675	6,399
Totals	22,013	33,358	26,369	81,740

*Beginning in 1969 only VCI receiving sentences of one year or more were counted.

Table A-2
Resource Allocations

Year	U.S. Advisers	U.S. Monetary Support (in millions)
1968	435 military/13 civilian*	1.53
1969	434 military/20 civilian	1.46
1970	704 military/2 civilian	.38
1971	397 military/1 civilian	.40
1972	125 military/1 civilian	.11
	Total	3.88

*Civilian advisory personnel numbers furnished by OSA and are probably low. The CIA was unwilling to give precise figures.

CENTRAL PHUNG HOANG COMMITTEE

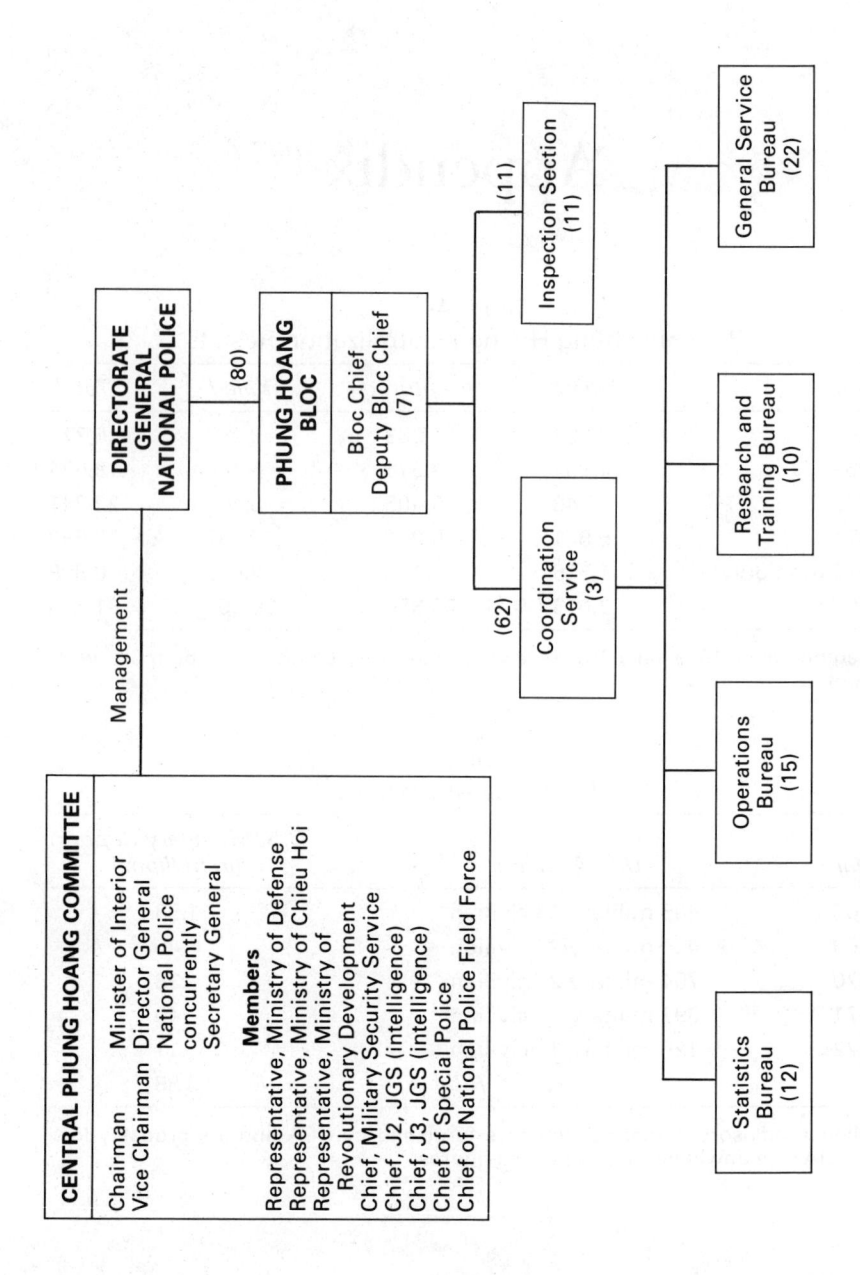

Chairman — Minister of Interior
Vice Chairman — Director General National Police concurrently Secretary General

Members
Representative, Ministry of Defense
Representative, Ministry of Chieu Hoi
Representative, Ministry of Revolutionary Development
Chief, Military Security Service
Chief, J2, JGS (intelligence)
Chief, J3, JGS (intelligence)
Chief of Special Police
Chief of National Police Field Force

DIRECTORATE GENERAL NATIONAL POLICE (80)

PHUNG HOANG BLOC (7)
Bloc Chief
Deputy Bloc Chief

Inspection Section (11)

Coordination Service (3) (62)

Statistics Bureau (12)

Operations Bureau (15)

Research and Training Bureau (10)

General Service Bureau (22)

Figure A–1. National Level Phung Hoang Organization

Appendix

COMMITTEE CORPS/MILITARY REGION
Commander (Chairman)

Region Director National Police
(Vice Chairman, Secretary General)

Members
CORPS/Military Region – G2 (intelligence)
CORPS/Military Region – G3 (operations)
CORPS/Military Region – Military Security Service
Region Chieu Hoi Representative
Region Chief, Special Police

Management

REGION PHUNG HOANG
Permanent Office

(25)

(3) Message Section
National Police – 3

(9) Planning and Program Section
National Police – 2
Military Security Service – 1
G2 (intelligence) – 1
G3 (operations) – 1
Political Warfare – 1
Chieu Hoi – 1
Vietnamese Information Service – 1
People's Self-Defense Force – 1

(3) Inspection Section
A.R.V.N. – 2
National Police – 1

(10) Training Section
Source of personnel not specified

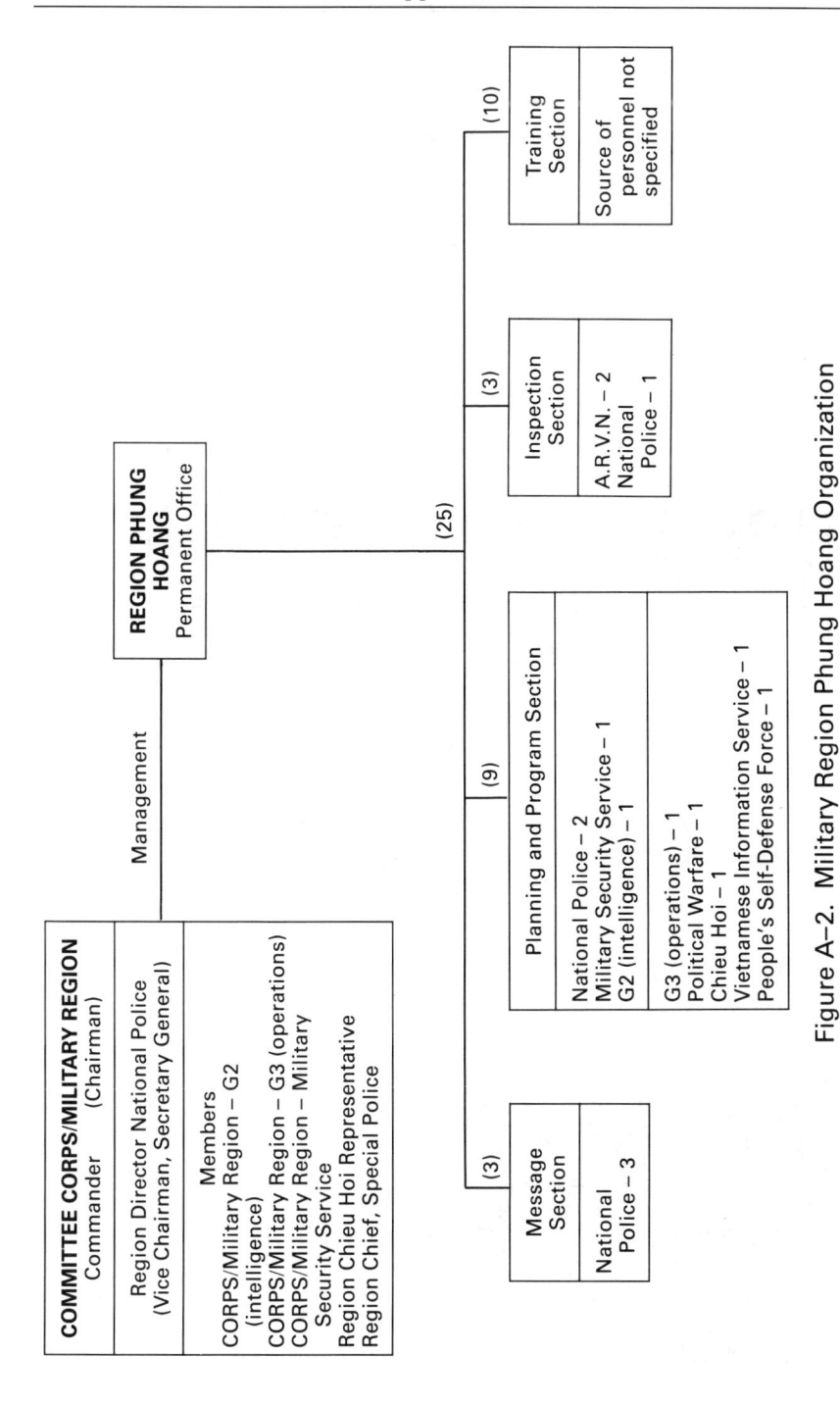

Figure A–2. Military Region Phung Hoang Organization

COMMITTEE

Province Chief (Chairman)
Province National Police Chief (Vice Chairman)
Sector S2 (intelligence)

Members

Sector S3 (operations)
Sector Military Security Service
Chief, Province Revolutionary Development Cadre
Chief, Province Chieu Hoi
Chief, Province Special Police
Intelligence (military units)
Commanding Officer, National Police Field Force

Management

PROVINCE PHUNG-HOANG PERMANENT CENTER

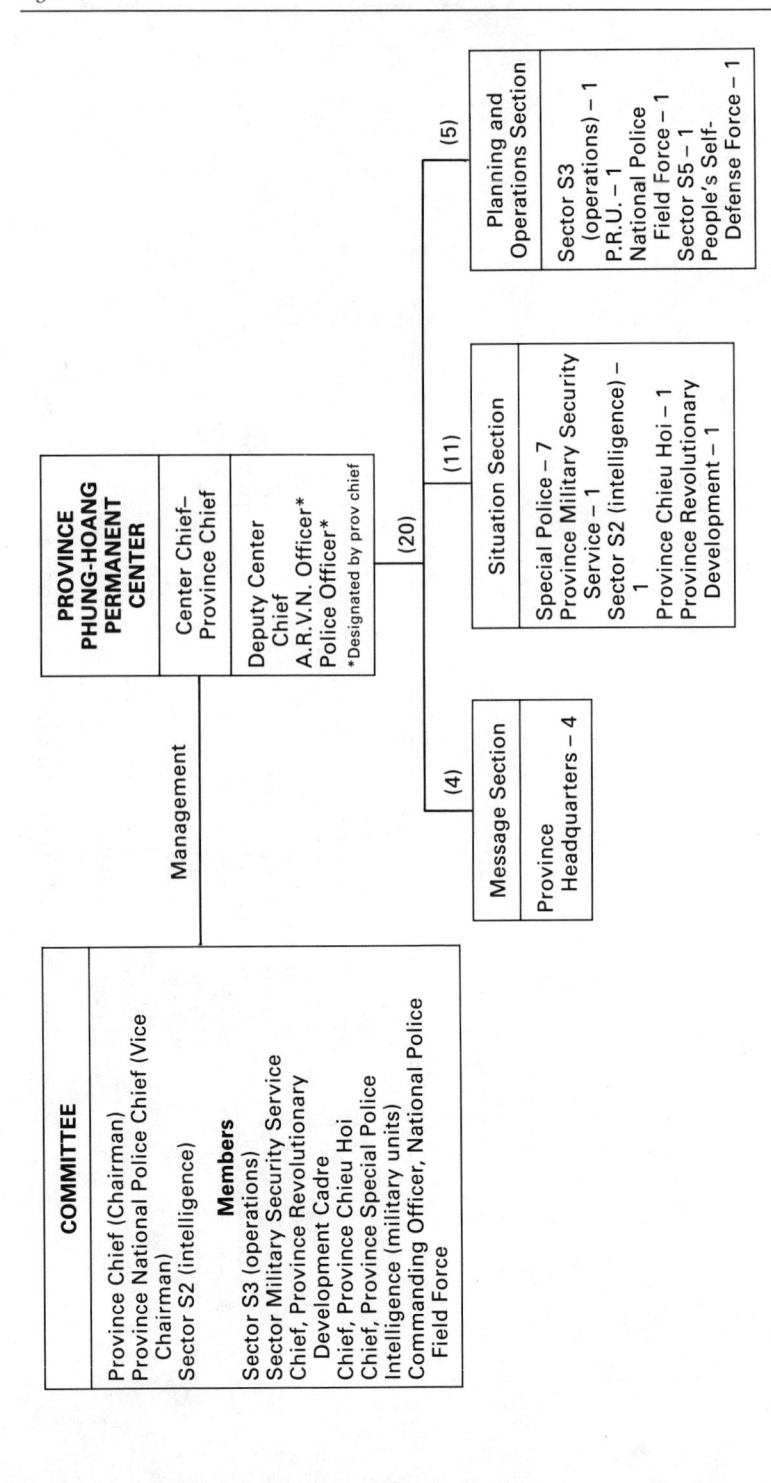

Center Chief – Province Chief
Deputy Center Chief
A.R.V.N. Officer*
Police Officer*

*Designated by prov chief

(20)

Message Section (4)

Province Headquarters – 4

Situation Section (11)

Special Police – 7
Province Military Security Service – 1
Sector S2 (intelligence) – 1
Province Chieu Hoi – 1
Province Revolutionary Development – 1

Planning and Operations Section (5)

Sector S3 (operations) – 1
P.R.U. – 1
National Police Field Force – 1
Sector S5 – 1
People's Self-Defense Force – 1

Figure A–3. Province Phung Hoang Organization

Appendix

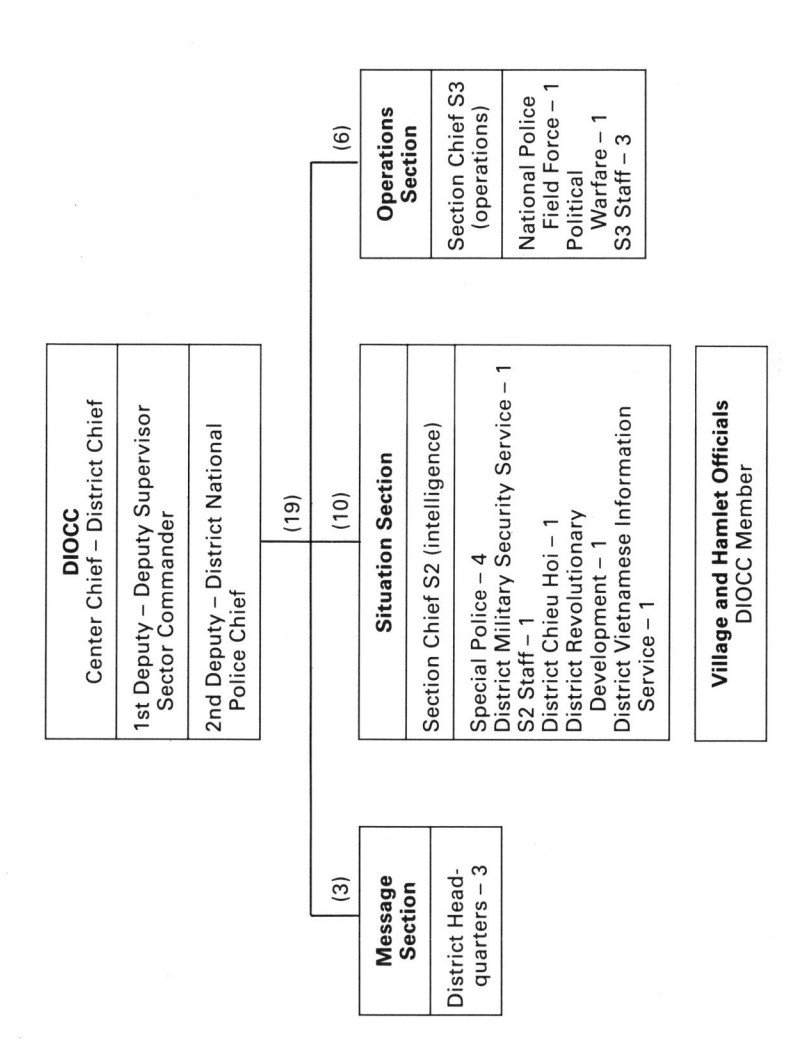

DIOCC
Center Chief – District Chief
1st Deputy – Deputy Supervisor Sector Commander
2nd Deputy – District National Police Chief

(19)

(3) **Message Section**
District Headquarters – 3

(10) **Situation Section**
Section Chief S2 (intelligence)
Special Police – 4
District Military Security Service – 1
S2 Staff – 1
District Chieu Hoi – 1
District Revolutionary Development – 1
District Vietnamese Information Service – 1

(6) **Operations Section**
Section Chief S3 (operations)
National Police Field Force – 1
Political Warfare – 1
S3 Staff – 3

Village and Hamlet Officials
DIOCC Member

Figure A-4. District Phung Hoang Organization

Notes

Chapter 1

1. "Interrogation Report from DIOCC, Duc Hue," conducted by Captain Stuart Herrington. Dated 11 April 1971.
2. Harry G. Summers, Jr., *Vietnam War Almanac* (New York: Facts on File Publications, 1985), p. 117.
3. George A. Carver, "The Faceless Viet Cong," *Foreign Affairs* 44, April 1966, p. 351.
4. Douglas Pike, *War, Peace and the Viet Cong* (Cambridge, Mass.: The MIT Press, 1969), p. 3.
5. Ibid., p. 7.
6. Douglas Pike, *Viet Cong: The Organization and Techniques of the National Liberation Front of South Vietnam* (Cambridge, Mass.: The MIT Press, 1966), p. 137.
7. Ibid., p. 147.
8. Pike, *War, Peace and the Viet Cong*, p. 18.
9. "Hanoi's Central Office for South Vietnam (COSVN): A Background Paper" (Saigon: U.S. Mission in Vietnam, July 1969), p. 1.
10. Ralph Johnson, "Phoenix/Phung Hoang: A Study of Wartime Intelligence Management," unpublished Ph.D. dissertation from The American University, 14 November 1984, p. 55.
11. "Hanoi's Central Office for South Vietnam (COSVN): A Background Paper" (Saigon: U.S. Mission in Vietnam, July 1969), p. 2.
12. Ibid.
13. Ibid. Also see Don Oberdorfer, *Tet!* (New York: Da Capo Press, 1971), pp. 42–43.
14. "The Viet Cong Infrastructure: A Background Paper" (Saigon: U.S. Mission in Vietnam, June 1970), p. 9.
15. Ibid., p. 12.
16. William C. Westmoreland, *A Soldier Reports* (New York: Dell Publishing Co., 1980), p. 187.

Chapter 2

1. Chester Cooper, et al., *The American Experience with Pacification in Vietnam*, vol. III (Arlington, Va.: Institute for Defense Analysis, International and Social Studies Division, March 1972), pp. 72–73. Hereafter referred to as Cooper.
2. Bernard Fall, *Two Viet Nams* (New York: Frederick A. Praeger, 1963), p. 107.
3. Philippe Devillers, *Histoire du Viet-Nam de 1940 à 1952* (Paris: Editions du Seuil, 1952), p. 176.
4. General Pierre Boyer de la Tour, "Evolution de la Pacification au Sud Viet-Nam," *Revue Militaire d'Information*, November 1949, p. 11.
5. Peter Paret, *French Revolutionary Warfare from Indochina to Algeria* (New York: Frederick A. Praeger, 1964), pp. 104–105.
6. Cooper, vol. III, p. 81.
7. "General X," *A Translation from the French: Lessons of the War in Indochina* (Santa Monica, Calif.: RAND Corporation Memo RM-5721-PR, 1967), p. 110.
8. Cooper, vol. III, p. 84.
9. Ibid.
10. Ibid.
11. See Cooper, vol. III, footnote no. 28, p. 85.
12. Cooper, vol. III, p. 85.
13. Jeane Leroy, *Un Homme dans la Riziere* (Paris: Editions de Paris, 1955), pp. 157–160. Also quoted in Cooper, vol. III, p. 86.
14. Philippe Devillers wrote that when French forces were transferred out of an area, the Viet Minh returned, "inflict[ing] terrible reprisals on those who cooperated against them." Devillers, *Histoire du Viet-Nam de 1940 à 1952*, p. 323.
15. Cooper, vol. III, p. 74.
16. Bernard Fall, *Street Without Joy*, 3rd rev. ed. (Harrisburg, Penn.: The Telegraph Press, 1963), p. 177.
17. Cooper, vol. III, p. 90.
18. Ibid., p. 91.
19. Donald Lancaster, *The Emancipation of French Indochina* (Oxford: Oxford University Press, 1961), p. 254.
20. Bernard Fall, *Street Without Joy*, p. 279.
21. Pierre de la Tour, quoted in Cooper, vol. III, p. 97.
22. Cooper, vol. III, p. 99.
23. General Henri Navarre, *Agonie de l'Indochine* (Paris: Librarie Plon, 1957), p. 317. Also quoted in Cooper, vol. III, p. 100.
24. Commandante Jacques Hogard, "Guerre Revolutionnaire et Pacification," *Revue Militaire d'Information*, January 1957, pp. 13–18. Also quoted in Cooper, vol. III, p. 105.
25. Capitaine Andre Souyris, "Les Conditions de la Parade et la Riposte a

Guerre Revolutionnaire," *Revue Militaire d'Information*, February 1957, p. 107. Also quoted in Cooper, vol. III, p. 109.
26. Malaya at that time was made up of about 49 percent Malay, 38 percent Chinese, 12 percent Indian, and 1 percent a combination of Europeans, Eurasians, and indigenous tribal peoples. From Richard L. Clutterbuck, *The Long, Long War* (New York: Praeger Press, 1966), p. 19.
27. For details on the organization of the MRLA, see Lucien W. Pye, *Guerrilla Communism in Malaya* (Princeton: Princeton University Press, 1956).
28. William L. Knapp, "Phoenix/Phung Hoang and the Future: A Critical Analysis of the US/GVN Program to Neutralize the Viet Cong Infrastructure" (U.S. Army War College, Carlisle Barracks, Pennsylvania, 8 March 1971), p. 12. Cooper puts the figure at ten thousand plus another fifty thousand to one hundred thousand supporters. Cooper's figure is probably closer to reality. Cooper, vol. III, p. 36.
29. Clutterbuck, *The Long, Long War*, p. 57.
30. Knapp, "Phoenix/Phung Hoang and the Future," p. 19.
31. Cooper, vol. III, p. 43.
32. Clutterbuck, *The Long, Long War*, p. 72.
33. Knapp, "Phoenix/Phung Hoang and the Future," pp. 22–23.
34. Cooper, vol. III, p. 39.
35. Sir Robert Thompson wrote the section on the Malayan Emergency in Cooper, vol. III, p. 58. Also see Thompson, *Defeating Communist Insurgencies* (New York: Frederick A. Praeger, 1966), p. 56.
36. Ibid., p. 85.
37. Edward Lansdale wrote the section on the Huk rebellion in Cooper, vol. III, p. 9.
38. Cooper, vol. III, p. 11.
39. Ibid., p. 15.
40. Ibid.
41. Edward Lansdale, *In the Midst of Wars: An American's Mission to Southeast Asia* (New York: Harper & Row, 1972), p. 43.
42. Cooper, vol. III, p. 16.
43. Napoleon D. Valeriano and Charles T. R. Bohannan, *Counter-Guerrilla Operations: The Philippine Experience* (New York: Frederick A. Praeger, 1962), pp. 83–85.
44. Lansdale, *In the Midst of Wars*, p. 63.
45. Cooper, vol. III, p. 16.
46. Lansdale, *In the Midst of Wars*, p. 48.
47. Cooper, vol. III, p. 16.
48. Ellen J. Hammer, *A Death in November: America in Vietnam, 1963* (New York: Oxford University Press, 1987), p. 68. Also Cooper, vol. III, p. 115.
49. Robert Scigliano, *South Vietnam: Nation Under Stress* (Boston: Houghton Mifflin Co., 1963), p. 167.
50. Ibid., p. 170.
51. Cooper, vol. III, pp. 120–121.
52. Ibid., p. 121.

53. Ibid., p. 135.
54. Ibid., pp. 152–153.
55. Neil Sheehan alleges that MSU advisory team members were in reality "CIA specialists." Many others disagree with Sheehan's assertion. Neil Sheehan, *A Bright Shining Lie: John Paul Vann and America in Vietnam* (New York: Random House, 1988), p. 187. Also see Cooper, vol. II, pp. 81–82.
56. Cooper, vol. II, p. 85.
57. Ibid., pp. 85–86.
58. Cooper, vol. II, p. 86.
59. See *Time* magazine, "We Were in Desperate Shape," 29 February 1988, p. 17.
60. *The Pentagon Papers,* Senator Gravel edition, vol. II, p. 123.
61. *Viet Cong* was a term coined by the Americans and was an abbreviation of "Vietnamese communist." The communists themselves as well as the people in the countryside still regarded the guerrillas as Viet Minh well into the 1960s, but by the early 1960s the term *Viet Cong* was widely used by the military, the press, and U.S. policy makers.
62. Blaufarb, *The Counterinsurgency Era,* p. 211.
63. Thomas Powers, *The Man Who Kept the Secrets: Richard Helms and the CIA* (New York: Alfred A. Knopf, Inc., 1979), p. 180.
64. Cooper, vol. II, p. 86.
65. Ibid., p. 87.
66. Peer deSilva, *Sub Rosa: The CIA and the Uses of Intelligence* (New York: Times Books, 1978), p. 216.
67. Ralph W. McGehee, *Deadly Deceits: My 25 Years in the CIA* (New York: Sheridan Square Publications, Inc., 1983), p. 141. Other sources less polemic than McGehee's generally concur that the CIA was solely responsible for the programs.
68. Powers, *The Man Who Kept the Secrets,* pp. 179–180.
69. Blaufarb, *The Counterinsurgency Era,* p. 213.

Chapter 3

1. Memo to Ambassador Komer from Richard Burnham and Richard Holbrooke, Office of Civil Operations, 24 May 1967, part II, pp. 1–2.
2. Ibid., p. 3.
3. Ibid., p. 5.
4. Edward Doyle and Samuel Lipsman, *America Takes Over* (Boston: Boston Publishing Co., 1982), pp. 83–84.
5. Ralph W. Johnson, *Phoenix/Phung Hoang: A Study of Wartime Intelligence Management* (The American University: Ph.D. dissertation, 1985), pp. 109–110.

6. Doyle and Lipsman, *America Takes Over*, p. 85.
7. William C. Westmoreland, *A Soldier Reports* (New York: Dell Publishing Co., 1980), p. 215.
8. Johnson, *Phoenix/Phung Hoang*, p. 116.
9. Chester L. Cooper, *The Lost Crusade: America in Vietnam* (New York: Dodd, Mead & Co., 1970), p. 255.
10. John Schlight, ed., *Second Indochina War Symposium: Papers and Commentary*, Richard Hunt, "The Challenge of Counterinsurgency" (Washington, D.C.: Center for Military History, 1986), p. 133.
11. Johnson, *Phoenix/Phung Hoang*, pp. 162–163. Also see Warren M. Milberg, USAF, *The Future Applicability of the Phoenix Program*, Maxwell AFB, Alabama: The Air University, master's degree thesis, May 1974), p. 24.
12. Ibid., p. 163.
13. Ibid., pp. 170–173.
14. Interview with Evan J. Parker, Jr., 17 March 1989.
15. Ibid.
16. Johnson, *Phoenix/Phung Hoang*, p. 177.
17. MACV Directive 381-41, "Military Intelligence: Coordination and Exploitation for Attack on the VC Infrastructure (C); Short Title: ICEX," 9 July 1967. Hereafter referred to as MACV 381-41.
18. Interview with Robert W. Komer, 13 January 1989.
19. Memorandum to Ambassador Komer, DEPCORDS COMUSMACV, "Action Program for Attack on the VC Infrastructure, 1967–1968," July 1967, p. 5.
20. Ibid., pp. 5–6.
21. Ibid., p. 1.
22. MACV 381-41, p. 4.
23. MACV MACCORDS Directive 381-43, 25 November 1967, p. 4.
24. Interview with Evan J. Parker, Jr., 17 March 1989.
25. Johnson, *Phoenix/Phung Hoang*, p. 191.
26. Ibid., p. 191.
27. ICEX Memo #6, "Financial and Logistical Support for District Operations," 28 November 1967.
28. John G. Lybrand, "Evaluation Report: Processing of Viet Cong Suspects," 11 December 1967.
29. Ibid., p. 8.
30. Ibid.
31. Letter from General Westmoreland to General Cao Van Vien, 2 Sept. 1967.
32. John G. Lybrand, "I Corps Provincial Prisons," 16 September 1967.
33. Memorandum from Robert Komer to "Heads of Involved Agencies," 6 November 1967, p. 2.
34. Ibid.
35. Ibid., p. 4.

Chapter 4

1. "Operation Phung Hoang: Rooting out the Communists' Shadow Government," Vietnam Feature Service (TCB-034). This was an unclassified and widely distributed document available to anyone. Although it glossed over many of the Phoenix program's problems and was overly optimistic in places, it gave a detailed description of the program. A covert operation would not have published such a document.
2. Danny J. Whitfield, *Historical and Cultural Dictionary of Vietnam* (Mefuchen, N.J.: Scarecrow Press, Inc., 1976), p. 229.
3. Interview with Robert Komer, 13 January 1989.
4. Ralph W. Johnson, *Phoenix/Phung Hoang: A Study of Wartime Intelligence Management* (The American University, Ph.D. dissertation, 1985), p. 210.
5. Transcript of taped interview with Major Edward L. Troubaugh, S-3 3rd Brigade, 1st Infantry Division, and Major Eugene D. Tapscott, S-2 3rd Brigade, 1st Infantry Division. Interview conducted 14 January 1968. Center for Military History, Oral History Collection, VNI-251. Hereafter referred to as CMH OHC.
6. Transcript of interview with Colonel George S. Patton, et al., 11th Armored Cavalry Regiment. Interview conducted 20 September 1968. CMH OHC VNI-185.
7. William C. Westmoreland, *A Soldier Reports* (New York: Dell Publishing Co., 1980), p. 333.
8. Ibid.
9. William Colby and Peter Forbath, *Honorable Men: My Life in the CIA* (New York: Simon & Schuster, 1978), p. 267.
10. Johnson, *Phoenix/Phung Hoang*, pp. 213–214.
11. MACV/MACCORDS, Decree No. 280-a/TT/SL, 1 July 1968, pp. 1–2. Hereafter referred to as Decree 280-a/TT/SL.
12. Ibid., p. 2.
13. Ibid., pp. 2–3.
14. MACV/MACCORDS, "Phung Hoang Standard Operating Procedure," 27 July 1968, p. 3. Hereafter referred to as SOP 1.
15. Many documents and province reports testify to specific examples of successful aspects of the Phoenix program. For a detailed account of the evolution of Phoenix in Hau Nghia Province see Stuart A. Herrington, *Silence was a Weapon: The Vietnam War in the Villages* (Novato, Calif.: Presidio Press, 1982).
16. Decree 280-a/TT/SL, pp. 3–4.
17. Johnson, *Phoenix/Phung Hoang*, p. 225.
18. MACV/MACCORDS, "Military Intelligence Coordination and Exploitation for Attack on VC Infrastructure (C) Short Title: Phoenix (U), Direc-

tive Number 381-41," 9 July 1968. Hereafter referred to as MACV/MACCORDS Dir. 381-41.
19. Ibid., p. 1.
20. Ibid., p. 2.
21. Johnson, *Phoenix/Phung Hoang*, p. 232.
22. MACV/MACCORDS Dir. 381-41, p. 8.
23. Lieutenant Colonel Leslie D. Carter, commanding officer, 1st Battalion, 502d Infantry, 101st Airborne Division, "Pacification of Quang Dien District—An Integrated Campaign," 1 March 1969. CMH.

Chapter 5

1. MACCORDS-PHD, "Phoenix 1968 End of Year Report," Appendix 2, Annex B, pp. 1–3.
2. Ibid., p. 1.
3. Ibid.
4. Ibid., pp. 2–5.
5. The author of the report on Operation Cutoff seemed proud that operations took only three hours. He noted that "the entire search/interrogation/PSYOPS phase of the operation required approximately 3 hours for the 'average' size hamlet (500 population)."
6. MACCORDS-PHD, "Phoenix 1968 End of Year Report," Appendix 2, Annex B, pp. 2–5.
7. AVDCMH, "Operations Against the Viet Cong Infrastructure—September 1968 to July 1969," After-action and intelligence reports. Data gathered by 18th Military History Detachment, 25th Infantry Division, 28 August 1969. CMH Oral History Collection, VNI-236.
8. MACCORDS, "Province Reports for Hau Nghia," Department of the Army, January through December 1969. On file at CMH.
9. AVDCMH, "Operations Against the Viet Cong Infrastructure—September 1968 to July 1969."
10. Ibid.
11. AVDCMH, "Intelligence Target Analysis, Operation Draw String," Headquarters, Military Intelligence Detachment, 27 March 1969.
12. The report makes no comment or speculation on the "light-skinned" soldiers. Reports concerning the presence of Chinese soldiers cropped up all over South Vietnam, but it seems far-fetched to assume that Chinese soldiers would be on tax collection duty in a predominantly GVN-controlled area.
13. AVDCMH, "Operations Against the Viet Cong Infrastructure—September 1968 to July 1969," p. 41.

Chapter 6

1. "Phung Hoang 1970 End of Year Report," 11 May 1971, p. 4.
2. Ibid., p. 5.
3. Ibid.
4. Ibid., pp. 5–6.
5. Ibid., p. 6.
6. MACCORDS-PHX, "Phoenix Accomplishments, 1969," 1 October 1969, pp. 1–2.
7. Ibid., p. 3.
8. MACCORDS-PHX, "Fact Sheet: II CTZ Phung Hoang/Phoenix Program During the Third Quarter of CY69," 9 October 1969.
9. MACCORDS-PHX, "Fact Sheet: III CTZ Phung Hoang/Phoenix Program During the Third Quarter of CY69," 9 October 1969.
10. MACCORDS-PHX, "Phung Hoang/Phoenix, Third Quarter CY69," p. 1. The document is a summary of a meeting held 25 October 1969. The written report was passed on to William Colby as a briefing paper.
11. Ibid., p. 2.
12. "Discussion Paper: Vietnamization of the Phung Hoang (Phoenix) Program," 18 September 1972.
13. John L. Cook, *The Advisor* (Philadelphia: Dorrance & Co., 1973), p. 55.
14. Exit interview with First Lieutenant Robert S. Hallock, Phoenix Adviser, Gio Linh District, Quang Tri Province. Interviewed 6 April 1970. CMH VNIT-763.
15. Exit interview with Warren Parker, Quang Nam PSA. Interviewed 26 September 1970. CMH VNIT-765, p. 26.
16. Ibid., pp. 26–27.
17. MACCORDS-PHX, "Fact Sheet: Phung Hoang/Phoenix, Third Quarter CY69," 25 October 1969, p. 1.
18. MACCORDS-PHX, "Fact Sheet: Phoenix Accomplishments," 1 October 1969.
19. MACCORDS-PHX, "Phoenix 1969 End of Year Report," Appendix 4.
20. Interview with IV Corps pacification officer, Vinh Binh Province, 20 October 1989.
21. "Discussion Paper: Vietnamization of the Phung Hoang (Phoenix) Program," 18 September 1972.
22. Ibid.
23. "Phung Hoang 1970 End of Year Report," 11 May 1971, p. 8.
24. Memorandum to secretary of defense, "Phoenix Program," 10 December 1970.
25. Thomas Thayer, "A Systems Analysis View of the Vietnam War: 1965–1972," vol. 10: Pacification and Civil Affairs, p. 65.

26. "Phung Hoang 1970 End of Year Report," 11 May 1971, p. 8.
27. Ibid.
28. Ibid., p. 9.
29. Ibid., p. 16.
30. Ibid., p. 17. The Congressional Hearings on pacification frequently brought forth the charge that most VCI neutralizations came about during troop sweeps by "conventional" forces.
31. MACCORDS, "Province Report: Kien Giang Province," 30 June 1970, pp. 2–3.
32. "Phung Hoang 1970 End of Year Report," 11 May 1971, p. 18.
33. Ibid., p. 19.
34. Ibid., p. 20. Also MSD/CORDS, "APT Handbook," revised edition 1970.
35. MACCORDS-PHX. "Fact Sheet: Phung Hoang Adviser Training," 1 December 1970.
36. Memorandum to secretary of defense from Secretary of the Army Stanley R. Resor, "Progress of Programs in Support of the Advisory Effort in RVN," 5 March 1970.
37. Memorandum to secretary of defense from Acting Secretary of the Army Thaddeus R. Beal, "Vietnam Adviser Program," 19 August 1970.
38. "Phung Hoang 1970 End of Year Report," 11 May 1971, p. 31.
39. Ibid.
40. "Discussion Paper: Vietnamization of the Phung Hoang (Phoenix) Program," 18 September 1972.
41. "Phung Hoang 1970 End of Year Report," 11 May 1971, p. 18.
42. Ibid., Appendix 6.
43. MACCORDS-PHX, "Phung Hoang Training for ARVN Officers Being Transferred to NP," 8 December 1970.
44. MACJOIR, "Fact Sheet for Ambassador Colby: PAAS (November) Results: Phung Hoang," 12 December 1970.
45. MACCZ-IV-80-PHX, "Consolidated VC Infrastructure Neutralization Report, An Xuyen Province," 30 March 1970.
46. Ibid.
47. Ibid.
48. MACCZ-IV-64-CR-PHX-088-70, "Consolidated VCI Neutralization Report, Chau Doc Province," 30 March 1970.
49. MACCORDS-IV-56-PHX, "Consolidated Vietnamese Communist Infrastructure Neutralization Report, Phong Dinh Province," 1 April 1970.
50. MACCZ-IV-65-PHX, "Consolidated Vietnamese Communist Infrastructure Neutralization Report, Sadec Province," 31 March 1970.
51. MACCZ-IV-PHX, "Consolidated VCI Neutralization Report, Vinh Long Province," 30 March 1970.
52. MACJOIR, memorandum to DEPCORDS Military Regions 1, 2, 3, and 4, "Phung Hoang Program," 14 December 1970. Also MACCORDS-PS, letter to DGNP BG Tran Van Hai from Frank E. Walton, director PSD, 19 September 1970.

Chapter 7

1. After-action report, "Operation Against HQ Co., 501st Main Force Battalion," 191st AHC, 1 February 1970. CMH VNIT-315.
2. Sir Robert Thompson, et al., "Report on the National Police, Republic of Vietnam" (Saigon, March 1971), p. 3.
3. Background paper, "Functional Brief: National Police Command," December 1971, pp. 2–3.
4. MACCORDS-PSC, "Guidelines for Advice of the National Police Field Force," 18 April 1968, p. 3.
5. Ibid., p. 4.
6. Ibid., p. 6.
7. SACSA, "Summary: Public Safety Program—Vietnam," 1972, p. 3.
8. MACCORDS-PSD, "Analysis—National Police Field Force—1969," 15 January 1970, pp. 1–2.
9. Ibid., p. 5.
10. Memorandum to DEPCORDS/MACV William Colby from Jean A. Sauvageot, CPDC Liaison Group, "Evaluation of Motivational Training for National Police at National Cadre Training Center," 16 March 1971.
11. MACJOIR, memorandum to ACofS CORDS William Colby from Robert Komer, "NPFF in Tuyen Duc/Dalat," 2 September 1968.
12. MACCORDS-PS, "Employment of 211 NPFF Co., Tuyen Duc, and 212 NPFF Co., Dalat," 20 August 1968, pp. 2–3.
13. Ibid., p. 4.
14. AVFA-DC, memorandum to DEPCORDS/MACV William Colby, "NPFF and National Police Situation in Dalat and Tuyen Duc Province," 11 November 1968.
15. MACCORDS/EVAL, "Evaluation Report: National Police Field Force, Thua Thien, I CTZ," 13 September 1968, p. 3.
16. Ibid., p. 8.
17. Memorandum to ACofS John Manopoli from Robert Komer, "Poor Employment of NPFF in Thua Thien," 19 October 1968.
18. MACCORDS-EVAL, "Evaluation of National Police Field Force RZ, Quang Nam Province, I CTZ," 22 October 1968, p. 4.
19. MACCORDS-EVAL, "Evaluation of NPFF in III Corps," 3 December 1968, p. 13.
20. Ibid., p. 19.
21. Memorandum to DEPCORDS IV Corps from Robert Komer, "National Police Performance in IV Corps," 25 October 1968. NPFF statistics in IV Corps dropped off by only 226 from 1,851 for the first six months of 1968 to 1,625 from 16 June to 5 October. To Komer, the problem was that the other three Corps had seen a rise in VCI neutralizations of between 30 percent and, in the case of I Corps, 350 percent.

22. MACCTZ-IV-DEPCORDS, memorandum to DEPCORDS/MACV William Colby from DEPCORDS IV CTZ, "National Police Performance in IV Corps," 13 November 1968. In October 1968 IV Corps reported 1,395 VCI neutralized by the Phoenix program.
23. "Phung Hoang: 1970 End of Year Report," 11 May 1971, p. 21.
24. Ibid.
25. MACCORDS-PSC, memorandum to DEPCORDS/MACV William Colby, "AIK Support for Special Police Training," 7 December 1968, p. 1.
26. Ibid.
27. MACJOIR, memorandum to chief of staff, "AIK Support for Special Police Training," 30 November 1968.
28. MACCORDS-PSC, memorandum to DEPCORDS/MACV William Colby, "AIK Support for Special Police Training," 7 December 1968.
29. Ibid.
30. *Washington Post*, "CIA Says Reds Infiltrate South Vietnam Government," 20 October 1970. The CIA reported as many as thirty thousand communist agents within the "South Vietnamese armed forces, police, and intelligence apparatus. . . ." GVN officials denied the report.
31. MACCORDS-PSC, memorandum to DEPCORDS/MACV William Colby, "AIK Support for Special Police Training," 7 December 1968, p. 3.
32. Ibid.
33. MACCORDS-PSD, "Analysis—National Police Field Force—1969," 15 January 1970, p. 12.
34. Interview, CIA PSB adviser, III Corps, 7 July 1989.

Chapter 8

1. Interview with CIA PRU adviser, 15 June 1989.
2. Ibid.
3. End of Tour Interview, First Lieutenant Robert S. Hallock, Phoenix Adviser, Gio Linh District, Quang Tri Province. Interviewed 6 April 1970. CMH Oral History Collection.
4. Interview with CIA adviser in IV Corps, 13 April 1989.
5. OPS IA SO, "Fact Sheet: Provincial Reconnaissance Units (PRU), RVN," 16 October 1969, p. 1.
6. Ibid.
7. Ibid.
8. MACJOIR, letter from COMUSMACV William C. Westmoreland to Chief JGS General Cao Van Vien, 27 February 1968.
9. OPS IA SO, "Fact Sheet: Provincial Reconnaissance Units (PRU), RVN," 16 October 1969, p. 1.
10. Ibid., p. 2.
11. MACCORDS, "NPFF/PRU Interim Report," 18 August 1969.

12. Interview with IV Corps CIA adviser, 13 April 1989. Financial figures from JCSM-752-69, memorandum to secretary of defense from CJCS General Earle G. Wheeler, "U.S. Military Involvement in the PRU Program in the RVN," 8 December 1969, p. 1.
13. MACCORDS, memorandum to COMUSMACV from William E. Colby, "Integration of NPFF and PRU," 18 October 1968.
14. MACCORDS, memorandum to Corps Phoenix Advisers, "Employment of NPFF," 24 August 1968.
15. RVN Prime Ministry Decree #044-SL/NV, 31 March 1969.
16. MACCORDS-PSC, memorandum to ACofS CORDS from William Colby, "NPFF/PRU," 9 August 1969.
17. OPS IA SO, "Fact Sheet: Provincial Reconnaissance Units (PRU), RVN," 16 October 1969, p. 3.
18. JCSM-752-69, memorandum to secretary of defense from CJCS General Earle G. Wheeler, "U.S. Military Involvement in the PRU Program in the RVN," 8 December 1969, p. 2.
19. Ibid.
20. Memorandum for the secretary of defense, "The Phoenix Program and Provincial Reconnaissance Unit Program in Vietnam," 20 October 1969.
21. Memorandum to CJCS from Secretary of Defense Melvin Laird, "Evaluation of U.S. Involvement in the Provincial Reconnaissance Unit Program in the RVN," 29 November 1969.
22. Interviews; CIA IV Corps adviser, 13 April 1989; Vietnamese PRU operative in Kien Giang Province, 23 April 1988.
23. JCSM-752-69, memorandum to secretary of defense from CJCS General Earle G. Wheeler, "U.S. Military Involvement in the PRU Program in the RVN," 8 December 1969, p. 1.
24. Ibid., p. 3.
25. Memorandum to Robert Komer from OCO, "Binh Chanh Province," 24 May 1967, p. 6.
26. Interview with Vietnamese PRU operative in Kien Giang Province, 23 April 1988.
27. Memorandum to Robert Komer, "PRU Analysis," 28 June 1968.
28. Thomas C. Thayer, ed., "A Systems Analysis View of the Vietnam War: 1965–1972," vol. 10: Pacification and Civil Affairs, 18 February 1975, p. 90. Also "Phung Hoang 1970 End of Year Report," 11 May 1971, Appendix 6.
29. Official cable to DEPCOMUSMACV Saigon from DEPCORDS IV CTZ. A copy was sent by William Colby to CIA Chief of Station Theodore Shakley, 22 December 1968.
30. Thayer, "A Systems Analysis View of the Vietnam War," vol. 10, p. 91.
31. MACCORDS-PHD, "Phoenix 1968 End of Year Report," Appendix 3, Annex B, pp. 1–2.
32. Command History for 1968, SEAL Team 2, p. 19.
33. John B. Dwyer, "SEAL Saga: North Africa to Normandy to Nha Trang," *Soldier of Fortune* magazine, October 1985, p. 54.

34. Command History for 1967, SEAL Team 2, p. 49.
35. Information on Detachments Bravo and Echo are still classified. Some units, particularly those advising the PRU, were attached directly to the CIA, not the U.S. Navy.
36. "Web-Foot Warriors," *Pacific Stars & Stripes*, September 1967.
37. There are no precise figures for SEAL manpower in Vietnam, but rough estimates can be gleaned from the SEAL Team histories.
38. Command History for 1968, SEAL Team 1, "Operational Summary Report: 7/29/68–9/14/68."
39. Dwyer, "SEAL Saga," p. 55.
40. Command History for 1969, SEAL Team 2, "Operational Reports," pp. 6–7.
41. Command History for 1969, SEAL Team 2, "Operational Reports," p. 6.
42. Command History for 1968, SEAL Team 1, "Operational Summary Report: 7/29/68–9/14/68."
43. Ibid.
44. Command History for 1969, SEAL Team 2, "Operational Reports," p. 8.
45. Command History for 1970, SEAL Team 1, "Operational Summary Reports: 3/1/69–12/31/69."
46. Interview with CIA adviser in IV Corps, 13 April 1989.
47. "Navy SEALs, Super-Secret Commandos, are Quitting Vietnam," *New York Times*, 29 November 1971.
48. Ibid.
49. Command History for 1971, SEAL Team 2.
50. Command History for 1970, SEAL Team 1. Casualty figures are not broken down into categories.
51. Quoted in Dwyer, "SEAL Saga," p. 55.

Chapter 9

1. "7 Women Viet Cong Suspects Sit and Wait," *New York Times*, 21 March 1970.
2. George G. Prugh, *Law at War: Vietnam, 1964–1973* (Washington, D.C.: Department of the Army, 1975), p. 23.
3. Ibid.
4. Ibid., p. 37.
5. Ibid.
6. Ibid., pp. 63–64.
7. Ibid., pp. 67–68.
8. MACCORDS, ICEX Memorandum no. 5, 2 November 1969.
9. William Colby and Peter Forbath, *My Life in the CIA* (New York: Simon & Schuster, 1978), pp. 230–231.
10. Interview with CIA ROIC of III Corps, 16 May 1989.

11. MACV Directive 525-36, "Military Operations: Phoenix (Phung Hoang) Operations," 18 May 1970.
12. Erwin Knoll, "The Mysterious Project Phoenix," *The Progressive*, February 1970, pp. 19–22.
13. U.S. District Court of Maryland, "Reitemeyer vs. McCrea," 302 Federal Supplement 1210 (1969).
14. Knoll, "The Mysterious Project Phoenix."
15. Guenter Lewy, *America in Vietnam* (Oxford: Oxford University Press, 1978), p. 287.
16. MACCORDS-PHD, "Phoenix: 1968 End of Year Report," 18 March 1969, pp. 12–13.
17. Ralph Johnson, "Phoenix/Phung Hoang: A Study of Wartime Intelligence Management" (Washington, D.C.: Ph.D. dissertation, The American University, 1983), pp. 401–402.
18. MACCORDS, "Handbook on Legal Processing of National Security Offenders," October 1970, p. 3.
19. Ibid.
20. Ibid., p. 5.
21. MACCORDS-PHD, "Phung Hoang Advisors Handbook," 20 November 1970, pp. 17–18.
22. MOI Circular no. 757, "Classification and Rehabilitation of Offenders," 21 March 1969.
23. MACCORDS-PSD, "Proposals to the Ministry of Interior for Improvements in the Processing of Communist and Political Detainees," 1969, pp. 9–10.
24. Thomas C. Thayer, ed., "A Systems Analysis View of the Vietnam War," vol. 10: Pacification and Civil Affairs (Southeast Asia Analysis Report, February 1975), p. 63.
25. Memorandum to Secretary of Defense Melvin Laird from Deputy Undersecretary of the Army John Siena, "Memorandum for the Secretary of Defense of Army Vietnam Trip," 20–28 August 1969.
26. Ibid.
27. MACCORDS-PHD, "Phoenix Comments on Internal Security Affairs: Internal Security Study," 16 July 1969, p. 1.
28. Ibid., pp. 2–5.
29. Thayer, "A Systems Analysis of the Vietnam War," vol. 10, p. 61.
30. MACCORDS-PSD, "Fact Sheet: Legal Processing of VCI Detainees," 8 June 1970, p. 2.
31. MACTRC-PD, memorandum to senior coordinator, Phung Hoang Division, CORDS MR 3, "Trip Report," 13 March 1972.
32. MACCORDS-PSD, "Fact Sheet: Legal Processing of VCI Detainees," 8 June 1970, p. 3.
33. Ibid., p. 1.
34. MACCORDS-PS, "Fact Sheet: Registrable Population—NIRP," 31 July 1971.
35. Ibid.

36. Memorandum to DEPCORDS, "National Identity Registration Program (NIRP)," 13 February 1971.
37. Memorandum to DEPCORDS, "Fact Sheet: Registrable Population—NIRP," 31 July 1971, p. 2.
38. Memorandum to DEPCORDS, "Fact Sheet: NIRP," 8 October 1971.
39. Summary Paper, "Public Safety Program—Vietnam," June 1972, p. 5.
40. Ibid.
41. MACCORDS-PS, "ID Card Allegation of Corruption," 19 December 1970.
42. Province Report, "Office of the Senior Adviser, MACCORDS, Kien Phong Province," 1 March 1971, p. 3. Entry on NIRP was sent separately to William Colby for comment.
43. Interview with National Police adviser, 6 November 1988.
44. Memorandum to Ambassador Colby, "The Geneva Convention and the Phoenix Program," 20 July 1971, p. 1. This document contains the original set of comments written by William Colby's legal staff to be read into the Congressional Record in July 1971. The Army JAG expanded on it for the final draft, which was subsequently presented to the House Committee on Government Operations.
45. Ibid., p. 2.

Chapter 10

1. Hoa Hao Buddhism, An Giang Province, *Letter of Protest—To the President of the Republic of Vietnam, no. 004/UBTD/AG*, "Protest Against the Local Phung Hoang Committee Which has Tread Upon the Law-Governed Democracy by Arresting and Torturing Until Death of Mr. N. H. Dang, a Civilian Working at the Long Xuyen Military Hospital and a Hoa Hao Follower," 20 November 1971, p. 1.
2. RVN, An Giang Province, "Announcement No. 7007-NA/CT/1," 29 November 1971, p. 1.
3. See note no. 1, p. 2.
4. Memorandum to Mr. Richard Thompson, Pol. Sec./US Emb. from Susan J. Walters, Pol. Officer/An Giang Province, "Follow-up on Anti-Phung Hoang Demonstrations in An Giang Province," 22 November 1971.
5. MACJOIR, "Phung Hoang Reexamination Study," 8 September 1971, p. 2.
6. MACCORDS-PHD, "Phung Hoang Reexamination (PHREEX) Study," 24 October 1971, Encl. 1, p. 1.
7. Ibid., p. 2.
8. Ibid., p. 1.
9. Interview with Phoenix adviser, III Corps, 19 February 1989.
10. MACJOIR—Memorandum to George Jacobson (DEPCORDS), "Phung Hoang Program," 10 November 1971, pp. 1–2.
11. Ibid., p. 3.

12. Briefing by Phung Hoang Director John Tilton to CORDS Quarterly Review Board, 8 September 1971, pp. 5–6.
13. MACDR-CR, memorandum to William Colby from Wilbur Wilson, deputy for CORDS, "Motivation of GVN Leadership in the Phung Hoang Program," 24 June 1971.
14. MACTRC-BT-PSA, letter to Richard Funkhauser, deputy for CORDS TRAC from Binh Tuy PSA, 26 May 1971.
15. AVFA-CORDS-PH, letter to William Colby from deputy for CORDS MR2, 4 March 1971.
16. MACDR-CG, report to COMUSMACV General Creighton Abrams from MG J. H. Cushman, "Phung Hoang Pilot Program in Vinh Long Province," 24 May 1971. Interestingly, the report placed the number of VC in the province at 1,017 and the number of VCI at 1,865. Considering the faulty intelligence capabilities in the province at that time, it is difficult to believe that Vinh Long's Phung Hoang program could be so exact at counting the enemy and yet incapable of selectively targeting.
17. MACCORDS-PHD, "Pilot Phung Hoang Program in Vinh Long Province," 3 June 1971.
18. MACDRAC-CR-PX, memorandum from DRAC PSAs, "Evaluation of the Phung Hoang Program," 18 May 1971, pp. 2–3.
19. Ibid., p. 33.
20. MACDR-CR, memorandum to William Colby from Wilbur Wilson, deputy for CORDS, "Motivation of GVN Leadership in the Phung Hoang Program," 24 June 1971.
21. MACCORDS-PHD, "Informant Rewards Program in RVN," 20 April 1971, pp. 2–3.
22. MOI memorandum no. 1223/BTL/CSQG/F1, "Rewards Program to be Put into Effect in Four Provinces to Support Phung Hoang Plan," 30 June 1971.
23. Ibid.
24. MACCORDS-PP&P, memorandum for Ambassador Colby, "Request for Funds—Phung Hoang High Value Rewards Program," 20 May 1971. Colby attached a typed response with his comments to the document front.
25. MACCORDS-PP&P-PD, "Request for Funds," 16 May 1971.
26. MACCORDS-PP&P, memorandum to Ambassador Colby, "Request for Funds—Phung Hoang High Value Rewards Program," Annex D, 20 May 1971.
27. MACCORDS-PHD, "Weekly Report of Significant Activities, 27 October through 3 November 1971," 3 November 1971.
28. Hearing before the Committee on Armed Services, U.S. Senate, 93rd Congress, "Nomination of William Colby to be Director of Central Intelligence," July 2, 20, 25, 1973, pp. 111–112.
29. Telegram from Ambassador Bunker to Department of State, "Special Phung Hoang Campaign in the Delta," 27 April 1972.
30. Ibid., p. 2.
31. Ibid., pp. 2–3.

32. Ibid., p. 3.
33. Letter to secretary of state, Washington, from Ambassador Bunker, "Phung Hoang Special Campaign (F-6) Ends," 5 January 1973.
34. Letter to Secretary of State William P. Rogers from Senator Clifford P. Case, 15 February 1973.
35. Letter to Senator Clifford P. Case from Marshall Wright, acting assistant secretary for Congressional Relations, Department of State, 13 April 1973.
36. USMACV Command History, January 1972–March 1973, vol. I, pp. D-33–D-34.
37. See note no. 35.
38. MACCORDS-PHD, "Fact Sheet: Phung Hoang Program," 2 July 1972.
39. "Phung Hoang Program Effectiveness During August and September 1972," undated.

Chapter 11

1. All material on the "B-3 Thought Reform Camp" is taken from a thirteen-page U.S. Army intelligence document submitted on 29 April 1971. The document was classified "Secret."
2. "Opposition to Accelerated Pacification Rising," Liberation Radio broadcast, 10 October 1969. Translated and released on 13 October 1969, p. 13.
3. "Coordinating Committee DH.52 Resolution," captured enemy document, September 1967.
4. Stephen T. Hosmer, *Viet Cong Repression and its Implications for the Future* (Lexington, Mass.: Lexington Books, 1970), p. 21.
5. Ibid., p. 103.
6. Ibid.
7. Ibid., p. 15.
8. Ibid., pp. 51–52.
9. "The Enemy in North Vietnam," undated, pp. 20–21.
10. Ibid., p. 30.
11. Ibid.
12. Ibid., pp. 51–52.
13. See note no. 2.
14. "Phoenix Plan Condemned as Terror Campaign," Liberation Radio broadcast, 24 October 1969. Translated and released on 27 October 1969, p. 1.
15. Ibid.
16. "Fundamentally Frustrate the U.S.-Puppets' Pacification Plan," *Quan Doi Nhan Dan*, 2 March 1970.
17. "Phung Hoang 1970 End of Year Report," 11 May 1971, p. 43.
18. Ibid.
19. Ibid., p. 44.
20. Ibid.
21. Ibid., p. 45.

22. Ibid.
23. Ibid., p. 46.
24. Ibid.
25. Defense Intelligence Agency: Intelligence Summary, 24 December 1970, p. 6.
26. "Phung Hoang 1970 End of Year Report," 11 May 1971, p. 47.
27. Ibid.
28. "Military Activity Plan of Sub-Region 5: July–September 1970, No. 25/KH," from Captured Document Log no. 09-1366-70, p. 3.
29. Ibid., p. 5.
30. Ibid., p. 8.
31. "Report on Enemy and Friendly Situation During the First Six Months of 1970," Security Section of Xuan Loc District Party Committee, Long Kanh Province, VC Region 7. Document released 16 February 1971, p. 3.
32. COSVN Directive No. 01/CT71, January–February 1971. From Gareth Porter, *Vietnam: A History in Documents* (New York: The New American Library, Inc., 1979), pp. 394–397.
33. "Resolutely Frustrate the U.S.-Thieu Clique's Criminal Phoenix Program," *Quan Doi Nhan Dan,* 4 November 1971.
34. D. H. Rochlen, "The Rochlen Report," 10 September 1972, pp. 1–4.
35. "Abduction Analysis, Tuy Hoa District, January–September, 1972," dated 8 December 1972, p. 1.
36. Ibid., pp. 3–4.
37. Stanley Karnow, *Vietnam: A History* (New York: Viking Press, 1983), p. 602.
38. "The Phoenix Programme and the Ashes of War," *Far Eastern Economic Review,* 2 May 1988, p. 40.
39. "We Were in Desperate Shape," *Time* magazine, 29 February 1988, p. 17.

Glossary

AGENCY Nickname for the CIA.
AID Agency for International Development.
AN TRI The special national security law that governed the sentencing of VCI.
ARVN Army of the Republic of Vietnam.
CHIEU HOI Literally "Open Arms," a program set up to encourage Viet Cong and NVA to defect.
CIA Central Intelligence Agency, also called the Agency.
COMMO-LIAISON Communications and liaison cadre. A common middle-level VCI position tasked with carrying documents and messages from village to village or district to district. Because they carried secret documents and knew who was whom in the VCI structure, they were considered a valuable catch by the Phoenix program.
COMUSMACV Commander U.S. Military Assistance Command, Vietnam. The commander of forces in Vietnam; he also commanded the pacification effort.
CORDS Civil Operations and Revolutionary Development Support.
COSVN Central Office for South Vietnam.
CPHPC Central Phung Hoang Permanent Committee.
CTT Counterterror Teams. The original name for the Provincial Reconnaissance Units.
CTZ Corps Tactical Zone.
DEPCORDS Deputy for CORDS. The head of pacification. He was second only to COMUSMACV in the MACV hierarchy.
DGNP Director General of the National Police.
DIOCC District Intelligence and Operations Coordinating Center.
GVN Government of (South) Vietnam.
HES Hamlet Evaluation System. HES was the monthly statistical report that provided the GVN and MACV with information on rural security.
HOI CHANH A communist soldier or VCI who surrendered through the Chieu Hoi program.

ICEX Intelligence Coordination and Exploitation. ICEX was the original U.S. plan for anti-infrastructure operations in South Vietnam.

KIT CARSON Former VC/NVA who surrendered through the Chieu Hoi program and volunteered to go back in the field to fight against their former comrades. Kit Carsons were used often by the Phoenix program.

MACV Military Assistance Command, Vietnam.

MOI Ministry of Interior.

NEUTRALIZE Word used to define putting the VCI out of action. Neutralize could mean kill, capture, or surrender through the Chieu Hoi program.

NLF National Liberation Front.

NP National Police. This included the NPFF and the PSB, as well as non-Phoenix-related policemen such as maritime officers and traffic police.

NPFF National Police Field Force. The paramilitary arm of the National Police aimed at the VCI.

NVA North Vietnamese Army.

NVN North Vietnam.

OCO Office of Civil Operations. Loose pacification organization that existed within the U.S. Embassy before the establishment of CORDS.

OSA Office of the Special Assistant to the Ambassador. A CIA position in the U.S. embassy.

PACIFICATION The program, which included Phoenix, designed to win the countryside from the communists.

PF Popular Forces. Part of the Territorial Forces designed to put rural defense in the hands of the population.

PHOENIX The American advisory side of the GVN plan to destroy the VCI.

PHUNG HOANG The South Vietnamese program to destroy the VCI.

PIC Province Interrogation Center. CIA-run interrogation centers, usually set up in each provincial capital.

PIOCC Province Intelligence and Operations Coordination Center.

POC Police Operations Center. Replaced the PIOCCs in 1972.

POPAT Protection of the People Against Terrorism.

PRP People's Revolutionary Party.

PRU Provincial Reconnaissance Units.

PSB Police Special Branch. The intelligence section of the National Police. Also called the Special Police.

PSC Province Security Committee.

PSD Public Security Directorate. U.S. AID-advised section within CORDS which included the National Police.
PSYOP Psychological Operations.
RDC Revolutionary Development Cadre. The RDC lived in the villages with the people. They sought to emulate the VC by using propaganda to rally the people to the GVN cause. The RDC program was run by the CIA.
RF Regional Forces. A regional local militia.
RF/PF Regional Forces/Popular Forces. The PF were recruited at the village level and tended to be less reliable than the RF.
ROIC Regional Officer in Charge. A CIA adviser usually stationed at the regional center of operations. Part of the ROIC's job was to aid and assist the Phoenix program.
SOP Standard Operating Procedure.
VC Viet Cong.
VCI Viet Cong Infrastructure. Used to define both the group and an individual member.

Selected Bibliography

A Note on Sources

THE Phoenix program is virgin territory for the historical researcher. Documents are not neatly cataloged and arrayed in boxes at the National Archives. Therefore, I do not have the luxury of citing box and file number. In fact, very few of the documents cited were found at the National Archives.

The U.S. Army Center of Military History has a sizable collection of documents concerning pacification in Vietnam, including the Phoenix program. Many of them are now unclassified. Unfortunately, they are mixed in with classified material and so are not cataloged by box and file. CMH also has an oral history collection containing some material on pacification and the Phoenix program.

The Military History Institute at Carlisle Barracks, Pennsylvania, keeps a collection of senior officer end-of-tour reports, many of which are from province senior advisers. They provide valuable insights on American military perceptions of the Phoenix program.

The Department of State has a sizable collection of documents on microfilm, as well as some recently declassified material still on paper.

Some material was obtained through the Freedom of Information Act, although the process is lengthy and not always productive. The various government branches have differing methods of declassification that can become cumbersome for the researcher. On numerous occasions I received a document from one agency with much of the detail blocked out for "security reasons" and the same document "unsanitized" from another agency.

Finally, I have relied on interviews with American and, in a few cases, Vietnamese participants in the Phoenix program. Most of them preferred to provide background details rather than specific quotes. In the case of higher-ranking figures, their connection with the Phoenix program is well-known and they are quoted and cited by name.

The journals and personal papers from some participants in the Phoenix program also lent valuable insight into the finer points of the program on a day-to-day basis. Except for a few instances, I have used this material for background research and have not made specific citations.

Books

Armbruster, Frank E., et al., *Can We Win in Vietnam?* (New York: Frederick A. Praeger, 1968).

Beckett, Ian F. W., and Pimlott, John, eds., *Armed Forces and Modern Counterinsurgency* (New York: St. Martin's Press, 1985).

Blaufarb, Douglas, *The Counterinsurgency Era: U.S. Doctrine and Performance* (New York: The Free Press, 1977).

Cable, Larry E., *Conflict of Myths: The Development of American Counterinsurgency Doctrine and the Vietnam War* (New York: New York University Press, 1986).

Carhart, Thomas, *The Offering* (New York: William Morrow & Co., Inc., 1987).

Chandler, Robert W., *War of Ideas: The U.S. Propaganda Campaign in Vietnam* (Boulder, Colo.: Westview Press, 1981).

Cincinnatus, *Self-Destruction: The Disintegration and Decay of the United States Army During the Vietnam Era* (New York: W.W. Norton & Co., 1981).

Colby, William, and Forbath, Peter, *Honorable Men: My Life in the CIA* (New York: Simon & Schuster, 1978).

Cook, John L., *The Advisor* (Philadelphia: Dorrance & Co., 1973).

Corson, William R., *The Betrayal* (New York: W.W. Norton & Co., 1968).

Davidson, Phillip B., *Vietnam at War: The History, 1946–1975* (Novato, Calif.: Presidio Press, 1988).

deSilva, Peer, *Sub Rosa: The CIA and the Uses of Intelligence* (New York: Times Books, 1978).

FitzGerald, Frances, *Fire in the Lake: The Vietnamese and the Americans in Vietnam* (New York: Vintage Books, 1972).

Fulghum, David, and Maitland, Terrence, et al., *The Vietnam Experience: South Vietnam on Trial* (Boston: Boston Publishing Co., 1984).

Herring, George C., *America's Longest War: The United States and Vietnam, 1950–1975* (New York: Alfred A. Knopf, 1986).

Herrington, Stuart A., *Silence was a Weapon: The Vietnam War in the Villages* (Novato, Calif.: Presidio Press, 1982).

Hosmer, Stephen T., *Viet Cong Repression and Its Implications for the Future* (Lexington, Mass.: Lexington Books, 1970).

Hunt, Richard A., and Schultz, Richard H., eds., *Lessons from an Unconventional War: Reassessing U.S. Strategies for Future Conflicts* (New York: Pergamon Press, 1982).

Isaacs, Arnold R., *Without Honor: Defeat in Vietnam and Cambodia* (Baltimore: Johns Hopkins University Press, 1983).
Karnow, Stanley, *Vietnam: A History* (New York: Viking Press, 1983).
Kinnard, Douglas, *The War Managers* (Wayne, N.J.: Avery Publishing Group, Inc., 1985).
Komer, Robert W., *Bureaucracy at War: U.S. Performance in the Vietnam Conflict* (Boulder, Colo.: Westview Press, 1986).
Kunstadter, Peter, ed., *Southeast Asian Tribes, Minorities, and Nations* (Princeton: Princeton University Press, 1967).
Lansdale, Edward Geary, *In the Midst of Wars: An American's Mission to Southeast Asia* (New York: Harper & Row, 1972).
Leites, Nathan, and Wolf, Charles Jr., *Rebellion and Authority: An Analytic Essay on Insurgent Conflicts* (Chicago: Markham Publishing Co., 1970).
Lewy, Guenter, *America in Vietnam* (Oxford: Oxford University Press, 1978).
Lipsman, Samuel, and Doyle, Edward, et al., *The Vietnam Experience: Fighting for Time* (Boston: Boston Publishing Co., 1983).
MacPherson, Myra, *Long Time Passing: Vietnam and the Haunted Generation* (New York: Doubleday & Co., 1984).
Maitland, Terrence, and McInerney, Peter, et al., *The Vietnam Experience: A Contagion of War* (Boston: Boston Publishing Co., 1983).
McGehee, Ralph W., *Deadly Deceits: My 25 Years in the CIA* (New York: Sheridan Square Publications, Inc., 1983).
Nighswonger, William A., *Rural Pacification in Vietnam* (New York: Praeger Publishers, 1966).
Palmer, Bruce, Jr., *The 25–Year War: America's Military Role in Vietnam* (New York: Simon & Schuster, Inc., 1984).
Porter, Gareth, ed., *Vietnam: A History in Documents* (New York: Meridian Books, 1981).
Powers, Thomas, *The Man Who Kept the Secrets: Richard Helms and the CIA* (New York: Alfred A. Knopf, Inc., 1979).
Pratt, John Clark, ed., *Vietnam Voices: Perspectives on the War Years, 1941–1982* (New York: Viking Penguin Inc., 1984).
Proffitt, Nicholas, *The Embassy House* (New York: Bantam Books, 1986).
Race, Jeffrey, *War Comes to Long An: Revolutionary Conflict in a Vietnamese Province* (Berkeley: University of California Press, 1972).
Ranelagh, John, *The Agency: The Rise and Decline of the CIA* (New York: Simon & Schuster, 1986).
Reston, James, Jr., *Sherman's March and Vietnam* (New York: Macmillan Publishing Co., 1984).
Shaplen, Robert, *The Road From War: Vietnam 1965–1970* (New York: Harper & Row, 1970).
Sheehan, Neil, *A Bright Shining Lie: John Paul Vann and America in Vietnam* (New York: Random House, 1988).
Snepp, Frank, *Decent Interval: An Insider's Account of Saigon's Indecent End* (New York: Random House, 1977).

Stanton, Shelby L., *Vietnam Order of Battle* (Washington, D.C.: U.S. News Books, 1981).
———, *Green Berets at War: U.S. Army Special Forces in Southeast Asia, 1956–1975*, (Novato, Calif.: Presidio Press, 1985).
Sullivan, David S., and Sattler, Martin J., eds., *Revolutionary War: Western Response* (New York: Columbia University Press, 1971).
Tang, Truong Nhu, *A Vietcong Memoir* (San Diego: Harcourt Brace Jovanovich, 1985).
Thayer, Thomas C., *War Without Fronts: The American Experience in Vietnam* (Boulder, Colo.: Westview Press, 1985).
Thompson, Robert, *Defeating Communist Insurgency: The Lessons of Malaya and Vietnam* (New York: Frederick A. Praeger, 1966).
———, *No Exit From Vietnam* (New York: David McKay Co., Inc., 1969).
Thompson, W. Scott, and Frizzell, Donaldson D., eds., *The Lessons of Vietnam* (New York: Crane, Russak & Co., 1977).
Trullinger, James Walker, Jr., *Village at War: An Account of Revolution in Vietnam* (New York: Longman, Inc., 1980).
Westmoreland, William C., *A Soldier Reports* (Dell Publishing Co., Inc., 1980).

Monographs

Davison, W. P., *Some Observations on Viet Cong Operations in the Villages* (Santa Monica, Calif.: RAND Corporation Collection, RM-5267/2-ISA/ARPA, May 1968).
Davison, W. P., and Zasloff, J. J., *A Profile of Viet Cong Cadres* (Santa Monica, Calif.: RAND Corporation Collection, RM-4983-1-ISA/ARPA, June 1966).
Lung, Hoang Ngoc, *Intelligence* (Washington, D.C.: U.S. Army Center of Military History, 1982).
Pike, Douglas, *The Viet-Cong Strategy of Terror* (Saigon: United States Mission in Vietnam, February 1970).
———, *The Viet-Cong Infrastructure: A Background Paper* (Saigon: United States Mission in Vietnam, June 1970).
Pool, Ithiel de Sola, *Village Violence and Pacification in Viet Nam* (Urbana, Ill.: University of Illinois, 1968).
Pye, Lucien W., *Observations on the Chieu Hoi Program* (Santa Monica, Calif.: RAND Corporation Collection, RM-4864-1-ARPA, January 1969).
Tho, Tran Dinh, *Pacification* (Washington, D.C.: U.S. Army Center of Military History, 1980).
Truong, Ngo Quang, *Territorial Forces* (Washington, D.C.: U.S. Army Center of Military History, 1981).
West, F. J., Jr., *Area Security* (Santa Monica, Calif.: RAND Corporation Collection, P-3979-1, August 1969).
———, *The Enclave: Some U.S. Military Efforts in Ly Tin District, Quang Tin Prov-*

ince 1966–1968 (Santa Monica, Calif.: RAND Corporation Collection, RM-5941-ARPA, December 1969).

Journal Articles

Drosnin, Michael, "Phoenix: The CIA's Biggest Assassination Program," *New Times*, 22 August 1975, pp. 16–24.
Geyer, Georgie Anne, "The CIA's Hired Killers," *True Magazine*, February 1970, pp. 38–105.
Komer, Robert W., "Clear, Hold and Rebuild," *Army*, May 1970, pp. 16–24.
———, "Pacification: A Look Back," *Army*, June 1970, pp. 20–29.
Popkin, Samuel L., "Pacification: Politics and the Village," *Asian Survey*, August 1970, pp. 662–672.
Treaster, Joseph B., "The Phoenix Murders," *Penthouse* magazine, December 1975, p. 76.

Government Publications

The Congressional Record, Hearings Before the Committee on Foreign Relations, U.S. Senate, "Vietnam: Policy and Prospects" (Washington, D.C.: U.S. Government Printing Office, 1970).
———, Hearing Before the Subcommittee to Investigate Problems Connected with Refugees and Escapees of the Committee on the Judiciary, U.S. Senate, "War-Related Civilian Problems in Indochina, Part I—Vietnam" (Washington, D.C.: U.S. Government Printing Office, 1971).
———, Hearings Before a Subcommittee of the Committee on Government Operations, U.S. House of Representatives, "U.S. Assistance Programs in Vietnam" (Washington, D.C.: U.S. Government Printing Office, 1971).
———, Hearing Before the Committee on Armed Services, U.S. Senate, "Nomination of William E. Colby" (Washington, D.C.: U.S. Government Printing Office, 1973).
"Psychological Operations," Department of the Army Field Manual FM 33-5 (Headquarters, Department of the Army, January 1962).
"U.S. Army Handbook of Counterinsurgency Guidelines for Area Commanders," Department of the Army Pamphlet no. 550-100 (Headquarters, Department of the Army, January 1966).
"Counterguerrilla Operations," Department of the Army Field Manual FM 31-16 (Headquarters, Department of the Army, March 1967).
"The Vietnamese Village, 1970: Handbook for Advisors" (published by Translations & Publications Branch, Management Support Directorate, CORDS, May 1970).

"APT Handbook, Revised Edition" (Translations and Publications Branch, MSD/CORDS, 1970).
"Phung Hoang Advisor Handbook" (United States Military Assistance Command, Vietnam, November 1970).
"Revised HES Handbook, Question-Set and Glossary" (MACCORDS, January 1971).
Cooper, Chester L., et al., *The American Experience With Pacification in Vietnam*, Vol. I–III (Washington, D.C.: Institute for Defense Analyses, International and Social Studies Division, March 1972).
"Territorial Security Advisers Reference Book" (MACCORDS, January 1973).
Marolda, Edward J., and Pryce, G. Wesley III, *A Short History of the United States Navy and the Southeast Asian Conflict, 1950–1975* (Washington, D.C.: Naval Historical Center, Department of the Navy, 1984).

Unpublished Material

Johnson, Ralph W., "Phoenix/Phung Hoang: A Study of Wartime Intelligence Management" (Ph.D. dissertation, The American University, Washington, D.C., 1983).
———, "The Phoenix Program: 'Planned Assassination' or Legitimate Conflict Management" (*Papers in Asian Studies*, The American University, Washington, D.C., vol. III, no. 1, Fall 1981), pp. 1–15.
Knapp, William L., "Phoenix/Phung Hoang and the Future: A Critical Analysis of the U.S./GVN Program to Neutralize the Viet Cong Infrastructure" (research report, U.S. Army War College, Carlisle Barracks, Pennsylvania, 8 March 1971).
Milberg, Warren H., "The Future Applicability of the Phoenix Program" (master's thesis, Auburn University/Air University, Maxwell AFB, Alabama, May 1974).

Index

Abrams, Creighton, 57, 182, 246
Accelerated Pacification Program (APP), 268
Agency for International Development (AID), 56–57
Agroville Program, 35–36
American Embassy, 48, 54
An Giang Province, 223, 252–253
An Nhon, cordon-and-search in, 100–103
An Nihn, 265
An Phu Dong, cordon-and-search in, 100–103
An tri laws, 216–217
An Xuyen Province, 143–144, 145
Anti-Communist Denunciation Campaign, 33–34, 83–84
Anti-infrastructure: CIA and, 57; CORDS and, 57–58; description of problem, 48–52; ICEX, 59–70; problem with civilian apparatus, 56–58; role of Komer, 55–56; search for a solution, 52–54. *See also* Viet Cong infrastructure
Armed Propaganda Teams (APTs), 138
Armed reconnaissance units (ARUs), 265
Army of the Republic of Vietnam (ARVN), 4, 8–9; pacification and, 53; problems of military service and preference for, 177–178; transferral of, from the army to the police, 142
Arrest, procedures for, 214–216
Assassination training, 211–213

Ba Xuyen Province, 269
Bac Lieu Province, 224–225, 269
Bah, Nguyen Thi, 190
Bandits: notes used by, 112–114; operations undertaken by, 114–122; Tropic Lightning and, 108–112
Banh, Vo Van, 188

Ben Cat, 75; PRU operation in, 188–191
Ben Cui village, 75–78
Bien Hoa Province, 130, 162, 244
Biet Hai, 192
Big Mack, 224, 252
Binh Chanh District, 48–49, 50, 185
Binh Dinh Province: ICEX in, 68; Operation Dragnet in, 67; reward program in, 244; VCI in, 145; VCI in prisons in, 221; Viet Cong purge of, 276
Binh Son Hamlet, 260
Binh Thuan Province, 128
Binh Tuy Province, 240
Binh Xuyen, 33
Bounty Hunters, 150, 151
Brickham, Nelson H., 58–59, 65–66
Briggs, Harold, 25
British in Malaya, use of pacification methods by the, 23–29; black tent operations, 27; Central Executive Committee, 24; infrastructure of the Malay communists, 24–25; Malayan Races Liberation Army, 24; Min Yuen, 24–25, 26–28; New Villages, 25–26; use of police, 26–27; War Executive Committees, 25
B-3 Thought Reform Camp, 256–262
Bundy, McGeorge, 53
Bunker, Ellsworth, 246, 248
Butto, Junichi, 63–64

Cambodia as a refuge for VCI, 3–4
Can, Ngo Dinh, 37
Cao Dai, 18, 33
Carter, Leslie D., 91–92, 95
Case, Clifford P., 249–250
Cay Trom hamlet, 116–122
Census/Grievance and Aspiration Program, 44
Central Office for South Vietnam (COSVN): creation of, 9;

Central Office for South Vietnam (*continued*)
headquarters of, 9–10; Phoenix and, 268, 273–274
Central Phung Hoang Permanent Office (CPHPO), 125–126, 141, 269
Chanh, Nguyen Van, 256, 258–259, 261
Chanh Luu village, 78–80
Chau Doc Province: F-6 program in, 248; intelligence program in, 242; Phung Hoang program in, 144, 241
Chien Tang-Hop Tac pacification plan, 43
Chieu Hoi (Open Arms) program, 4, 94, 132, 138
China, intervention by, 52–53
Chot, Nguyen Van, 101
Chuyen, Muoi, 259, 260, 261
CIA: Census/Grievance and Aspiration Program, 44; contributions of, 45, 57; Counter Terror Teams, 41–44; Komer and, 57, 58; problems with PSB created by, 168–170; Province and District Intelligence Coordination Centers, 42; PRUs and role of, 176–177, 178–179, 182, 184; statistics on, 43; transfer of Phoenix operation from, to MACV, 133–134
CIO (Central Intelligence Organization), 43
Civic Action Teams, 34–35
Civil Guard (CG), 35, 37, 153, 154
Civil Operations and Revolutionary Development Support (CORDS): creation of, 45, 47, 57; PRU and, 186; PSB training and, 166; refugee problem and, 74; reward programs and, 243; Standard Operating Procedure, 86
Co, Nguyen Huu, 53
Cochin-China (southern Vietnam), use of pacification methods by the French in, 15–23; Garde Republicaine de Cochinchine, 18; Garde Republicaine de jaunir, 18; lack of reforms, 19; Mobile Administrative Groups for Operations, 21; Mobile Units for the Defense of Christendom, 18–19; oil spot method, 17–18; in Tonkin, 20–21; Viet Minh victory, 15–16
Cohn, Michael J., 212
Colby, William E., xviii, 60; Geneva Convention and Phoenix program and, 226–227; intelligence extracted under torture and, 210; National Police and, 85; PRU effectiveness and, 187; PRU legality and, 180; PRU name and, 43; reward program and, 245; sanctioning of Phung Hoang and, 83; sentencing of prisoners and, 217
Combat Police, 154
Combined Campaign Plan, 136
Cong, Huyen Tan, 197–198
Cordon-and-searches: in Ben Cui, 75–78; in Chanh Luu, 78–80; in Gia Dinh, 100–103; problems with, 96–97; in Quang Dien, 91–96
Counterinsurgency, 191–192
Counter Terror Teams (CTTs), 41–44, 172
Cu, Nguyen Van, 118
Cu Chi, 111, 112; Operation Draw String, 115–122
Current Affairs Committee, 9, 11
Cutoff I, Operation, 105–106

Dai, Bao, 32, 33
Dang, Nguyen Hong, 231–234
Dang, Nguyen Van, 188
Dang Lao Dong, 7
Decree, Thieu's presidential, 82–85; American reaction to, 89–91
de la Tour, Pierre Boyer, 16, 18, 21–22
Detention system, 202–206
Di An District, 130
Diem, Ngo Dinh, 3; Agroville Program, 35–36; Anti-Communist Denunciation Campaign, 33–34, 83–84; Civic

Action Teams, 34–35; Civil Guard, 35, 37, 153, 154; GVN Intelligence Service, 38–39; legal system under, 208; Mutual Aid Family Groups, 34; National Police force and, 39, 153–154; pacification and, 32–40; proclaimed president, 33; Self Defense Corps, 35
Dinh, Nguyen Thi, 278
Dinh, Tran Kim, 205
Dinh Tuong Province, 145, 164, 269, 271
Dinh Tuy Province, 128
Directorate General of National Police (DGNP), 141
District Intelligence and Operations Coordinating Centers (DIOCCs): change in name, 60; divisions of, 88; interrogation and, 213; ratio of military to police personnel in, 141; relations with PRUs, 137–138, 174; role of, 88–89; source of advisers for, 139
District Intelligence Coordination Centers (DICCs), 42
District Operations and Intelligence Coordinating Centers (DOICCs), 60
Do, Tran, 278
Draw String, Operation, 115–122
Duc, Cao Van, 232
Duc Hoa, 111, 112; Operation Draw String, 115–122
Dung, Bay (camp director), 258
Dung, Bay (prisoner), 259–260
Dung, Thuong Thi, 204

Easter Offensive, 247, 275–276
EDCOR (Economic Development Corps), 31

Fall, Bernard, 16
Force Populaire, 37
Forces Terrestres Sud-Vietnam (FTSV) (Ground Forces in South Vietnam), 18
Foreign Operations and Government Information Subcommittee, xv

IV Corps: effectiveness of NPFF in, 162–163; effectiveness of Phung Hoang in, 137, 143–145; Navy involved in operations, 147–148; PRU advisers in, 178; PRU agents in, 186; PSB training in, 165, 167; ratio of military to police personnel in, 141; reward funds in, 246
French in Indochina, use of pacification methods by the, 15–23; Garde Republicaine de Cochinchine, 18; Garde Republicaine de jaunir, 18; lack of reforms, 19; Mobile Administrative Groups for Operations, 21; Mobile Units for the Defense of Christendom, 18–19; oil spot method, 17–18; in Tonkin, 20–21; Viet Minh victory, 15–16
F-6 program, 246–250

Galbraith, John Kenneth, 40
Garde Republicaine de Cochinchine, 18
Garde Republicaine de jaunir, 18
Geneva Accords, 5, 6
Geneva Convention, Phoenix and, 226–227
Gia Dinh Province: cordon-and-searches in, 100–103; description of problem in, 48–52; effectiveness of NPFF in, 162; effectiveness of PRU in, 185
Giang Ca Loc, raid on, 149–153
Gio Linh District, 130
Go Cong Province, 132, 194, 241, 252
Go Vap district, cordon-and-searches in, 100–103
Government of South Vietnam (GVN): intelligence collation center between U.S. and, 50; Intelligence Service, 38–39; NLF and, 6–7; problem of military service requirements, 177–178; reaction of, to Tet Offensive, 74, 81–82; reaction of, to Viet Cong in villages, 3; support for Phoenix, 124–127

Green Berets, 191
Gurney, Henry, 25

Harriman, Averell, 53
Hart, John, 176
Hau Nghia Province, 68, 162, 221, 269
Helicopters, importance of, 111
Hiep, Pham Van, 198
Hinh, General, 32, 33
Ho Chi Minh, 6
Hoa Hao, 18, 33, 231–233
Hoi Chanhs, 94, 95, 109, 110
Hon, Nguyen Thi, 204
Honolulu Conference of 1966, 53–54
House Committee on Government Operations, xv
Huk rebellion, 29–32, 243
Human rights abuse, 209, 210
Hung, Pham, 10

ID card system, 223–225
Informant and reward programs, 242–246
Intelligence, problem with Vietnamese, 49–51
Intelligence Coordination and Exploitation (ICEX): advisory structure of, 90; creation of, 59, 60; effectiveness of, 68–70; guidelines for the implementation of, 60–61; organization, 63–65; problems with, 61–63, 65–68
International Red Cross, 208–209
Interrogation: American involvement with, 209–213; problems with, 65–68

Jacobson, George D., 235
Johnson, Lyndon B., 45, 47; Honolulu Conference of 1966 and, 53, 54; Office of Civil Operations and, 54; pacification and, 52–53

Karnow, Stanley, 278
Kennedy, John F., 191, 192
Khiem, Tran Thien, 244

Khiem, Tran Van, 83, 125, 127
Kia, Nguyen Van, 189
Kien Giang Province, 137, 185, 223
Kien Hoa Province, 145, 268
Kien Phong Province, 225
Kien Phong Province Interrogation Center, 203–205
Kit Carson Scouts, 109
Komer, Robert, 55–56; Brickham and, 58; CIA and, 57, 58; creation of CORDS and, 57; creation of ICEX and, 59; evaluation teams for NPFF and, 159, 161
Ky, Nguyen Cao, 53

Lac, Nguyen Huu, 232
Lai Khe, 75
Laird, Melvin, 183, 184
Lam Dong Province, 128
Lang, Nguyen Van, 181
Lansdale, Edward, 29, 30–31
Lao Dong Party, 7, 9, 10
Lau, Ha Van, 270
Legal system: detention camps, 202–206; early prisons, 208–209; evidence needed for arrest/conviction, 216–218; human rights abuse, 209; National Identity Registration Program, 222–225; power of arrest, 214–216; problems within the, 218–220; statistics on VCI in prison, 220–222; under Diem, 207; use of interrogation, 209–213
Lenin Institute, 29
Leroy, Jean, 18–19
Liberation Radio, 267
Lien Doi Nguoi Nhai, 192
Loan, Nguyen Ngoc, 50
Lodge, Henry Cabot, 53, 54, 55
Long, Nguyen Van, 258–259
Long An Province, 128, 221
Long Khanh Province: ID cards issued in, 223; operations in, 103–108, 128

Mach, Bay, 259, 260, 261
Magsaysay, Ramon, 30, 31

Mai, Dang Van, 188–189
Malaya, use of pacification by the British in 23–29; black tent operations, 27; Central Executive Committee, 24; infrastructure of the Malay communists, 24–25; Malayan Races Liberation Army, 24; Min Yuen, 24–25, 26–28; New Villages, 25–26; use of police, 26–27; War Executive Committees, 25
Malayan Races Liberation Army (MRLA), 24
Mau, Nguyen Van, 50
McCloskey, Paul N., Jr., xv, 226
McNamara, Robert, 53
McNaughton, John, 53
MEDCAP (medical civil action program), 80, 106
Mekong Delta, SEALs in, 193
Michigan State University, 37
Military Assistance Command, Vietnam (MACV), 45; prison system and, 208–209; PRUs and role of, 177–179, 181–182, 184; SOG (Special Operations Group), 193; torture and, 211; transfer of Phoenix operation from the CIA to, 133–134
Military Assistance Security Adviser (MASA), 140
Military Intelligence Detachment (MID), 109–112
Military Intelligence Service (MIS), 31
Military Security Service (MSS), 106, 213
Min Yuen, 24–25, 26–28
Ministry of Interior (MOI), 125
Mission Council concept, 54
Mobile Administrative Groups for Operations (GAMO), 21
Mobile I, Operation, 104–105
Mobile Units for the Defense of Christendom (UMDC), 18–19
Moorehead, William S., xv-xvi
Mua, Phan Van, 190
Mutual Aid Family Groups, 34
My Hanh, 109, 114
My Lai massacre, 179, 212, 213

National Armed Support Bloc, 157
National Identity Registration Program (NIRP), 222–225
National Liberation Front (NLF): creation of, 6–7; problems with, 7; relationship with PRP, 8
National Mobilization Decree, 81
National Police Academy, 142
National Police Field Force (NPFF): chain of command, 155–156; classifications of, 155; creation of, 154–155; effectiveness of, 141–142, 159–164; Operation Cutoff I and, 105; Operation Mobile I and, 104; purpose of, 148, 155; raid on Giang Ca Loc, 149–153; relations with PSB, 156–157; training and recruitment of, 155, 157–159
National Police force: cordon-and-searches in Go Vap District and, 100–103; creation of, 39, 153–154; ineffectiveness of, 49, 103–104; integration of Phung Hoang and, 126–127, 140–142; integration of PRU and, 181; Operation Cutoff I and, 105; Operation Mobile I and, 104–105; role of, 84–85, 89–90
National Security Laws, 202
Navarre, Henri, 20, 22
Neutralizations, statistics on, 135, 143–146, 287
Nha Be District, 50
Nha Trang, 128
Nhu, Ngo Dinh, 36–37, 207
Noh, Tran Van, 119–120
Noi, Hyunh Thi, 116, 117, 118
North Vietnamese Army (NVA): Easter Offensive, 247, 275–276; invasion of, after American withdrawal, 230; role of, after Tet Offensive, 82
North Vietnam's Worker's Party, 7

Office of Civil Operations (OCO), creation of, 54
Office of the President, 125
Oil spot method, 17–18

I Corps, 68; effectiveness of Phung Hoang in, 130–131, 145; Marines involved in operations, 147; PRU advisers in, 178; PSB training in, 165, 167; ratio of military to police personnel in, 141; reward funds in, 246
Operation Dragnet, 67
Operation Recovery, 74
Operations, Phoenix: cordon-and-searches in Go Vap district, 100–103; Cutoff I, 105–106; Draw String, 115–122; in Long Khanh Province, 103–104; Mobile I, 104–105; SARC X, 107–108; Undertaker, 114–115
Osborn, K. Barton, xv–xviii

Pacification: Americans in Vietnam, 40–45, 52–53; ARVN and, 53; British in Malaya, 23–29; Diem and, 32–40; Filipino army and Huk rebellion, 29–32; French in Indochina, 15–23; ingredients for a successful program, 22–23; Johnson and, 52–53. *See also* Anti-infrastructure
Paris Peace Accords, 251
Parker, Evan J., 59–60, 63
Patton, George S., 78
People's Liberation Army Forces, 81–82
People's Revolutionary Party (PRP), 3; creation of, 7; district committees of, 8; headquarters of, 8–9; ineffectiveness of, 49; Phoenix and, 268; purpose of, 8; relationship with NLF, 8
People's Self-Defense Force (PSDF), 81; cordon-and-searches in Go Vap district and, 100–103; importance of, 137
Phelps, William E., 109
Philippines, Huk rebellion in, 29–32
Phoenix Coordinator Orientation Course (PCOC), 139
Phoenix mistresses, 259–262
Phoenix program: administrative structure of, 87–89; American public opinion on, 229–230; American troops participating in, 147–148; American withdrawal from Vietnam and effects on, 229–231, 241–242; areas emphasized by, 85–87; background of name, 72–73; classification of, 90; creation of, 72; definition of VCI, 84; effectiveness of, 86, 127–129; effects of, on tax revenues going to the Viet Cong, 271; effects of Tet Offensive on, 71–72, 81; example of the shortcomings of, 231–235; Geneva Convention and, 226–227; high-ranking views of, 124–127; importance of having good informants, 132–13; National Police and, 84–85; problems with, 123–124, 240–242; problem with cordon-and-searches, 96–97; province and district views of, 129–131; statistics kept by, 123, 124, 128, 129, 131, 134–135; termination of, 250–253; Thieu's presidential decree, 82–85; training facilities, 128; transfer of operations from the CIA to MACV, 133–134; Vietnamization of, 138–140. *See also* Operations, Phoenix
Phoenix program, communist reaction to: after the war, 278–279; measures used against, 264–266; in 1970, 272–273; in 1971, 273–276; Phoenix mistresses, 259–262; Phoenix prison camps, 256–262; Phoenix propaganda leaflets, 261; post-Tet communist reaction to, 268–272; Viet Cong propaganda statements regarding, 262–264, 266–268
Phong Dinh Province, 144
Phu Yen Province, 277
Phung Hoang, 73, 83; administrative structure of, 87–89; adviser classifications, 139; American withdrawal from Vietnam and effects on, 229–231, 241–242; Central Phung Hoang Permanent Office, 125–126, 141;

committees, 84, 85–86, 87–88; district organization, 291; effectiveness of, 135–136, 142–146; example of the shortcomings of, 231–235; importance of National Police in, 84–85; integration with the National Police, 126–127, 140–142; military region organization, 289; national level organization, 288; operational capability of, 136–138; province organization, 290; reexamination study, 235–238; termination of, 250; training for, 138–140
Phung Hoang Management Information System (PHMIS), 135–136
Phung Hoang Reexamination (PHREEX) study: description of, 235–238; effects of, on VCI, 238–240
Phuoc Long Province, 128
Phuoc Yen, 91
Police Operations Centers (POCs), 251
Police Special Branch (PSB), 106, 141; counterintelligence (CI) section in, 166–167; creation of, 164–165; effectiveness of, 168–170; relations with NPFF, 156–157; training and recruitment of, 164–167; women in, 166
Popular Forces (PF), cordon-and-searches in Go Vap district and, 100–103
Porter, William J., 54
Protection of the People Against Terrorism (POPAT), 250–251
Province Intelligence and Operations Coordination Center (PIOCC): Operation Mobile I and, 104–105; ratio of military to police personnel in, 141
Province Intelligence Coordinating Committee (PICC), 61
Province Intelligence Coordination Centers (PICCs), 42
Province Interrogation Centers (PICs), 210

Province Security Committee (PSC), 203, 204, 215, 221
Provincial Reconnaissance Units (PRUs), 3, 90; American advisers and, 176–179, 181–184; charges of brutality and torture, 174–176; CIA role, 176–177, 178–179, 182, 184; creation of, 41, 44, 172; effectiveness of, 137, 171–172, 185–188; integration with National Police, 181; intelligence gathering, 174; legality of, 179–184; MACV role, 177–179, 181–182, 184; Operation Cutoff I and, 105; operation in Ben Cat, 188–191; Operation Mobile I and, 104; recruiting for, 173; relations with DIOCCs, 137–138, 174; structure of, 172–174
Psychological Operations (PSYOPs), 105, 106

Quan Doi Nhan Dan, 267, 274–275
Quang Dien District, operation in, 91–96
Quang Duc Province, 240
Quang Nam Province: neutralization rates in, 131; NPFF in, 161–162; reward program in, 244; VCI in, 145; VCI reaction to Phoenix in, 270
Quang Ngai Province, 145, 223, 271
Quang Tin Province, 145, 163–164
Quang Tri Province, 68, 130

Ranh, Nguyen Thi, 204
Recon by fire, 92, 101
Regional and Popular Forces (RF/PF), 49; effectiveness of, 92, 137, 147; helicopter operations and, 93–94; Operation Cutoff I and, 105; in Quang Dien District, 92–96; SEALs and, 197
Reid, Ogden R., xv
Reitemeyer, Francis T., 211–212, 213
Resor, Stanley R., 182–183
Resource allocations, 287
Revolutionary Development Cadre (RDC), 49

Revue Militaire d'Information, 22–23
Reward programs, 242–246
Ria, Nguyen Van, 116, 117, 118, 119
Rung Sat Special Zone (RSSZ), 193, 270
Rural Development (RD) cadres, 53
Rusk, Dean, 53

Sadec Province, 145, 241
SARC X, Operation, 107–108
Sau Tau, 2
Screening committees, 215–216
SEALs (Sea, Air, and Land teams): creation of, 191–192; effectiveness of, 171–172, 195–199; RF/PF and, 197; role of, 192–194
Self Defense Corps, 35
Senate Committee on Armed Services, xviii
Sharp, U. S. G., 53
Siena, James V., 218
So, Huynh Phu, 231
Special airmobile resources control (SARC) team, 107–108
Strategic Hamlet progam, 24, 26, 85
Supplies, interdicting, 107–108
Swans, 166

Tactical Operations Centers (TOCs), 136
Tam, Le Van, 232
Tan, Bui Ngoc, 197
Tapscott, Eugene D., 76
Taylor, Maxwell, 53, 54
Tem, Tran Van, 1–5
Tet Offensive, 3; effects of, on the communists, 73–74; effects of, on Phoenix program, 71–72, 81; GVN response to, 74, 81–82; NVA after, 82; VCI after, 82, 97
Thach, Nguyen Co, 278
Thanh, Nguyen Chi, 10
Thanh, Tam, 119–121
Thanh Loc, cordon-and-search in, 100–103
Thanh My Tay, 102
Thieu, Nguyen Van, 53; presidential decree, 82–85; support for Phoenix, 125; Tet Offensive and, 71–72, 81
Thompson, Robert, 28, 126
III Corps, 48, 99; effectiveness of NPFF in, 162; effectiveness of Phung Hoang in, 128, 130; PRU advisers in, 178; PRU agents in, 186; PSB training in, 165, 167; ratio of military to police personnel in, 141; reward funds in, 246; VCI in prisons in, 221
Thua Thien Province, 160–161
Tin, Bui, 278
Ton, Nguyen Nghiem, 50
Tonkin (northern Vietnam), pacification methods used by the French in, 20–21
Torture, use of, 210–211
Trieu Phong District, 130
Tropic Lightning, Bandits and, 108–112
Truong, Ngo Quang, 242, 247
Tuan, Nguyen Thanh, 197
Tuy Hoa District, 277
Tuyen Duc Province, 159–160
II Corps, 68; effectiveness of Phung Hoang in, 128; PRU advisers in, 178; PSB training in, 165, 167; ratio of military to police personnel in, 141; reward funds in, 246; VCI in prisons in, 220–221
Tydings-McDuffie Act of 1934, 30

Undertaker, Operation, 114–115
U.S. Assistance Programs in Vietnam, xv
U.S.-GVN intelligence collation center, 50
United States Overseas Mission (USOM), 41

Van, Nguyen Ngoc, 115–116
Vann, John Paul, 48–49
Vien, Bay, 33
Vien, Cao Van, 67
Viet Cong infrastructure (VCI): after the Tet Offensive, 82, 97; armor used against, 78–80; Bandits effects on, 108–122;

categories of, 217; formation of, 5–7; life of a VCI, 1–5; operations and activities of, 10–12; Phoenix definition of, 84; position of, after Quang Dien, 95–96; in prison, statistics on, 220–222; problems in replacing their losses, 276–277; purpose of, 1; statistics on, 83, 220–222; Westmoreland's views of, 12–13. *See also* Anti-infrastructure
Viet Cong Military Region, 50
Viet Minh, 33–34
Vietnam: A History (Karnow), 278
Vinh Binh Province, 213, 244

Vinh Long Province, 145, 196, 240–241
Volunteer Informant Program (VIP), 243–244

Westmoreland, William C.: at the Honolulu Conference, 53; Komer and, 56, 57; PRUs and military service and, 177–178; SEALs and, 199; VCI and view of, 12–13, 47, 67

Xay, Nam, 120, 121

Zinman, William H., 211

About the Author

Dale Andradé is a historian specializing in special operations. He received his B.A. and M.A. from the University of Colorado, Boulder and now works as a Vietnam War historian for the U.S. Army.

SOUTH VIETNAM
POPULATION AND ADMINISTRATIVE DIVISIONS

Persons per square mile: 0, 50, 300, 1000
Persons per square kilometer: 0, 19, 193, 386

Population data based on estimates by districts for 1960 and January 1965

- — · · — International boundary
- — — — Province boundary
- ⊛ National capital
- ⊙ Province capital
- **DA LAT** Autonomous municipality

Scale: 0 25 50 75 100 Miles / 0 25 50 75 100 Kilometers

BOUNDARY REPRESENTATION IS NOT NECESSARILY AUTHORITATIVE

57978 12-67